DEVELOPMENTAL PLANNING

McGRAW-HILL SERIES IN INTERNATIONAL DEVELOPMENT

DEVELOPMENTAL PLANNING

RICHARD L. MEIER

*Associate Professor of Resource Planning, School of Natural Resources
and Research Social Scientist, Mental Health Research Institute
University of Michigan, Ann Arbor*

McGRAW-HILL BOOK COMPANY
New York London Sydney Toronto

DEVELOPMENTAL PLANNING

41337

PREFACE

THIS BOOK IS INTENDED to introduce a different kind of discussion of economic and social development. Instead of describing how such a program should be carried out on the basis of theoretical models of rationality evolved in Western Europe and the United States, it starts with a more skeptical and pragmatic view and depends heavily upon observations of success and failure in recent times among countries which have been attempting to expedite economic development. It starts also from the premise made by economists and others that economic development depends to a large extent upon a number of noneconomic factors.

Economists have arrived at quite explicit ideas about what constitutes economic growth and are able to propose procedures for its estimation; but the equivalent concepts of social growth, political growth, and cultural growth—the noneconomic elements—have not been sufficiently illuminated. This study applies the simple processes of economizing to the noneconomic sectors. It thereby seeks to describe procedure by which a people may freely organize themselves so as to achieve a more desirable style of living. The recommendations are not those of an economist but of a student of organization, technology, and planning.

The stimulus for writing this book arose from my peripheral contacts with an unprecedented success in development in one country. A cooperative arrangement between the Puerto Rican government, particularly the Planning Board, and the University of Chicago was arranged by Harvey Perloff in 1950 and continued to 1955. Documents and statistics were provided by the government which were used for teaching and for research in planning. I collaborated in that educational project, and on two occasions (1952 and 1958) I served for a few months on the Island as a planning consultant. This was not an unusual arrangement. All during the period following World War II, Puerto Rico was the object of many academically oriented studies; altogether the number of monographs and books must already exceed one hundred, so that the successive states of existence of these 2,300,000 people have been analyzed in greater detail than other liberating transitions, except possibly the American Civil War. The detailed studies have ranged from agriculture and medicine to industrial planning, from prehistory to contemporary cultural differentiation, and from tourism to tax policy.

Not being involved deeply in any single program, I purposely sought the underlying changes that appear to be the reasons for growth, tried to identify the policies and techniques that were responsible for stimulating these changes, and then to judge whether the concepts could be transferred to other parts of the world. The prodigious amount of investigation undertaken by predecessors and colleagues, most of it of a highly sophisticated nature, was particularly useful in illuminating the structure of this society.

Concepts of development and growth, however, focus upon *change;* modern institutions rise, and many traditional ones decline. As to what these changes were and how they came about, the available academic analyses were exceedingly vague and inadequate. Government statistics had been designed to measure progress toward certain goals which had been set in the national planning, so that some features of change (for example, industrial production and school enrollment) were highlighted while others of a cultural nature were obscured (for example, the shift in vocabulary). In my quest for concepts I became a sleuth, seeking out change in this society wherever it could be detected, then discussing directly with knowledgeable persons what were the properties of one and another change and, further, of *associated* changes. Hypotheses produced about the source and significance of a change were tested against statistics (which were extraordinarily good for a developing area) and more interviews.

What I found was very exciting. Much of the change followed patterns that were recognizable in the history of economic and social development in Western countries and Japan, but the pace in this case had been speeded up. Present technology had pushed some factors ahead much more speedily than others; consequently the new structures that this society was assuming were strange and somewhat unexpected. It turned out that American advisers, steeped in the history of Western economic development, were often poorer judges than the Puerto Rican politicians and civil servants as to what kinds of policies would produce new growth in this environment, even though the native planners had little specialized education. Here a small group of public servants in highly responsible positions were inventing techniques and policies as they went along, to meet problems that were foreseen a year or more in advance. Their decisions brought about a three-fold increase in the level of living in about fifteen years, without any evidence that there was borrowing against the future. This was accomplished without any significant endowment of natural resources or any major windfalls. To a very large extent everything was centrally planned, but in such a way that the planners and entrepreneurs rarely came into open conflict; instead they tended to reinforce each other. Both public and private ends were simultaneously served.

A significant feature of the program is that notable changes in social structure, language, belief systems, and political participation accompanied improvements in welfare. The transition from abject poverty to relative adequacy was so rapid for the majority of citizens that it might be called revolutionary, yet for most people living and working within the society, the expectations have expanded at least as rapidly as achievements. For the people themselves the pace seems to be faltering and slow, and there is fair cause for dissatisfaction. For each unusual success I uncovered—instances which demonstrated the value of the planning procedures that had been adopted—the local experts could (and did in private sessions) point out a failure of proportions that bordered on scandal. The experts themselves were proving that the planning was not perfect. This difference in view-point makes it difficult for the outsider and the insider to agree in their assessments of the same body of facts. Actually the Puerto Ricans, with their advisers, are very proud of their achievements and have advertised them in a very clever fashion, so that it is not easy to draw the most highly informed and responsible persons into sessions of frank self-criticism.

The object of my explorations, however, was the identification of transferable techniques and procedures. These are fragments and sequences of institutional behavior which are expected to fit into a wide range of social systems and yield similarly rewarding results. Programs and strategies cannot be transported to a new environment *in toto,* even from a highly successful operation. The process of transfer requires an equivalent amount of information concerning the structures of the societies which are the potential imitators. Are the expected consequences of what the Puerto Ricans invented and applied likely to be as revolutionary elsewhere? On this point it is worth quoting Kenneth E. Boulding, who viewed the Puerto Rico phenomenon mainly from the vantage point of Jamaica, where its influence was increasingly felt. His phrases are eloquent:

> . . . There is a type of revolution which does not fit comfortably into any of the above categories (Malthusian or Marxist) and which may be the most important of all in the long run. I call it the "Fomentarian revolution" in honor of a remarkable institution in Puerto Rico which embodies it, known

as "Fomento." The Fomentarian revolution has four aspects. Its prerequisite is some kind of political consensus in the society. It cannot develop if a society is wracked with internal conflicts and factional fights, whether these are between races, cultures, classes, or political groups. There must be some widely shared vision of the future and an image of the way in which the society can move towards its future. This usually has to be the work of a charismatic leader who can inspire large numbers of people with a vision of the future. Sometimes a succession of leadership is required. The charismatic but unrealistic leader may awake the people out of their apathy and give them a sense of identity and purpose. For the revolution to be accomplished, however, a new type of leadership may be necessary—more sober, less dramatic, and with a clearer and more realistic vision.

The second pillar of the Fomentarian revolution is the stress that it lays on education and the development of human resources. If necessary, a society must be prepared to accept some sacrifice of quality in education in the interests of quantity. The developing society not only requires literacy of the mass of the people, it requires a certain type of moral education in inculcating a favorable attitude toward work and austerity and it requires technical education appropriate to the modern world. Higher education of the right kind occupies a key position in this process.

The third pillar of the Fomentarian revolution is the skill to strike clever bargains with foreign capitalists. Genuinely bootstrap development is possible, as the history of Japan showed. The development of Japan came almost wholly from internal reorganization and by the acquisition of knowledge rather than capital from abroad. For this recipe to be successful, however, a fairly authoritarian social structure seems to be necessary. Whether this is feudal as in the case of Japan, or Communist as in the case of China, bootstrap development means holding down consumption, holding down real wages, and squeezing the farmer as hard as he can be squeezed in order to extract every last ounce of subsistence for capital accumulation. In looser and more democratic societies this is hard to achieve. It is hard to resist the clamor of the people for a present share of future benefits. Under these circumstances it is hard to keep real wages from rising which means it is hard to keep consumption from rising which means it is hard to accumulate. Under these circumstances a careful use of foreign investment seems almost necessary. If the investor can be rewarded with friendly attitudes and with long-term security, the recipient society will not have to pay so much hard cash. With an unfriendly and querulous attitude, on the other hand, foreign investment can only be attracted at a high price. The ability to make good bargains with foreign investors is a very important element in the success of the Fomentarian society.

The fourth pillar of Fomentarianism is the most difficult of all to establish. This is the ability to effect a sufficient cultural change at the level of the individual, the family, the neighborhood, and the small group so that the gains of development can be reasonably permanent and acceptable to the society. This brings us back to Malthus, for unless the revolution encompasses some kind of control of the population the revolution is doomed to failure. The control may simply be the ability to emigrate in the case of Puerto Rico. This, however, is a solution which is not open to the world at large, and it cannot be regarded as permanent. Nevertheless, the ability to emigrate from an already over-populated area may be the key, paradoxically enough, to a process of development which will eventually enable it to support a much larger population.

If a society is to enter the modern world, there must also be changes in the attitudes toward the family, toward work, and toward income and saving. All these changes, perhaps, can be summed up by saying that the transition from the traditional culture to what we call an "economic culture" will have to be made. In this process something inevitably is lost. One hopes that the gains are worth the cost.

> —"The United States and Revolution," Center for the Study of Democratic Institutions, Occasional Paper, Fund of the Republic, Santa Barbara, Calif., 1961.

The Fomento took the lead in dealing with the outsiders. It developed slogans which lent impact to its advertising and public relations policy. Therefore it played a central role in constructing the popular image of Puerto Rico that has been created overseas, representing it as a bold experiment in social and economic development. As Boulding implies, the social and economic planning that underlies the Fomentarian Revolution must be done quietly, responsibly, and without continuous publicity. The Fomento had little responsibility for the background work and intervened only if the work threatened the industrialization program. Other governmental departments carried responsibilities that were often equal to those of the Fomento. Indeed, the emphasis has recently shifted, since the leaders of the Fomento have moved on to take bigger jobs. Other agencies now are setting the pace; their experience deserves to be taken into account as much as that of the Fomento, but because these background techniques are less publicized, they are more difficult to borrow and install elsewhere.

This preface may have dwelt too long upon the initial stimulus and the origins of this study. The work itself certainly generalizes far beyond the experience of Puerto Rico. It assembles useful ideas from all points of the compass and attempts to construct a body of reasonable procedures for developmental planning. In a favorable environment the procedures described should yield much better results than those experienced in Puerto Rico. To put it another way: the outline for planning described here should be able to overcome more difficult environments than those presented by Puerto Rico and still manage to get the process of growth going. This does not mean that it—or any body of recommendations—could be applied everywhere. In my opinion, the Malthusian pressures are so strong in some parts of the world that present technology, regardless of the efficiency of the planning and administration, is unable to cope with the problems presented. Our only hope is to improve our knowledge by observation, analysis, and experiment. If this growth of knowledge proceeds rapidly, it is possible that major catastrophes can be averted and that the tools available to planners will be powerful enough to deal with the most difficult cases.

The recognition of this need for more efficient technology and more adaptive and farseeing organization has forced me to employ theory that has not yet been very well developed. The Puerto Rican experience brings home forcefully the value of access to *information* prior to the irreversible decision; in turn, this makes mandatory the searching out of procedures for measuring information and examining models which relate accumulation of information to the growth of some social, economic, or cultural characteristic. If any abbreviated label is to be attached to the theory that is implicit in the following chapters (it is explicated to some extent in Chapter 3), it is perhaps best called "an information theory of social and economic development." It attempts to describe the best institutional environment for "learning by doing."

Processes and techniques require an equal amount of emphasis. Developmental planning is an endeavor of rationalization that can be undertaken once the image of a developed, welfare-oriented state has been accepted as a goal worthy of collection action. The process cannot be dissociated from the methods of modern public administration and constructive politics; indeed it requires these forms of reorganization and reform in order to be effective. Planning, as visualized here, is a programmed drive to higher levels of living, of national self-respect, and of greater freedom of choice in cultural affairs. All the available resources are mobilized to reach preset targets, without exhausting reserves and without increasing the likelihood of catastrophes. In these terms, developmental planning may also be described as a calculated effort toward removing impediments to economic, social, and cultural growth.

Planning is an activity that is notoriously difficult to define because the term is applied so broadly. It may refer (1) to a set of theoretical procedures that conform to the socialist ideologies, (2) to the practice of resource allocation and programming of production as typified by the Soviet Union, (3) to the use of long-range forecasting devices and administrative controls in large organizations, in order to avoid pitfalls and prevent substantial losses over the long run, and (4) to the orderly exploration of alternative paths of action by government, such as those undertaken specifically by military staffs who test proposed alternatives by laying out the logistics and making assessments of feasibility. Since all these are valid meanings of the term (there are many more besides), no attempt will be made here to assert a narrower definition. We shall instead synthesize from the recent experiences of nations a set of policies and administrative processes which, once presented, would normally be referred to as a kind of planning and should lead to development.

The language employed in what follows is deliberately simple because it is expected that many readers will not have mastered the nuances of technical English. Many crucial arguments are intentionally stated from different standpoints; hence it is unavoidable if at times the points made seem to be redundant. The choice of emphasis is based upon hundreds of hours of discussions with advanced overseas students and with scholars visiting in this country. I am greatly indebted to them for their forbearance as I tried out on them many unsuccessful approaches which had to be discarded before more persuasive arguments were sustained.

Some explanation must also be given for the way in which reference is made to prior work by others. Citations are rarely given because the establishment of fact outside of one's own system is seldom important to the formulation of rules for procedure. Nor was it possible to document comprehensively all the clues that preceded an insight and the evidence that seemed to confirm the hypotheses. Formal scholarship keeps us too long in the preliminary stages; it contributes little to an attack on the central problems of decision making for the long run. Thus this work has become a discourse on the art and method of developmental planning. The various pillars upon which it rests are still much more in the nature of wisdom than of knowledge. Most of the chapters have been provided with an annotated list of works which contain either some parallel arguments or various relevant background analyses. The list is not intended to be comprehensive, but it does provide a fair sample of the readily available material. A critical comment is provided for each. The bibliography should serve as the basis for a small institutional collection.

Much credit for a balanced discussion must go to the interdisciplinary faculty seminar maintained by the Center for Research in Economic Development at the University of Michigan. By inviting a broad spectrum of scholars, Professors Samuel P. Hayes and Antonin Basch kept introducing new sets of facts and ideas and new challenges from all parts of the world, so that none of us who were trying to arrive at generalizations were permitted to rest easy. I also owe a great debt to the Mental Health Research Institute of the University of Michigan, which has brought together a small body of scholars with an extraordinary range of interests and skills. The Social Change Seminar conducted by the Institute enabled me to bring the theories of growth and conflict, evolved in the other social sciences, into a framework that invited systematic comparison. The discussions of social communications and nationalism were particularly rewarding. The studies on urbanism were assisted by Resources for the Future, Inc. I am indebted to Dr. Harvey S. Perloff and Professor Lee Martin for their critical reading of parts of the manuscript and to Mrs. Claire Adler for her assistance with the editing and typing.

RICHARD L. MEIER

CONTENTS

PART ONE

ORGANIZATION FOR PLANNING

1

RECENT EXPERIENCE WITH
ECONOMIC DEVELOPMENT

THERE HAVE BEEN many surprises and disappointments in the progress
toward higher levels of living since World War II. Great expectations
were generated at a time when peoples were trying to rebuild an economic
system ravished by war. International organizations for economic and
social cooperation were created, and paths to self-government were charted
by the leaders of formerly colonial peoples who saw the bonds of empire
dissolving. The policies of economic development then adopted reflected
these new expectations or, in a few instances, some that were left over
from a previous generation. As time went on and results could be identified, the policy mix was, of course, changed.

Now, roughly two decades after the first postwar plans were laid,
what has been the experience? This added knowledge has a great deal
of bearing upon the formulation of recommended procedures for planning
in the near future. Analysis of recent history cannot yield firm conclusions
regarding development policy, though they may be desperately needed.
It can only overturn preconceptions and direct attention to those parts
of the world where certain common problems seem to have been solved.

Surprisingly, countries that were expected to develop most rapidly—
those with relatively abundant natural resources—have not fared so well.
The reasons that can be found for their halting progress are diverse,
although most fall into the category of internal political problems or have
stemmed from the changing terms of trade. In most countries, nationalists
played upon a morbid fear of being cheated out of priceless assets.

3

Virtually any agreement with a technically competent group was vulnerable to attack, with political gains going to the critics. The bargaining power of the representatives of the developing country was correspondingly reduced. When arrangements for resource exploitation were finally worked out, outside sources of capital showed reluctance to follow through with the advanced processing, refining, and resource-oriented manufacturing that is normally associated with the resources. Neither local politicians nor foreign corporations could be reasonably sure that a deal would be carried out as agreed over the long run. Effective public opinion on the resource issues was volatile and unpredictable. The multipliers and accelerators that were expected to bring about progress have not taken hold in this environment.

In the spectrum of politico-economic organization that puts the socialized states at one extreme and the predominantly capitalist countries at the other, there have been some consistent trends that were equally unexpected. The most spectacular shifts have centered around the development of soil resources. The repeated failure of socialized countries to meet rather modest production targets for food and other agricultural products, while the countries having subsidized capitalist forms are plagued with unprecedented surpluses in food and fiber, signifies a difference in attitude toward transforming the rural society. Either of these experiences, shortage or surplus, can hold back overall growth. Both kinds of societies have miscalculated the incentives that were needed to get the agricultural production desired. In other areas of production, the socialist countries have emphasized heavy manufacturing, often resource-oriented, while the capitalist countries have been more successful in expanding consumer-oriented industries. Neither of the extreme versions of organization for production has demonstrated any clear superiority in the period since the war, so the increasing tendency to employ a mixed strategy—a blend of institutional types—seems quite reasonable. Both these modern forms of political organization, however, are clearly superior to the traditional societies in their capacity for bringing about growth and development.

Population growth rate has produced the most threatening deviation from expectations. In both developed and newly developing countries, and probably even in the few remote territories that do not yet aspire to develop, the growth in numbers is at least double what had been anticipated. Still worse, an age structure has been created in the interim which will result in growth of population for as long as a generation beyond the time that adequate measures for control take hold. As a consequence the rather remarkable increases in production that have been achieved in the interim have been dissipated for the support of more people instead of producing significant improvements in welfare. Whole continents, already close to the poverty line, have probably slipped backward in terms of per capita consumption. While the distribution of poverty is better regulated so that actual starvation is rarer, at the same time the occasions for surplus are more seldom encountered.

Many people survive today because governments have managed to improve the efficiency of the distribution of essential goods. Thus gaps in the local food supply caused by natural disasters, such as floods and droughts, are filled by temporary surpluses generated elsewhere. Since more people can survive on the same production of food and other necessities, it is not surprising that the gap in welfare, between the mass of the population of the world living close to subsistence and that of advanced countries, has widened substantially.

THE INTERNATIONAL ENVIRONMENT

In the period since 1945 the world has experienced almost continuous expansion of trade between nations, along with increasing interdependence of economies, and a rapid diffusion of modern technology. Various methods were worked out for expediting the transfer of goods; some were implemented by mutual reduction of tariff barriers and quotas, others by moving toward convertibility of currency, while the increasing availability of credit probably was more responsible than any other factor. Figure 1 portrays the trend of the war and postwar periods, together with the expectations for the near future. Thus it might be concluded that political boundaries were becoming more permeable to economic and social exchanges.[1]

During the same period, colonialism collapsed to about 5 percent of its former dimensions, leaving behind it more than forty new nations. Each of these new nations now must surround itself with a properly trained customs service and border guards. It must collect customs duties, issue licenses, and enforce quotas. Thus barriers between peoples are being raised, at the very same time that the older boundaries separating the more developed nations are being penetrated. Progress has its paradoxes: as economic nationalism is being rejected as a contributor to war and a deterrent to growth, and the imperialistic aspect that built up self-contained worldwide blocs has collapsed altogether, its features are being adopted as a matter of political necessity in the bright, new states that have just been created.

Much more spectacular than the growth of economic interchange has

[1] For a longer-term view see the analysis of K. W. Deutsch and A. Eckstein, "National Industrialization and the Declining Share of the International Sector, 1890–1959," *World Politics,* vol. 13, pp. 267–299, 1961; G. Haberler, "Integration and Growth of the World Economy in Historical Perspective," *American Economic Review,* vol. 54, pp. 1–22, 1964.

been the flow of persons and cultural materials. New methods of passenger transportation and communications are far more economical of time and money than their predecessors. People the world over have been taking advantage of these opportunities, as evidenced by Figure 2. This acceleration of interaction, for purposes of diplomacy, foreign study, business, and pleasure, means that an international version of civilization is being increasingly diffused throughout the world; in each country at least one city has absorbed part of it. For parts of the world which previously had little contact with the outside, the resulting participation in the modern

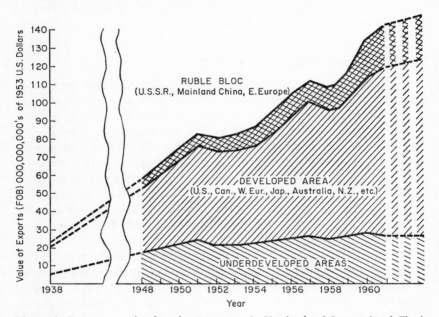

Figure 1. Postwar trends of trade. Source: 1961 Yearbook of International Trade Statistics, 1963.

world culture has brought about the establishment of airports, radio communications, hotels, hospitals, printing facilities, schools, and (to a lesser extent) harbors, roads, factories, telephones, offices, and public health programs. Through these affected cities the underdeveloped areas of the world are being pricked by pinpoints of modernism; rapid change of some kind seems inevitable.

How long can this favorable climate for exchange be expected to continue? What factors are operating to sustain it? Many proposals for reducing tariff barriers have been produced by individual nations and blocs, intended to create conditions equivalent to those of the Common Market in Western Europe. Some of the less ambitious of these seem likely to be expedited. Proposals for promoting tourism, overseas study, and work permits for nonresidents are being implemented. The movement of persons across national borders is making the production and consumption of exportable services a much more significant factor in the balance of payments than before, but the effects upon commodity flow are diverse. In some cases the flow of expertise will substitute for sizable quantities of imported goods; more often it serves to introduce new wants into a society, and these wants can only be satisfied through increased trade.

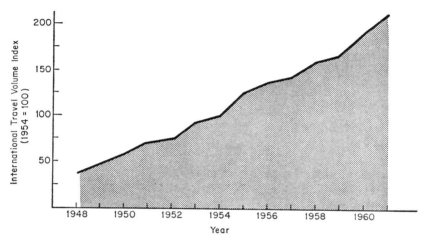

Figure 2. International travel. Source: International Tourist Travel, U.N. Statistical Yearbook, 1962, for basic data.

An important factor limiting the growth of trade is the orientation of the national economic specialization toward the markets provided by the original seats of industrialization—an outgrowth of colonialism and historic spheres of interest. Thus neighboring countries in the less developed parts of the world are more likely to produce competitive export items than complementary ones which could be conveniently exchanged. Therefore, if foreign commerce were to be encouraged, it could easily create the conditions for cutthroat competition between neighboring countries, with the result that virtually all the benefits that flow from trade go to the consuming nations that are already on the road to affluence. This would merely repeat conditions similar to the overproduction and intense competition during the later part of the 1950s that afflicted the nations whose primary exports were coffee, cocoa, and sugar.

Another cause for the slowing down of the rate of growth of international trade arises from the need of many nations to conserve foreign exchange, limiting its use to the purchase of only the most necessary items. The reserves of foreign credits that accumulated during World War II, because there were no suitable goods on the market, were largely spent by 1950. Countries whose exports were at a low level, or for whom markets were not expanding, were forced to restrict their expenditures because credit was usually available only for special projects. Thus the prospective scarcity of foreign convertible currencies led developing nations to give high priority to proposals for import substitution. The most common industries that were encouraged were cotton textiles, wood products, and automobile assembly.

It is to be expected that eventually all the nations of the world will have their own garment-making industries, paper mills and printing plants, as well as the skills for fabricating shapes and machines from iron and steel. It would then be supposed that all trade in these items would stop, but that is not the case. People exchange goods for the sake of variety as well as efficiency. There would still be a demand for exotic styles and forms that could not be conceived in one's own culture. This all-too-human dissatisfaction with the routine fulfillment of needs, and sharpened interest in other peoples' tastes and talents, will probably become a major motive for trade after all the opportunities for import substitution have been exhausted. The increasing variety and sophistication in consumer tastes are stimulated and sustained by the growth in the exchange of persons.

Technological innovation also tends to depress the needs for trade. At a given level of economic activity there will be less exchange across national boundaries when substitutes for the foreigner's goods are invented. Perhaps the most notable example in the postwar period is that provided by synthetic rubber. Were it not for the development of several kinds of synthetic rubber during World War II and some spectacular achievements in high polymers during the 1950s, rubber would have experienced a boom at least as great as that of petroleum, since the expansion of both is strongly linked to the spread of automobile transportation. But as things stand, in the near future almost any country will be in a position to supply raw materials for the production of butadiene and process it into synthetic rubber, and almost all industrialized countries have already installed some plants to supply at least part of their own needs. Therefore the price of rubber has tended to drop down to the price of the synthetic, even though the supply of natural rubber is not significantly augmented. Much the same story could be told regarding the world market for fats and oils, for the detergents have accounted for an even greater share of consumption in the soap market in industrial countries than have synthetics in the rubber market. Wool, too, has experienced strong substitution pressure from nylon, dacron, orlon, and other synthetics, and silk has been reduced to virtually an oddity in the course of its contest with nylon.

One consequence of the tendency toward substitution has been to reduce the relative dependence of the industrial nations upon the commodities exported primarily by less developed countries. Thus since 1954, after the burst in demand induced by the Korean conflict had settled down, the value of commodities declined as compared with the value of machinery and equipment. The terms of trade turned against the raw-materials-producing countries (Figure 3). Moreover, the value of the

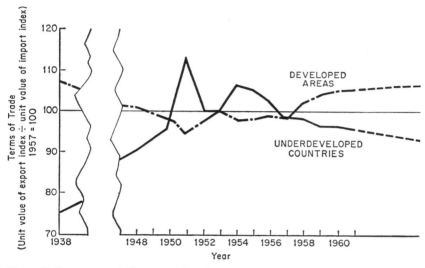

Figure 3. Postwar trends in terms of trade. Developed areas include North America, Western Europe, Australia, New Zealand, South Africa, Japan. Source: 1961 Yearbook of International Trade Statistics, 1963.

highly fabricated products being exchanged accounts for a steadily increasing proportion of world trade, and it appears most likely that capital goods and durable goods will continue to increase in importance as long as the international monetary system holds up and long-term credit is being granted for the purchase of these items.

Flows of capital goods are stimulated initially by international comparisons made by travelers, and subsequent installations involve many additional trips. Simultaneously the cost of travel, expressed in terms of money and particularly of time, has been diminished by investments in air transport and the building of highways. These movements have by no means yet run their course; on the contrary, they provoke further acceleration in the transfer of equipment across national boundaries. Continuous growth of international travel at a rate of 10 to 15 percent may be anticipated for decades to come, barring any intervening catastrophes, while export of equipment is expected to expand at half that rate.

To sum up, the climate for exchange in the world now seems to have shifted from "commodities" to the movement of sophisticated goods and educated people. Caused in part by increasing foreign aid and technical assistance, it provides many opportunities for development, which will be explored in the following section on industrialization.

DEVELOPMENTS FROM ADVANCED TECHNOLOGY

The outstanding performer among the various commodities in world trade during this postwar era was petroleum. It was the bonanza resource, a source of wealth as good as the possession of gold. Oil was needed in almost all the developed parts of the world, its price being determined to a large extent by the price of coal. The cost of coal, including the subsidies, was steadily rising in Europe. In contrast, the fluid state of oil made it simple to transport on land and economical to move by sea. More than half of all the funds expended upon resource development poured into petroleum exploration and production.

Oil is virtually unique among natural resources for its technological requirements. Very high levels of technical skills, combined with remarkably large amounts of risk capital, are needed for exploration and drilling. Very few countries which possess oil-bearing strata have both the skill and the capital. Moreover, once oil is found, subsequent transportation, refining, and marketing stages require equally advanced skills and even larger amounts of capital. Thus it is not surprising that more than 90 percent of the world's oil production, and virtually all the pioneering in the development of new fields, is undertaken by billion-dollar corporations that operate internationally through subsidiaries, affiliates, and consortiums with governments. Many of the oil-rich countries have been forced to collaborate with extremely modern business firms operating on a scale larger than the country's own national economy. The oil countries have become technologically dependent upon the companies, not only for managing petroleum production but also for many modern services, such as public health, fresh water, and transportation.

Most of the countries that presently export oil were colonial or had been placed under the protection of Western powers in a semicolonial status. Thus the international oil companies usually started with preferential status, and they could depend upon military protection by the interested powers. The rise of nationalism in the postwar period changed that relationship. The respective oil countries proceeded to remove all the symbols of political dependency, to build up their own armies and administrative bodies, and to extract better terms from the companies.

The technological dependence, however, remains as strong as ever. Extraordinarily expensive failures of national oil enterprises suggest that no country lacking a long petroleum tradition can develop its own oil with its own skills and organizations, even if, as in Brazil, the country has already made substantial technological progress. The recent instance of Argentina is equally emphatic in confirming this dependence upon the international firms. For political reasons this country made extended attempts, unsuccessfully, to develop its own oil potentials by itself. Argentina changed its position from a significant oil importer to that of exporter within a few years after the international firms were admitted, and as a consequence saved hundreds of millions of dollars' worth of foreign exchange each year. The rapid expansion in the U.S.S.R. cannot be claimed as an exception, since Russian experience with petroleum began with the Baku fields at the very beginning of the evolution of the technology; its organization should have accumulated knowledge and experience equal to that of the large international firms capable of undertaking petroleum development elsewhere in the world.

The technical competence of the oil companies is based upon outlays for research and development on a scale that cannot be matched by the oil-exporting countries. Increasing company research is now going also into the marketing of petroleum products and into human organization, but the oil companies' investigations of governmental processes remain uninspired and deficient. They have developed a technique with a strong bias toward engineering. It is only in the past decade or so that they have turned their attention to the other key variables that affect the efficiency of resource development.

The principal reason for the heavy demand for oil is the convenience of the internal-combustion engine for power vehicles and the high quality of hydrocarbon fuels. Gasoline and diesel oil contain roughly 50 percent more energy per unit weight than competing fuels—an important consideration when it is remembered that it costs fuel to carry fuel; and the poorer the energy content of the fuel, the more frequent are the halts for refueling and reconditioning. Dieselization of railroads and ocean shipping, for example, has brought about remarkable operating economies. Electric power production in the harbor cities has shifted to the use of low-cost petroleum residues, and even the steel industries have found ways of saving part of the declining supply of coking coal by heating the furnaces with oil and gas. Superimposed upon all these industrial uses is the increased household utilization of oil, mainly in the form of kerosene and fuel oil, although natural gas is replacing coal gas in the larger cities and low-pressure gas (LPG) is being introduced wherever higher incomes are prevalent. While the petroleum chemicals, plastics, synthetic-rubber, and synthetic-fiber industries are indeed huge and almost completely dependent upon oil as a source of raw materials, their contribution to the increased demand for petroleum is still almost trivial by comparison with the demand for fuel. Consumption of petroleum should increase in the future with the spread of industry, but natural gas will play a bigger role because methods have now been developed for its economic shipment in a condensed, or liquid, form. Gas is even more likely to be converted into chemicals and then into the other ultramodern industrial products; it will therefore be the basis for large industrial complexes arising near the major oil and gas fields over the next several decades.

The capital cost of petroleum refining and further chemical synthesis is very much the same per unit of capacity, regardless of the site of operations. The cost of transporting petroleum products, however, is several times greater than that of moving crude oil. Therefore these facilities tend to be located at points which minimize transport costs over the lifetime of the installations (which are normally amortized over ten to twenty years) and more often than not located close to the industrial users of the components of the product mix.

The initial removal of the petroleum from the ground, however, requires a variable amount of capital. In its report "The Economic Development of the Middle East, 1958-9," the U.N. Department of Economic and Social Affairs estimated that the gross cumulative investment in the production of one barrel per day of average quality crude oil was $350 in the Middle East, $1,700 in Venezuela, $3,300 in Europe, and $4,000 in North America. The average cost of production during the 1949-1958 period showed a similar pattern, with $0.16 per barrel for the Middle East, $0.57 in Venezuela, $0.87 in the Far East, and $1.66 in the United States. The cost differential has been greater than the cost of transporting petroleum to the principal markets in Western Europe and the United States, and therefore the Middle East in particular greatly increased its share of the market during the 1949-1958 period. Its competitive advantage has been maintained since then despite the entrance of the U.S.S.R. into the market. However, the profits of most of the international firms fell off sharply toward the end of the decade as the competition increased. Price instability brought a reaction in the form of the Organization of Petroleum Exporting Countries (OPEC), an agency which has been seeking with some success a larger share of more monopolistic prices for the producing countries. This policy, however, may stimulate a new flow of "hot oil." Bonanzas are difficult to bank.

THE VALUE OF RESOURCES

What is the effect upon development of the possession of a balanced complement of resources? Let us turn from a focus upon oil and its peculiarities to a survey of the stock on hand of all the recorded resources, taken country by country. Such an assessment of assets should include the other major fossil fuels, especially coal, hydroelectric power, the chief ferrous and nonferrous minerals, and the agricultural soils, timber, and other living resources. This is not a complete list of resources; climate, for example, can be exceedingly important, and so is accessibility to the rest of the world, but the market value of these latter assets is less readily assessed.

A country-by-country evaluation of the stock of available resources encounters many difficulties in assessment. Most of the problems arise from the need for definitions of what constitutes an extractable resource and what remains a low-grade unusable potential. What degree of certainty is acceptable that the superficial probings reflect actual strata or ore bodies? The various resource specialists and the agencies responsible for resources have no set standards for reporting the results of their explorations.

For the purpose of systematic development planning, the viewpoint of this study toward resources is that of the prudent and responsible appraiser who realizes that some risk of being proved wrong is inevitable. He must contend nonetheless that it is foolhardy to depend upon speculative, and often self-serving, reports (typically the rumors that are responsible for the booms and rushes that so often fade out). International statistics, which are more and more being put upon a comparable basis, provide the best basis for intercountry comparison. It should be borne in mind that these statistics do not tell us the whole story. Their main defect is that many of the least developed countries have not reported what their own resources are in one or more categories. Nevertheless, the ultimate test of prudence still applies because such countries are with few exceptions unable in their present position to develop their own resources, or even to measure them with some degree of confidence, without the participation of external groups. And natural resources cannot be counted upon for purposes of development until the know-how needed for their exploitation is at hand.

The set of calculations compiled (Table 1) represents a series of approximations which lead to an estimate of the aggregate value of resources on a per capita basis. The most serious difficulties encountered were with the pricing of commodities produced directly from the resources because proved and probable deposits represent materials to be used not now but in the indefinite future. In general the supply-and-demand outlook that lies behind Table 1 is the same as that arrived at in a recent study of the American economy.[2] That assessment is highly relevant

[2] H. H. Landsberg, L. L. Fischman, and J. L. Fisher, *Resources in America's Future*, The Johns Hopkins Press, Baltimore, Md., 1963.

Table 1. The Stocks of Natural Resources Available on a Per Capita Basis in Selected Countries of the World

Rank	Country	Population	Agricultural forests and fisheries	Coal reserves	Iron ore	Oil	Nonfuel, nonferrous	Hydro	Total
1	Kuwait	220,000				$210,000			$200,000
2	Qatar	40,000				75,000			75,000
3	U.S.S.R.	210,000,000	$ 70	35,000	240	9,000	6	490	44,000
4	Norway	3,600,000	790	5,600	520		100	2,100	10,000
5	Rhodesian Federation	8,100,000	160	2,200	3,000		100	3,500	9,000
6	Colombia	13,800,000	280	4,900	16	82		2,500	7,800
7	Venezuela	6,500,000	50	2	610	4,400		2,000	7,100
8	Poland	29,300,000	60	5,100	20		870	1,400	7,300
9	Bahrein	140,000				6,300			6,300
10	Cuba	6,600,000	860		5,000		310	2	6,200
11	Iceland	170,000	510					5,000	5,500
12	Saudi Arabia	6,000,000				5,000			5,000
13	Czechoslovakia	13,600,000		4,200	40			30	4,300
14	Iraq	6,900,000	30			3,800		11	3,800
15	Ecuador	4,200,000	303			21		3,000	3,400
16	Costa Rica	1,100,000	700					2,200	2,900
17	British Guiana	550,000	770				500	1,600	2,900
18	Malayan Federation	6,700,000	890	4	40		13	1,700	2,600
19	Brazil	64,200,000	170	170	1,070	50	10	1,080	2,600

No.	Country								
20	Chile	7,500,000	37	37	106	240	1,000	970	2,400
21	Liberia	1,300,000	280		130		33	2,000	2,400
22	Peru	10,500,000	130	480	12	43	75	1,571	2,200
23	Denmark	4,500,000	1,980				60	140	2,200
24	Iran	20,100,000	60			1,940		40	2,000
25	Honduras	1,900,000	340	1.3	60			1,500	1,900
26	Argentina	20,600,000	610	6.6	47	35		670	1,370
27	Spain	29,900,000	100	670	300		17	140	1,230
28	Trinidad	820,000	360			920			1,220
29	Finland	4,400,000	880					150	1,050
30	Mexico	33,300,000	130	230	100	120	21	390	1,040
31	Ireland	2,800,000	820				70	130	950
32	Burma	20,500,000	100			7	4	800	910
33	Philippines	24,700,000	200	5	450		27	200	880
34	Sierra Leone	2,400,000	60		460			250	770
35	India	402,000,000	13	340	260		3	80	700
36	Uruguay	2,700,000	360	590				300	760
37	Korea	23,800,000	2	9	32			5	630
38	Algeria	10,900,000	280	220	89	30	6	215	630
39	Tanganyika	9,100,000	150				160	105	630
40	Nicaragua	1,400,000	400					190	590
41	Japan	93,700,000	43	440		1		73	570
42	Uganda	6,500,000	390					120	510
43	Israel	2,000,000	360				32	90	480
44	Ethiopia	21,800,000	30					400	430
45	Ceylon	9,600,000	380					45	420
46	Yugoslavia	18,400,000	110	5	33	62	5	195	410
47	Greece	8,300,000	210		66		33	95	410

Table 1. The Stocks of Natural Resources Available on a Per Capita Basis in Selected Countries of the World (Continued)

Rank	Country	Population	Agricultural forests and fisheries	Coal reserves	Iron ore	Oil	Nonfuel, nonferrous	Hydro	Total
48	Lebanon	1,600,000	$ 130					160	$ 290
49	Portugal	9,000,000	130	6	61		14	59	270
50	Italy	49,100,000	120	8	13		14	110	270
51	Turkey	26,900,000	120	37	9		9	80	260
52	Afghanistan	13,200,000(?)	49					200	250
53	Formosa	10,200,000	150					87	240
54	Bulgaria	7,800,000	180				24	34	240
55	Thailand	21,900,000	140		1		20	44	210
56	Egypt	25,400,000	140		6	$ 21		13	180
57	Indonesia	90,300,000(?)	65	11	12	33	8	12	140
58	Viet-Nam	13,800,000(?)	52	5				52	100
59	Pakistan	86,800,000	24					70	100
60	Sudan	11,500,000	16					13	30

because the United States is by far the largest consumer of raw materials, and price changes in North America cause worldwide shifts with insignificant lag. An upward trend in the prices of mineral commodities (except iron ore) is anticipated for the 1970s and 1980s, but not acute enough to make it pay to engage in stockpiling above the ground. Increases in value of the basic commodities would be far greater were it not for the cost-reducing innovations now in the laboratory that should soon affect the production of some of these commodities. Those products which are not susceptible to technological improvements will be indirectly affected by the shifts in consumer choice brought about by differential price increases.

In these calculations the values assigned to the respective resource stocks are set at the lowest regional prices during the 1962–1963 period. True, these prices include some transport charges and variable amounts of extractive costs. For that reason, we must speak of resource assets in a gross sense. For example, the sale value of the land containing the resource, but otherwise in an undeveloped condition, would normally be somewhat less than the value assigned in Table 1 if actually put out for bid. Nevertheless the existence of the resource in one land area adds also to the value of other lands and properties that lie between it and the important markets. Careful planning enables a society to take advantage of this extra value. The potential return to the economy can be significantly greater than merely the value added in the course of producing the basic commodity. Therefore the figures employed represent a reasonable approximation for national comparison.

This appraisal also puts emphasis on the long pull in development, which means placing a high value on opportunities that are available a generation or more hence. Coal supplies, for example, are assigned a value of $5 per ton, which is the approximate contract price in the vicinity of the best coal fields. However, the value of coal at the older European mines, around which many industries and human settlements have grown up, runs $12 to $20 per ton. But even such prices, when discounted at the present rates of return on capital from dates of mining 30 to 100 years hence, rarely yield a present value as much as $5 per ton. Thus, the price assigned reflects in considerable part the value of the opportunities made available to a country as a result of the possession of coal seams. The values are real and fairly attributed to the resource.

The stocks of a resource-rich nation, such as the United States (not represented on the chart), may well be overstated by these assumptions. Calculated by the same method, they come to the amazing figure of $30,000 per capita, owing primarily to the extensive coal reserves that have been surveyed. Similarly, the intensive exploration that is being conducted in the U.S.S.R. (said to cost more than a quarter of all mineral production charges) has yielded reserves which would be assessed at an even higher sum.[3] But the Soviet resources are, to an important extent, inconveniently located, so that costs of exploitation and transport will be high and the potential net contribution to income may be no greater than those to be developed in North America.

A novel balancing feature has been incorporated into this accounting of resources. Soil resources have hitherto been set aside or treated separately in assessments of natural-resource endowment because they are believed to have quite different effects. It is recognized that countries such as Denmark, New Zealand, Malaya, and Brazil have achieved significant economic progress by developing soil resources. On the other hand, the huge output of agricultural products in China and India barely keeps their population alive. It is apparent that soils used for export crops (to other countries or other regions in the same country) can provide the potential for economic growth, whereas those used for subsistence do not. Therefore a reasonable appraisal of soil resources relevant to development, comparable with the appraisal worked out for minerals, is the economic value of the land required for the production of exports; it is approximated by taking ten times the value of the annual exports as established at the time and place of shipment. Since land is predominantly a renewable resource, its properties are very similar to those of hydroelectric power, where, according to a popular convention for achieving comparability, the undeveloped capacity was multiplied by ten years of production in order to estimate a present value of output. Fisheries are trivial in almost all cases (except in Norway and Iceland), but they are treated in the same manner as output from the soil. This manner of defining soil resources implies that if the institutions lack the capability for switching into new export crops, the resource might as easily disappear through a deterioration in the world market for certain commodities (this has occurred for indigo, and may soon be the case for butter) as through a decline in the fertility of the soil.

The gross estimates in Table 1 are low in some instances. They do not include contributions to internal growth where they can be identified. Nor do they take into account the proposed land-development schemes and irrigation projects that already are generating speculative land values in countries like Pakistan, Sudan, Mexico, etc. As already noted, the prudent appraiser discounts speculative land booms as a source of real development. In any case most of the expected output of such projects will go into local consumption to meet the demands of the increasing population, so the contributions of these new projects to world trade should not upset the rankings to any considerable degree.

[3] J. A. Hodgkins, *Soviet Power,* Prentice-Hall, Inc., Englewood Cliffs, N.J., 1961.

Among all the resources, by this evaluation, coal remains the most valuable. This condition is likely to last for at least another century or two. Geologists recognize that among the fossil fuels in the world at large, coal is ten to thirty times more abundant than petroleum and natural gas. Similarly, the coal reserves of last resort—the brown coal, lignite, and peat that are presently uneconomic but likely to be used on a large scale when present fuel sources have been exhausted—are perhaps a hundred times as great in quantity as the oil shales and the tar sands from which petroleumlike products can be extracted. The value of uranium is not a very significant factor when putting a dollar value upon fuel reserves. This is true despite the anticipation that nuclear fuels will become the principal source of electric power by the end of the century because the cost of capital is the primary determinant of the cost of electricity drawn from nuclear energy. Further, its widespread deposits suggest that monopoly pricing will not be possible, in contrast to the fossil fuels, which will be found primarily in two countries after the turn of the century. For purposes of this study uranium is included in the nonferrous, nonfuel component of natural resources.

At present it is expected that the fossil fuels will achieve their highest value as materials for the synthesis of transport fuels (aviation and marine) and as reducing agents for oxidized ores. Fossil fuels therefore provide a resource base for developed economies specializing in heavy manufacturing, whereas soil resources and water resources should lead to a developed economy based upon food processing. Those areas with very poor resources will be forced to specialize in light-to-medium industries and in services.

NATURAL RESOURCES AND ECONOMIC GROWTH

Is the ranking of a nation with respect to its stock of resources in any way correlated with its performance as a growing system? Andic and Peacock [4] have compared the per capita income of countries in 1957 which also reported their incomes in 1949 (Figure 4). These statisticians demonstrated that the oft-observed trend for the gap to widen between the rich and the poor nations continued through this period. The comparison is made upon income data obtained for thirty-five of the countries in Table 2, much of it admittedly of poor quality but certainly no worse than the resource data for the same countries. In any case some sources of error are canceled out by the fact that the per capita income of a country is compared only with itself at a prior period. A high correlation between resource level and the level of per capita income ($r = 0.90$, $p < .00,001$)

[4] S. Andic and A. T. Peacock, "The International Distribution of Income," *Journal of the Royal Statistical Society,* ser. A, vol. 124, pt. 2, pp. 206–218, 1961.

was found, thereby reinforcing the generalization arising from theoretical and historic analysis that a high-resource level has in the past promoted opportunities for economic growth. No satisfactory sample could be obtained, however, for computing a correlation of resource level with recent growth rates.

When comparing one list of nations ranked according to resource level

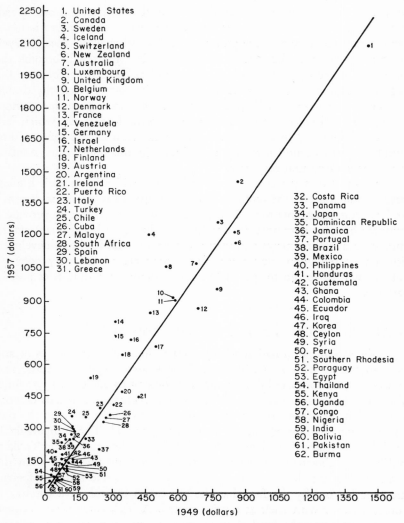

Figure 4. National per capita incomes reported to the United Nations. Source: Yearbook of National Accounts Statistics, 1959. Regression of 1957 data on 1949.

with another graded according to the income level achieved, it is useful to identify the exceptions to the rule. What happened in those instances? The countries that managed to reach unusually high incomes ($250 to $350 per capita) despite a paucity of resources were Israel, Italy, Japan, Turkey, and Lebanon. For quite different reasons Israel and Lebanon had found means of obtaining capital and skills from overseas through the use of family and ethnic ties. Italy and Japan have built up manufacturing enterprises which compete for price and quality anywhere in the world, even though almost all the value of the raw materials other than fuel is based upon mechanized agriculture. All these countries except Lebanon received rather large infusions of foreign aid in the period since World War II; Lebanon obtained its capital mainly from individuals by providing banking and investment services.

The scattered and still incomplete reports of economic growth as they are accumulated reveal a strong association between rapid growth and the receipt of substantial amounts of foreign aid. On the other hand, countries like Burma and Ceylon, which have refused aid of many kinds, have fared rather poorly. The success of the Marshall Plan is self-evident, but the postwar comeback in Japan, the Philippines, Formosa, Malaya, and Greece has recently become at least as impressive.

The high-resource-level countries that have not exhibited income growth commensurate with expectations include Colombia, Ecuador, Peru, Burma, and Iraq. A review of recent history in these places suggests that their pace was particularly sluggish in the postwar period. For the greater part of this period all these countries were controlled by political groups which were not sympathetic to the international enterprises that were skilled in resource development. None gave a high priority to education in their national programs until the end of the period. Colombia, Iraq, and Burma were racked by civil war; the other countries were faced with repeated threats of armed rebellion. It might be reasonably concluded from this small sample of nations exhibiting low growth that social and political conflict kept them at levels very much below what would have been expected on the basis of their respective resource endowments.[5]

[5] It should be remembered that statistics regarding resources are not available for about forty nations and self-governing territories, and that the data on per capita income reported to the United Nations for 1957 omitted about seventy political units, or more than half. Therefore statistical conclusions must remain suspect. It is a fact that reporting countries almost always have reasonably efficient statistical services, and that these services are a consequence of both extensive foreign trade and organized development programs. Contrarily, those countries that do not report are almost surely lagging in economic development. This inference does not alter the conclusions which have been put forward in these paragraphs.

EXPERIENCES OF THE OIL COUNTRIES

How has the availability of rich resources affected the process of national development in recent times? By far the best examples of the special hazards of wealth are provided by the experiences of the oil-producing countries.

The relationship between oil and national economic development is very simple: oil provides foreign exchange in an economy where it had previously been very scarce. But how has the money obtained from the export of petroleum been used? What kind of development has resulted from this new potential for capital formation? Where has the money derived from oil been invested?

Each country in question presents a different picture (Table 2). Oil money in Kuwait, for example, provided almost every basic service free to the small populace: education, technical training, fresh water, clinics, hospitals, roads, public facilities, some housing, etc. Teachers were imported from all over the Arab world at attractive rates of pay, and contractors were brought in also to get the construction done quickly. Adults brought up to live in a traditional manner were slow to change, however, so the results are still not evident to any casual visitor. The remainder of the oil money—about two-thirds of it—has accumulated in London, awaiting prudent methods of expenditure to be developed. Part will eventually go into a special fund for the development of Arab countries, but this project moves slowly.

In Saudi Arabia the impact has been felt somewhat longer and the compromise with tradition remained closer to the established mores. A substantial share of the returns from the wells has sustained the legends of luxury and extravagance in the life of the royal household. Saudi Arabia being more independent, its funds were handled according to values that were traditional for royalty in the Near East. Economic development was not a goal espoused by the King in the period immediately after the war; instead pan-Arabism was an end sought after, but only on the King's own terms, so that it developed into an antinationalist Islamic league that encompassed far more than the jealously nationalistic Arab world. As a result, only a nobility and elite have profited significantly from oil, although Aramco has done its best to encourage the expansion of a tiny middle class committed to enterprise as a way of life. Poverty is perhaps even more visible now than before the large-scale exploitation of the oil, because the nomads have been settled upon the land and peasants are crowding into the cities. A public works program accelerated belatedly in 1960–1961 should make some visible impact by the end of the decade.

Table 2. Economic Development of the Territories Rich in Petroleum Resources

Country	1960 population *	1960 petroleum production,† barrels/day	1960 value per capita	GNP invested, %	GNP education, %	1960 per capita GNP ‡	1950–1960 growth of per capita GNP, % ‡
Saudi Arabia	6,000,000	1,395	$ 70	5§	1–2§	$ 169	3–5
Kuwait	200,000	1,600	1,400	35	10	300§	10
Venezuela	6,800,000	2,850	550	25	3	1,019	4–5
Iraq	6,800,000	965	9	10–20	5–7	160	3–4
Iran	20,000,000	2,050	15	?	2.5	145	1–2
Indonesia	110,000,000(?)	2,110	1	?	5 ¶	59	None

* Estimated from data presented in the *U.N. Demographic Yearbook* for earlier years.

† As reported in *Oil and Gas Journal*, Jan. 29, 1962, p. 183.

‡ Estimated from various sources, but depends especially upon: Benjamin Shwadran, *The Middle East: Oil and the Great Powers*, Frederick A. Praeger, Inc., New York, 1959. A balanced historical review of the development of petroleum in an area where petroleum issues have dominated the development.

W. A. Leeman, *The Price of Middle East Oil*, Cornell University Press, Ithaca, N.Y., 1962. A discussion of the world petroleum market during the postwar period.

Life-Rand McNally Atlas, New York, 1961. The GNP data are based upon 1956–1960 averages as reported by nations, but adjusted by local specialists when dubious.

H. R. Labouisse, *The Economic Development of Venezuela*, The Johns Hopkins Press, Baltimore, Md., 1961.

§ Estimated from various qualitative descriptions cited in the monthly *Middle East Affairs*.

¶ Estimates arrived at by observers in Indonesia. The contributions of the family and the community to education are quite significant but are not budgeted and not included here. Allocations to education have been declining since 1960, mainly because of armament and inflation.

Iran is a much larger country and is not wholly dependent upon oil. It has funneled its own share from the oil wells and refinery into physical development of many kinds—dams, roads, airports, universities, irrigation projects, factories, etc. However, the social structure and the behavior of property owners have proved to be remarkably inflexible, so that the reforms of the traditional way of life that usually precede rapid economic development have been slow to appear. The politics of Iran was focused upon the oil-development issue all during the decade, generating the extremism of a sincere nationalist, Mossadeq, and delaying constructive programs. Thus far, the possession of oil has probably done more harm than good to Iran because the development rate has been very slow and no formula has been found for stepping it up; yet there is a real opportunity for the future.

Iraq's experience has been similar in that the share of oil profits, the use of these funds, and the acceptance of advice and protection from a foreign power have all stirred up continuous agitation and bloody revolutions. Much of its returns from oil have been put into education, irrigation, and miscellaneous other projects which are finally beginning to produce extra income in the population. But again, it is primarily the educated classes that are profiting at this point; the majority remains unaffected.

In Venezuela the amount of money left in the country from the sale of oil is the greatest of all, and the influx of receipts has been building up over decades. Much of this wealth has been acquired by the political families and transferred to Europe. Most of the remainder was invested by a dictator in monumental structures for the major cities. The building of property that produced such low rates of return on capital led to a financial crisis when income from oil declined because of changes in the world market. A sizable population in Venezuela (in the hundreds of thousands) live at a North American level, which costs 10 to 20 percent more there than in North America, while others, numbering millions, remain at levels close to subsistence. A major share of the oil income was spent in a manner that permitted this differential to be maintained. Nevertheless the basis for rapid growth now exists. Urbanization of the poor rural population, enlarged expenditures for education, and the modernization of agriculture make it possible. However, the violent political divisions inherited from the past must be held in check.

Indonesia is hardly to be ranked with the others because its population is much larger and its oil exports are smaller. Yet it, too, suffers from the disease of "oil politics." The uprisings in Sumatra were based to an important extent upon a feeling that the resources which "belonged" to the people in those areas were yielding no local advantage but only supporting the central government and the Javanese. Oil revenues were not being returned in the form of extra education and other services. The central

Indonesian government barely managed to survive the many challenges it faced during the 1950s while the nation was being knit together. Development has had to be postponed until the nation is complete and secure.

Evidently the riches derived from oil have not been very efficiently channeled into development programs and therefore have produced very little economic development. Although most of the diversions may be traced to characteristics of the traditional society and its government, some may be traced to the special technology of oil. A large oil field requires first a camp in which drilling and construction crews live at a high level of consumption. Later, when operations have been firmly established, small cities must be constructed which operate at standards very close to those set by upper-middle-class suburbs in the United States and Great Britain. The residents train native counterparts, who, when they take over responsible positions, cannot afford to live at a markedly lower level of consumption because they would lose status in their relations with foreigners. Oil thus propagates a style of life which a newly developing country cannot really afford to have transferred to the whole of its civil service (except in Kuwait and now, perhaps, Libya).

Even more important than status problems are the psychological effects of possessing exportable quantities of oil. The development of petroleum reserves excites fears of being robbed or exploited, suspicions of the motives of any local promoter, and feelings of grandeur that lead to extravagance. It induces obsessions, and these crystallize into political factions and even guerrilla bands. Petroleum extraction is the most highly civilized of any resource-development activity, and yet it induces something akin to the "gold fever" of the nineteenth century, which affects both a floating population of sharpsters and confidence men attracted to the scene and the nationalities that are represented as the owner. This disease causes a striking increase in irrational behavior, or at least what appears as such to outside observers.

A third source of difficulty lies in experiences encountered by perhaps half the countries when actually applying the oil funds to major projects. It is desirable to obtain visible improvements in transportation, water supply, electric power generation, and the school system as quickly as possible. This means committing the funds to fully prepared projects as soon as they are earned. The resulting program is acutely vulnerable to an upset in oil prices in the world market and to interruptions in oil transportation (as in the Suez crisis). These disturbances are relatively frequent and completely unpredictable. To accumulate an adequate foreign exchange reserve might delay the program several years; yet, if an adequate reserve had not been built up, at each such crisis the construction projects must be halted. Then the contractors disband their organization and go home. So, while oil offers one of the steadier sources of foreign exchange (its continuity of income is quite good as compared with nonferrous metals and agricultural products), it is not nearly as dependable as a varied mix of manufactured goods.

In the countries discussed, except possibly Indonesia, the underground reserves are so large that petroleum production is likely to double over the next decade and continue to increase for a while thereafter. However, sometime within the next generation it will take a sharp downturn. The history of the early oil fields ultimately must be repeated because oil is not a renewable resource. What will happen to these areas then? In Texas, Mexico, and elsewhere, the oil producers (both private and public) obtained subsidies for the marginal wells, but in these areas the rest of the economy was large in comparison with the oil industry. Plans for building up, or becoming attached to, large economies have not yet been undertaken by the oil countries, although Kuwait may be able to make such moves with its new development fund. Some of the most foresighted planning has been undertaken by the international companies. Their horizon is limited, however, to five to fifteen years, so they are not concerned with the prospects of decline.

A review of the experiences of these societies suggests that a diet of rich resources is rather indigestible for a poor, traditional society and that the resulting upsets inhibit the development of modern institutions. The social, cultural, and political variables throttle the growth rate to a modest level even when there is no scarcity of capital or high-level technological skills.

FRUSTRATIONS IN THE COMMUNIST BLOC

The most striking shift in growth patterns in the post-1957 period had little to do with the resource structure itself. Rather it reflected a new ideological approach to development. China mobilized a Leap Forward which aimed at accelerated industrialization, particularly in basic commodities. But the confusion that resulted in the coordination of production efforts, particularly in the programming of transport movements, caused great wastage, especially of fossil fuels and agricultural produce. During the period 1960–1964 the Communist regime ceased publishing statistics. Growth in overall output per capita probably ceased (although there is evidence that some sectors were still expanding) and food became particularly scarce, despite improved weather for crops.

In Cuba similar policies have had even more catastrophic effects. A precipitate socialization of the economy has resulted in a decline in per capita income—once the second highest in Latin America—at the rate of 5 to 10 percent per year, despite extensive foreign aid. In the first three years the Castro regime managed to reduce consumption by one-quarter. The effect of income distribution was not quite as bad as these figures would indicate because virtually all luxury consumption was cut out; but the flight of the professionals, such as doctors, engineers, and teachers, has reduced the quality of social services available to the whole population. The organization of agriculture suffered, cash crops did not reach commitments, and strict rationing had to be instituted.

The economies of North Viet-Nam and Albania also stagnated during this period. The backwardness here, however, may be ascribed to political decisions being made without reference to their economic effects. In other words, in these countries it was more important to be dialectically "correct" than to make progress economically.

In Poland, Czechoslovakia, Hungary, and Yugoslavia the treatment of agriculture became more flexible during this period and the emphasis upon heavy industry was somewhat reduced, so that substantial improvements in the level of living were recorded. Food-production trends were more favorable than in the U.S.S.R., where after 1960 they appear to have failed to keep up with population growth. In all these Central European countries one new factor favors future development efforts: ways have now been found to reduce the birthrate. (The abortion rate is very high despite the entrenched opposition of the Catholic Church; yet the drop in birthrate occurred at the same time that the Church seems to have remained influential in many other matters.) In China and Cuba the structure of the family has been such that it successfully resists attempts to reduce fertility.

The basic difficulty for the Marxist-Leninist socialized systems, which distinguishes them from some other politico-economic systems, is that no incentives have been found which motivate a poorly educated people to produce an increasing agricultural surplus, i.e., commodities which can be exported to the urban sector. Nationalism has provided a cause which induces hundreds of thousands of people to sacrifice their careers and even their lives, but it does not seem to be the kind of force that makes farmers more efficient. These Socialist regimes believed that the elimination of landlords would provide both incentives for the farmers and surpluses for the cities, but this policy has worked out badly in the long run. Yet in other situations ideological commitments against market forces have been known to affect soil resource development constructively. The Mormons, for example, have done an outstanding job in the American desert, as compared with others coming from the same culture but not possessing the Mormons' religion-based political system. It is possible that the Marxist ideology may yet find a formula that fits within their political beliefs (the contemporary Polish situation is still a compromise with capitalism) because they are very willing to undertake experiments with whole economies. However, recent history does not suggest what the formula will be; the failures have been highly consistent.

Three countries that narrowly escaped the threat of Communist domination have experienced rather unexpected growth in the latter part of the 1950s and the 1960s. In Malaya growth was unexpected because synthetic rubber was making huge inroads on the natural-rubber market and threatening even greater replacements in the future. In Greece the contribution of natural resources seemed trivial, but its enterprising citizens had begun to develop agricultural exports to the Common Market countries, to undertake fisheries off the African coast in the Atlantic Ocean, and to attract capital for modern manufacturing. South Korea has begun to develop manufacturing enterprises at a rapid rate, while agriculture has not particularly lagged. Part of the explanation may lie in the fact that each of these nations suffered severely from military aggression (also described as "assistance to revolutionary forces") much later than the rest of the world, so that much of what was witnessed during this 1957–1963 period represents the kind of rebound after conflict that was demonstrated in Western Europe, Japan, and the U.S.S.R. somewhat earlier. All these countries (Malaya, Greece, Korea) were recipients of large quantities of aid from the outside, both military and economic, and each of them had previously put an emphasis upon education that was unusual for its part of the world. As a consequence, each was in a position to adjust rapidly and take advantage of economic opportunities.

THE ENTREPRENEURIAL SOCIETIES

During the postwar period some countries have exhibited the most prodigious spurts of economic development ever recorded in history. Japan has been most outstanding; Puerto Rico comes very close; and Hong Kong, Singapore, Italy, and Greece seem to be equally astonishing. These exceptional bursts of industrial expansion are resource-independent in that they involved no significant resources other than locational factors. How have such societies managed to do so well?

Japan has had a high rate of saving, a high level of education, and an orientation toward international trade for a long time. In the late 1950s Japan established itself as a technically sophisticated nation in the manufacture of synthetic fibers, specialized ships, automobiles, and pharmaceuticals. All these activities matured within a few years, using designers and technicians trained after the war. Many of the new industries quickly took over an important share of the world market. The underemployment in agriculture and the supposed overproduction of high school and college graduates permitted rapid recruitment of needed personnel. Japan's birthrate had meanwhile dropped closer to the level needed for replacement than had any Western country's in the postwar period. Thus Japan could register 7 to 11 percent per year or greater growth rates for several years consecutively.

In Puerto Rico many of these factors are seen at work. Roughly 10 to 12 per cent of the commonwealth income has been expended on education since World War II, and large amounts of assistance had been given to local educators before the war. Since most of this assistance was given for education in a foreign language (English), it was not received very well. The Puerto Rican sophistication appeared in certain unusual areas of government, such as planning, industrial promotion, tourism, and welfare administration. The government worked out an ingenious set of incentives for attracting entrepreneurial talent. It did its utmost not only to bring in new industry but also to see that high levels of worker productivity were achieved as quickly as possible, and everything was done—short of subsidizing gross inefficiency—to keep the enterprise alive and thriving. Much was done also to promote the efficiency of construction and service activities through improvement of transport and communications and through careful urban planning. The population pressure was relieved by emigration that was indirectly encouraged by the government.

In Puerto Rico the growth rate on a per capita basis ranged from 5 to 9 percent per year. All income levels in the population benefited, so the growth has been more balanced than in Japan. Puerto Rico is unable to use infant-industry protection, or other forms of discrimination in favor of home manufacturers (such as quotas), and so is presumably susceptible to the swings of the business cycle in the United States. Nevertheless, the economic planning has worked out strategies which enable the island economy to take advantage of downturns as well as upturns in the American economy. During downturns firms became very sensitive to labor costs and were therefore much more willing to investigate alternative locations for a projected expansion. During an upturn the policy was to attract the stablest and best-managed firms. Two different classes of firms could be fitted into the Puerto Rican economy, and two quite different sets of arguments, data, and incentives had to be formulated. Behind these policies has been a fact-oriented pragmatic institution, the Fomento, backed up by the economic division of the Puerto Rico Planning Board. The expertise in initiating new enterprise and promoting efficiency has, in effect, insulated the economy from the rather irregular growth of the United States as a whole.

Hong Kong's astonishing economic growth is sometimes attributed to a series of accidents. Industrialization was given a considerable assist when textile machinery bound for Shanghai, and ordered well before the Communist takeover, was held at Hong Kong. The hoarded capital that escaped from China was placed in banks that sponsored entrepreneurs in garment manufacture, toys, plastics fabrication, light machinery, batteries, etc. The levels of education in Hong Kong were higher than in China, and this local labor force was bolstered by refugees, which constituted a much more vigorous than average element in the inland Chinese population. There are no adequate summary figures to document the recent development in Hong Kong, but the scraps and fragments that do get published confirm the qualitative impression.

The government of the Crown Colony of Hong Kong previously thought its duty to be limited to maintaining public order so that trade could proceed. The transition to manufacturing required government attention to housing, water supplies, education, and other services. It has not yet faced up to the high fertility rate and the fact that the Chinese on this peninsula have no place to which they can migrate. (Arrangements arrived at in 1962 for emigration to the United States and Great Britain were a beginning, but insignificant as compared with the need.) Altogether Hong Kong's 3 million inhabitants have done remarkably well, despite the absence of natural resources and the leveling off of world trade. Its businessmen have shown remarkable capacities for overcoming the protectionist obstructions that arise as soon as they have borrowed a technology and set up an increasing flow of exports.

Singapore thus far has remained more of an entrepôt and has only half the population of Hong Kong, but it, too, has embarked upon a program of planned development of housing, education, and services. Singapore is able to maintain close connections with a Malayan hinterland with large export crops and large important demands, and its businessmen have shown astonishing capacity for recognizing economic opportunities and exploiting them, so the urban community is incidentally advanced. The population growth is so great, however, that it threatens to exceed any possible prospective returns from commerce. Only a limited amount of space is available for overspill in the form of housing and industry. Sites have been laid out for manufacturing, and some processing has begun, but the future remains unclear even if the union with the Malaysian territories to the north and on Borneo persists.

There are probably only a few other places in the world that could apply the government-assisted entrepreneurial formula that has worked so remarkably well for Hong Kong and Singapore thus far. Curaçao in the Caribbean is perhaps one possibility, Malta in the Mediterranean, or even cities like Aleppo in Syria, or Athens, Greece.

In the case of Italy quite a different pattern seems to have been responsible for the remarkable growth. Northern Italy had been even more developed than Japan, so that the basic managerial and technical skills were already present, while central and south Italy lived very close to subsistence in villages, towns, and urban slums. Modern industrial management took hold and improved worker productivity between 1952 and 1959 even more rapidly than it was increased in Japan. International markets were found for Italy's output of typewriters, motorbikes, automobiles, plastics, and other consumer products. By the 1960s some of the branch plants moved south to the Mezzogiorno, while at the same time the migration to the north became substantial. The planning carried on by the government was more extensive than any carried out in Japan, but its effectiveness seemed to be reduced by the political necessities facing the government. The state-sponsored efforts of the major entrepreneurs must be given the principal credit for the new prosperity in Italy.

In any country a relatively advanced stage in development can be said to have been reached when a growing society provides more technically trained people to other countries than it draws to itself to maintain its own growth. Although the exact date is difficult to establish, it appears now that about 1960 Japan started again to export more technical know-how than it received (it had previously done this during its attempted development of Manchuria, but this was a relationship imposed by military control). Its transfers of technical capability are made to less developed areas, such as Hong Kong, Thailand, and India, but various countries in Africa and Latin America were also significant recipients. The United States also recruited hundreds of Japanese scientists and engineers for its most advanced technical work.

In Puerto Rico also this reversal of the overall flow of technically competent people occurred about 1960. At the same time that the Puerto Ricans were still hiring statisticians, engineers, and university staff from all over the world, a majority of doctors, educated at great cost to the society in the local medical school, were taking posts in the United States as specialists and researchers or moving to practice in other parts of Latin America. Its best administrators were pulled out of local positions by the Kennedy administration and assigned much greater responsibilities representing the United States government. Thus the prior expenditures upon education, combined with the experience obtained in creating and managing economic growth, have changed external relationships for such societies as Puerto Rico from those of dependency to those that imply interdependency with the "great powers."

EXPERIENCES WITH DEVELOPMENTAL PLANNING

In this review of the postwar experience with economic growth, frequent mention has already been made of various planning efforts. A great many societies claim they are "planning," but in most of them the success of the planning in reaching the announced targets has been indifferent at best. How have the various "schools" of planning policy and technique fared during this period? Can anything be learned from the experience? The answer to these questions requires a categorization of approaches to planning. They are simple enough to identify historically, but the procedure results in increasing confusion as the review is brought up to date. Many hybrids and special cases are coming into existence. Each time the planning within a nation is reorganized, it draws upon the newest techniques and ideas.

Present conceptions of the process of national planning originated in the 1920s and 1930s. Although originally couched only in dogma and verbose theory, these conceptions have culminated in administrative frameworks with procedures, regulations, documents, and a body of law to back them up. The history of the early struggles of a national planning organization is still reflected in its doctrine and the recommendations made to new nations regarding how to start to plan. The members of the present planning organizations are rarely conscious of the reasons for the evolution of their particular structures. The demands of the situation must be distinguished from the personalities of the chief actors.

In the Soviet Union, for example, the plan was the policy instrument which guided the drive to create a heavy industry. The resources allocations were calculated to create an industrial establishment of the scale and type that promised to enable the state to defend itself from its enemies, which existed both within and beyond its borders. It was necessary to equip and supply a powerful military organization and to build industrial cities. Both, it was hoped, would make possible the transition from the local version of socialism to the Communist ideal, where each person receives goods according to need. Hostility outside its borders made it necessary to eliminate every dependency upon supplies from the outside. Therefore Soviet planning was autarchic. It created a large planned sector that was publicly owned and managed, leaving only a minor free market for the distribution of garden products and household manufactures. It instituted a system for direct allocation of expected supplies of basic manufactures and elaborated complex accounting systems for preventing misuse. This same method of planning was transplanted to Poland, Czechoslovakia, Hungary, Romania, and elsewhere after World War II, and with it went the inherent bias toward heavy industry and relatively integrated and self-sufficient industrial complexes. This outcome occurred despite the general agreement that a trading bloc should be created, based upon differentiated and complementary economies, which might be expected to compete successfully against the Marshall Plan program. Russian planning is designed so that when a shortfall from targets does occur, it will appear in light manufactures, agriculture, and sometimes transportation. These were the most traditional and least modern sectors of production.

Yugoslavia started with the Soviet model for planning but broke away while it was being installed. A shortage of trained personnel was the principal reason given for the decentralization of much of the planning to the regional and provincial level. Smaller industrial firms were managed by worker committees. Many other innovations were introduced in the "socialized sector," but almost all agriculture was left out of it. Thus Yugoslav planning became a distinct subspecies. It has now been transmitted, with important infusions from French, English, and Scandinavian schools, to Egypt, where an Arab form of planned socialism is emerging.

The simultaneous evolution of planning in Great Britain and Scandinavia was primarily concerned with that great evil of the depression years in capitalist economies—urban unemployment. Its real aim was social justice, so that other problems and scandals that exercised the moralists in the society at the time, such as the conditions in the slums and the access to health and education, also became the direct responsibility of the state. This planning proceeded in a more gradualistic and less totalitarian manner, moving from reform to reform without need for violence. It was the Fabian approach to planning. The mixture of idealism and practicality incorporated in the design of laws and the procedures for administrative implementation is best discovered by sampling back issues of *Political and Economic Planning* and *Town and Country Planning*. One is impressed with the extent to which their dreams have been realized in the postwar period and with the evidence that new dreams are necessary to maintain the dynamic elements in their planning systems.

The British system of planning has been adopted by many of its colonial peoples, once they achieved their independence. The social justice and welfare orientation was attractive. Many of the Scandinavian ideas have been propagated through the United Nations, mostly piecemeal rather than as a planning system. It is interesting to note that in those new countries where underemployment is massive and unemployment has a very different meaning, an exaggerated concern for unemployment may be detected in the public discussions of the plans. Again the carry-over of the historic bias is evident.

Few are aware of the school of planning created in the United States. The origins may be traced back to concepts of organizational efficiency promoted by F. W. Taylor, whose thinking culminated in the modern assembly line and industrial design process, which were further developed in theories of public administration. The ideals were those of the reformers in Roosevelt's New Deal and Truman's Fair Deal, and the programming techniques were those developed in the large corporations. The planning was rarely centralized or comprehensive, yet it often achieved what it set out to do because it collected the necessary information and worked with precision toward limited ends. American planning evolved to a large extent in those corporations which were forced to adapt rapidly to small changes in the business and political climate and to the great mobility of the American population. American approaches to planning became centrally coordinated only when combined with Latin institutions in Puerto Rico and, to a lesser extent, in the Philippine Republic. They are reflected in the kind of advice given by technical assistance teams to scores of other nations, in the procedures for administration installed in other countries by the international corporations originating in the United States, and in the recommendations to governments made by the dispensers of the foreign-aid funds. Now the United States technique is being merged with all other kinds of planning in different degrees of mixture in many places in the world. Similar attempts at general synthesis are being made in the course of creating functioning planning agencies in places like India, Israel, Nigeria, France, and elsewhere.

One conclusion may be drawn from the trends. Autarchic approaches to planning are no longer developmental. They are defensive and result in little or no social and economic growth. The attitude that one's nation must be able to carry out all the essential tasks for maintaining a modern civilization, ranging from agricultural production through manufacturing to the various arts and sciences, and be potentially self-sufficient in all of them is appropriate only to nations with large and varied reserves of natural resources. It is not a practical policy even for those countries like China, India, and Brazil, which do have the necessary variety in resources, because it can only be accomplished at considerable cost to overall growth.

The inefficiency of allocating funds and scarce skills to the exploitation of submarginal resources does not prevent autarchic propositions from being made; they capture the attention of the most nationalistic elements and are highly susceptible to use for political purposes. Everywhere in the world since World War II, peoples' attempts to be self-sufficient, for purposes of national integrity alone, have created industrial organizations that remained sick, immature, and wasteful. Perhaps the most expensive projects of this sort, which proceeded to completion in quite a few countries, are the steelworks that have been built where there is neither adequate ore nor coking coal (and it turns out that even the generation of scrap iron for remelting within the economy was estimated much too liberally).

In the planned society there is a law of diminishing returns in the use of authority, the restraint of liberties, and the exhibition of pride. The excessive use of authority results in resentment and a legalistic tendency to follow orders to the letter rather than carry through their obvious intent; it may even stimulate some of the more open forms of sabotage.

Abnormal restraint of liberties causes a paralysis due to fear, an unwillingness among the rank and file to point out mistakes, distrust of the police, and emigration of professional people to other countries. The pointing with pride to the accomplishments of one's own people is pardonable until it results in the dismissal of useful information produced by others and in the construction of unnecessarily grandiose monuments. At the other extreme, the kind of society that has very little authority, restraint, and pride may be expected to be loosely organized, anarchistic, humble, fatalistic, and unable to develop many of its own natural resources. Such a decentralized society may be able to raise a few specialties to a surprising level of expertise, but it would not be able to use the full range of technologies that need to be introduced. For example, ironworking over a forge in small independent workshops may reach as high levels of skill as anywhere in the world, but the production of consistently good-quality iron and steel requires larger organizations and more discipline. The type of society that approaches either extreme tends to waste scarce natural resources and equally scarce economic opportunities.

BIBLIOGRAPHY   1311699

Barnett, H. J., and C. Morse: *Scarcity and Growth: The Economics of Natural Resource Availability,* The Johns Hopkins Press, Baltimore, Md., 1963.
Takes up the application of the law of diminishing returns to the utilization of natural resources and shows that the law does not apply so long as society can make adequate investments in technological innovation.

Basch, Antonin: *Financing Economic Development,* The Macmillan Company, New York, 1964.
Self-sustaining growth depends upon an enhancement of international trade, which in turn requires a program for the liberalization of the internal economy and must take advantage of a wide range of sources of capital and expertise.

Ginsburg, N. S.: *The Atlas of Economic Development,* The University of Chicago Press, Chicago, 1961.
A statistically sophisticated presentation of the spatial distribution of resources, population, income, transportation, communications, and other factors involved in the economic development of nations.

Levin, J. V.: *The Export Economies: Their Pattern of Development in Historical Perspective,* Harvard University Press, Cambridge, 1960.
Describes earlier forms of resource exploitation, as typified by Peruvian guano, and those characteristics which have changed in modern times as a result of national attempts to capture a large share of the profits.

Rosenstein-Rodan, P. N.: "International Aid for Underdeveloped Countries," *Review of Economics and Statistics,* vol. 43, pp. 107–138, 1961.
A country-by-country estimate of the need for capital goods from the outside,

based upon prospective growth rates, propensity to save, investment rates, and an algebraic formula of dubious applicability.

Spengler, J. J. (ed.): *Natural Resources and Economic Growth,* Resources for the Future and Committee on Economic Growth of the Social Science Research Council, papers presented at a conference in Ann Arbor, Mich., Apr. 7–9, 1960, Washington, D.C., 1961.

> Brings up to date the advanced economic arguments regarding the role of resources in economic growth, in theory, in history, and in prospect; should be used as a comprehensive review of current economic doctrine regarding resources that makes it unnecessary to repeat the standard arguments here.

The Worldmark Encyclopedia of the Nations, Harper & Row, Publishers, Incorporated, New York, 1960.

> An enormously convenient compendium of United Nations statistics and related information organized by country or territory.

2

POLITICAL PRECONDITIONS
AND DEVELOPMENT STRATEGY

THE POSSIBLE STRATEGIES for development can be classified according to the degree they depend upon opportunities originating from outside the national boundaries. A continuum of possibilities exists, ranging from the free port city-state to the Shangri-la whose isolation is reinforced by mountains, deserts, or inaccessible seas.

The extreme in closed strategies for development imposes strict control over the influx of persons, ideas, and products. It prohibits the entry of multinational corporations. It employs unique institutions of local design for dealing with economic, social, and cultural opportunities. No relevant experience exists for guiding such development. The Chinese Communists, for example, have already flatly declared that Soviet strategies do not fit Chinese problems, and therefore doctrine must be reinterpreted. The result is a strategy which, if anything, is more closed than the Soviet's. The conclusions arrived at by the Chinese are equally true for countries which seriously consider either a closed strategy for development or a dependence upon Soviet bloc assistance. *The relatively closed strategies are, almost by definition, so unique that few procedural recommendations can be formulated which are relevant to the category as a whole. A country employing such a strategy is committed to a trial-and-error kind of evolution based upon an unbalanced resource endowment, rather than a well-considered imitation of the successful programs elsewhere, which employ the resources of the rest of the open world almost to the same extent as those at home.*

The most powerful generalizations, incorporating the broadest range of experience, are accessible to the relatively open society. The degree of closure required is simply that needed to commit resources to national purposes and to implement plans once the decision has been made to proceed with a project. Perhaps a third of the political units containing about half of the world's population do not qualify as "open," or potentially open, by the standards laid down here. These include:

First, at least a score of self-governing territories which have been bypassed in the rise and decline of empires and *have not been strongly affected by technological ideas.* These territories are still shackled by tradition. Some are chiefdoms and sheikdoms occupying deserts, jungles, and islands that do not contain natural resources of importance to the rest of the world. Their tradition is largely oral rather than written, their contacts with the outside world are casual and irregular, and population changes are almost as likely to be downward as upward, although the actual statistics are rarely available. Their history is made up to a large extent of sagas relating the heroic exploits of past leaders. These societies pose special problems in political organization and ethics that need to be treated separately.

Second, a few states which *have virtually sealed up their borders and look with suspicion upon outsiders and their ideas.* The name of this sociopolitical disease is xenophobia, and it is normally contracted by tightly knit traditional societies that have had some painful experiences in the course of dealing with outsiders. Their ruling groups are determined to prevent any repetition of similar experiences, and so take extreme measures to restrict communications and trade.

Third, a few states which *do not recognize the value of efforts of international agencies (public or private) or of international firms working inside their borders.* The reasons for such limitations are various. In some instances the legal systems prevent the ready application of formulas for corporate organization which have been in force elsewhere; in others large segments of the population are actively unsympathetic and are able to harass such organizations with boycotts and strikes. A few countries, such as Yugoslavia and Egypt, may yet devise procedures for close collaboration with external corporate groups possessing vital expertise.

Other conditions may prevent an application of the formula for open development. The recent history of a society determines to an important extent what is possible in the future. There are several kinds of "underdevelopedness," and the prescriptions that follow should not be administered to the wrong patient. This chapter is particularly concerned with defining what kinds of histories are incompatible with the policies that can be proposed.

There are at least two hundred societies for which histories need to be written; of these societies nearly 90 percent may be said to be still un-developed or in various early stages of economic development. Only for a few of the latter have histories been assembled and written, and even fewer are found between the covers of books. Therefore, as an indicator of suitability for an open program of development, this study is forced to depend upon the "typical" history that qualifies a society. A member of the elite of any given society which is undertaking the task of economic development will not find this portrayal very satisfying; he will detect immediately the ways in which his homeland differs significantly from the type, and such observed deviations loom very large. For purposes of study, however, the similarities are what should be noted. The installation of modern planning and organizational techniques depends most strongly upon the existence of similarities to the prototype experience; the dis-similarities suggest primarily the kinds of adjustments and modifications which need to be introduced in each case in order to fit the techniques to a new and particular environment. The history of the typical society proceeds through a sequence of identifiable stages, and well over a hundred of the societies of the world resemble this line of development strongly enough to support the conclusion that the mode of planning which grows out of it is applicable in large part to each of these societies' own circumstances.

THE PRELIMINARIES TO MODERN DEVELOPMENT

Development sprouts from a seed of modernism that has been intro-duced into a traditional society. By *modernism* is meant a body of concepts concerning qualities of life and social organization typical of the era of electricity. These concepts have been conveyed primarily by members of the society who acquired a higher education during this period, or by products of the technology. The recorded contacts with the modern world usually have been initiated as by-products of commerce, occasionally the outcome of invasion, and in the remaining instances resulted from the mobility of certain kinds of individuals (adventurers, missionaries, refugees, and outcasts).

Each human society develops a standard response to the appearance of a complete stranger and the goods he brings with him. Normally he is treated politely and regarded with curiosity; some fantastic rumors are generated, and an attitude of skepticism and toleration eventually results. When such contacts are repeated over time, the traditional society develops specialized groups for dealing with the outsiders. Some of the local mer-chants, for example, may turn to external trade. The wise men make efforts to become acquainted with a wide spectrum of alien concepts. Ministers of state, being alert to potential threats to the regime, are inclined to add a new branch to the intelligence service. Those persons making continuous contacts with the aliens assume roles that are the nearest counterpart of the presumed roles of the outsiders. Thus merchants deal with merchants, the seagoing population mixes with sailors, military officers negotiate with other officers, etc. A mutual exchange of information between insiders and outsiders results, which is as symmetrical as circumstances permit. History is replete with such contacts, and some of these exchanges had reached very substantial proportions prior to the era defined here as modern. The volume of trade and the diffusion of culture through Europe, America, and the Far East, for example, became very extensive in the nineteenth century and was a major preoccupation of the ruling classes in all the societies concerned.

Continuous contacts with outsiders led to an active two-way cultural exchange. Trading families sent sons abroad to study the customs of the principal commerce-oriented nations. The Christian missionaries produced teachers, nurses, and ministers locally within a decade or two after they had established themselves, and they sent other promising students out for further education. The centers of political power needed competent emissaries; therefore children from the royal family, the chiefs' sons, and a few others were trained at elite educational institutions abroad (Eton, Sandhurst, Oxford, Cambridge, Harvard, Yale, MIT, École Polytechnique, the Sorbonne, the leading *hochschulen,* etc.). This transfer of persons for educational purposes was particularly common in countries subjected to indirect rule by colonial powers, but the outside education of military men also was very common in states that managed to remain independent. The foreign ideas brought back were sifted, and while many were rejected, many were adopted by the elite. The still newer typically twentieth-century ideas flowed in a channel from the outside cut by the older ones and were deposited most often where nineteenth-century ideas had gained a foothold.

Thus, by various routes, in each of these countries or societies, a group of persons came into being who were conversant with the achievements of modern science. To some extent these same groups had become dependent upon the goods and services produced in Western Europe and America. The people comprising these groups were chosen largely by accident of birth, being present in the right household at the time when a nomination had to be made. Such a group attracted to itself a body of hangers-on, largely self-taught, strongly opportunistic, and usually unprincipled. They are the kinds of people who are fascinated with the novelty and apparent power of modern ideas. The whole assemblage—leaders, dilettantes, self-made men, and shallow opportunists—comprised a tiny community that maintained itself in the capital city and chief ports.

In this way, as a consequence of these contacts and of the use of

techniques which depend upon borrowed principles, one or more expanding microcosms of the outer world are created in the midst of the traditional society. These microcosms do not constitute a full-fledged social
system but a series of overlapping circles of associated individuals, each
circle with its own focus of interests. Some specialize in science, others
in literature, several in ideologies, and a few in the technologies. They
will be referred to as a *modern* elite, to distinguish them from a land-
holding, somewhat militaristic *traditional* elite, when discussing the wield-
ing of power in the society. In other connections, as when considering
the impact of the modern elite upon government administration, education, and social welfare, they will be referred to as the *progressive group*.

A seed cannot sprout until it encounters the proper germinating conditions. The small circles of well-born individuals described here can
dabble in foreign ideas for decades without causing any significant imitation and change if their overall society is neither disturbed nor divided.
Prospective leaders in a disturbed society, however, recognize that some
kinds of changes, either in leadership (the most common panacea), in
governmental methods, or perhaps even in religion, must be initiated in
order to reduce the sense of injustice, the feelings of inferiority, and the
general unrest that prevail. In the midst of disintegration and insecurity
it is impossible to avoid taking into account new potentials for action that
are at hand. The effectiveness of such measures elsewhere in the world
offers a real incentive for putting them to work in a traditional economy
which is beginning to lose its coherence. The seeds of modernism therefore take root in a time of troubles, and real growth begins after the crisis
passes.

Once modernism has put down roots, it must extract nutrients from
its environment, grow, bloom, and cross-pollinate with distant members
of the species if it is to become permanently established in the new
environment. The narrow range of contacts previously established within
the traditional culture is expanded by installing modern transport. Railroads (if they existed at all before) are dieselized, electrified, and reorganized. Telegraph and wireless connections are extended far beyond the
rails. Roads are built and buses begin to ply them. Next, foreign-language
schools are founded, a few of them at the university level. Small libraries
are created, and acquisition of periodicals containing news and comment
becomes much more ambitious. Hotels and resorts conforming to various
popular international styles are built, and modern fashions in clothing,
food, and drink are adopted for most kinds of public events. Modern
medicine is particularly popular, and its prestige is so great that it is
possible to prevent epidemics among the population as a whole, modern
and traditional, through immunizations and improvements in sanitation.
An exchange of cultural characteristics is expedited as numbers of the

populace are sent abroad to study, at the same time that foreigners arrive
from the outside to assist in the construction and management of the new
facilities.

Modernism costs the "old" society millions of dollars yearly to buy
the needed equipment and supplies obtained from the modern countries.
Therefore exports must be developed to pay for them. The indigenous
commodities suitable for export almost always extend the market economy, causing it to encroach more deeply into the traditional economy.
Thus the progressive group is joined not only by imperfect imitators but
by a third contingent—its direct and indirect suppliers. They too accumulate a stake in the modern economy even though they do not personally
accept its system of values. Similarly a collection of scholars, commercial-
izers, missionaries, and sympathizers comes into being overseas which
has developed economic and emotional ties to the progressive group; they
often take the initiative in expanding the range of external contacts.

Thus far the most potent source of change has barely been mentioned—a means by which a modern elite can win the acquiescence of the
tradition-oriented population. The modern world has modern weapons.
Once modern equipment is introduced into any struggle and is contested
with weapons of the nineteenth century or earlier, the decision is never
in doubt. If in a contest for power within a country the modern elite is
split, the costs of the conflict will be very high indeed.[1] Further development is delayed until the issue is settled. If the military threat comes from
the outside, however, the modern elite assumes rather complete authority,
and the recruitment of new members for the progressive groups is
accelerated.

The majority of newly developing societies have experienced colonialism, a condition that yielded a sequence of typical responses. Accommodation with the imperial power was the first reaction. As the modern elite
grew larger, it began to protest; later it organized independence movements, and its members often undertook armed resistance.

In a typical colony the first individuals to acquire modern culture
were alienated from their own society and therefore had little choice but
to collaborate with the occupying power. Often they took the role of
translators and mediators of conflict between the old ruling classes or
mercantile families and the representatives of the colonial power.

A succeeding generation, sometimes appearing on the scene as little
as ten years later, could not accept the unequal privileges assumed by or
granted to foreigners. The strikes and protest demonstrations they organized were quickly channeled into a movement for political independence.

[1] The relationship of such conflicts to growth is taken up in a more thorough
fashion in Chap. 3. A theory based upon ecological considerations is introduced
there.

Curiously enough the number of natives collaborating with the colonial power also increased during this period. These were drawn largely from the flow of graduates from secondary schools who were then given civil service jobs and accorded membership in the "civilized" contingent within the population. Their outlook was thoroughly bourgeois, but it was brittle, and a personal slight often converted a willing functionary into a rabid revolutionary.

Almost always the enlarged modern elite in a colony split three ways on the independence issue: collaborationists, modernist-moderates, or revivalist-extremists. The first needs no explanation; generally they switched their sympathies when it became apparent that the independence movement would win. The second attempted to use force only after negotiation failed; they were willing to borrow institutions and ideas wholesale from the occupying power. The extremists lived on hate and sought to destroy the evidence of occupation and to restore the nation to some previous condition of glory and eminence that was fabled in legend and saga. If the extremists came to power at the time of independence, the nation was unlikely to make economic progress because progress has never been the aim of extreme nationalists. They were more likely to create monuments, spend government funds on great national pageants, attempt to establish thought control through the use of police power, and reduce participation in world trade out of fear of exploitation. Under extremist regimes, businessmen were forced to operate on wide margins and in the short run only, because risks of inflation and seizure of property were so great. Accordingly, businessmen gave the appearance of being irresponsible profiteers. Sieges of dictatorship often followed the ascendancy of the extremists. Typically, a decade or two after independence had been achieved it became widely realized that the romantic idea, the "golden age" that was to be reconstituted, was an unsuitable goal for national policy. The existence of the extremist element, which represents a strong emotional rejection of all symbols and all reminders of injustice rather than a constructive response, explains why—in many "national independence" achievements—the process of economic development has not proceeded up to the level made possible by the resources, population, and capital equipment available.

Yet, despite the injustices and the violence attending colonial relationship, modernism was injected into a traditional society by colonialism more quickly and completely than through the normal processes of trade and acculturation. (The principal exception to this assertion is Japan.) Features of the modern society that are fundamental but cannot be perceived at a distance were installed in colonial areas at the behest of the colonial administrators. Such projects would not be considered important by the indigenous authorities in a poor but sovereign state. Thus colonies acquired meteorological stations, pest-control centers, agricultural experiment units, soil surveys, decennial censuses, mineralogical surveys, research laboratories concerned with the improvement of natural products, disease-control units, university colleges, technical institutes, etc. None of these facilities were very large in scale. Sometimes decades passed before the knowledge that was accumulated was put to direct use. Many such projects failed altogether, were dissolved and then forgotten. Nevertheless, surviving installations continued to supply explicit information about conditions in the environment, and their reports enabled the decision makers in the progressive group to assess the risk involved in various proposals and to conserve scarce capital. As a consequence of the availability of a wide variety of information, the former colonies today have more opportunities available to them and are exposed to less risk of loss, once they have committed themselves, than are areas which had not been integrated into empires.

THE DUAL SOCIETY

Scholars speak of a dual economy, or a dual society, when two coherent views of social organization prevail in the same population and many among the inhabitants are put into the position of having to live within both and find appropriate compromises. The concept itself is highly simplified; each time an empirical social scientist assembles material from any part of that half of the world under discussion, he finds not two societies, but several. Usually more than one traditional culture is present, often also some other nonmodern cultures that have made intrusions from the outside, besides one or two communities of modern culture, and occasionally some hybrid or compromise. Each tends to dominate a segment of economic specialities in the production process, and each has a typical pattern of consumption that can be distinguished from the others. Plural cultures are the rule in the world today; pure cultures are an extreme rarity.

Nevertheless the model of the dual society is not so limited as it sounds. Most often an individual, a family, an enterprise, and even a community is caught between only two cultures. And as long as the structure of the tradition-oriented society is not specified, the duality concept applies to most of the decisions that are made which affect development. It is possible, therefore, to consider the interaction of an integrated traditional cultural system with the modern viewpoint and encompass almost all the choices which set the stage for planning. This means that for each human need—whether medical assistance, nutrition, or parental control of children—there are likely to be two distinctly different approaches to satisfying the individuals concerned. Inevitably there will be acceptable mixtures and combinations as well.

It is vitally important to consider how the dual society appears from the position of people who are completely embedded in the tradition-bound culture. Their viewpoint is often misconstrued and not easy to obtain in unbiased form. As long as the strange new way of life of the modern community threatens nothing sacred or vital, it is regarded as an opportunity to be exploited. The newcomers seem to have a mysterious set of values that induce them to offer unusual prices or rewards for commodities that heretofore were of little value. Similarly a villager may accept employment in town, or with one of the projects in the field, but will normally apply his cash wage to the improvement of his social standing, if that is possible, or to the security of his family's position in the traditional society. He may accomplish this end by buying land, arranging favorable marriages, or acquiring work animals. Thus the modern society is exploited by members of the traditional society to further their own welfare and that of their households.

The exploitation is mutual, of course. Since the progressive groups need products for trade on the world market, they obtain them by trading with rural peoples for minerals, agricultural surpluses, fibers, skins, logs, handicrafts, etc. Because the supply is not very dependable when obtained through barter and trade, a growing modern community will attempt to set up mines, plantations, ranches, sawmills, and factories and take on members of the traditional community as laborers. If the peasants nearby are not sufficiently interested in the jobs, or want too high pay, others are imported from a distance. Enterprises of this sort are extremely risky; therefore to succeed they must exhibit high profit margins to counterbalance the failures and add to the wealth of the community. The firms that survive are exploiting the differential between the values attached to goods and labor by the two societies. Mutual exploitation is usually not a bad thing, provided the political power of the two societies remains roughly balanced, but a condition of equality seldom lasts more than a few years. For one thing, the weapons technology of the intruding Western society has been vastly superior to the traditional arsenals since the time of the Renaissance and the *conquistadores*. Once the new weapons have been introduced and armed force has been mobilized, a remarkably small modern group, whether indigenous or alien, is able to dominate the exchange situation.

The asymmetry in the balance of power between modern and traditional societies has allowed the surplus values accruing from the exchanges to be appropriated by the modern society. The latter has immediately reinvested its profits in enterprises in a manner calculated to expand its scale of operations, while the losses caused by oversupply of products available for exchange (and by acts of God) had to be borne by the traditional society. The laws controlling the market, the ownership of property, and the dispensation of justice were revised so that they favored members of the modern society, and the police (often in concert with contingents from the army) were ordered to enforce the changes. The immediate effects of this arbitrary use of superior power by individuals and corporations have been such that the foundations of the traditional society eroded away. The natural outcome of such treatment has been resentment, the withdrawal of friendly cooperation, sabotage, and eventually the onset of guerrilla-type rebellions. Experience shows that this destructive interaction can be prevented only by carefully formulated law covering the exchange relationship, together with self-discipline on the part of the modern elements.

The net effects of exploitation are not always profitable for those who hold political power. Dividends from British investments in the twentieth century in the colonial areas were markedly less than those obtained from enterprises at home. To this must be added the extraordinary cost of maintaining troops and naval units at great distances and of supplying civil servants for administering the law that was imposed. Colonialism has passed well beyond the point of diminishing returns. These fruitless investments in extensions of the empire very likely cost Great Britain its world leadership in science and technology. The economic losses accruing from the much smaller American ventures into colonialism are even more evident. The French are still paying very large bills that are coming due, so that the returns cannot be calculated as yet. The Italian attempts were catastrophic, and the German colonial enterprises were abortive. The Dutch, Belgian, Portuguese, and Spanish experiences in this century are difficult to assess; for them there might have been an economic motive for maintaining colonies, as long as the cost of military control did not rise too high, but the cost of letting go and moving out has been extraordinarily high. It seems likely that, looking backward, no colonies have been paying propositions since well before World War I.

This view of the yield on investments made in colonies has, of course, been arrived at decades after the fact. At the time the new enterprises were launched, there was an expectation of very considerable profit. What the promoters failed to take into account was the rise of sentiment favoring self-government and the conflicts resulting from incompatible points of view. In the course of the ensuing rebellion both modern and traditional sectors of a colonial society were mobilized for the purposes of building a nation.

Almost all colonies remaining after the war became nations between 1945 and 1964. Now the problem is to create a viable state and a continuing growth of the modern sector by reducing to a minimum the costs of conflict between the modern and traditional sectors. A formula for mutual exploitation must be found which enables the dual society of the present to evolve into a single integrated society in the future.

THE STRUCTURE OF THE MODERN SECTOR

The existence of a dual society is a precursor to a period of economic development. However, not all dual societies have structures suited for planning future development. It has already been suggested, for example, that former colonies are more likely to be ready than other parts of the world experiencing the same levels of living. A minimum, or prerequisite, structure can be described. If the modern sector does not contain all the elements specified, then highest priority must be given to filling the gaps. Elaborate development plans are meaningless as long as this foundation is not available.

It is simplest to begin with size. Before it can even exist as an independent, self-governing political unit in the world today, a country needs at least one hundred persons with varied professional training, regardless of the gross size of its population. Then, for each million population, it needs at least thirty more of these same kinds of professionals. Thus, for a population of ten million persons, a progressive group containing four hundred active persons with college training or equivalent seems to be essential. A greater number are required if the population is dispersed or speaks several languages and if internal communications are difficult. Then, for each professional at hand, five, ten, or twenty more are needed who have completed secondary school or have acquired equivalent training. These latter can accept responsibility for government and administration; they can manage local enterprises, and do most of the teaching. Additionally, for each person with a certificate or a diploma, there should be three to ten others who have some secondary training and who can be used to keep records and operate the transport, communications, and other services needed by the modern society. At the base of this social pyramid are still larger numbers who are barely literate but have ambitions which propel them more in the direction of the modern than the traditional. If they do not succeed in acquiring a foothold for themselves, they try to make sure that their children will.

Anyone can corroborate the magnitudes of the structure given above simply by reviewing the offices, or posts, implied by the existence of an independent state. For example, at the top there are a dozen or so ambassadorships and ministries which must be filled, plus additional need for those who will be responsible for the principal trade relationships, for the United Nations representation, and for maintaining the policy-making process at home. The treasury requires persons who understand finance, foreign exchange, monetary policy, and public budgets—all subjects demanding knowledge of modern concepts. The collection of customs and taxes may well be left to traditional methods for a while, if they existed before. But communications and transport are government responsibilities in such countries and each separate system (telephone, telegraph and cable, postal service, radio, air transportation, shipping, roads, etc.) requires a small group of trained people to direct its activities and keep the equipment functioning. The military and public health functions are equally demanding, and electric power production certainly needs a team of specialists. Then, there must be some functionaries who work elsewhere than in the capital on principal income-earning projects and in provincial administration. This rule-of-thumb estimate of the minimum number of trained or otherwise able native personnel needed for a functioning state was arrived at essentially by reviewing reports from such places as Libya, Afghanistan, Bolivia, Ethiopia, Kuwait, and Somalia, where the sovereignty of the nation is limited in various degrees precisely because of the lack of native personnel with modern training.

The most common deficiency in a modern (native) elite is the lack of engineering and other technological skills. Apprentices to the technical trades—the understudies of the technologists—are also scarce, and many of those that do exist have learned only obsolescent skills. It frequently happens, on the other hand, that the prestige of government service results in an oversupply of persons trained in law and whatever other kinds of education were considered suitable for administration (mainly classics, history, and foreign languages). This bias occurs primarily because the families in the traditional elite and the property-owning classes have invested in a "modern" education for their children, but of a kind that fulfilled the requirements of posts that existed a generation or more ago. Curiously enough, in most countries, military officers now are more flexible and better able to keep up with modern requirements for administration in an atmosphere of change than the average member of the elite. The principal reason is that export of military technology since World War II has proceeded more rapidly than virtually any other form of technology. Moreover, it has been concentrated heavily upon weapons systems using much communications equipment and the kind of organization required to operate such equipment. Thus, career officers are likely to be found in public works departments and other national ministries. Their background rarely equips them, however, for operating subsidiary political units.

The modern sector needs at least one region equipped with urban services. Such a region needs all-weather roads that connect with nearby regions, a harbor for deep-draft vessels, an airport, a bus and jitney service, etc. For communication it needs a postal system, a radio station, a telephone exchange, several newspapers, a magazine and book-printing establishment, a library, and a source for overseas publications. Soon television and computers also will be necessary. In the area of health it needs a general hospital, specialized clinics, a source of pure water, and a public health service for the control of epidemics. For structures it needs a few modern office buildings, a few major retail establishments, a hotel, modern warehouses with refrigeration, a sewage and trash-disposal system, etc.; several neighborhoods with dwellings that permit people to live in the international style; bridges, terminals, stadia. It needs a police force, a set of judicial courts, and municipal law; an education system that reaches up to university college and technical college levels. A central bank and a monetary system are necessary. So also are recreational centers such as parks, cinemas, swimming pools, gymnasiums, tennis clubs, and beaches.

Thus far little has been said about manufacturing, which in most cases was retarded in dual societies of the twentieth century as compared with commerce. The slow introduction of manufacturing was in part due to the shortage of appropriate skills in the newly developing society and in part attributable to the advanced stage of the cottage industries in the populous agrarian societies, but there is evidence also, in the form of legislation and the resolutions of trade associations and labor unions, that potent interests conspired to prevent industrialization in the colonial territories, or at least to slow it down. Yet modern industries have arrived, principally as offshoots of international trade or the necessities of world war. With few exceptions these factories were established in cities other than the country's capital or seat of government. Very often they were started close to the home and business location of the chief entrepreneur. (More will be said about recent patterns of industrial location in Chapter 5.)

The manufacturing plants made an impact upon both the modern and traditional economies. They introduced another opportunity whereby the traditional society could exploit the modern. Young men and women undertook factory work in the cities for a few years and sent remittances to the families remaining at home. Similarly, members of the modern sector made good use of their knowledge about local styles and prices of consumer goods, developed the local market by displacing cottage industries with either a much cheaper product or one of much better quality, and proceeded to expand production to meet the demand.

The first factories were not very modern; they used second-hand machinery and whatever buildings were available. But those that succeeded moved out from behind the marketplace or the edge of the harbor district, where the original sites were usually found, to convenient new addresses; in the last decade they have been attracted to planned industrial estates. New equipment in new locations forces manufacturers to seek sharp increases in productivity through rationalization of production. It presses the owners, whether government or private, to assemble a modern management—most of which will be college-trained—and a considerable number of technicians and foremen who aspire to modern ways even though many, if not most, cannot make the full step. The young labor force thus collected by modern industry is susceptible to new ideas, but at first its loyalties still rest firmly with the family and the village. As the laborers' efforts become increasingly productive and management learns how to coordinate effort in factories, the bonds with the rural regions are correspondingly loosened; the result is another increment to urban population and the modern sector. Often it takes the form of an unstable, insecure, turbulent proletariat.

The culture of the modern elites in the dual societies is normally vigorous, innovative, but tinged with the emotive elements of the traditional society into which most of its members were born, and incomplete in many of its features. The formal culture is modeled after the British, French, or American versions of the international style. Thus, in parlor and club, and on state occasions, the give-and-take in conversations and in the comportment of individuals cannot easily be differentiated from some of the other variants of the international style. The speech may be accented in some unique fashion, the talk may be a few months behind (or ahead) of Paris, London, or New York, and the etiquette may be a bit more "proper," but these differences are minor. However, in the informal life of these elites—in the kitchen, the bedroom, and the wineshop—members of the progressive groups are forced to come to terms with the traditional way of life.

Families make transitions much less readily than individuals. Therefore, if a man commits himself to a new way of life within a society and achieves a position that merits respect within it, the rest of the family may be proud, but it is also mystified, confused, and suspicious of the new customs. Divisions of opinion arise about what should be the careers of younger members of the families. The modern man often is expected at the same time to play the role of elder brother and uncle in the traditional society, and sometimes he inherits a chieftainship or a feudal title, which brings additional responsibilities for whole communities. Not infrequently he is forced to maintain two households, one modern and the other traditional. In these circumstances he must compromise when planning the careers of his own children. Therefore the modern elite is made up mostly of persons who must live in two worlds and must repeatedly decide, when local customs require quite different responses to a situation, which shall prevail. Such conflicts build up great stresses; it is not a surprise that the frequency of stomach ulcers and mental breakdowns is very high. These same stresses also create unusual sensitivity, and can be expected to result in extraordinary contributions to literature and the fine arts if the time to develop them ever becomes available. The interaction between cultures is also the principal source of the invention of new images and concepts.

Modern elites must borrow as opportunities present themselves and gaps in their acquisitions leave equivalent gaps in the local version of modern culture. The serious cultural media, including music, painting, literature, and architecture, find devotees but no creators. Such masterpieces of maturity are not the idiom of a modern elite struggling to develop a nation. There is a place in the small progressive circles for the specialist interpreter of local traditions, but the man of books, the philosopher-critic of newly exposed ideas, is rare. (The nearest approximation is an editor of a newspaper read by the modern elite.) Creations in only one or two of the fine arts may be taken seriously. The sciences are not better represented. They, too, are largely irrelevant for the tasks at hand.

The lesser bureaucrats, the subprofessionals, the teachers, the technicians, and the businessmen serving the progressive groups, most often live in the modern society only while at work and in company of fellow workers. The rest of the time is spent in environments which have become acculturated to various degrees but still represent tentative compromises. More often than not these elements of the elite postpone the hard decisions, or avoid their consideration, with the result that the frustrations are not turned inward, as among the leaders, but outward, and a sullen sabotage of the production system and the bureaucratic functions results instead of illness due to internal stress. In consequence, institutions that worked very smoothly in the countries of origin operate haltingly in the new environment, and the reasons are often due to the undetected presence of certain culturally ambiguous behavior which impedes the performance of tasks.

The traditional cultures are not left unchanged by the rise and expansion of a modern elite. The populace who exploit the modern sector in order to take the profits back to the village are simultaneously infected by some of the modern ideas. They bring back to their villages not only goods that are potentially useful but also others that are merely pleasing. Views of the world are enlarged, shifts in social status are more common, political power is transferred to new groups, and the values that were held most dear in the traditional way of life are reshaped. Parents are unsure how to raise their children; the old codes of behavior no longer elicit the responses they did in the past. As a result the traditional society is more susceptible to a charismatic leader who promises a more stable order in the patterns of life. Portions of the society may change their religion, accepting a more codified doctrine, while other segments will reject the foreign images and attempt to revive a classical community structure; still others decide to abandon the old ways altogether and move to the city to escape from tradition.

So much for the typical history. It explains the origins of the problems that politicians and planners inherit. The evolution of the dual society generates all sorts of instabilities which must be brought under control by means that economize on time and scarce manpower. Control, it appears, can be achieved only by constructing a political unit, a nation among nations, which acquires a monopoly of coercion but uses it sparingly.

THE MAKING OF A NATION

Among the various preconditions to social and economic development, the most elusive is the establishment of a national state. If the state does not exist yet, the first order of business for a modern elite is to create such a political unit. No one presently seems able to conceive a self-help approach to development without the presence of a self-governing state. A colonial form of dependency may bring about the large-scale introduction of capital and technology, but the relationship is politically unstable and in the long run it has an extremely high likelihood of dissolution. The trusteeship arrangements devised during the last several decades for the administration of dependent territories produce insufficient incentive to bring about the radical changes that are necessary for development to get under way. Subnational political units such as chiefdoms and kingdoms are archaic. The most promising political unit by far is the modern national state, but the present-day modern state was originally constructed upon a set of premises regarding the nature of sovereignty that has recently become obsolete. The national states of long standing are on their way to becoming something else as yet indeterminate; therefore a modern elite endeavoring to create such a state finds itself aiming not at a stable stereotype but at a moving target.

Nations originally came into being when cities were no longer able to defend themselves. The technology of war had made their walls useless. Security then lay in the use of natural barriers to invasion, such as mountains, rivers, and seas. Thinly populated space was an equally useful deterrent. Then the cities in the valleys and on the coasts were protected by a defensible shell, and the power was lodged in a central government. But the technology of war did not stand still. Security from invasion became increasingly difficult to maintain, since now both buffer areas and natural resources were required, and security in the old sense disappeared altogether with the coming of the nuclear age. The nuclear weapons, along with the sciences which underlie them, are primarily responsible for the obsolescence of the states which presently exist.

The states that we know (there are about fifty fully formed examples) evolved during a period when the following elements were required:

1. A territory with certain boundaries established by the former rulers that remained unchanged from predecessor political units, and others that were established by treaty, often after military conflict
2. A common language, or set of languages, in which to conduct both official business and informal communication
3. A complementary set of social institutions for carrying on production and engaging in cultural activity
4. A popular demand for political independence and self-government
5. A belief system (often religious) that embraced the great majority of people, one which encouraged them to assert that they had a common origin and a common destiny
6. A strong preference for living at home with other people who belonged to the territory rather than for migrating elsewhere
7. A manifest pride in the achievement of one's own people and a commitment to the future this aggregation could make for itself
8. An insistence upon sovereignty in the event of conflicts with outgroups and other nations, and a hostility toward anyone who would not acknowledge such sovereignty

These elements are less evident constituents of the image of a nation today because an international system of nations is coming into being, and the United Nations Organization is attracting increasing loyalty to itself, most noticeable during times of crisis. The present international system operates in part as an assortment of regional blocs, as with the Soviet coalition and the Common Market arrangement; the remainder functions primarily through the United Nations and its specialized agencies. As a consequence, while boundaries between nations remain important, they are becoming more permeable.

Aspirations for social and economic development (resulting in con-tinued growth in the case of states that are already well established) must also change the concept of the national state. For example, an internal order must be brought into existence which permits looking forward to the long run (say, ten years or more) with some confidence that the contractual arrangements which have been made and the agreements which have been arrived at will persist, so that new possibilities which assume the presence of a structure of obligations can be explored with profit. A higher degree of organization and self-control is required to bring about growth than to maintain equilibrium. Politicians and civil servants must weigh their actions more carefully to achieve conditions of growth, and the political structures needed for assuring this extra consideration are to be found in only a few of the newly developing countries.

Though the meaning behind the term *nation,* or national state, may change and become more diffuse, the general concept is likely to be with us for a long time to come. *Nationalism,* the sentiment that is responsible for bringing a nation into being and supporting its sovereignty, may not last long, however. Nationalism is a mode of political thought which focuses and unifies most of the aspirations that extend beyond the welfare of family, clan, and immediate community. Thus nationalism mobilizes the fervor and commitment of individuals in a manner that very much resembles a modern religion. The political leaders of the nation take on roles similar to the hierarchy of a church. National images, such as flags, evoke reverence. Indeed, in many nations both new and old, church and state are inextricably intertwined. The Moslem faith, for example, is tied to the political structures of more than a dozen new countries. It is quite possible that once an enduring nation has been built, the sentiments may shift to some other focus, but the nation would still continue—just as many of the established churches continue even though few people attend their services or observe their rituals.

Nationalistic movements are built around leaders who inspire people about them to work for a cause rather than for self-interest. Such leaders are basically reformers. They encounter many instances of mistreatment and injustice, and they work out programs designed to remove the apparent sources of injustice. These leaders need advice about how to formulate programs in such a way that the most important ones can be carried out. It is entirely characteristic of nationalistic leaders that they are more interested in righting wrongs and in teaching their followers than in consistency of argument or in efficiency. The wisest of them know they need advice in most of their undertakings, and it is forthcoming from persons who are imbued with the same ideals but are willing to work as unsung heroes in the back rooms, assembling the facts and preparing recommendations for action. Leaders need staffs, and when they are building nations they need political staffs.

What are the duties of political staffs? A primary one is that of recruitment. The brightest and most ambitious of the young potential leaders need to be contacted, persuaded to join the movement toward building the state, educated in their responsibilities, and assigned tasks that will make contributions toward national ends. A mass political party must be established, if none existed before, capable of funneling protests about injustice to centers where their intensity can be appraised; often action can be undertaken immediately to alleviate the inequities. As a mass party matures, it becomes more rigid. Then it fails to serve its function of reducing conflicts and tensions unless it grows new arms or divisions which concentrate upon the new problems. (Again a good example is drawn from analogy with the organization of churches, where new monastic orders and service organizations recruited able young people to work on serious new problems.) The new organizations must have representation in the top councils of the party, and the leader must spend a great share of his time finding appropriate adjustments between action that needs to be taken on new problems and prior procedures adopted on prior occasions. The party and its adjunct staffs are seen here as an information-gathering agency and an organization devoted to the resolution of local grievances. The evolution of the mass party into a more structured political organization will be taken up after some of the central problems of combining nation building with development are introduced.

Fragmentation into factions is evident in political parties after a period of time and constitutes one of the most serious problems. It occurs even if the political heretics who lead the factions are persecuted, exiled, or otherwise removed from the scene. Then the nation-building efforts are transformed into a series of compromises between the leaders of factions, or are postponed while the contest for power and control remains unsettled.

Nevertheless, some developmental planning can proceed even during periods of irreconcilable political strife. Improvement of the public utilities, for example, can usually be agreed upon by all principal parties and factions. Features of natural resource development that are not too greatly influenced by foreign interests are rarely controversial. The physical equipment and staff of the schools can be expanded (but curriculum reform usually adds fuel to the conflict and therefore should be put off to a later date). Some industries may get established, but in general few new starts are made under unsettled conditions. Progress in public health can be achieved quite readily in death control, but often not in birth control. Thus, as long as political disunity exists in a condition short of civil war, the planning function can operate. But the limitations put upon new programs make it increasingly sterile because political leadership sets the goals and priorities for the plans, and political staffs smooth out the difficulties associated with the launching of new programs.

THE IMAGES OF NATIONHOOD

The political unit ideally suited for development would use a minimum of scarce resources for maintaining the party, the army, the borders, and the rituals of independence. This is not easily accomplished because over the past several decades older practices of nationhood have been transmitted to developing countries and have become embedded in the political thinking of members of the elite. Occasionally the party in power errs by following wasteful Western precedents and launches a program of self-glorification and conspicuous consumption. In such cases an election is considered merely a climactic affirmation, concluding a series of parades and celebrations. The military, with its uniforms and mobile equipment, is most likely to be the object of extravagant spending to dramatize the existence of the state. Declaration of a series of patriotic holidays that did not exist before also increases the cost of nationhood through the resulting loss in industrial output. In the creation of new nations with development and growth potentials, some substitute procedures must be found for these historic approaches.

The significance of national boundaries reveals quite clearly the forces at work. One of the principal images of a nation is an outline map of the territory it controls. National identity is associated with a set of borders. Border disputes with countries having roughly the same military capability constitute an issue seldom compromisable. If national identity is threatened thereby, the fact that the economic value of the disputed area is much less than the cost of its defense is irrelevant. Maintaining a full complement of images of nationhood has primacy over economics, social standing, and even the lives of individuals. Indicators of the importance nations attribute to the maintenance of borders are everywhere evident. Among them are the procedures for entry and exit, the equipment and personnel for manning checkpoints, the architecture of customs houses and airports, and the siting of military installations. Politicians find that national solidarity is most readily achieved when defending previously accepted boundaries. This means that the majority of the society is willing to set aside private concerns and make sacrifices to prevent the destruction of their image of the nation. The nation thereby becomes a part of the personality of the citizen as well as that of the political leader.

One explanation for rapid development in Puerto Rico is that the agonized search for identity (*puertorriqueñismo*) felt by a large segment of the elite was channeled into framing and implementing a constitution that attempted to combine the best features of democratic politics, as evolved in the United Kingdom and in the United States, with the special properties of Latin culture. Pye (1962) points out that in Asia there is no doctrine of democratic development that could be contrasted with Marxist and Soviet doctrines, and this lack of political prescriptions creates a bias toward closed and authoritarian measures.

The Puerto Ricans found such a doctrine on their own initiative and proceeded to carry it out (Friedrich, 1959). The intelligentsia seeking national identity were challenged to put their images of nation into communicable form. Serious histories needed to be written, basic ethnological and archeological materials collected, textbooks written, modest museums and public parks equipped, and institutes of national culture organized. The otherwise aimless polemicists and extremist groups were thus submerged in work of a kind they claimed was important, and they had little time to organize sentiment against the government. The political leadership surrounding Muñoz insisted upon respectable performance on small tasks that used up little capital and other scarce resources before large-scale support would be undertaken. The leadership took the trouble to keep prodding in public and initiated a series of queries from budgetary and planning agencies which required brief reports on progress. Because the work was meaningful, it succeeded in large part in deflecting the rising younger generation from wasteful ultranationalistic agitation.

POLITICAL ORGANIZATION

If the party in power needs support in the form of votes, it must first acquire information about the issues. Because very little of the effective communication in the rural areas is written and the specific issues vary from place to place, the party must set up many local secretaries and representatives who can continually interact with the populace on a face-to-face basis. It is then up to the man on the scene to do everything possible to rectify misunderstandings and to prevent conflict between the government policies and community or private interests. He must also remain in regular contact with regional and provincial centers. In addition, the roots of this organization of representatives must be supported financially in such a fashion that the channels of communication are not corrupted; the party representative must not be permitted to become someone else's agent.

In the cities a political party is organized in several ways. Much of the population that has recently migrated is segregated into communities of households which have their origin in the same tribe or area in the hinterland. Dialect, customs, religion, and kinship bring them together. The party would naturally attempt to create a secretariat in each such community that will permit it; the party representatives could function very much as in the villages, except that the problems to be coped with are more complex. They are associated most often with employment, housing, and health, and the dimensions of the evident needs often appear to be overwhelming. Other secretariats function in universities, trade unions, cooperatives, sports clubs, and the associations that transcend the spatially delimited communities. All groups are represented in the central committees of the party.

In many political parties the gulf that separates the modern leaders, most of whom expect to hold office, from the partially politicized tradition-oriented members is so great that very little cross communication occurs. This is a dangerous situation because the modern elite often deludes itself about conditions that exist in the society outside its own circle of acquaintances and contacts, and the barrier prevents sufficient contradictory information from entering to arouse doubts or inquiries. In Puerto Rico, Muñoz recognized this danger from the beginning and therefore required his university-trained cabinet to leave the major cities and tour the countryside in the months before elections. This experience made them much more sensitive to the notes of urgency in petitions forwarded to the government, hence less likely to permit a local situation to get out of hand. In between elections also, Muñoz's programs of community education employed carefully designed methods for discovering new aspirations, new leaders, and tasks which could be transferred to the communities as "self-help." Parties in other countries that have made rapid social and economic progress have found similar techniques for building political bridges within the dual (or plural) society.

The government that best assists development is a stable, representative, and responsive political system. The transfer of power from one party or coalition to another should be effected constitutionally and without destruction of the machinery or dissolution of organization. Recent experience shows that these properties are highly dependent upon institutions which expedite communications flow.[2]

Perhaps the best rule to apply in the development of governments of nations and of nationalist political parties is that the emphasis should remain upon borrowing and adapting ideas and methods. The modern elite should systematically choose countries to learn from which have similar problems but are preferably somewhat more advanced and have demonstrated their capacity for growth.

What techniques can be used for dealing with the respective problems there? How can that technique be improved? What is the best place in one's own country for testing it? Such borrowing cannot be carried out

[2] A remarkable study of 77 nations for the period 1940–1960 shows that an index of political development is much more closely associated with an index of communications development than with available indexes of urbanization, education, or non-agricultural employment. Altogether 65 percent of the variance around the mean of the political development score could be accounted for by the scores on communications development. There was also an indication that those countries which deviated most from the regression line were under stress and have since 1960 moved either toward simpler political organization (Indonesia, Burma) or toward enhanced communications (India, Philippines, Spain). Also, the countries that have done well in political development during this period have good to excellent prospects of economic development. See Phillips Cutright, "National Political Development: Measurement and Analysis," *American Sociological Review,* vol. 28, pp. 253–264, 1963.

merely through the exchange of reports and correspondence; it requires a two-way interchange of *persons*. It also requires cordial relations between the respective countries.

THE SOPHISTICATED EXPLOITATION OF DUALITY

A still more difficult problem is that of recruiting personnel from the traditional culture for tasks that have little or no prestige in the traditional society but are essential for modern government. Sometimes the task does not even exist in traditional society, but superficial appearances may cause it to be linked with a low-status occupation. These jobs must be filled with competent individuals, and the particular competence is most likely to be found in the lower-status ranks.

One of the most promising locations for conducting the training and selection of this type of personnel is in the military services. For one thing the accent upon modernization is much greater among the military forces, and promotion to noncommissioned officer is a standard procedure for rewarding special skill and zeal. Another access can be set up in a factory hierarchy, using short courses and diplomas from a vocational school as indicators of increasing competence of individuals who are moving out of the traditional society into the modern. What happens, then, is that children from relatively poor families are step by step moved into the scarce trades and professions, each stage selecting the most promising youngsters from the previous stage by using the most appropriate rewards. The apparent success of those that are chosen leads other ambitious youngsters to attempt the same path to prestige, but the process can be very much enhanced if appropriate publicity is given to the achievements of persons in the hard-to-fill positions. When the tide has turned and the flow of recruits has increased significantly, it is time to establish high standards of performance. At this point aid from other countries may be crucial, particularly in the form of students from among the modern sector who have studied the appropriate subject overseas. At the same time, examinations and other tests of competence must be drawn up so that they are meaningful to the tasks that must be carried out and lead to an upgrading of performance; they should depend minimally on the memorization of textbooks and lectures and maximally upon problem solving of all kinds, including the technical, practical, theoretical, organizational, etc.

What does this argument mean for the planners responsible for the growth of the modern economy? Take a specific factor that will become important in many societies: the substantial income generated within the ranks of the traditional society after it has been successfully exploiting its contacts with the enterprises of the modern sector. That income often causes price instability, and in many instances inflation results. The moment it happens is an appropriate time for the imposition of taxes to siphon off the excess funds. For example, if the price of land is being bid up to unprecedented heights, a direct or indirect tax upon land would be appropriate. Then a cadre of tax collectors is needed who have accumulated among themselves the skills of accountants, assessors, surveyors, and detectives who cannot be bribed. Since tax collectors universally are not well liked, it is not exactly the kind of career that young men aspire to. To attract them, the planners might turn first to the military because the basic skills are needed there also. A body of such men can be developed in the military before the tax is imposed and then transferred to the treasury department when needed. Since the military draws heavily from almost all elements of the traditional population, it will have available a significant number of poor boys who have become literate and are eager to obtain higher skills and positions. Such persons contribute an extra capacity: they are quite familiar with the devices used by peasants to avoid paying taxes.

A tax collector should be given good pay in order to prevent the temptation to accept bribes, and he must also have a chance to associate with others of equal status. If possible he should teach in the appropriate educational institutions and help identify the most promising youngsters. He should be encouraged to devise and test new procedures for conducting his job. A particularly prestigeful activity would be the identification of new commodities upon which a new excise tax could be based. Tax collection would then become professionalized; yet it remains the kind of profession that, while always bringing up new talent from the traditional sector, does not attract the children of tax collectors (who acquire more education and move into more attractive professions in the cities). This "social climber" inclination makes it easier to maintain a reasonably honest and effective tax-collection agency. The handling of money and the assessment of value make up the most obvious responsibilities of this profession, but the planners find that a good corps of tax collectors can play a vital role in development programs. Because they gain wider knowledge of local economic affairs than anyone else, the reports they prepare and statistics they collect have great bearing upon the appraisal of costs and benefits of various projects. The aggregate findings of tax collectors will very often determine the economic feasibility of a resource development or an industrial project. Close relationships with planners would also serve to add extra prestige to alleviate the rather lonely, isolated posts that tax collectors have.

Notice what happens in this proposition for the recruitment of tax collectors: First, a new arm of the modern sector is created which develops specialized skills and functions. Second, a "learning by doing" system is created which should improve in competence over time because of professionalization and the importation of standards of performance from more developed societies. Third, a device for recruitment is invented which should keep many professional and subprofessional people in the hinterland, where there is a great scarcity of them, rather than luring them to the capital. Fourth, a means is provided for transmitting more information about the state of the economy to the planning staff, the administrators, and the party organizers. Fifth, by encouraging recruits to teach part time in local schools, on subject matters pertinent to their specialization, a way is found for detecting talent and thereby supplying an opportunity for efficient recruitment of promising youngsters into the modern sector.

In any given situation, a number of other policies associated with modernization and development may be advanced by modification of this proposition. It should be noted that it will take from five to fifteen years to implement even the main features of such organization as outlined here, the actual amount of time depending upon the human resources available, the quality of the outside assistance obtained, and the number of unpredictable crises that may intervene.

It is not possible, of course, to set down even a checklist of all the new problems that must be attended to when organizing a modern self-governing nation that is ready to grow. The foregoing discussion has attempted to convey a *style* of organization which seems to be appropriate, rather than to treat the whole subject in detail. In relatively poor countries which have achieved steady growth, many institutional variations are found that are typical of this style. In relatively stagnant countries, however, there are very few examples of highly adaptive institutional behavior.

PRIORITIES OF READINESS

Up to this point the preconditions have been stated in such a manner that, if fulfilled, the likelihood of rapid growth is maximized. While inadequate fulfillment of the preconditions does not entirely preclude growth, extra hazards are introduced and it is to be anticipated that the full potentials will not be realized. Political and social priorities for development can be brought out by a brief recapitulation of the key arguments.

The procedures for stimulating growth to which Boulding applied the term *Fomentarian Revolution* were found to apply to only a part of the world, but it happens to be the part which can be discussed in operational terms. Excluded are (1) self-governing territories that have not achieved some initial modernization, (2) states which have virtually sealed their borders and have insulated their population against contacts from the outside, and (3) countries that do not recognize the right of international companies and consortia to conduct business inside their borders. Therefore perhaps half of the world's population can avail itself of these procedures to at least some degree.

Societies in the best position to use such techniques are those which have evolved a plural society, with one component oriented to a world-wide flow of ideas, modern technology, and an international style of life. The remainder of the people in the society live according to one or more sets of traditions that have been used to their utmost already and no longer possess the capacity to grow and expand. Thus the most appropriate simplified theory is that of the *dual economy,* which finds the traditional sector exploiting the modern in order to improve family security and status in the community at the same time that the modern sector uses tradition-oriented persons for resource development, construction work, services, and some manufacturing.

The modern sector of a dual society must construct a national identity capable of operating as a unit on the international scene. A modern elite recruits from the rest of the population through the educational system, coopting the promising and energetic persons into its agencies—the military, industry, political parties, and civil service. It organizes the government, expands international contacts, extends transportation and resource development, and builds up popular support for its programs. Most of the growth of modernism is concentrated in a few cities. Provision must be made at such centers for rapid agglomeration of population.

Building a nation is made difficult by the obsolescence of historic examples in Western society at the time that many new nations are attempting to model themselves after such examples. There is a tendency toward excessive politicization, designated as ultranationalistic behavior, which requires internal discipline. What is needed now, instead of fervent patriotism, is ingenuity in creating organizations that are highly adaptive, accumulate experience rapidly, reinforce the parts of the educational system that produce scarce skills, and cannot be corrupted through bribery. If it can be assured that fairly suitable organizations will be on hand for taking advantage of opportunities, and that the society is indeed ready, it is possible to turn to the theory behind the plans that such organizations might undertake in order to optimize the overall growth process.

BIBLIOGRAPHY

Almond, G. A., and J. S. Coleman (eds.): *The Politics of the Developing Areas,* Princeton University Press, Princeton, N.J., 1960.
 A systematic review of the process of change, political groups, political functions of governmental structures, authority functions, and political integration in various parts of the world, based upon a theory of comparative politics.

Apter, D. E.: "Nationalism, Government and Economic Growth," in *Economic Development and Cultural Change*, vol. 7, 1959, pp. 117–136.
   An analytical paper that draws together most of the generalizations that can be made about political parties, nationalism, elitism, resource allocation, etc., in newly developing societies.

Boeke, J. H.: *Economics and Economic Policy of Dual Societies*, Institute of Pacific Relations, New York, 1953.
   The classical formulation of the theory of the dual economy based upon experiences in Indonesia during the colonial period.

Friedrich, C. J.: *Puerto Rico: Middle Road to Freedom*, Holt, Rinehart and Winston, Inc., New York, 1959.
   The political doctrine evolved in Puerto Rico analyzed by Harvard's specialist in constitutional government.

Lerner, Daniel: *The Passing of Traditional Society*, The Free Press of Glencoe, New York, 1958.
   An evaluation of the dual society in the Middle East, employing tools of social analysis.

Popper, K. R.: *The Open Society and Its Enemies*, 2d ed., Routledge & Kegan Paul, Ltd., London, 1952.
   A trenchant dialectical defense of the concept of the open society.

Pye, L. W. (ed.): *Communications and Political Development*, Princeton University Press, Princeton, N.J., 1963.
   Case studies and theory supporting the close connections between national political development and the adoption of modern communications systems.

———: *Politics, Personality, and Nation Building*, Yale University Press, New Haven, Conn., 1962.
   The most advanced analysis of the task of nation building, but the Burmese case which illuminates the discussion was unfortunately stagnant during the period of observation, so that nation-building theory has not yet been connected with successful development.

Rosenau, J. N. (ed.): *International Politics and Foreign Policy*, The Free Press of Glencoe, New York, 1961.
   Advanced theory on policy making, the actions of states, and methods of analysis; 55 contributions.

3

OPEN SYSTEMS FOR GROWTH AND DEVELOPMENT

WHEN MONETARY RETURNS are obscure, the dual-society concept can be fitted very readily to the tasks of decision and action. Politicians and administrators have already been sensitized to the differences between modern and traditional approaches to problems and can confirm from personal experience the value of many of the prescriptions that may be inferred from the existence of the dual society. The concept is nevertheless a simplification of the real world and may sometimes mislead in the course of the search for suitable policies. Still more frequently, it has little relevance to many significant issues that arise. Therefore it is worthwhile to consider several complementary conceptualizations of growth and development which make it possible to render more than one judgment of a proposed line of action for a nation.

A reconsideration of the other well-known concepts underlying economic and social growth has been undertaken recently by Hagen in his book *On the Theory of Social Change*. He has endeavored to probe more deeply into the behavioral sciences in order to identify the processes of growth after accepting the conclusion that knowledge about resources, technologies, and organizations must grow if the socioeconomic system is to develop. Essentially, his interest is in the manner in which knowledge is used to promote growth.

Hagen is concerned, for example, with the reasons for the stability of the traditional society. Why are the outlooks and the behavioral patterns transmitted from one generation to the next with remarkably little change? Under many circumstances, we now know, it is quite normal for the younger generation to rebel and reject the social roles and some of the values of the parents, but this reaction seldom ever occurs in the traditional agrarian society. The latter has shown a strong tendency to breed true and replicate itself generation after generation.

Traditional society, as Hagen depicts it, is an ultrastable system where, each time a deviation from the norm is detected, a force (as often unconsciously directed as conscious) is set into motion to restore the original conditions. Unconscious forces are at work mostly at the level of child training and cultural indoctrination (the "little tradition"). A conscious force is the use of authority by an elite which is regulated by a great historically oriented tradition. Thus the mass of peasants and artisans are kept in line by the principles of behavior transmitted from parents to children, but the exceptions are dealt with by intervention of the military leaders, the priests, and the nobility, who comprise that part of the elite which is granted authority. (Hagen does not give the frequency of exceptions, but one would judge from the instances cited that they might range from 3 to 10 percent, and of these many more among males than females.) Such a strong interdependence between the elite and the masses has been established that the support of the elite falls off, and its ability to fulfill traditional obligations is constrained, if obedience to tradition by the peasants declines. On the other hand, temporary surpluses produced by the masses are properly (according to the "great tradition") consumed by the elite in feuds, affairs of honor, quests for power, or ostentatious display. Knowledge can accumulate in such a strongly interdependent system, particularly when the elite is intent upon restoring a prior state of affluence that had been interrupted by a catastrophe, but the rewards obtained from the possession of knowledge are meager. The traditional agrarian society uses the family enterprise and the chronicles of the royal courts for the preservation of information. These are rather inefficient institutions for that purpose, so it is not surprising that many productive concepts need to be rediscovered repeatedly.

Change most often comes to traditional societies in catastrophic form: invasions, epidemics, earthquakes, floods, famines, etc. Large portions of the elite may be lost, and significant fractions of the rural population may disappear with them, but regrowth occurs—usually by incorporating invading or subject tribal elements—so that the economic base and the social structure are restored to the same dimensions and outline. Reconstruction and some new growth may continue for a generation or even more, but the profiteers join the gentry and invest in land, and the surpluses are thereafter consumed. A traditional agrarian society is thus brought into being again, although it is somewhat modified by the new cultures assimilated during the regrowth phase.

Despite their ultrastability, traditional societies are passing. Hagen emphasized the effects of innovations, which are now coming in larger numbers than can be accommodated by the restoring forces that are present, as the triggers of change. The upbringing of children has been disturbed, the frequency of youthful rebelliousness is increasing, and there are at least a few ways of making a living within the society while still rejecting its traditions. Thus innovations can persist, and may reinforce each other.

Whereas in former times traditional societies responded to challenge by *retreatism,* a move toward fantasy, or a rigid *ritualism,* depending upon the degree of shock, nowadays they more frequently undertake an innovational or reformist tack. Innovations, when adopted, represent shortcuts to accepted ends within the existing social framework, but reforms require an overhauling of the institutional structure, including forms of government, religion, education, and etiquette, in an attempt to modernize the society.

When Hagen's recapitulation of classical theory is fitted to case studies, which range from (1) modern Burma, (2) twentieth-century Colombia, (3) nineteenth-century Japan, (4) fifteenth- to eighteenth-century Britain, to (5) contemporary Sioux Indians living on a reservation, it is seen that there are many loose ends and indeterminate factors. None of these instances of development (or lack of it) was *planned* or even guided in the direction of a goal, so that one gets the feeling that random elements are dominant.[1]

A much more explicit behavioral explanation of development is to be found in McClelland's book, *The Achieving Society.* It starts from the measurement of human motives and behavioral characteristics. Motives, he has argued, can be gauged by reviewing the spontaneous thoughts and by analyzing the resultant freely produced visual and verbal images. The interests that seem to be guiding the transitions from one image to the next can be standardized to some extent by asking people to write out their impressions of specific pictures. From the flow of ideas produced it was discovered that at least three motivational themes can be identified: (1) a need for achievement, (2) a need for affiliation, and (3) a need for power.

A scale can be constructed by counting the number of ideas related to a given theme that are produced in the spontaneous response. This

[1] A reconstruction of Hagen's theory using more operational forms of psychology was undertaken by John H. Kunkel in "Psychological Factors in the Analysis of Economic Development," *Journal of Social Issues,* vol. 19, pp. 67–68, 1963. His version offers a persuasive explanation but is no more useful for planning since it is concerned with the conversion of a traditional society into a transitional society, while planning can begin only after this modification is well advanced.

scale can be connected to other scales based upon the public imagery employed in the society that is available for analysis—the art, poetry, drama, street ballads, popular novels, sermons, etc. In brief, McClelland found that nAchievement (the index measuring the prevalence of the achievement motive) was a predictor of development, that nAffiliation was negatively correlated with development, and that nPower seems to be irrelevant.[2]

These studies (which have been carried out on a wide variety of societies, contemporary and historical) suggest that a society-wide enhancement of nAchievement is a necessary but not sufficient cause of economic and cultural development. People must feel that the struggle to reach personally set goals is more important than pleasing members of the family or friends in the community; they must also feel it to be more important than controlling the behavior of others. When an increasing number of persons in the population accept these value orientations, it becomes possible to promote development.

McClelland's most spectacular success in illustrating the significance of the relation of nAchievement to development was obtained in quantitative studies which explain the golden age of Athens in classical times. He and his collaborators also worked out methods for comparing many different contemporary cultures by analyzing the content of the readings presented to elementary school children in 1925 and 1950. After considering 65 to 70 different discriminations, it was discovered that many of the attitudinal requirements for economic development, previously hypothesized as necessary by sociologists and economists, were not connected with growth; but it was found that achievement motivation images (e.g., hard work is a means to an end, action is more important than interaction, large long-range goals are to be preferred over others) and "other-directed" indicators (demanding cooperation of others, being aware of the signals that call for conforming to styles set by peers, rapid borrowing of good ideas, etc.) alone seemed to exist *before* a society began to develop rapidly. A shift from tradition-directed behavior to a dependence upon public opinion has a much greater likelihood of producing conditions conducive to rapid growth.

How is the achievement motive enhanced in a society? Most commonly, the idea of achievement is encouraged through the educational system. Chances to travel and make comparisons need to be greatly improved because many people discover goals worth working toward in this manner. Opportunities to improve social status through effort must

---

[2] A moderately high nPower index may not be irrelevant to the existence of the nation as an independent unit, another prerequisite for development in most parts of the world, but McClelland collected his data in such a way that the connection between this motive and the development of the nation would not be revealed.

be provided also. Once change has begun there is likely to be a wave of religious reform which takes hold and reinforces a *protestant ethic,* a pattern of beliefs founded upon achievement.

Other-direction—the second key to growth—can be strongly increased by mixing up the new immigrants to cities with the established urbanites while they are at work and when they are purchasing household goods. Watching how other people respond to social situations is a rather obvious means of resolving one's own doubts about how to behave.

The affiliation motive can be suitably reduced by setting up national interests as superior to family and community, by giving responsibilities to youngsters at an earlier age, and by inducing a sensitivity to public opinion. Attempts to reduce the rate of population growth should also be influential. However, McClelland points out that low nAffiliation indices combined with high nPower tend to lead to dictatorship and an authoritarian form of society. He did not suggest in his own study how the nPower could be affected by reforms of social institutions, but this objective has been the focus of attention of a considerable group of social psychologists, so there is no scarcity of suggestions. What is lacking, however, is an effective procedure for intervention in child raising, so this authoritarian hazard of development promotion can only be noted in passing. Recommendations for action in the typical situations cannot be formulated at this time.

Studies of the behavioral policies prerequisite for development are still sketchy and incomplete. In any society, some individuals are high in nAchievement, regardless of the strength of tradition. This cluster can be encouraged to propagate and diffuse; normally, the middle classes embrace it first. Then, if political circumstances do not interfere and the natural resources situation is not too adverse, an accumulation of skills and capital should result. *Thus these isolated reservoirs of nAchievement should be considered a special resource which needs to be discovered, assayed, and exploited for growth purposes.* The policies intended to affect motives and attitudes when redirecting society should enable it to expend governmental effort with greater assurance of desired results. Each instance, however, deserves closer study because the nAchievement score is an even grosser concept than the economists' per capita–income index, and it is therefore more susceptible to misuse when guiding the programs and plans of a society.

THE IMAGE AND THE PLAN

McClelland's discovery of achievement motivation as a force for producing growth and development is only a beginning. Also necessary is (1) an image of a more desirable future, (2) at least one course of action that enables the society to achieve it, and (3) hierarchical ordering and structure. Miller, Galanter, and Pribram, in their collaborative book *Plans and the Structure of Behavior,* have borrowed some terminology from Boulding and have designated the first of these the *Image* and the second the *Plan*. The third characteristic represents an insight into the requirements for organization of higher order. Their study explores the relation between the Image and the Plan at the level of individual behavior. Their mode of thinking is quite appropriate also for the behavior of groups, institutions, and nations.

The Image they consider actually embodies the sum of the knowledge that a person has accumulated. All the past experience affects directly or indirectly the view of the future, much of it in the form of preferences about what should not *recur* in the future. The Image is a mosaic of facts that are ordered and arranged by values. The Image is organized by concepts into a set of hierarchical levels, but the strata are frequently disturbed and sometimes interleaved. The concepts are not entirely consistent and unambiguous. This is mainly because the housekeeping in the Image is always running behind the accumulation of experience, so that some facts have not yet been put into their proper places. The Image is made up of a series of memories of environments containing both physical and social elements, and each of the environments is made up of a series of typical situations. The latter may be further subdivided into messages and impressions that are both sent and received (transactions). Messages carry imagery that fits into hierarchical arrangement even more neatly. Their structure will be analyzed later in this chapter.

The Plan is the process which controls the order of a sequence of operations to be performed. If the Plan is to be feasible, the respective operations must already be part of the Image. However, an outline for a course of action, with details unspecified under some of the headings, can still be a Plan because during the latter stages of execution one may choose any of several operations on the basis of opportunism. The Plan can be outlined because it also is hierarchically organized, the levels being programs, projects, and lesser units of behavior. The sequencing of programs in the Plan is usually termed *strategy,* that of the subsidiary projects within a program is called *tactics,* while the execution of the minor elements will be referred to here as *actions.*

Miller, Galanter, and Pribram identify the building blocks of action as a cybernetic loop as shown in Figure 5. They then demonstrate how this elementary unit can be assembled into hierarchical structures such that the next highest level in the hierarchy will have the same kind of loop but may process different inputs. Thus the Plan consists of tests and operations, the tests being part of the Image that is desired for the future. The more complex the Image, the more multitudinous and exacting are the tests. Similarly, the operations that go into the Plan need to be more precise.

These authors are highly conscious of the fact that the scope of individual Plans is limited by the capacities of a human being, in the same manner that the plans of a society are limited by its history and its resources. The constraints they identify are under such headings as (1) source of the Plan (borrowed, adapted, or invented), (2) time span (also called horizon), (3) internal consistency (has it been "debugged"? [3]), (4) interchangeability of parts (flexibility), (5) speed of construction, (6) information retrieval, and (7) the "stop orders" (which determine

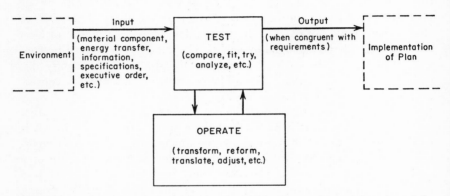

Figure 5. Requirements for organized action. This diagram is an elaboration of the model of Miller, Galanter, and Pribram. An input from the environment is tested for suitability for standard actions, accepted tactics, and the strategy agreed upon earlier. If it does not fit, it is operated upon and modified. It is then retested. This recycling may be repeated several times until a satisfactory output is found or the attempt is abandoned. This element can be made a component of a hierarchy.

when a given Plan is obsolete and another should take its place). These constraints have equivalents in the plans drawn up for societies. This analysis directed them to the essential subprocesses of communication that underlie the Plan—remembering, speaking, searching, etc. Communication is even more fundamental to the preparation of national plans.

Finally, there is the question of the construction of Plans. These authors ask themselves, "Where do personal Plans come from?" They answer their own question by noting that Plans are usually made up of old Plans that have been assembled in a new way. They are very much aware of the fact that the goal-directed problem-solving computer pro-

[3] A term used by engineers who at one time attributed the inoperability of new equipment to the presence of "bugs"; the word was borrowed by computer programmers and has now become a part of standard nomenclature.

grams have been built up in the same manner. But this is not enough. There must be a plan for Plans (what the philosophers would call a *metaplan*) which contains rules that do not always work but still apply much more often than chance would permit (the proper name for such a rule is *heuristic*). They recognize that Newell, Simon, and Shaw's "General Problem Solver" program for a large computer serves as a generator of programs by using heuristics which have worked well in the past even if not universally. Heuristics could find proofs to many theorems in *Principia Mathematica,* or find many good moves when playing a chess master, but are not universally successful. Presumably there are other heuristics, less well known to ordinary problem solvers, which need to be added to the General Problem Solver before it can handle the remaining problems with the computing resources at hand. The metaplan, therefore, suggests tentative Plans, which must be tested by the information at hand for appropriateness to the problem.

A book on developmental planning must be just such a metaplan. It must start from insights derived from observing successes and failures. It should concentrate upon heuristics that would apply to open societies because that is the only kind of society that will draw extensively from such experience. It ought to produce suggestions for constructing explicit national plans at the level of strategy and incorporate some of the tactics and actions that seem to be required if the key programs are to succeed.

It should be pointed out at once, however, that at least one grave deficiency can be found in the modeling of Plans after computer programs. When a conflict develops within the program, or between programs that are being run simultaneously, the computer stops, and a debugging operation begins. Living systems, such as individuals or societies, cannot afford to cease operations in that manner. They must find ways of resolving conflicts before the breakdown occurs. Successful plans foresee conflicts and avoid them or, if the conflicts already exist, find ways of bridging over the difficulties.

In Chapter 1 it was demonstrated quite clearly that countries fortunate enough to have rich reserves of natural resources are also subject to internal conflicts. Less fortunate countries have inherited historic feuds which are no less troublesome. It is evident that growth has been forestalled by such conflicts. Surprisingly, until now no social scientist aside from Boulding has analyzed conflict in a systematic way, so we may draw upon Boulding's observations.[4] Because of the paucity of prior work, a brief review of the basic considerations of the dynamics of conflict, and

[4] K. E. Boulding, *Conflict and Defense,* Harper & Row, Incorporated, New York, 1962. However, Boulding mixes competition with the conflict situation where adversaries are mutually aware of an incompatible Image and both are determined to have their way.

their effects upon growth, is needed before the growth process itself is elucidated.

CONFLICT SYSTEMS

Conflict between individuals and between organizations is extremely expensive. If one adds up the losses from family feuds and communal struggles, the waste due to bureaucratic wrangling, the inefficiencies due to cutthroat competition, the strikes and slowdowns of organized labor that protest injustice on the part of employers, the cost of the military budget, and the destruction of war, it will be seen that vast sums are dissipated in conflict and preparations for conflict. In most parts of the world this inability to prevent the threat of conflict uses up a quarter to a half of the income potential.

In order to understand conflict, the typical environment in which it occurs must be described: Take a territory of some sort with natural boundaries imposed by history; this territory is occupied by organizations of various sizes which are loosely coordinated into a society. Some organizations are being formed, others are dying, but most are in a steady state with fluctuating fortunes. Boundaries of the total system may also expand or contract, thus changing the interaction between the organizations and the area occupied by each. Of particular concern is what happens under conditions of growth.

Organizations that grow within a given social environment cause increased conflict. The basic reasons are readily apparent. Growth brings with it increased flows in and out; and therefore increased demands for channel capacity in transport and communications; it may also introduce potentials for action in a new domain. If the space for maneuver was almost fully occupied before the growth occurred, a contest develops wherever two or more organizations seek to grow into the same space. A similar situation is encountered when expanded transport and communications flows are required to support a larger-size organization, but competing organizations make demands upon the same capacity in order to meet their own needs. How shall the limited capacity be divided? Finally, growth may bring an organization to a level where it operates no longer within a community or region but in the nation, and there it comes into contact with a new circle of competitors and must battle with the giants for its place in the sun.

In the course of development the organizations within a society have a broad range of growth rates. Some expand much more rapidly than the society itself (these are one set of troublemakers), others at about the same rate, others at a slow rate; quite a few are not growing at all (another set of troublemakers), and some are visibly declining in size and capability. Organizations with exceedingly rapid growth contribute most heavily to the development process, but they also may trigger off conflicts which tear the whole social system apart. On the other side of the spectrum, the shrinking organizations tend to evade or postpone conflict until they are cornered and forced to face a threatened take-over by an aggressor organization, often a potential predator type that would extract the liquid assets and leave the shell. Occasionally all the remaining assets are wasted in conflict. Nevertheless, declining organizations contribute little to the level of conflict encountered during general social and economic development.

A typical conflict arising from growth has to do with the fixing of boundaries and the possession of territory. A static organization almost always has stable boundaries, or limits, to its activity, which are well recognized by the members of the organization. It is challenged by an upstart, with no recognizable tradition behind it, which wants some territory or share of the market presently under the control of the static organization. In its comparatively long history a static organization has developed a series of alarms graduated to meet the scale of the perceived threat. Alarms are set off which impel the organization to mobilize its liquid resources, which may be manpower reserves, mutual-help obligations owed to it by other organizations in the vicinity, or cash. The simple objective is to repel the invaders, obliterate the sources of their power, and secure the traditional boundaries. This model fits closely the behavior of city-states in ancient history.

Recall that many kinds of organizations exist in society. Some, such as ethnic communities, occupy territory. The picture described above would apply very well to ethnic communities in a crowded metropolis. Business firms are drawn into similar conflicts for a part of the market. Government agencies fight their battle for a proper share of the budget and for authority to act; nevertheless, the conflict can be analyzed in an analogous fashion. Voluntary organizations often get involved in vicious conflicts while trying to obtain "their share of the private donations and public charities." Thus there is always a "conflict field" similar to land upon which the battles are fought. Organizational resources are converted into leverages (power and influence) which operate on that field. Victory implies undisputed control of the field in question. Defeat implies not only a loss of control, but also a loss of viability, which could result in the disappearance of the organizational entity.

If growth and development are the prime objective of the whole society, action to diminish the cost of conflict will be taken at the national level. All wasteful destruction of valued resources on the part of the respective organizations must be curbed. Rules are therefore laid down for the resolution of conflicts before they get out of hand. Society is willing to invest in police systems, one for each well-known field of conflict, in order to make sure that its rules are obeyed. Conflict resulting from aggressive and rapacious behavior can then be deterred. A regulated competitive system results, with concepts of justice, propriety, and fair play determining the relations between organizations.

A strong tendency exists for the rules designed to prevent conflicts to yield a system which moves rapidly toward equilibrium, a condition of nongrowth. A growing society must bias its rules in favor of growing organizations. Vigorous organizations are to be deterred only when several neighbors feel threatened, and are likely to form a coalition to fight back even if it means going outside the law. Both capitalist and socialist societies have provided such biases in favor of the growing units in the modern sector of the society. It is often done through forbearance to prosecute for small offenses. In the field of conflict represented by the market, preference is shown through the choice of excise taxes, tariffs, subsidies, and incentive payments.

Another procedure for preventing destructive conflict and maintaining civil order is the development of a modern system of corporate law. Then the injured parties have access to the courts in order to reestablish control over lost "territory." In effect, a new field for conflict is created which uses the services of well-trained advocates as contestants. Property is not destroyed, lives are not lost, but still a significant fraction of the time and effort available to a society is spent in the creation and maintenance of a system of law. (Usually in the range 1 to 3 percent of the productive activity is committed to these purposes in human society, not counting education and indoctrination in the schools.) Some fights are thereby reduced to debates.

Many expensive conflicts continue outside of the law. They include feuds, destructive competition between firms, political clashes in the course of seeking popular support, and struggles between ethnic communities. Their cost may be reduced through identifying the common sources of conflicts, the kinds of gains and losses incurred, and the mechanisms of the spread of the conflict that tend to involve more organizations than those originally concerned. For the settlement of such conflicts a series of peacemakers or mediators must be supported who go into a conflict situation and attempt to get the parties to give up fighting and find some compromise which is acceptable for the moment. The compromise might easily also become a convenient precedent for settlement in the future. Certainly any society attempting to minimize the cost of lawless conflict, as a component of its development program, would make plans of this sort.

Some kinds of conflicts are more significant than others, and it is possible to sort them out by the frequency of appearance and the damage that results. Collisions between two rapidly growing organizations are more common than would be expected on the basis of random interactions between organizations because rapidly growing organizations tend to be concentrated in the same vicinity, they are often neighbors, and they see roughly the same opportunities at the same time. Growing organizations tend to have several options for action open to them. Therefore it is relatively easy for them to bargain *quid pro quo;* both organizations can find a way of getting much of what they want by giving up a little. Problems of conflict between rapidly expanding organizations in a growing society are matters of concern for the government, but they are not likely to build up to such a scale that the bases for overall growth are destroyed.

Static organizations have a more jaundiced attitude toward conflict; they have been sparring with their neighbors over some time and therefore have arrived at a fairly accurate appraisal of relative power. Static organizations bordering on other static organizations have the most stable boundaries. Occasionally they do get thrown into mortal combat with each other, where only one can win. This means that the immediate social and economic environment has become less favorable and only one organization can survive where two or more existed before. These circumstances are common in depressed regions or markets, or when sources of support are dwindling. Such battles affect the rates of growth and development very little.

In the typical dual society—the modern-traditional dichotomy—conflict is polarized around the new versus the old. The challenges stimulate the modern organizations far more than the traditional. The modern have a much larger body of experience to search for bringing new tactics and new resources to the attention of the decision makers than has the typical traditional organization. Nevertheless, the history of war suggests that many traditional organizations grasp the significance of innovations in a conflict situation when at any other time the potentials would have been ignored. The traditional units adopt the innovations in the emergency, one innovation leads to another, and the unit starts undergoing rapid modernization. More often, however, chaos results, owing to the "retreatism" of traditional organizations, which proceeds at an even more rapid rate than the advance of the modern agencies in the same field. Individuals without their organizations, or with impotent ones, feel a normlessness, or *anomie.* Some of the major costs of growth and development in a society are borne by members of organizations which fight modernism and lose. Special welfare organizations, such as the Salvation Army and the settlement houses, may need to be created in the cities which recruit these displaced individuals into the low-skilled services for the modern sector of the society.

Until this point in the analysis, conflict has been regarded as destructive of resources, but it has a constructive contribution as well. Just as in biological societies, the rank of an organization among its peers is determined by its apparent ability to damage competitors and not be damaged by them. Its capability is judged in the course of sparring for superiority. Both the contestants and observers arrive at similar conclusions, but the contestant's information about relative strength is far more explicit and more likely to affect its decision making. Once the rank, or pecking order, as it is called in a flock of birds, has been clearly established in a population of organizations or individuals, the amount of conflict diminishes to a relatively low but not insignificant level. Some conflictful interaction is apparently necessary to expedite the gradual changes in relationships due to accident, maturation, and aging. The continuous friction keeps the individual organizations alert, and it requires a repeated search of the environment for resources that may be useful for self-defense.

IMAGES AND ORGANIZATION

It is time to put together the subassemblies of argument that have thus far been introduced. The procedure employed for unraveling the principles for planning over the next decade or two has involved a consideration of the factors that hinder growth and development. It was seen that the presence of natural resources is less necessary than in the past, while the settling of disputes before they become destructive is more necessary than ever. The presence of an achievement-oriented, other-directed contingent in the society seems to be needed, and it must have in addition a modern, organized Image of the future which serves as a goal. The image of the sovereign nation, capable of interacting as an entity with other nations and attracting the loyalty of its citizens, has been introduced. Actually, if the parties in power within a nation are attempting to foster development, they must grant highest priority to the growth of a great variety of groups, circles, departments, bureaus, companies, and institutions in the modern sector. The degree of interaction of these components must increase.

A company or institution may be regarded as a special kind of machine which uses men as replaceable parts, but these social machines are so marvelous they do not yet have adequate analogues in the mechanical world. One unusual property they have is that they are self-constructing; they were started when one or more of the "parts" went forth and recruited others to carry out complementary and coordinated behaviors. These companies are to a high degree also self-repairing systems; when damage is sustained, they will readjust the relations between the parts in order to maintain as much output as possible under conditions of stress.

When conditions in the national environment become more favorable, the output of most of the various organized units should expand at a greater rate than their recruitment of participating individuals. When such a marked advance in productivity per head can be discerned, it is highly probable that development is proceeding rapidly.

An astonishing property of the majority of the new human organizations which need to be propagated is that they are primarily concerned with intangibles. Even the attention paid to the output by consumers is rarely associated with the necessities of life, but deals with side issues. For example, food has always been prepared from certain natural materials by time-tested recipes, but in order to preserve food and reduce spoilage, a food processor must come into being. This new processor must standardize the shape, texture, and taste of the product, package it, and put a printed label on the package. Most of the organizational activity concentrates on these aspects. Success for a food processor depends much more upon his taking cognizance of these qualities of the output than the price differential he is able to maintain.

Another example of the importance of the external qualities of the product can be drawn from the institutions providing for living accommodations and shelter. Many buildings have been raised in the traditional society, either by those who wished to live in them or by craftsmen who were acquainted with traditional materials and forms. However, development implies that architectural and engineering firms would come into existence which pay special attention to structure and configuration. Individualized appearances are superimposed upon buildings to signify their unique uses. These intangible elements, the patterns that may be either unique or standard, are recognized by a portion of the population coming into contact with them; they stimulate predictable behavior on the part of the population that identifies them. Such intangibles are most often transmitted by means of speech and writing, although quite a few may have visual form alone, or primarily affect the senses of odor and touch.

These particular intangibles will be called *images* because they are tiny fragments of what Miller, Galanter, and Pribram—also Boulding some years before them—have called the Image. By successive stages of clarification, their qualities will be made so explicit that the images can be counted and the size of the repertoire of images assembled by individuals or institutions can be measured. The size of the inventory of different images recognizable within a society will be shown to be an indicator of its social and cultural wealth. It is probably a more significant index than the accumulation of livestock or property, which have been used to measure wealth in the economic sense. The variety of images available to a social unit reflect its capabilities for responding to its social and physical environment. They indicate the degree to which it has become organized.

Images are all-important in the creation of new organizations. The natural history of any social unit from the time before it was conceived to the time it expires can be explained in terms of the images that are readily recognized by its members and its clients. Image sharing is the basis for the coherence of the organization. The following brief description of the evolution of a well-organized modern social unit illustrates the manner in which images function.

Long before any social organization can come into being there must exist in the milieu some unfulfilled service or collective need. How can such an idea of need arise? Primarily from making comparisons, often between himself and strangers, an individual is stimulated to imagine a new state of affairs—different from anything he ever observed or experienced before—that ought to be distinctly preferable to the present. This concept may be the consequence of dissatisfaction, or even envy of some other person, but it is also invention. An immediate outcome of invention is a reconstruction of the inventor's Image. He feels he knows a future that could well exist. If the idea can be communicated to other people, the inventor must describe it in terms of images he already shares with them. If they are able to transmit the idea to others in an essentially accurate form, the reconstructed Image is likely to survive for a while in the population as a hypothetical ideal.

Imagine, for example, that the reconstructed Image allows for the possible prevention of a well-known disease. Sometime later (the amount of time may range from seconds to decades) the discrepancy between what is observed to exist and what is contained in the Image about a possible future is evaluated morally. The gap is felt to be unnecessary. Then the actions of individuals that maintain the present state of affairs suddenly appear stupid, evil, reactionary, primitive, etc. These moral judgments are rendered by reformers. They call attention to the value differences between the standard traditional Image and the new one. They assert loudly that the gap is scandalous and that society should reform itself. Many people take delight in scandals; they recognize the possible validity in the arguments but do nothing about the inconsistency themselves. They do not have the motivation to right wrongs or achieve a new state of affairs. The reform is discussed abstractly, as a matter of public morals and justice, which is someone else's responsibility.

However, some persons may see this gap, the inconsistency in the mosaic that makes up the Image, as an opportunity. They survey the situation to discover whether the necessary resources can be assembled, a staff can be hired and trained, and the means for closing the gap in at least one locale can be produced. Thus a new social unit is created. Unsuccessful promoters of new organizations lose their time and capital and disappear from the scene. Successful units, however, accumulate over time.

Achievement of the objective creates a valuable outcome in the social milieu. At least a part of this value can be measured in monetary terms— dollars, pounds, yen, etc. In a market system much of the value is returned to the organization, which then pays the participants and yields a profit to the promoter. Whatever remains stays with the part of the public that has benefited. In a bureaucracy the successful promoters are paid off in prestige if they create a new activity or service for the institution. Thus a fragmentary image of what the future could be has been converted into an image whose meaning is being experienced in the present.

As promotion expands and is imitated, an increasing proportion of the public shares in the experience and in the benefits. In the example of disease prevention, they have taken their immunization shots, or decontaminated their water, and thus have taken effective action to prevent the contraction of the disease. Ultimately people will come to depend upon the absence of the disease and improve the organization of their production system, educational system, and other institutions wherever they were affected.

As soon as a novel image is introduced in this manner, and a working organization has appeared to propagate it, inefficiencies become obvious to persons with calculating minds. These managerial types find shortcuts and make minor inventions which "improve the art" and reduce the cost of the service provided by the unit. New subsidiary images are created in the process. Thus the degree of organization is enhanced; the unit may become indefinitely viable. Again in the case of disease prevention, the small inventions that become minor images may be clinical test routines or procedures for treatment. Managers who seek these improvements are found in public health services and in hospital staffs.

Thus an image acts as a social propellant. It triggers specific actions on the part of many people. It gets modified in meaning by the accumulation of experience, and, as it is increasingly employed in communication, it may become fuzzy and indefinite at the fringes, but it stands distinct from all other images in the mosaic. The added images are the intangibles that pull a society out of the rut of tradition. They represent something of great value to individuals and organizations—valuable enough to stimulate effort.

INNOVATION AND THE FLOW OF INFORMATION

Emphasis thus far has been placed upon images—their origins, role, function, and identification. These intangibles in social process have been singled out and made discrete. Now attention must be paid to the transmission of images, or communication.

A communications system is constructed to transmit *messages*. Whatever else may flow over a communications channel, and is not understood, should be regarded as noise. Messages contain *terms* that are understandable to both sender and receiver(s). As noted before, a term may be a word or a group of words representing an image. A term may also be a pattern incorporated into a picture. Terms are built up from *symbols,* which have no meaning (i.e., concrete referents) of their own but can be manipulated readily for tests and operations (as in Figure 5) carried out by the receiver. This hierarchy is completed by noting that symbols can be defined as a *set of stimulus patterns* for an organism. The transmission of any member of that set conveys the symbol, and a pattern of symbols similarly conveys a term, while an assembly of terms is needed to convey a concept. This mode of organization of communications has resulted from the scarcity of human time that could be allotted to social endeavors. Pictorial channels have been left open for the fuzzier and less explicit images, but language has become a medium for precise communication. A good language is one that reflects the degree of imprecision in the minds of the senders and receivers regarding the concepts in a message and at the same time permits exact statements. Mathematical notations are extensions of language with some of these constraints removed.

Now, reconsider briefly the flow of communication required for invention, the adoption of invention, the production of a new product, and the development of expanding uses for the new product. Whenever the message content has recognizable value to the receiver, it will be called *information;* information flow in this context first occurs when some messages interact with a felt need. If the messages were novel, or the need was new, a new concept might well result. Such a concept, if it is to be manipulated with ease, must be represented by a new image. This is an invention. Inventions, it must be noted, are preceded by flows of information, and the speeding up of invention requires increased communication.

Still larger flows of information are required for comparing the invention with alternative means for achieving the same ends. If an entrepreneur makes an energetic search for satisfactory alternatives and fails, he is then encouraged to innovate. An innovation extracts social value from an image. An innovator must switch to the role of sender and persuade suppliers, workers, wholesalers, retailers, sources of credit, and customers to accept the implications of this innovation. He sets off a wave of communication much larger than what is needed to maintain the less useful alternatives. An invention, therefore, is an image that acts as a trigger.

Information that has been distributed in a society by these processes is likely to be useful in carrying out tasks that are assigned at a later date. Learning is involved. The third or fourth occasion that the innovation is used should take observably less time to implement. As that task is repeated, the time to completion will be shortened until fatigue or some other limit becomes significant. After many such experiences with innovation and the acquisition of information, most people "learn how to learn," so that most novel situations are handled with dispatch. The people carrying out instructions have come to trust their sources of information, and so are not held back by doubt and suspicion. They make fewer errors in interpreting the messages they receive. Any information acquired relating to innovations and changes in the society should then result in more output in less time. *In general, the greater the innovation rate and the associated flow of information, the greater is the rate of social improvement.* This relationship holds until fatigue, or confusion, sets in and effective responses are inhibited.

This argument can be stated in the inverse: An increase in economic efficiency requires at least a shift in the flow of information in the economic system. People must know more in order to manipulate the factors of production and obtain greater output. More often than not, the extra messages needed to acquire the knowledge are added to the regular transmission so that, in sum, an increase in information flow is to be anticipated.

The inverse argument can also be put in sociological terms. In the course of social development a great many important new organizational roles are created outside of the family. If these organizational roles are to be filled, people must learn to carry out explicit tasks. The more information a person has at his disposal, the more likely he is to perform these tasks competently. By so doing he would meet the expectations of others and obtain their approval.

If a person wishes to gain prestige, a society usually offers several routes by which he can move into such roles. In a developing society it appears that information, either in the form of educational preparation or knowledge obtained by other means, has become a principal means for getting and holding prestigeful positions. The other methods, which include conspicuous consumption, landownership, saintliness, and prowess in battle, require less information and are less effective during a period of growth.

A parallel argument connecting information flow to cultural development starts with a body of cultural traits. For each of these traits there will almost certainly be found at least one word or term in the vocabulary of the society. Development implies that the range of these traits (which include rituals, symbols, styles, techniques, and types of artifacts) must be increased and the number of ways they are combined must increase even more. Communication is required for the diffusion of these traits through the society so that most persons have a wider range at their disposal. For the word "traits" the word "images" can be substituted to give a still more general cultural proposition.

Administrative systems are also capable of development. Their progress depends upon the creation of large institutions. New activities, such as central government, integrated transport service, electric power production, water supply, medical service, military defense, and municipal administration, require larger and more intricate organizations than existed before. Before these bureaucracies can function and provide their designated services, they need quite large numbers of educated persons to fill the respective positions. They also need modern media of communication, such as a postal service, a telephone system, news publications, and banking services. Thus administrative development demands an accelerated buildup of communications through the educational system, as well as a set of public carriers with very much enlarged capacities.

A close connection between political development and enhanced communications has already been introduced in Chapter 2. Politicians who wish to retain the backing of their supporters will employ every new medium of communication as a means of making contact with potential supporters. As soon as a new medium, such as television, has become available, the successful politician is the one who rebuilds his party organization around the special advantages offered by the new medium. A two-way communication system results, with appeals, promises, and informing statements flowing from the political leader to the public, and the concerns, fears, petitions, and suggestions being transmitted by the public to the politicians. The superior, or dominant, political organization over the long run is the one that has perfected this communications circuit so that large amounts of information flow in both directions.

Review for a moment the concepts that exist in each of the social sciences as encapsulated in the preceding paragraphs. They suggest that development cannot be achieved over the long run without very substantial increases in communications flow and large-scale accumulations of knowledge, both in people's heads and in collections of books and files. If people improve their economic productivity, advance their social status, enrich their culture, organize themselves for large tasks, and make their political action more sensitive, they cannot avoid placing more emphasis upon the quantity of messages that is received and sent. The respective systems—economic, social, cultural, administrative, and political—require it.

Outside of these systems, the psychology of the individual in the developing society must be considered. He has aspirations of some sort for the future. Some individuals particularly value freedom of choice in the marketplace; they would naturally work specifically to increase their money income. For most individuals, however, the urge to acquire a higher income is regarded only as a means to some other end. Very frequently, for example, the end is family security. For some others the extra product would go toward the creation of an effective nation that could command the respect of other nations and no longer be dominated by outsiders. Some individuals belong to oppressed minorities, and they aspire to gain higher social status and to occupy professional roles hitherto denied them. Still others yearn for a cultural life, rich in imagery, that will offer continual opportunities to experience new aesthetic creations. Having more money does not automatically assure one of achieving such aspirations, but wealth greatly increases one's chances.

To realize his aspirations, the individual must be alert to opportunities. He becomes interested in education because it guides his progress. He is also interested in the news because it brings information about possible opportunities. But the ordinary individual in the society remains a poor judge of what he needs to know. The student of the development process will be able to infer from comparisons of several societies in various stages of development what the curriculum should be, approximately how much effort should be expended in purveying the news, and what kinds of content would be the most informative.

Because the history and the aspirations are different for each country, it is not feasible to lay out an explicit plan for information-gathering systems. Differences in attitude toward information and concerning means for its distribution are among the major reasons why nations remain separate: they do not see any identity of aspirations and approach. Otherwise nations might easily federate and amalgamate in their efforts toward development. There is, however, a central core of information and procedures which is expected to be common to all nations and which embraces more than just science, technology, and world affairs. Therefore this study will concentrate upon a typical scheme for communicating the known body of needed information while being mindful that there is a unique component within each society as well which must be dealt with in the actual planning.

Thus far, information has been treated as a commodity which could be created, transmitted, stored, accumulated, bought, and lost. All this implies that information is something which can be handled quantitatively, and that there must be some sort of physical unit, similar to *tons* or *ergs,* by which to measure it. It is therefore proper at this point to consider carefully the logical foundations for relating information to growth, which should lead to the most relevant procedures for measurement.

THE PROPERTIES OF INFORMATION SYSTEMS

Underlying the foregoing judgments concerning the properties of communication and information are some basic principles connecting social change with the state of information. They cannot be proved in any scientific or philosophic sense of the word, but they can be shown to be logically consistent as well as representative of the true state of affairs. These principles, extricated from their immediate context, may be stated as propositions.

Proposition One: Social control requires prior knowledge. Increasing control of a situation by human organization requires information useful for a short-range forecast of the future as well as knowledge of new opportunities for preventing threatened losses.

An executive group, charged with directing an organization, must know trends in the social, physical, and political environment before it can act in a reasonable manner. It must ask questions and collect data before reaching a decision. The questions executives pose to assistants and to the people around them cause the latter to generate many more questions. With this aggregate information, the opportunities for controlling a situation will be either equal to or greater than the ability without it. Almost always, then, any attempt to control the environment should be preceded by the collection of more facts than were already on hand.

Proposition Two: Economic growth is preceded by the acquisition of new information. Each increment of new economic growth and social organization requires prior infusion and diffusion of new information into the economic system.

Before steady growth can be recorded in any sector of the economy there must be a surge in the marketing of a line of products and services. Expanded use must be preceded by new information regarding the potential value of the product or service.[5] People rarely modify their consumptive choices upon the receipt of a single message with a new image; they almost always wait until they have had many confirming signals. The expansion also requires that needed workers be trained a year or so beforehand and new production and distribution services be organized at the same time. New facilities would have been designed two to five years earlier, and investors persuaded to commit their savings to the projects.

[5] Economic theorists can show there is a logical possibility that this statement is not necessarily true, but the exceptions are trivial cases.

All these new activities require a level of communications far beyond the national average. It is true that there may be some offsetting loss of information about the displaced activities, but such knowledge is slow to disappear completely because the backward areas of society retain knowledge of the former activities for generations after they have been abandoned in the modern component. Thus economic growth presupposes rapid advances in public information in some sectors and only a slow erosion of tradition generally.

Proposition Three: The present stock of natural resources is an outgrowth of accumulated knowledge. Any addition that is made to the reserves of natural resources is obtained through the use of reconnaissance, prospecting, surveying, and assaying the opportunity provided by nature. The value, which ultimately depends upon human wants, must also be ascertained. In addition, the technology for transforming the resource into useful products must be reasonably practical.

A given ore deposit, waterfall, or fishery cannot be considered a resource until the knowledge has been acquired which allows its conversion into products whose value exceeds anticipated expenditures. An increasing body of technological knowledge leads to opportunities for substitution and interchangeability, so that on the world scene there are already substitutes available, at a not impossible cost, for all the exhaustible resources.

Proposition Four: A decision system consumes information. Many decisions make some information obsolete and useless because alternatives that were investigated are no longer possible.

A functioning decision center is fed with information. If it is to generate growth, it must have a varied diet and plenty of action. It should be noted, however, that once an irrevocable decision has been made and the consequent action taken, the decision becomes history and the bulk of the information produced to inform the decision makers becomes virtually valueless. Hence all the original information collected can be quickly buried, except possibly for an otherwise useful principle or generalization that might have been formulated along the way.

Proposition Five: Knowledge must be renewed. Many random factors, such as fire, accident, death, and forgetfulness, combine to reduce the body of knowledge over time, and only new observations, inventions, and concurrences can increase the stock.

Contemporary knowledge exists as the memory of individuals, much of which has been transcribed to paper, film, or magnetic tape. Knowledge is considered here as only those memories with which other observers agree as to their correctness. It includes information about the states of nature and the structure of social action. Recorded knowledge is therefore several steps behind the actual state of knowledge in the society. For example, many specialized food-processing crafts will vanish in the course of a famine; or political knowledge will disappear upon the death of a great leader and the dissolution of his circle of advisers, so the total know-how of the culture would diminish more and more over time unless some source that produces new knowledge is present. It seems likely that many more societies in the historic period have regressed over time than have progressed. The losses are more often attributable to the consequences of conflict than to any of the other causes mentioned—one of the principal reasons for giving an unusual amount of attention to the resolution of conflict elsewhere in this analysis.

Proposition Six: Scientific findings are systematized knowledge. Science, both fundamental and applied, attempts to establish relationships between phenomena so that various observers can agree upon facts and relationships as being true enough to act upon. Its more important contribution is the development of theories which collect most of the facts together into several meaningful, teachable systems that save time and trouble in discerning details.

Scientists are specialists in the creation and preservation of knowledge that promises to be of value to people in general. They take great care, when reducing their observations to some published form, to employ words with precise, unambiguous meanings. Methods of observation are specified, and the relationships to prior works are almost always established. As a result much less of the scientific information is consumed in the course of institutional decision making (most of which is applied science) than of other forms of information (including judgments of motivations of people, temporary scarcities, the implications for setting certain precedents, etc.).

Behind these propositions exist two fundamental concepts—information and knowledge—which are ultimately capable of quantification. *Information* is defined as the content of a message or a signal which permits the recipient to make what he feels are better choices in subsequent behavior. The interpretation of the message may tell him (1) more about the ends or outcomes of the decisions, (2) more about the risks associated with alternatives already being considered, (3) some hints of new paths of action of which he had previously been unaware, and (4) warnings of new kinds of choices which may soon need to be made. The transfer of information, therefore, is a property of communications of all kinds, including observations made upon features of the surroundings. Information flows are a direct outcome of communication rates. *Knowledge* represents stored information, remembered primarily because it is believed that sometime in the future it might be useful. Knowledge takes the form of a series of statements which are felt to be true and pertinent to the actions of individuals, groups, institutions, and sociopolitical systems at the national and international level. The amount of knowledge that a person has acquired about a given subject (say, international affairs) can be judged by the score he makes in a comprehensive examination on that subject. This might be called personal knowledge, as distinguished from public knowledge which can be drawn upon by referring to an encyclopedia or a library.

In science, over the past fifteen years or so, methods have been devised for measuring the amount of potentially useful information that is contained in a message, and generalizations have been reached regarding typical human rates for absorbing information. The same measures can be applied to the stored messages residing in files and in libraries. The advantage of measurement is that it establishes whether or not growth in information flow and storage has occurred over time. If it has, then one of the prerequisites for social and economic growth will have been met. In practice, however, it will be advisable not to make extensive measurements of total information flow but to find a few simple indexes which reflect growth and decline of message flow in important sectors of the culture. Such statistics are even more fundamental to a growth-promoting policy than most financial data that are being collected today.

INFORMATION, IMAGES, AND GROWTH

Consider a typical struggling society when it is looked at through this new lens provided by modern information principles. What is its current state of affairs? It is improper to invade privacy and look behind the walls of the household, but it is possible to scrutinize what transpires in public, because all significant social, political, and cultural phenomena must eventually be detectable in public transactions. By definition, the actors in public are in a fishbowl and are fair game for systematic observation.

It will be noted that people frequently come together and exchange remarks. They send mail to each other and make telephone calls. Apparently these interactions have utility. There is a pattern to these interchanges also, which changes with the time of day, the day of the week, and the season. Each person outside of his household may engage in scores or even hundreds of such "public" transactions per day. Often, through newspapers, radio, and television, the public world is brought into the household itself so that public transactions may occur there also. These transactions bind households together into a much larger unit; they comprise attempts on the part of individuals and households to explore and adjust to the external realities. The market, the government, the job, the cultural events, and the educational system, each and all, are included in any comprehensive survey of the public communications transactions.

In a society based upon an oral tradition, the spoken interchanges provide the supports for cooperation and integration. Even in these societies there are some accessory supports and images, such as temples, rituals, tribal emblems, and artistic forms which are not oral, but the inscriptions and signs enter into only a trivial fraction of daily activities. The stock of knowledge in such a society resides in the memories of its respective members. The skills of the artisans, the techniques of agriculture, the history of political and social organization, the framework for public service, all of these must be known to at least a few people who must pass their own knowledge down to the next generation by teaching. The key to the stock of knowledge in such a society lies in the language— it needs a word for almost everything that is preserved. The capacity for rote learning and remembering of designated names of things in such a society is often phenomenal by present standards.

The use of writing, the scriptural tradition, because of the impersonal means of communication afforded by writing and ciphering, brings about a major advance in the society that adopts it. Many more facts and ideas can be transmitted from one generation to the next, and the likelihood of loss is greatly reduced. However, it has been the introduction of printing that has wrought the most powerful revolution in societies. With printing, writing could be multiplied and put into many hands; it could be stored simultaneously in many different places, and so it led the way to universal literacy. The stock of knowledge then could be built up many times over and be diffused much more widely through the population. With the flowering of science and technology, much of the knowledge rose to levels of generality and applicability which were recognizably higher than folk wisdom and the handicrafts. Thus the basis is provided for modern society. Modernity consists of participating to a very marked extent in world culture and drawing upon the rapidly growing body of knowledge that is internationally valid.

Thousands of images are acquired at an early age in family life, but tens of thousands are learned in public life. One learns, for example, to link thousands of names to an equal number of faces and to identify their kinship and social role. Each item in the marketplace carries with it not only impressions of its shape, design, and purpose but also the process by which it is used. Thousands of addresses are known, and are distinguished both by location and by peculiarities of the structure at the given address. Many thousands more images cover concepts of public behavior, customs, rituals, routines, and issues. Thus a person may be able to recall to consciousness any of tens of thousands of images, contrast them, rank them, use them to work out tentative solutions to problems, and communicate them to others in order to gain approval and cooperation. The same person can recognize several times more images with which he has less familiarity and confidence, and his curiosity, if nothing else, will induce him to cooperate when exposed to them in human associations so long as there is no indication of threat.

Images are the object of cultural play. Each person reassembles them in his thoughts and his dreams. Novelists are adept at presenting them with words that evoke a segment of life that presumably could have been lived. Musicians play with variations in timing and tone. Cinema directors string together visual images, backed by speech, in a persuasive fashion. Poets invent new images by making deft contrasts between old ones and put into words subtleties that had previously escaped description. All of these artistic skills are directly concerned with imagery. They fill in gaps and round out the spectrum of the possible images that can be based upon mutual experience.

The most numerous body of images by far is provided in science. Each distinct species and strain of organism represents a different image for which a verbal designation exists. There are many millions of these alone. Compositions of matter, inorganic and organic, make up another set of images, and there are millions of these, too. There are other images of relations between images, and so scientific principles come into being. Principle can be piled upon principle, so that a huge intellectual structure of images has been built up in science. Most of a scientist's training is spent becoming acquainted with the logic of this structure so that he can find his way to the specific images that are of interest and trace their connections with the others. Science has gone so far, far beyond the capacity of the human memory that the basic strategy is to establish paths for getting around in the records, almost always in a highly specialized region, of knowing *how* to find past observations rather than remembering in detail *what* has been found. Research adds to both the number of images and the number of relationships that are known to exist between them.

Each of the images in the repertoire of people may be assigned a market value, an emotional value (a feature deliberately removed from scientific images in order to reduce the likelihood of costly conflict and misunderstanding), and an information value. These properties are quite convenient for persons who think like economists. For example, the more frequently an image is used in communications, the less likely its use will convey anything new (and therefore informative) to the recipients; as a consequence, less information is diffused by its transmission. Hence the growth of information transmission cannot be based upon the simple repetition of messages. On the other hand, the precisely defined image used only on rare occasions results in a very high level of information transmission, provided that an appreciation of the precision exists at the point of reception. The same arguments can be made for market value (because supply is restricted) and for emotional value (because satiation is not a factor).

Thus a society has a stock of knowledge, made up of the combined repertoire of images available to its members together with the relations of the images to each other, and this stock is diffused through a population according to need and interest.

The stock has properties similar to those of an inventory of capital goods in economics, and the flow has properties similar to a consumption function. Yet the whole system of market transactions taken up in economic studies ordinarily makes up only a minor part of this cultural flow. Despite the preconceptions of economists, most images do *not* have explicit money prices attached to them—in fact, in many societies it is often judged to be immoral if money is charged or paid. Nevertheless, the utility of the images can be measured. This eiconic view of society and culture resembles the economic picture, with each image representing a commodity that is being exchanged, but it can be far more general.

A repertoire of images is a *living* system. In a body of images that is shared by a given society some images are being born, others are being adopted, and many are dying of neglect. Images come into being when observers agree that it is convenient to make distinctions between stimuli originally lumped under a single image. It might be said that such images have undergone fission, much as bacteria reproduce. Others, when contrasted with each other, yield a new concept whose parentage is obvious. Sometimes an instrument, or a technique of exploration—a single image— may generate a whole string of new images. All such offspring images have to be re-used occasionally, otherwise they will be lost. Even the most esoteric scientific image must be republished every half century or so if it is not to be lost. Images die largely because they are obsolete; other images have been found in their stead which convey more value.

A traditional society has a small repertoire of shared images, and most of the possible relationships between them have already been worked out. The images it has are relatively infertile and are rarely split into new ones. New images that are formed usually are balanced in number by others which disappear owing to accidents or lack of concern.

In the dual economy—after noting all the reservations introduced earlier when the term was defined—the modern sector is aware of most of the images of the traditional society within which it (the modern sector) is embedded; but it has downgraded the value of most of them and is concerned with establishing connections with images borrowed from outside the society. It discovers that a rich variety of images has been brought into existence in the modern cultures and that these are for the most part freely available; one need only take the time to study and to acquire copies of the written record.

Yet a creative effort remains. It is that of merging the traditional system with those parts of the modern that are accessible. These combinations must be tried out by experiment, and most of the experiments will end as failures. The literature and art associated with these initial attempts at synthesis are, with few exceptions, exceedingly poor. The newly created images intended to connect the old with the new are crude, clumsy, and shallow in conception during the first stages of this acculturation process. But, first in the large organizations with on-the-job teaching programs (government and industry), then later in the schools and studios, suitable compromises are eventually found and the results can be very exciting indeed. Thereafter the stock of images available to the whole society can be expanded by accelerated borrowing. The diffusion process into the traditional sector can be subdivided into easy steps which allow the ambitious youth to break out of the confines of the traditions within which he was raised and move into far more imposing edifices of images which are shared in a large part with the rest of the world. This cultural hybridization is most evident in Japan over the last two decades.

MEASURES OF GROWTH AND OPENNESS

If the accumulation of a stock of new images and their distribution through the population are highly indicative of social and cultural growth and a determinant of economic growth potential, what indexes should be used for the measurement of this very basic kind of growth? What implications are suggested for governmental policy?

These questions point up a deficiency in developmental planning as presently practiced. They are questions that have never been adequately approached before in publications and have never been undertaken in practice, yet they follow logically from the principles that have already been expressed.

The basic data are supplied by a lexicon—a list of words employed in a society at a given time. On the theory that a term must exist for every significant phenomenon, a lexicon should provide a fairly comprehensive list of images current in the society. If in addition a dictionary of local usage has been prepared by a team of linguists, the list would also contain idioms, phrases, and the multiple meanings of some overworked words for each dialect. It would be much more complete than a lexicon and would constitute a bench mark against which subsequent measures could be made.

Linguists in their fieldwork try to identify new usages for words that are currently being employed for human activity in public. Their ears are tuned to discovering new slang, new loan words from the outside, new word arrangements, and new intonations. A few of these word mutations are traceable to the natural drift of the language and to the flow of events within the society, but most are due to outside contacts and the importation by such routes of viable images. Some may be attributed to the strains set up in the language by earlier borrowing; people, in order to be perfectly clear in their expression, tend to modify it accordingly so as to emphasize key phrases. Thus the changes in the popular language tend to reflect very sensitively the images being added to the stocks previously available to the society.

Ordinarily linguists would prepare notes on each new usage and its context each time some innovation in language is detected. Such notes, however, represent nominations for change, since poorly educated persons may make errors which are corrected as soon as the deviation is brought to their attention. Only after a new usage has been noted in a given number of independent contexts (three would be sufficient) would it be formally designated an addition to the language and be recorded in the next comprehensive dictionary. If the new usage can be traced to the appearance of a new image that is growing in significance, frequency of use, and utility, it can be expected to be introduced then into a still wider range of contexts.

Perhaps an example would be helpful to demonstrate the subsequent proliferation. Take the image of "fertilizer"; it has probably already entered the repertoire of virtually every society at one point or another. But the subsidiary concepts will enter later—superphosphate, urea, ammonium nitrate, potash assay, spreaders, and various trade names of premixed fertilizers on the international market. Each time any of these words are used they disseminate a unique image about a specialized fertilizer or its constituents and imply possible advantages that follow upon the acquisition of this knowledge. Repeated demonstrations of Western technology show that this knowledge of fertilizers itself promises eventually to produce a striking increase in agricultural production; but before this can occur there must be modifications in the practice of traditional agriculture. These improvements in agriculture can only follow arguments presented by leaders and specialists who are likely to invent a new term or two to summarize their recommendations. Increases in the yield tend to require emergency storage and transport, and these makeshifts also are likely to introduce additions to the language. In the end, scores of images would be contributed to the society merely by the introduction of synthetic fertilizer.

In a comprehensive dictionary of the terms employed in the spoken and written language of a specific society, linguistic specialists can identify quite closely the dates of appearance and the probable source of each term. When studying the language of a developing society, one expects to see the rate of appearance of new terms increasing. The source of the terms is also important. An open society will be borrowing terms from the contacting societies that provided the image. Thus the borrowing rate of loan words over time should be an indicator of openness. The borrowing process goes on most rapidly at the borders of a country and in the centers of its cities. Oppositely, the loss of an image is not so easily established in any society because usage retreats from the cities to the most isolated regions, where it may persist for centuries. The total size of the lexicon, therefore, is more difficult to measure than the rates of accretion.

The growth rate of indigenous terms, drawn from the slang and the argot of specialized groups, should rise in response to urbanization and to the diffusion of local interpretations of modern culture. The adoption of new terms with internal origins should therefore accelerate sometime after the rate of adoption of loan words had begun to increase. The ratio between these two rates—internal versus external—should be a still more sensitive index of openness. It would be interesting to compare this ratio with internal versus external intercity travel (an indicator of the growth of larger social organization), and internal versus external sources of capital.

The linguistic connections between cultural growth and economic growth follow directly from the foregoing propositions. They deserve a great deal of research similar to that on motivational factors coordinated by McClelland. This lexicographical research is vital in a newly developing country and need not be expensive. A society of amateurs made up of newspaper reporters, writers, editors, printers, policemen, social workers, teachers, and similar people will do the bulk of the work with enthusiasm. Only a small committee (drawn from among university staff, technicians, and statisticians) is then needed to supervise the accumulation of materials and rule on doubtful inclusions. True, some countries are forced to maintain a larger organization if, like Indonesia and Israel, they need to *create* a national language and produce a full range of textbooks in that language.

There are no arbitrary values for these indexes depicting growth of the repertoire of terms, or images, which can be compared across cultures. So much depends upon each country's history of colonialism, invasion, foreign aid, discovery of natural resources, and its location, that counts of new terms introduced have meaning only when viewed in the perspective of the country's own evolution.

The cross-national transfer of lexicographical terms signals the beginning of a new type of influence, or a greater depth for well-known types of influence. The influence is never unidirectional because the developed societies also pick up many novel images in their contacts with the less developed societies. The developed societies have the most to learn in the areas of plant and animal ecology, herb medicine, linguistic variations, art forms, and geography.

This complementarity in the exchange of images often can cause misunderstandings among the new nations. Most ultranationalistic elites try to guard the national language as expressed in schools, newspapers, and books against contamination. They decry the use of loan words. They also resent the interest of inquisitive, camera-carrying foreigners in the backward portions of the society, and even may legislate against foreign contacts. They thereby reduce both the openness and the growth of the society.

MORE PRECISE MEASURES OF GROWTH

There is a way of starting from the study of language and obtaining a measure of growth of communications and knowledge which can be used for comparisons *between* societies. It requires estimations of the frequency with which the respective terms in the repertoire turn up in the public communications.

The background arguments and a description of the methods to be employed for obtaining an index of cultural growth are provided in a previous book by the author, *A Communications Theory of Urban Growth*. The technique has not been applied to any countries as yet (except in outline as an academic exercise to discover its properties), nor could it be carried out with any real precision until the latter part of the 1960s. The principles upon which the proposed technique is based are quite new. An outline of the relevant elements can be presented here.

Once a reasonably complete lexicon of terms in a given society has been assembled, the public communications of the society need to be sampled. The sampling cannot follow the areal divisions of the census because the highest rate of communication is reached away from the residence. The proper unit for sampling is a metropolitan area combined with the hinterland that it dominates. The sample should be stratified according to the kinds of public communications engaged in: reading, television and films, radio and recordings, social discussions, telephone conversations, observations of the environment, etc. A sample can also be based upon measures of the time spent by the population while engaging in these various communications.

The crude index of information flow can be obtained by finding the number of times each term is being received in the society per unit of time, multiplying by $p \log p$, where p is the frequency of appearance, and summing up overall terms in the message flow. The crude index overstates the flow of potentially useful information, but equilibration forces in social institutions almost always act so as to assure that potentially useful information remains a relatively constant proportion of the total.

Estimates of the potentially useful information flow can be obtained by carrying out experiments upon typical receivers of the transmitted communications: Which of the terms employed were repetitive, unnecessary, or redundant; which were not recognized at all? It is also possible to obtain by experiment the receivers' judgment of the likelihood that the respective terms would appear in the context that they do. Then, by substituting the subjective probability of the appearance of a term into the mathematical phrase $p \log p$, a more realistic measure can be obtained of information actually transmitted. The cost of obtaining such statistics is at present quite high, but it can be reduced by careful planning of the routine accumulation of statistics (as discussed in Chapter 4). The primary value of the statistics is for the guidance of investments in education and urban services.

One meaning that can be attached to the numbers obtained in this index is that it represents the number of *bits* of mechanical memory that would be required for storing the content of the communication after it had been translated into the most efficient possible binary code, where the units employed are *bits*. Knowing the capacity of magnetic tape, for example, it is possible to calculate how much tape would be required. However, when dealing with human memories for the frequency of terms in the repertoire within environmental contexts—a far more subtle storage device—the unit of information is called a *hubit*.

Preliminary estimates of net information flow in various societies, drawn from descriptions of public life and social interactions within them, have been calculated. Residents of the large cities of the poorest societies (Indonesia, Ethiopia, etc.) appear to transmit 100,000 to 1,000,000 hubits per capita per year. Completely modernized, urbanized, and literate societies exceed 100,000,000 per year. Recall, for purposes of comparison, that per capita incomes for these same societies range from an estimated $40 at the bottom to a measured $1,000 to $3,000 per year at the top, a ratio of at least one to twenty-five but not exceeding one to seventy-five. The corresponding ratio for information flow is much greater, being more nearly one to five hundred. This means that growth rates in the transmission of information must be greater than those exhibited for income, as well as being registered sooner in the growth process—an argument that has already been emphasized.

Some indication of the significance of these indexes of knowledge (as demonstrated by the lexicon size) and of the transmission of information is provided by reconsideration of the war-damaged countries in the process of reconstruction discussed in Chapter 1. If samples had been taken of the vocabulary employed even at the period of greatest suffering and deprivation, there is little doubt that the range of images employed still would be many times greater than that of an underdeveloped country at the same consumption level. Gradually the communication rate climbed, organizations were recreated, and the gaps in them were filled by quick retraining of persons. In reconstruction, the knowledge that resided in the memories of men and the surviving records of their organizations were reconstituted first in concrete, steel, and glass, and later in the form of marketable goods built to specifications that had been established as suitable to the climate and the culture years before. The war-damaged countries did not have to take time to innovate or test other people's images for suitability to the environment; they needed only to recapitulate what already existed in the culture, and fit the pieces together into plans which were much more rational and laborsaving than the hodgepodge that existed before the war. During this period of exceedingly rapid economic growth, therefore, the stock of knowledge index would show a much slower rate of growth of images and only a rather ordinary growth in the flow of information index after radio and newspapers had been reestablished and television introduced. The poetry, novels, and music would be quite dull—in the main merely affirmations of what had been felt to be valuable decades earlier. Some images were lost forever in the destruction, and some others needed to be denied; as a result the working vocabulary might display some significant gaps during the reconstruction.

This slowdown in cultural growth during reconstruction disappears when increased leisure, mobility, and security permit large interchanges of population. Then many new images are borrowed, and satisfaction with one's own cultural heritage is challenged. The success of the postwar reconstruction period in Western Europe has provided a foundation for a ferment that is already detectable in the spoken languages and in the kinds of discussions underway in periodicals. The acceleration should be measurable by applying the kinds of indexes described here. Current measurements, however, could give no indication of the bloom of cultural creativity that should result when the dispersion of images across national boundaries has been digested.

Thus the argument is made here that *the image must precede the physical reality, and that, as long as the image remains, the physical reality can be quickly reconstituted.* Development, then, is fundamentally a mental task requiring first the assimilation of new images and then the reconstruction of relationships between all the images. The images may be distinguished from one another and counted, primarily because language is such a precise instrument, and the accessories to language—pictures and diagrams—can be catalogued in a manner closely resembling methods used for language. An enrichment of the culture presages the formation of social organizations which are able to translate the images into physical reality.

A RESTATEMENT IN EVOLUTIONARY SEQUENCE

Anyone who has studied *growth phenomena* in economic systems, in businesses, in service organizations such as hospitals or libraries, in learning processes, or even in biology, will quickly discern the universal applicability of the central arguments presented in the foregoing "information theory of development." There seem to be general principles of growth that apply to all living systems, but some systems are more elaborate and complex than others. In no case, however, is the knowledge about the components of a system combined with the knowledge of the principles sufficient for one to instigate and direct growth at will. Our understanding is presently a few steps ahead of what was available before, but in all these areas of expertise it still falls far short of what is needed for reliable control over the development process.

Growth has its origins in some system that has matured and come into equilibrium with its environment. A seed of change is introduced and a new system grows up to displace the old because the new is better able to cope with the challenges presented by the environment.

In our typical case of social-political-economic-cultural growth, we begin with a territory with a human population living within it. The human population has found a *modus vivendi* at its existing size by employing tools that it has known for a long time. Thus it has achieved a kind of equilibrium within itself as well as with nature. The seed of change, as was said before, is information about conditions outside the territory. Some information diffuses in from the edges of the territory so that people on the borders come to accept some of the customs and techniques of peoples in neighboring territories, even if they are enemies. News about the outside world, and cultural influences emanating from foreign capitals, converge upon the decision-making centers, usually the residences of chiefs, kings, or chief ministers and their advisers. If there has been a radical transformation in the parts of the world making contact, then the change may significantly affect the security and welfare of the more knowledgeable people, either for better or for worse, before it affects the others. Part of the governing elite worries about whether it should or should not adopt some elements of the change.

Once such contact has been made and the seed of change has begun to swell, attention must be paid to structural details within *the system* under observation, as well as its environment. Our instrument for observation must have four focuses: one for the assemblage of nations and territories; the second for the territory with the properties already given; the third for groups and organizations within the territory; at the fourth level we scrutinize the behavior of individual human beings that is being coordinated through the groups and organizations. Change becomes apparent at each of these levels in the course of the growth process.

The developmental stage following upon the introduction and adoption of new ideas is the formation of the dual society, as depicted in Chapter 2. The image of the future that comes into being in the modern sector of the dual society is based upon a composite of the images of the modern nations with which its members have had direct and indirect contacts. The traditional sector senses the change, regards it as a disturbance with mixed good and bad aspects, and tries to abolish the undesirable results without having very great knowledge regarding either the immediate causes of the change or the effects of attempts to repress it.

Following this is a period of wholesale borrowing of foreign images. The languages and culture of foreign countries are learned, and as many as possible of their artifacts and styles are introduced. The latter choices are usually made by individuals and families, without much subsidy from the government. As noted earlier in this chapter, the greatest friction is between the growing modern organizations and the relatively static but powerful traditional institutions.

With the formation of the dual society comes nationalism, and ultimately the creation of the nation-state. The new state requires the invention of scores more of new images, mainly calculated to induce unity of purpose in the population and to suggest equivalence to other states in the world arena. These new images include flags and other insignia, postage stamps, uniforms, constitutions, roles of leadership, etc. Attempts are made to legitimize the new by borrowing images from tradition. Then, shortly after nationhood is achieved, an architectural style for public buildings is chosen for many of the same reasons: a history of the nation must be synthesized which befits its self-image.

The proliferation of images that occurs at this stage is to be found primarily in the political sphere because they are needed as a means of orienting loyalties. Those adopted are hybrids of various sorts, invented to reduce conflict and assist in the creation of institutions. Thereafter undisciplined acceptance of foreign images is frowned upon by those in power, the xenophobic versions of nationalism being quite extreme in their prohibition of outside images. But such attitudes are unproductive.

After the inception of the nation, when the planning begins in earnest, the natural resources and the goals of the people determine the value of the respective images. Certain international specializations must be learned in all their technical details, so that this particular nation is as likely as any other to produce innovations which are imitated by other nations. Thus, nations that plan become quite selective concerning what images shall be systematically borrowed. If organizations do not already exist for acquiring and installing a body of technical knowledge, they are created by fiat and carefully nurtured with grants and subsidies until they can operate independently. If an insufficient number of individuals had not acquired the basic technical skills during the period of wholesale borrowing, the nation might have to start with selecting students for foreign study and postpone the creation of the organizations for five to ten years.

In the organizing process of developing a national institution, an extra burst of communications activity is experienced. It is exceeded in volume only by the "public information" that is later undertaken to sell the increasing quantities of the product or service.

Thus, the Image of the nation in a developed state—with all its implications for behavior—comes first. Next—if there are no mistakes or interruptions—come the modern manufactures and associated services, such as medicine or radio broadcasting. Finally comes the actual consumption and adjustments in the pattern of living by households and individuals.

Therefore, if a nation wishes to know how well it is doing in preparing for the succeeding decade of growth, rather than for the next few years, it would do well to sample the images that are distributed through the various agencies in the society. Where there is growth in the variety and frequency of modern images, expansions in physical capacity are likely to follow—provided they are at all advantageous economically.

A nation has at best only partial control over the *social* communications of its citizens. There is a strong temptation to manipulate the press, the textbooks, and public statements so that only the "right" images are transmitted. Such procedures are not easily administered in a liberal fashion; they are either ignored (and the force of law is weakened by the winks of the officers), or they are too strictly interpreted and the growth of imagery is stunted.

The supply of images, and the behaviors associated with them, existing within a population operate as a kind of reserve for meeting emergencies and opportunities. Maintaining a stock of images is equivalent in many respects to holding substantial inventories. If the prerequisites for meeting an emergency require existing products and components, the challenge can be met. A society's stock of images serves much the same purpose. Its repertoire covers all the monetized sector, besides a large area in addition where respect and cooperation cannot be obtained with monetary payments. The possession of a *balanced* supply of images can in fact contribute more to the creation of a flexible, adaptive, and growing society than would a plentiful supply of cash. Indeed, the chief problem of the countries richly endowed with natural resources is to find a reasonably efficient (i.e., conflict-free) means for converting hard currency into *social* resources of this kind.

As the images are employed in an institutional framework, they assist in the making of decisions at every level. The internal structure of the enterprises, government bureaus, schools, and other organizations that aid the short-range decision making can also make a difference in how effectively the images are used. Structure determines the *speed* with which the stock of images can be mobilized and directed to the challenge that has arisen. For enterprise, the quicker the response, when in competition with other countries, the more likely the country is to obtain the first fruits rather than the leavings. The institutions related to planning, however, are expected to take many more facts into account and to make the long-range decisions affecting the allocation of resources after several alternatives have been compared. Thus, rather than quickness of response, it is the *breadth* of adequate response that is emphasized in plan-oriented organizations.

At the final stage in development (this is the one that Japan is presently entering and Italy is not far behind) the distinctions between modern and traditional begin to disappear. The peasants have television sets and small tractors; the poorest people in the cities have unions, churches, political associations, sports clubs, and community-improvement organizations. The social structure contains many intermediate roles which are neither modern nor traditional, but instead represent various kinds of compromises. As growth continues, the educational requirements and technical ability demanded of persons filling the more common roles are increased. This is another way of saying that comprehension of a larger repertoire of modern images is needed to fill the post satisfactorily. Standards of performance are being raised. The *quality* of the goods and services produced becomes a matter of grave importance.

Growth can continue for a long while thereafter, as the Western European and American economies have demonstrated. Communications flow in urban areas may increase by five to fifty times beyond what it is now in these advanced countries, before human limits are reached. The number of images that may be added to the repertoires from science and the arts appears to be close to infinity; but as the number is enlarged, human beings will need machines to sort out the images, identify those that are of particular interest, and submit them to the study groups in some convenient manner. Therefore, image-processing machines seem to constitute a prerequisite for growth in advanced societies. Computers are now being used for these purposes, but they are still exceedingly clumsy.

When the "information theory of development" is stated in this evolutionary form, it appears less formidable and more like common sense. Its propositions and computations are more useful for the fine calculations needed to choose the best projects and to assess the needs of programs already under way. This evolutionary form is more convenient, too, for understanding the strategy of development and the more specific needs for "openness."

BIBLIOGRAPHY

Boulding, K. E.: *The Image,* The University of Michigan Press, Ann Arbor, Mich., 1957.
> An elementary discourse on the properties of images and the systems that encompass them.

Hagen, E. E.: *On the Theory of Social Change,* Dorsey Press, Homewood, Ill., 1962.
> A reconsideration of the major extraeconomic factors underlying economic growth.

Hoselitz, B. F.: *Sociological Aspects of Economic Growth,* The Free Press of Glencoe, New York, 1960.
> Connects social change and economic development with the classical theories of demography, social structure, and organization.

Kuhn, Alfred: *The Study of Society: A Unified Approach,* The Dorsey Press and Richard D. Irwin, Inc., Homewood, Ill., 1963.
> A reconstruction of economic, social, and cultural theory around the concepts of transactions and organizations.

Lewis, W. A.: *The Theory of Economic Development,* George Allen & Unwin, Ltd., London, 1955.
> This book introduced and gave strongest emphasis to the importance of education, administrative institutions, and knowledge for the process of economic development in mixed economies.

Machlup, F.: *The Production and Distribution of Knowledge in the United States,* Princeton University Press, Princeton, N.J., 1962.
> Concludes after wide-ranging empirical assessments that 29 percent of American GNP is expended for communication, education, research, and other knowledge processes, which grow twice as fast as the rest of the economy.

McClelland, D. C.: *The Achieving Society,* D. Van Nostrand Company, Inc., Princeton, N.J., 1961.
> Isolates the "need for achievement," a psychological factor necessary for rapid development, in historic and contemporary societies, and describes how it can be measured.

McLuhan, Marshall: *The Gutenberg Galaxy,* University of Toronto Press, Toronto, Canada, 1962.
> A humanistically oriented analysis of the transformation in social structure brought about by the transition from oral to printed images in the Western world, which in turn was caused by a technological transition.

Meier, Richard L.: *A Communication Theory of Urban Growth,* The M.I.T. Press, Cambridge, Mass., 1962.
Lays foundations for the identification of images and the measurement of information flow.

Miller, G. A., et al.: *Plans and the Structure of Behavior,* Holt, Rinehart and Winston, Inc., New York, 1960.
A systems theory approach to the essentials for organizing individual and social behavior.

Ornstein, Jacob: "Patterns of Language Planning in the New States," *World Politics,* vol. 17, pp. 40–49, 1964.
Lists factors determining success of second-language programs and language synthesis.

Polak, F. L.: *The Image of the Future: European Aspects,* transl. by Elise Boulding, Sythoff, Leyden, The Netherlands, 1961, 2 vols.
A humanistic and cultural assessment of the futures that have engaged European intellectuals.

Zollschan, G. K., and Walter Hirsch (eds.): *Explorations in Social Change,* Houghton Mifflin Company, Boston, 1964.
The most wide-ranging up-to-date review of the present thinking about social change, whether revolutionary, evolutionary, or induced.

4

CONSTRUCTING AN ADMINISTRATION
FOR PLANNING

ECONOMIC AND SOCIAL PLANNING in a developing society is administered initially by organizations created for purposes of control, by the palace, the presidency, or the cabinet. However, information about the existing state of affairs must precede effective control. Thus information gathering and supervision are closely linked, with the information being sought at the outset being primarily relevant to control. Later the two functions become separate and self-sustaining. The preparation of a budget, for example, is seen as a means for maintaining the control of the executive over a bureaucratic administration, but the need to justify requests for increased funds and additional personnel requires the assemblage of standardized information.

It is not surprising, then, that the roots of planning lie in the budgeting process. In effect, each organizational unit prepares a one-year plan when it arrives at its estimate, and extra factors are taken into account as the estimate is reviewed by division heads and ministers. Revenues are estimated independently from the reports of the revenue-collecting branches. If prospective income is insufficient, proposals must be produced for cutting back or for coping with the deficit. Most budgets require enabling legislation on the part of the legislature so as to give them the force of law. Finally, a reporting system is set up which uncovers deviations from expectations so that adjustments can be made in the implementation of this "administrative plan." Periodic reviews uncover certain recalcitrant areas of administration which demand a longer time perspective. Either more information needs to be collected and processed prior to the submission of estimates or, as with construction projects, the staging is not conveniently broken down into annual packages. A capital budget, for example, soon receives separate treatment, and it provides a principal support for long-range planning.

The planning *function,* however, must diffuse far beyond the confines of the budget, and even beyond the specialized agencies to which planning is entrusted. Planning must spill over into nongovernmental organizations, firms, and households, where it introduces goals and constraints regarding production, consumption, and program choice. The actual controls applied in such areas cannot be as direct as those of the budget; preferably they would remain as invisible as an indirect tax or the regulation of public utilities. Thus a satisfactory range of options is left to each unit. Every group should do some planning; every organization should look ahead. That they look in roughly the same direction simultaneously is the responsibility of the various planning and information agencies.

Each central administration for planning will adopt procedures for comparing the long-range goals and objectives for its society. Tests for compatibility and relative importance must be found. The administration would prefer that a simple scale of collective preferences be constructed because an optimal strategy can then be computed; but the society that undertakes development is never simple. Instead the planners must live with a constellation of ends or goals upon which consensus is always shifting. The priorities administrative units employ in exerting their powers of regulation and direct control normally reflect which goals are ascendant.

Another aspect of planning, which follows directly upon the setting of priorities for the nation, is that of resolving conflicting demands for limited resources. Information about alternative technologies and the possibilities for substitutes must be collected to enable the planning staff to estimate the contribution to national growth made by one use of resources against another. For scarce commodities, whose price might be bid up, a planning staff may have to resort to allocation procedures similar to rationing. In designating the use to which land may be put, it may restrict the competition to categories of activities which reduce the likelihood of congestion, physical incompatibility, and political disorders.

Each central planning unit must identify the directions for expansion, propose realistic rates of growth and development, resolve conflicts for scarce resources, publicize the priorities, discover the incentives that motivate the independent decision makers, and resort to various devices of indirect control which will prevent waste. The overall administration for planning is charged with preparing many plans, large and small, and with supervising their implementation, but its organization must be constructed so that most of its responsibilities can be delegated. The decentralized planning utilizes published information about projected government action and about the prospective supply of the respective resources by laying out programs of action that promise to yield increasing quantities of services and goods if extra production appears profitable. It will therefore rely heavily upon informal controls and regulation.

In developing countries, planning advances through its participation in short-run crises (with readily apparent long-run consequences), in budgetary allocations, in the allocation of space, and in the construction of strategy. Crises serve as visible evidence of deficiencies both in the information that is accessible and in the capacity for implementation; they can be used to justify the changes that had already been felt necessary but had not yet received attention by decision makers at the top.

History shows that the early needs for planning frequently result in the formation of a council of advisers to the heads of state. In an open society there are enough issues involving international relations to make it necessary that some noncitizens be included among the advisers. In the period since World War II the noncitizens have been primarily economic policy specialists. The advisers have the task of feeding in information and proposed policies. Any proposal they make necessarily goes beyond the boundaries of traditional considerations.

Invariably advisers find they must spend a great deal of time "maintaining relations" with the decision centers if the policies recommended are to have any real chance of being implemented. Because advisers then have insufficient time to do all the information collecting, they often train a local staff much larger than is actually needed to replace themselves. The extra personnel are expected to collect the needed data. Multilingual young men with better-than-average education are selected. Almost always the recruits are zealous adherents to the modern points of view. The initial assessment of alternatives is *ad hoc,* but it soon becomes evident that bench-mark data, which describe in considerable detail the structure and organization of the society on a given date, must be obtained before trustworthy quantitative estimates can be prepared. Thus before this advice giving can be converted into planning, institutions for the collection of such data need to be put into operation.

Often there is also an ideological demand for planning, several features of which were discussed in Chapter 2. The members of the modern component in the society are prone to think of planning as a means for creating a strong nation. Also, the introduction of planning incidentally makes openings for jobs with good pay and high status requiring persons with skills similar to their own (although they are slow to admit this selfish interest). Usually the ideological demand is quite superficial and is satisfied for some time with paper plans which cannot be implemented. The pressure of this unsophisticated nationalistic fervor disposes the government to establish institutional shells which claim to plan but, in fact, can do no more than the advisers mentioned above. Often such pseudo planners lack the trust of the decision makers, and so accomplish even less.

Effective developmental planning needs a full complement of institutions, most of which are not publicized in socialist tracts and therefore are not accorded adequate political priorities. The planning group must use data collected by public and some private agencies; it must also influence the procedure by which data are collected so that the needs for long-run projections are met as well as those of day-to-day administration.

Each of the planning institutions, most of which are government agencies, must be constituted so that it fills some essential short-term need which cannot be dispensed with. Then the agency cannot be readily abolished, and its members feel reasonably secure. It should fit into some internationally recognized pattern so that, when the opportunity arises, it can claim most of its new responsibilities without interagency argument.

For certain problems of development no adequate technical and organizational solutions have thus far been found (examples: fertility control, large-scale low-cost urbanization, reprocessing polluted water, international relations with aid-giving countries, etc.). The approaches to their long-term solution will generate new responsibilities for fact gathering, and these facts would be used to *regulate* the crucial activities.

Regulation smooths out the peaks and valleys in the demand for services. It reduces the frequency of bankruptcies and unearned windfall gains in the economy. It constrains the speculative aspect of any kind of enterprise and provides a basis for calculating relative gains and losses. Regulation works only when sufficient knowledge is available to the policy makers regarding supply, demand, price, and interruptions, to enable them to predict how the bulk of the people and their associations will react to typical situations. Regulation normally begins with efforts aimed at the prevention of minor disasters and then adds new rulings calculated to remove bottlenecks in production and commerce.

ESSENTIAL INSTITUTIONS: STATISTICAL

Any advisory council in the modern era will find it necessary to review the flow of funds. Reports of accountants can be aggregated so that exports, imports, government expenditures, and certain other activities can be followed on a month-to-month basis if necessary. The preparation of economic statistics which are used for the purpose of designing fiscal controls has been introduced into virtually all countries, and the United Nations has assisted in the establishment of reasonable standards for overall accounts. Governments are conscious of their needs for control over finances, and they recognize that the power of the pocketbook can be used to influence bureaucratic behavior. Therefore the basic statistics can be found in perhaps 90 percent of the countries and the procedure for acquiring them is being installed in the remainder. There is no need to take up the subject in detail here. It is assumed that such data will be supplied with increasing reliability through the combined efforts of the country's treasury and its bureau of the budget.

The institution having the next highest priority is a central statistical office. Budgetary controls and executive directives require background information that approximates the precision of the allocations. The various United Nations agencies (such as the World Health Organization and the Food and Agricultural Organization) press countries to adopt standard reporting schemes for incidence of diseases, mortality figures, crop production, educational enrollment, etc. The emphases of the United Nations agencies upon statistical standardization are not misplaced, for a newly formed central statistical office is likely to receive technical assistance of a type to enable comparisons between nations. The assistance may not necessarily be best adapted to the *immediate* problems of the country's developmental planning, but in the long run the standardization of statistical procedures enables the country to draw upon international science and technology with greater confidence and to get greater value from technical assistance which is accustomed to the international methods.

The proper design of a statistical office in the 1960s is changing a great deal from the approach applied in the previous decades. The international shortage of statisticians and clerks is such that the mechanical core must be considered from the very beginning, or reconsidered if a false start has been made. The day is virtually past when the routine statistical work was done completely by hand. A basic installation for card punching and tape processing must be installed to handle at least some fundamental duties, such as the census, land-use maps, etc. For a while the extra capacity of the mechanism can be used for special projects and new services, but expansions in the basic facilities and additional accessory equipment will soon become necessary.

A curious anomaly often arises when statistics processing is considered. The production of tabular data is almost always separated from the consumption of data. For virtually any statistical operation, at the start a manual procedure will appear to be the more flexible and economical. In newly developing countries this is in part due to the low cost of clerical labor using an abacus or hand computer. Yet, if growth occurs, within a few years the enlarged production of figures will cause increasing delays in their availability and perhaps also reduced reliability. And it is during this same period that a demand develops for *early* estimates and more precise measures at the decision-making level. As an example, census data made available a few months after collection are worth many times more than the same data published several years later; but because this extra value of the information is hard to assess, there are disagreements among specialists who refuse to look at the larger picture and therefore do not see the need for rapid processing.

The transition to a mechanized data-processing system is often painful, too, because types of errors change; new rules for their detection and prevention take time to work out, and in the meantime the trust in the system declines. Resistance to required job changing and reorganization will be encountered also. But within a few years a reasonably well-designed system will be handling the routine data very smoothly and accepting new tasks at regular intervals.

For the organization that is given the responsibility, the design of data-processing systems is no easy job in circumstances where the production of statistics is growing rapidly and irregularly at, say, 10 to 40 percent per year. The number of failures in the design of these systems is significant, since even in advanced countries it runs perhaps as high as one in five. Often the best compromise is one in which a crew of clerks is used to reduce the data processing to a kind of routine which could easily be transferred to the mechanical data-processing equipment. The clerks then would be reassigned to tasks associated with the latest emergencies.

The validity of the data, i.e., whether they reflect actual conditions at the time they are collected, is a property that will concern every user of the information. From their experience professional statisticians are able to supply some techniques for internal checking. Accountants and economists have identified certain ratios that are permitted to vary between known limits. When inconsistencies are found, an investigation must be made to discover whether some error has crept in. Improvements would normally be made in the procedures for *collecting* the data. Over time, therefore, the information would become more reliable, so that resurveys would yield very nearly the same figures. The role of the statistician is primarily that of the borrower and adapter; most of his effort would be directed to the task of producing local data of a kind that is already being published and used elsewhere in the world.

What kinds of data have highest priority in the development process? On the economic side, anything that contributes to the understanding and control of foreign exchange will be important. Highest priority would be given to statistical series on exports, imports, prices, inventories, tourism, emigration, harbor and airport use, manufactured products, banking operations, along with a few unique items that would be significant for the particular country in question. Indicators of inventories and crucial flows are needed on a month-to-month basis in those countries which are forced to operate with relatively low reserves.

A second body of statistics having high priority are those associated with the appraisal of the limiting constraint upon growth. If it is food production, for example, figures are needed relating supply to demand. Fertilizer production, weather, water reservoir levels, migratory labor, transportation flows, and the location of consumers for the respective products are also likely to be extremely relevant.

Yet another body of statistics high on the list is concerned with foreseeable problems that must be viewed in perspective. For example, most newly developing countries have a population problem which is brought about by the disparity between low or declining death rate and a relatively unchanged birthrate. The causes may be traced to disease prevention, in which case morbidity statistics assist in predicting where, and by how much, the population will grow. The efforts at fertility reduction will need statistics on the urbanization process, on the recording of new households and births, the estimated population of contraceptors by locale (a statistic rarely available anywhere today), and the changing content of communications. Developing countries will have to pioneer in devising methods for the collection of most of these data because there are few models; modern countries have been slow to develop such statistical procedures.

Priority would also be given to those statistical series which permit the construction of medium-range five- or six-year plans. In the course of fitting together a bundle of projects, many questions develop regarding the costs and returns that may be attributed to each of them. The statistics collected in response to this need may not be very adequate at the start, but data collection can be made a part of the Plan, so that appraisal of the impact can be deduced from the improved series of statistics that result from carrying out the project.

A central statistical office is essential, but it does not collect and process all the statistics. It will have certain basic responsibilities for bench-mark data and for data processing, but other than that its main responsibility is in supervising the collection of operating data by departments, making sure that the data are reasonably comprehensive, and that the outcomes are compatible with each other. The central statistical office may possess the initial large data-processing system, but soon others will appear in other agencies of the government. The central office usually undertakes the publication of a statistical yearbook, a copy of which ordinarily is to be found available for ready reference in the office of any civil servant involved in planning or in the higher levels of administration. Over time, then, statistics collection and processing permeate the whole government, although the focus remains in the central statistical office.

It will be noted that no specific place in the hierarchy has been assigned to this office as a prerequisite for efficient functioning. This is a political question, and greatly depends upon personalities and issues at times of founding and reorganizing.

ESSENTIAL INSTITUTIONS: SURVEY

The most familiar statistics for understanding what is happening over time in a society are based upon comprehensive *counts*. An enumeration is made of people, dwellings, shipments, transactions, or events. Counts could be carried out in most cases by relatively unskilled persons who were literate enough to fill out an official form. Long-range planning has need to know of other kinds of trends which are indicative of the choices that people are likely to make on their own initiative in the near future. These trends are based upon opinions and attitudes which very easily may change before the choices themselves are recorded.

In states that have installed the popular franchise for political parties which compete for public favor by promoting different policies, perhaps the greatest priority in the survey of opinions will go to the study of the factors that affect who will go to the polls and how they will vote once they are there. Political leaders want to know what promises to make to the electorate in order to attract those willing to change their political affiliations, without losing too many of those voters whose support they already have. Normally the leaders consult the local political chiefs and depend upon their judgment, but in times of social change the opinion of the small politician is often faulty. The wise national politicians look for some independent source of information, and most often they find it in whatever near approach to the Gallup Poll springs up in their own country. Polls are private organizations that sell their services to newspapers, magazines, firms, and political parties. They interview perhaps 3,000 randomly selected individuals, code the replies, make deductions about preferences by sex, income, residential location, education, etc. The preferences may be expressed for candidates, parties, policies, or products. The distribution of these attitudes toward a forthcoming choice usually enables a forecast to be made of the aggregate outcome, which can then be verified. A series of successes in prediction builds up confidence in the procedure.

Administrators will want to have a polling organization of their own which will forecast the kinds of acceptance and resistance a new policy may be expected to meet. Or they may wish to fill in with survey data on occasions for which no reliable statistics could otherwise be collected,

A survey organization designed to serve the bureaucrats will normally be constituted in the agency that is best able to make use of the information that can be produced. But the findings sometimes come as a shock to officials; the latter naturally react by suspecting a conspiracy of some sort, and the measures taken by aides of the officials often restrict the freedom to report an unbiased result. The problem of assuring objectivity may cause the survey organization to be established as an independent institute, or a research bureau of a leading university.

In the past the first surveys undertaken in a country have usually been studies of household expenditures. A sample is chosen which reflects the distribution of households in the country. A series of questions is asked about sources of income—which tend to be severely understated—and about expenditures over the previous week. (The choice of the particular week for survey is a special problem in itself; it may contain too many fiestas, marriages, holidays, or fast days, and thus not be representative of the year.) Most information about age of members of the household and relationship to each other can be checked against the census. Estimates are made of the self-produced food, clothing, and shelter that are consumed by the respective households. These forms are coded, tabulated, and then used in planning new services, designing new taxes, and in laying out the curriculum for the schools.

Hitherto most such household surveys have neglected to ascertain how people spend their time either in the household or outside. The use of commodities, public services, and money has been emphasized but *the use of labor or the expenditure of time* has rarely been explored, except in local agricultural surveys. Much has been written about underemployment in poor economies, but practically nothing has been discovered about the patterns for the use of time. In the future these surveys may be used, but *in conjunction with other sources of data,* to prepare a *reference system,* which will be explained later, in Chapter 13. A time budget for the population is such a reference system that would be extremely useful. Behavioral changes are best described quantitatively through changes in the time budget.

Surveys have been used for other purposes of great interest to planning. The rate of capital formation in the traditional sector of the dual economy, for instance, can be determined only by survey techniques. Also, the need to discover the receptivity to a given set of innovations associated with development was one of the first reasons for developing survey research procedures. Marketing introduces a series of very closely related questions. The progress of members of the population toward understanding complicated subjects presented in the educational system or in the mass media is also readily estimated by survey. Informal organization in the society as a whole and the effects of such organization upon behavior can be illuminated. Intensive interview techniques have even been used with marked success in the study of sexual relations and the attitudes toward controlling the size of family. The accumulation of trend data on this last subject alone should be sufficient to guarantee the establishment of an institute for survey research because the population problem is almost universal.

Survey work is quite specialized and requires postgraduate training, but to an increasing degree technical assistance is available. Access to punched-card-sorting machinery is necessary from the start, and in later stages it is advisable to use a computer. The statistical techniques are applicable anywhere in the world, but the meaning of the individual questions put to the respondents is known to change from one culture to another. Therefore each country is forced to carry on a considerable amount of fundamental research on the matter of *how* one can ask questions which elicit reliable responses. This kind of investigation is closely related to the linguistic measures of cultural growth described in Chapter 3. The two subject matters are likely to reinforce each other to an increasing degree in the future. Expenditures required for surveys are highly variable and cannot be estimated for the typical case.

ESSENTIAL INSTITUTIONS: DOCUMENTARY

All the institutions discussed to this point are designed primarily to *acquire* vital quantitative information, describing conditions in the present or very recent past, that was previously available only in the form of qualitative appraisals made by decision makers and their staff or supporters. Attention now is turned to institutions which *preserve* specific bits of knowledge, or a body of useful experience, and make it accessible for the studies which prepare the way to the formulation of development policies.

The lore of the traditional society can be preserved in museums. The typical contemporary museum contains not only the outstanding art and treasures of the past but also recordings of the songs and the storytelling, pictures of the leaders and the communities, films of the rituals, and descriptions of the customs.

The backlog of experience in the modern society is retained in the archives. Personal papers of the leaders, communications between nations, memoranda circulated between agencies, secret reports, and internal orders as transmitted down the line are all deposited in the archives.

The maps sometimes are found in special collections, occasionally in archives, but more often the most complete set is possessed by the military organization. Maps portray the features of the land and the structures that have been placed upon it. They are necessary for military operations, and detailed maps are prepared by the military aerial photographers, surveyors, and cartographic units. It is not unusual for the military to forbid civil use of such maps, not realizing that the whole construction program associated with development may be delayed and made more costly as a consequence.

Access to maps must be given high priority in any society that is endeavoring to plan. Fortunately map-reproducing techniques have been greatly improved in quality over the past few years and the cost has been reduced; therefore it is possible to have several libraries and map rooms with relatively complete sets of maps. Maps constitute a set of bench marks for physical planning. Decisions regarding the precise locations of roads, bridges, harbor installations, new settlements, forests, reservoirs, marketing centers, irrigation projects, and similar developments depend to a very great extent upon the details presented only in maps.

Library systems are becoming the most complex and expensive institutions for documentation. The elements of planning that emphasize technological, social, political, cultural, and economic affairs will require the accumulation of a stock of books and research periodicals of the present and recent past. The knowledge accumulated in the outside world must be brought in and made readily accessible. Equally important are any locally published reports that describe attempts to apply such knowledge. A collection of books initially numbering 100,000 carefully selected titles should be sufficient to take care of the immediate needs of planning, administration, and higher education. The cost is likely to run from $3 to $5 million for books, building, and cataloguing, and a half million dollars a year for operating expenses to make the materials accessible. Fortunately the drain on foreign exchange is not so great as it seems from these figures because several countries are more than willing to put their aid into the form of books and technical assistance for ordering, cataloguing, and storing them. Few developing countries have adequate libraries at present, and few of their civil servants or students of higher education know how to use this extraordinary stock of knowledge. It would be invaluable to the foreign adviser and to many of the students returned from study overseas, who would know how to use it to good advantage. Moreover, the proper design and implementation of new projects worth many more millions of dollars depend greatly upon having such a resource available.

The dimensions of the library depend heavily upon the size of the country and upon whether the chief commercial city is identical with or different from the capital city. Countries having more than 10 million population will undoubtedly need a system containing several major libraries with equivalent coverage, but each may also assemble specialized collections.

An official library in a country (usually also the most comprehensive) is commonly designated a *library of record,* in which copies of all copyrighted publications are stored. Arrangements are often made also with printers to obtain pamphlets and news sheets which are uncopyrighted. The political, cultural, and social analyses are very much assisted by the possession of a relatively comprehensive collection of this sort. The content of public communications (which, it was pointed out in Chapter 3, should become richer and more diverse a few years prior to a period of real economic growth) is revealed to a large degree by the study of these materials.

Libraries keep accounts on the number of persons who are eligible to borrow books (individuals who hold library cards) and also register the number of loans made to each. Some major libraries find theft and irresponsibility to be so prevalent and damaging that they require all materials to be used within the premises. Where this is necessary, such libraries should be equipped to provide reproductions of selected pages, diagrams, and pictures at reasonable cost so that the crucial materials for any report or study can be assembled outside the library.

As time goes on, the library is likely to become a center for advanced education. It is a natural place for people to congregate who are reading for external degrees or seeking diplomas from correspondence schools. These ambitious young people constitute one of the most valuable segments of the modern sector. New political factions are likely to be born in the tea shops, coffeehouses, Coke bars, and bistros in the shadow of the library. These individuals and groups reflect the energy of the rapidly rising intellectuals who prefer educational channels to military promotion or commercial success as means for improving their own social status, and they are very useful to the planning and other staff agencies. Therefore the library provides a double reinforcement for planning, contributing to both the information resources and the development of human resources.

THE PLANNING COMMISSION

A planning commission must above all maintain the trust of the executive—or whatever focus of political power exists. Without this trust the commission is likely to be supervising studies and speculations on the future which have only occasional opportunities for implementation, the overall outcome being very different from what had been anticipated. In retaining a position of trust, the planning commission needs a base of power that cannot be easily challenged, and so it must provide a useful service for the executive in disposing of day-to-day issues that have long-run consequences. It also needs a base of expertise that is not found elsewhere in the government. Thus a planning commission is an agency that should report directly to the executive, or to someone who must be in the immediate circle of policy making.

This closeness to the center of decision making means that the professional ideal, which excludes politics and its compromises from technical optimization, can never be realized at the level of the commission itself. Planning issues are settled in a political context; any attempt to ignore this reality makes the planning effort irrelevant and ineffective. Hence the planning commissioners themselves must be chosen so that they combine both professional and political skills. The chairman, in particular, should have the ability to gain and maintain trust. The staff of the planning commission, however, needs to be shielded from politics so that the technical and factual bases of its recommendations are clearly understood. This relationship between planning and politics, which enables the job to get done, is a matter of experiment and adjustment as time goes on. It is not something that can be "installed," like a computation center or a power plant, with the expectation that it will continue to operate without further attention except for routine maintenance. With this in mind, experts should refrain from making arbitrary recommendations for changing the structure and responsibility of the planning agency. With few exceptions, outside consultants will endorse a system that varies only slightly from that with which they have become familiar. The executive body of a developing country must form the planning commission so that it fits the style of political decision making that has been adopted. The structure, responsibilities, and powers should be so conceived that there is considerable latitude for evolution.

In this connection the Puerto Rican experience is very valuable. The legislation by which the Planning Board was brought into being was carefully prepared after thorough review of worldwide experience up to about 1940. In the course of passage certain compromises in the legislature brought changes which the authors of the bill feared would emasculate it, but ten years later, upon reviewing the rapid development of effective planning in Puerto Rico, one of these authors (Tugwell, 1958) admitted that the changes might well have reduced friction with individual politicians, communities, and special interest groups, thereby enhancing effectiveness. There were three commissioners, one of whom was designated chairman and maintained a position of authority over the staff as well as acting as the liaison with the executive. The commission had responsibilities for the preparation of *master plans* integrating the work of the respective departments of government; it supervised the land-use plans for communities; it retained control over building permits for privately owned structures on private land, and reviewed each petition. Each year it threshed out with the various departments of government a six-year financial program which reset priorities and scheduled capital spending;

it made economic, social, and cultural analyses of issues facing the government in the forthcoming year or two (thus taking over the task of a council of economic advisers); it laid out *perspective plans* for the growth of the overall economy fifteen or more years in advance; it prepared project designs for public housing, rural resettlement, public facilities, recreation, etc. Later on it even took the responsibility for the central statistical service because it needed the data earlier than other agencies, and was more concerned about validity and consistency.

Despite its rapid growth and the extent of its responsibilities, the initiative for planning did not always rest with the Planning Board. For perhaps half of its first twenty years of existence (at the time of writing) most of the initiative rested with the Economic Development Administration, popularly known as the Fomento. The reasons may be attributed in part to dynamism of the Fomento leadership and also to the fact that the Fomento dealt with the rest of the world and was the first to be aware of opportunities for growth that made it highly attractive to the ambitious young men. The major planning responsibilities of the Fomento were for industrialization, tourism, transport, and communications, but these often spilled over into education, statistics, finance, public relations, scientific research, and other peripherally related activities.

The Fomento also demonstrated a central principle in planning, namely, that the strategic thinking in planning goes on in conjunction with the greatest opportunity that has presented itself, or with the most difficult problem that must be solved before growth is possible. Often the society moves from one crucial problem to another every half decade or so. Then the body of knowledge and skill required for making the next step will be different, and the focus for developmental planning may easily move to another institutional group. In Puerto Rico the major opportunity was created by the Fomento when it found the proper combination of incentives for attracting and installing outside entrepreneurs. For the most part these businessmen brought their own capital with them, so capital scarcity disappeared and productivity (in physical terms) needed the most attention. These entrepreneurs could create a modern industrial establishment and an up-to-date distribution system, and introduce a wide range of high-quality commercial services in a partially developed environment. Therefore many of the proposals for new social overhead items were worked out by the Fomento but reviewed by the Planning Board, as with others generated in Puerto Rico's departments of agriculture, health, public works, etc.

Often the Planning Board raised sufficient questions regarding the implications of the respective proposals for ongoing programs so that they would be taken back for restudy and resubmission. When the Fomento projects really fitted into the economy and used scarce sources to the greatest imaginable advantage, they were likely to obtain the highest priority and proceed rapidly to completion. The scope of the thinking in the Fomento during its apogee made it possible to detect technical faults and misdirection of attention in other departments of government which were not being answered satisfactorily by the departments or their advisers. Thus an often forgotten point is emphasized: *high-level competence in planning prevents large-scale waste more often than it achieves preset objectives.* The Planning Board in Puerto Rico carried on this waste-reducing function in an inspired way over most of its history.

One feature of Puerto Rican planning can be imitated to advantage elsewhere. It was installed there after the survey of planning institutions around the world, an effort which revealed three main sources for techniques and procedures for planning. The earliest of these arises from architecture, civil engineering, and landscape architecture. It is variously called town-and-country planning, physical planning, or city planning. Another develops from financial advice, the control of credit and foreign exchange, together with a concern for problems of full employment and industrialization. It is usually referred to as economic planning. A third evolves from the steady improvements in public administration which follow upon the establishment of a civil service and a budget. It less often has a name, since national administrative traditions (British, French, Spanish, Scandinavian, Italian, etc.) differ to a greater extent than do the principles of national economics and civic design. It will be referred to here as *administrative planning.* Harvey S. Perloff, in his book *Education for Planners,* has described these three streams, in the American context, with great clarity, and points to the need to fuse them when solving American planning problems—the techniques of land-use analysis need to be combined with cost-benefit analysis and tests of administrative feasibility when a project is designed. No feature can be skimped in favor of another. The structure of planning in Puerto Rico, both in the Planning Board and in the Fomento, encouraged this fusion. Integrated planning was sometimes insisted upon before the appropriate skills existed within the society, but such mistakes are seldom very costly. There are few parallels as yet in the world as a whole.

THE DISSEMINATION OF PLANNING

One of the first duties of a planning commission is to teach the planning process to others so that they acquire the know-how and the necessary techniques are diffused through many layers of personnel. Gradually, then, the commission can become an agency which supervises and coordinates the plans of others, reserving to itself the preparation of plans for those projects which seem to be no one else's responsibility. A planning commission set up with broad enough authority and a comprehensive set of interests can be a very powerful agency. It is able to exert its power upon the various departments of government, and the respective provinces or states contained within the nation, through its veto power over the capital budget and its proposing of priorities for development.

Basic policies are decided at the executive level (often in the presence of the heads of government departments), but the details are worked out in sessions between the department heads and the planning commission. Educational processes begin at this level. The planning commission must discover in each of the various arms of the administration what capabilities exist for carrying out programs; the departments in turn must learn how to prepare projects that integrate with the various objectives of the development program and use scarce resources to advantage.

Much of the power of a planning commission derives from its familiarity with a manifold body of information in dealing with people whose experience has been limited to one or two fields. It must work out channels for distributing this information and the techniques for fitting it to long-range problems. These channels are normally established when a staff member of the planning commission is given an opposite member in a department with whom direct communication can be made. This tactic eliminates going up to the top, being referred to the responsible agency head and then passed down to the subordinate. Such a relationship assists the planning commission in expediting its responsibilities and the departments in putting forward acceptable projects.

Large-scale projects, such as irrigation schemes, industrial complexes, or express highway systems, require much more planning effort on the part of the government departments most concerned. These ministries recognize their inability to cope with the problems they face owing to inadequate experience and insufficient access to the main bodies of worldwide experience. They ask for technical assistance of a kind which would modernize their design and planning section. If they are fortunate in getting it, planning can then gradually take hold at the departmental level. At the same time, junior civil servants can be taught to use statistics and libraries; they will then eventually be able to prepare proposals that withstand criticism. They acquire this ability not only by practice on the job, but also by participating in meetings of professional groups, by taking evening courses presented by technical high schools and universities, and by studying technical books. The first professionally trained staff members of the planning commission, more often than not, are the teachers of the courses. Even more frequently, planning commission staff members are found in positions of leadership in the newly formed professional societies. Many contact points like these are needed for rapidly educating the personnel of the key departments of government.

Contacts with the managements of whatever large international corporations have operations within the country also figure in the educational process. These firms seek secure futures and conditions of steady growth, preferring to avoid risks of any sort with which they have had no experience. Therefore, when national planning gets established, a counterpart plan is often framed within the corporation, proposing the role of the firm in the development. In these sectors each is capable of teaching the other.

The largest of these international firms deal in petroleum, but the mining and refining of ores, the marketing of fats and oils, rubber and chemicals are represented very widely. So are automotive, airlines, shipping, and utilities companies. Such firms have significant opportunities to shift their expansion from one country to another according to the relative prospects. To these firms, a country's commitment to open development is, of course, enormously encouraging. Equally so are indications of responsible action toward development, which promises low risk of abnormal inflation. Negotiations between the planning commission and these firms may be carried out in very much the same way as with departments of government, except that the relative levels of information available to bargainers are more equal. The outcome is likely to be a modified project more compatible with the strategic features underlying the national planning.

In countries where no long-range governmental planning gets done, and improvements arrive haphazardly, the "compounds" run by the international firms appear to be models of order and competent administration. However, once development planning has begun, these same firms, accustomed to a slower pace, tend to lag. Unless special incentives are offered, calculated to change attitudes in the firm as a whole, the long-resident international corporation will proceed skeptically and only at a moderate pace. The technical capacity to plan is there, however, and an influx of several new international firms brought in to expedite major projects will either cause the competent men to be hired away from the older firms or stimulate them to do better. So planning for the business sector of the economy is often expedited by bringing in new competition with high technical competence.

A most significant feature of this process of dissemination of planning concepts is that planning soon becomes part of the technique of the modern sector of the society and is applied to the private sector almost to the same degree as to government. There remains the task of describing the planning process itself. The preferred institutional framework for the "big push" into exponential growth has been elaborated; now the *methods* for using these sources of knowledge and coordinated action must be introduced.

THE ROUTINES OF PLANNING

In the kind of planning commission that has been described—buttressed by the beginnings of information-gathering and knowledge-accumulating institutions which also have been described—there are certain duties that should be carried out continuously and repeatedly. If they are neglected, the power of the planning commission will erode away and be reduced to meaningless gestures in the face of pressing problems.

Perhaps the most significant of these duties (where it is constitutionally feasible) is the control over urban land use through the granting of construction permits. This exercise of power is necessary for introducing modern streets, rapid transit systems, water storage, sewerage, harbors, and similar installations at a reasonable cost. As the respective master plans for services evolve, land use can be appropriately controlled, speculation can be restrained, and the cost of demolition involved in changes in land use can be reduced.

One or more members of the planning commission, preferably those with experience in law or in building, would review petitions for changes. For administrative convenience it is desirable to limit petitions to some minimum value which is less than the cost of a very cheap dwelling, yet greater than most renovations, thus obviating the necessity of controlling house repairs. If plots have not been properly surveyed, and the deeds recorded, the task will be very complicated and difficult to administer. The planning commission will then have an immense backlog of work to make up and will have to limit itself at first to supervising the development of areas of high-density settlement. It will also give high priority to the control of new land being subdivided for housing and industry.

Experience must be accumulated regarding the effects of various construction methods upon neighbors, upon safety, and upon the provision of urban services, as new proposals accumulate and are accepted, rejected, or sent back by the commissioner for amendment. The commission is enabled from this experience to set standards which save scarce resources and supply better shelter at the same time. These standards would be approved as working rules by the full commission, often with the public backing of the executive. The change, and reasons for it, should be given as much publicity as possible. In this way the larger builders are quite certain to be informed, and the small builders more likely to know what is prohibited. Thereafter petitions that fall below these standards can be returned to the petitioner for revision. As further experience accumulates, more controls will be suggested which not only improve the cities but also are easily administered. As time goes on a body of rules and minimum standards will come into being which then can be printed and distributed.

What evolves here is *planning by regulation*. Perhaps 90 percent of the petitions for permits to build or demolish will pass with no more revision than amendments suggested and accepted at the time of hearing. For the remainder, which conflict either with the regulations or with plans that have been approved by the planning commissions, the builders and proprietors will be told how they can conform to the regulations. Most will undoubtedly make appropriate revisions and conform; or if they feel the decision of the planning commissioner to be unjust, it can be brought before the full commission. If the commission agrees with its member's decision, the petitioner can bring the case to court. The need to justify itself eventually before an independent court of justice prevents the planning commission from becoming too arbitrary and dictatorial.

Planning regulation may also be introduced into a society by direct order. A code can be borrowed from some more developed country, revised at some points, and adopted. Then the staff of the planning commission and the builders will have to learn together how to work within the code's limitations. But it is not easy to abide by a new set of controls, so there is likely to be some collusion between the commission staff and the proprietors—an arrangement which is convenient to both, but bypasses the law. In that event the published standards must be changed in acknowledgment of their defeat—which is not a good beginning for an agency that intends to implement the plan that is finally drawn up! Evasion of the land-use rules and building codes results in an improper fit between projects which had been carefully designed to integrate with each other. A directed society can accept authoritarian planning, using borrowed codes, if it has previously become used to accepting orders from above, but the efficiency, as judged by actual implementation, tends to be low.

The planning commission cannot afford to have its rulings disobeyed; if nonconformance were permitted its very reason for existence would soon disappear. Thus building inspectors become necessary, and a set of reports upon compliance are also accumulated. Elaborate measures need to be taken to prevent the corruption of these inspectors because they are extremely vulnerable to bribes.

The planning commission gains the respect of the public if it also makes suggestions which clearly save the proprietors and builders time and money. With the information that it accumulates, it can act as an instigator of technical improvements in building through these contacts with the building industry.

Another source of routine for the planning commission is the preparation of reports. (In many countries five-year plans complete with all the preliminary and supporting statistical tables are fashionable, and a five-year publication cycle develops for the top planning staff. The capital budget, which is an annual affair, may be undertaken by the same staff as part of this cycle.) At a specified time of year (some months before the various departments have finished preparing their own budgets) a circular is prepared in conjunction with the budgetary authorities, laying out the middle-run shortages and priorities and guiding the various departments in the formulation of changes in expenditure. The principal points in the document are likely to appear in a speech by the executive, usually well reported in the press, so that the private sector is informed of the decisions at virtually the same time as the departments of government. As a consequence of these allocation decisions that underlie the budgetary policy, adjustments in expectations are made all through the economy.

Later in the annual routine it becomes necessary to formulate the annual revision of the middle-run plan. This involves the preparation of a four- to six-year plan for capital improvements. The capital budget makes up the first year of this plan. The succeeding years take into account the need for funds required for completing projects already begun and for starting successor projects which take advantage of opportunities presented by those completed.[1]

These reports and proposals are analyzed carefully by representatives of the stronger interests in the society, both public and private, and they are circulated all over the world for inspection by other countries and outside interests. Therefore extreme care must be taken in the preparation and publication. All inconsistencies and mistakes of fact should have been eliminated before they are published. For this task experienced civil servants are needed, and technical assistance is extremely valuable in setting standards for quality in the first one or two of a series of planning documents.

Another routine is necessitated by the flow of questions raised in deliberations at the executive level or in negotiations with other countries. Before a decision or a position can be reached, more information is needed in the form of memoranda. Often these questions carry a short deadline. The staff of the planning commission is likely to be given the responsibility for some of the most complex questions because these usually involve several departments of government, or none of them, and the planning commission is expected to be familiar with a wider range of data than other agencies and departments. Especially under conditions of rapid growth, when new and urgent questions continue to appear with accelerating frequency, more than half of the staff time in the planning commission is likely to be spent answering brief inquiries.

[1] For example, when the oil refinery is finished, the chemical plants should be started; when these are ready, the polymer plants would go up; and when the latter are producing, the rubber and plastics forming factories would be installed. A sequence like this may take ten years to complete and the schedule would need revision almost every year.

In circumstances like these, the professional and technical staff of the commission feel extremely harassed. There is no time, they complain, to get the "real planning" done. Rarely do they consider how catastrophic it would be, on the other hand, if the questions ceased arriving! It would mean that the planning agency had lost the trust of the executive, in which case the preparation of the more polished and sophisticated planning proposals and documents they are concerned about would be meaningless. Actually, the contents of the plans, proposals, projects, and revisions are themselves shaped by the questions that are received and the answers that are found. An active inflow of questions and outflow of memoranda make it possible to assemble realistic plans in a very short time when it becomes necessary.

The routines of planning described could easily occupy all the time of a steadily expanding staff, and many of the assigned tasks could use much larger effort in order to avoid the chance of error. Yet, in addition, the planning commission is usually also the designated arm of the executive for coordinating and implementing large and complex projects with long-range consequences. While it is true that these projects interfere with orderly growth of the planning staff, they also enrich it with experience that extends its competences into unexpected areas. This function of the planning commission also needs to be explored.

THE SPECIAL PROJECTS

The contributions of the planning function to development are best observed when a relatively large and complex project is being advanced. The routine reports discussed above emphasize one facet or another, ranging from data gathering to establishing requirements for achieving proposed targets, as well as setting standards, targets, and priorities, enforcing and implementing rulings, etc. But these actions, at the time they are taken, cannot be seen in perspective as shaping the new social and physical environment that is coming into being. Only in retrospect is a professional planner able to trace the growing experience of his agency and discover the ever widening repercussions of diligent work done upon rather repetitive tasks. The organization *does* learn, even while it fumbles. The lessons are more explicit and the learning more evident, however, when a major project is launched and the organization's experience is focused upon a connected set of problems.

Perhaps the best demonstration is to choose a typical case. It should be of a variety that is faced at least once in every developing country (for which there are many examples and will be many more) and one that cannot be accomplished without reasonably adequate planning. After considerable search it appears that river-basin development offers the best possibilities for clearing away the clichés and misconceptions that surround the planning process and illuminating the methods that are productive. Although the example is a hypothetical one, drawn from dozens of reports of an almost equal number of projects, it could have happened in almost any country with a competent planning group.

Each river-basin development scheme began with dreams. They were the dreams of a peripatetic engineer who could see a falling, rushing river and convert the image into a figure for the kilowatts of power that could be generated. This huge, unused potential he contrasted with the needs of the peasants for energy to pump water to the fields below and for the light that would enable them to read after dark. Why not put the river to work in the service of man? The engineer took a few sightings with surveying instruments and sketched out a proposal for harnessing the river. The sketch was not made to scale, the figures were only approximate, but the idea was clearly expressed.

Most basin developments have been more than one engineer's vision, and their visits were separated by years. Most of the dreams were first disclosed in the 1920s and 1930s, but many new versions appeared during the last war, when trained men found themselves in unexpected places. At about this same time other professionals with wanderlust came upon drought-stricken and flood-ruined lands and saw all the attendant suffering. Surely the river could be controlled so that it provided water almost around the calendar! Reservoirs established in the foothills could release the water when the irrigators were ready. These men, too, could make calculations. They estimated what a second and a third crop might yield, and the savings that might accumulate if the plains were not struck with disaster every few years.

Such dreams were exciting enough to be widely discussed among the elite. Schoolboys were fascinated by the romanticized possibilities of technologically induced prosperity. A new image of the future had been created. Some officials, too, showed serious interest in the possibility of river development. But in the first years little or nothing could be done about it. It became part of the lore of the educated classes, one among several items demonstrating the richness of the natural resources in the interior. Various conspiracies were even invented to explain why nothing was done to develop these resources.

Sometime along the way these dreams encountered the TVA ideal. Here was a similar body of images that had been successfully transformed into concrete and steel; that took the form of an institution as well as a power-producing system. Overseas students in North America felt compelled to make pilgrimages to Knoxville, Tennessee, and the Norris Dam. Their papers and self-chosen exercises at school were concerned with fitting TVA concepts to their rampaging river at home. They discovered that an exact fit could not be made; the TVA was not concerned with major irrigation districts, and somehow the Negro-white relationships in the Tennessee Valley did not at all resemble the language and ethnic differences at home. Yet many features did appear to be transferable. When the students returned home, their technology-based idealism infected a great many others who were inclined to see the possibilities politically. The river could be used to build a socialist state! The image was cleaner and more modern than a steel mill. Thus, river development gained status as the kind of project that a progressive government should advance. It was one of the first tasks that was handed to a newly founded planning commission in the late 1940s and the 1950s.

The initial step was to get a facts-and-figures proposal by an engineering team which completed first a reconnaissance and then a preliminary design. In so doing, these engineers asked questions which had never even been considered before: Where are the meteorological stations? What are their records for precipitation and evaporation rate? How far back do these records go? Organized records, it was discovered, did not exist, but scattered data were rounded up that had been collected by hobbyists and small foreign enclaves. A few villages had records of the times the river was in flood stage. All this made it clear that an official system for gathering meteorological data had to be set up, not only for this project but also for the airports, the agricultural experiment stations, and other modern activities in the country. Thus came into being a new meteorological bureau; then a coordinating center for the statistics from this new bureau also became necessary.

More questions were raised about the runoff of the precipitation, erosion, soil types, geology, etc. Only a few guesses could be made from aerial photos; specialists had to be found to make such surveys.

Then locations for the reservoirs were tentatively drawn up. Grazing lands, garden plots, whole villages even would be submerged. How were the inhabitants to be moved out and compensated? Already not a few political problems came to the fore!

Downstream new land would be brought under cultivation. How much water should be provided per acre per year? What crops should be grown? How would they be shipped to market? Indeed, how is the market likely to respond to extra supplies?

At the same time large supplies of electric power would be generated. Who would use it? Presumably peasant demand would grow slowly. This meant that an aluminum or fertilizer plant could be planned along with the hydroelectric installation. Very likely only one generator could be installed initially, and two or three others would be brought in as the demand for power increased. But this policy greatly increased the cost per kilowatt-hour. So how could greater demand be stimulated? The imponderables were about to swamp the project.

After four or five years of such debate and discussion, the planning commission and its staff members acquired a vocabulary suited to the range of issues that had arisen. The departments of government most involved in the project developed their own experts. Some of the surveys were finished. The routine meteorological and industrial statistics were being collected and integrated into maps and tables. The planners were then ready for the first cost-benefit analyses that would distinguish which of several subsidiary alternatives was superior. Some of the most romantic and imaginative proposals were sternly ruled out by these calculations. But there were still serious imponderables. Should food production be given higher priority than power? What were the rights of the bargemen downstream during a period of drought? What groups in the population at large were expected to profit from the development, and which ones would lose something?

As the finer calculations were being made, disturbing reports began to come from the valley itself. Speculators had become aware that big changes might occur and so they started bidding up some of the land. As a result many of the cost assumptions underlying the cost-benefit analyses were rendered obsolete. Any new surveys now would only add fuel to the bidding-up process, and therefore could not be undertaken. Instead the land-use and building-permit side of the planning commission was consulted. Could some feasible means be invented for reserving land for this project at present values? Eventually a law had to be formulated that applied to rural land as well as to urban, and under the law the planning commission extended the scope of its land-use controls to handle other situations. Another disturbing factor was the general land-reform ferment stirring the rural areas; it presaged a land-redistribution scheme but that issue could not be taken into account at this stage.

Apparently a whole series of surveys were needed. What is the level of living of those people who dwell in areas to be covered by the reservoirs? What is the pattern of irrigation agriculture that is most similar to what is proposed for the irrigation district? What do people want that can be provided economically by electricity? It was evident that in this project the government would have to take many steps into the unknown and it needed some indication of possible political reactions, both favorable and otherwise. Guesses were likely to be faulty; public opinion surveys of the effects upon political support also appeared advisable.

The dam, the power station, and the irrigation canals would require millions of dollars worth of specialized equipment and services. How would the bills be paid? These questions required a new study of the allocation of foreign exchange in the decade ahead. It was discovered that dams and power-production facilities that promised to generate cheap electricity could be financed on credit. A proposal was drafted for the

International Bank, and another was addressed to one of the advanced countries that was willing to grant long-term loans. Many months later new teams arrived which asked more questions pertinent to economic and financial feasibility. What would be the alternative costs of power if produced in thermal plants near the cities? Similarly, agricultural data, previously reliable only for export crops, needed improvement so that prices and volumes of production could be reported throughout the year.

Inevitably serious questions arose about the original engineering designs. It was possible that several small dams would be more economical than one big dam. New sets of alternatives had to be explored, and a new team of experts was requested. They arrived on the scene a year or so later, and another round of evaluation began.

When the papers were finally signed, the loans obtained, and an "authority" set up to administer the developments in the basin, the underlying questions were still only partially answered. The respective reports and other documents did not make identical assumptions about the variations in rainfall, the industrial demand for power, the kinds of facilities to be built, or the prices attributed to the increased output. The whole project had to be reformulated as a plan which stated exactly which facilities would go up at what times; what pieces of land would be used and what others would be affected; what people would have to be resettled at what times; what investments would have to be made in what years; what "choice points" existed along the way in the development where further decisions needed to be made—and what data would be needed to make good decisions then. With outside technical assistance this report was completed; the gaps in the data were filled in with the best estimates available.

But it was only when this project was fully committed and its total demand upon the supply of professional personnel, upon the sample survey organization, and upon the statistics-gathering capability was ascertainable, that the planning commission realized the extent of the overcommitment of scarce *human* and *institutional* resources to the river-basin development. The real returns to the society were rather far in the future, while many pressing questions were raised each month which could use these same resources and promised quicker returns.

As a consequence, many of the capital budget items in the succeeding reviews had a tendency to be incorporated into the voracious valley-development project. Agricultural experiment stations, building research stations, forestry training, and many other proposals of this sort were thrown into the basin to help solve the problems that were already evident. Industrial location decisions were also seriously affected because the potential linkages of a modern factory with the river-development schemes and related installations were always calculated. The valley tended to get more than its share of such installations because the information about the area was far more detailed and therefore fewer risks were involved.

And so it was that the planning commission discovered, perhaps ten years after it began to promote river-basin development, that it had committed itself to a "most favored area" policy for development. One area had been selected—unwittingly—for more intensive development than the others. The state guaranteed most of the necessary social overheads in order to assure completion of the facilities for controlling the water. The strategy is a defensible one; many good theoretical arguments can be made for it; but in most countries it creates conditions which foster costly regional conflicts.

PLANNING UNDER STEADY-STATE CONDITIONS

It takes a long time to construct institutions. If, at the start, a country has only a budgeting system and a group of economic advisers, and then it decides to proceed at full speed in the direction of development, the complete set of organizations that has been described here could not be brought into existence as functioning units in less than ten years. Allowing for the normal setbacks and unforeseen distractions, a period of twenty years is a more realistic interval. A country like India, with a large population and an endowment of trained personnel from the colonial period, managed in little over a decade to forge a complement of institutions that handled all the functions described earlier as being necessary for developmental planning. While it is true that the respective agencies in India still do not coordinate very well, each one pursuing a relatively independent program, nonetheless the civil servants are aware of these deficiencies, and the goals have already become synonymous. Other countries are likely to encounter more severe problems in staff training, since scores of persons would need to be sent overseas for study for several years and then (after perhaps half had been found unsuitable) trained on the job for a year or two more before their accomplishments began to advance the development program.

The institutional framework in India is much too gigantic to be considered as a suitable model for planning, while Puerto Rico and Israel offer instances that are too special to be discussed at length. Let us instead imagine a nation of 3 to 50 million people that has the following institutions in working order:

1. The Bureau of the Budget
2. The Council of Social and Economic Advisers
3. The Central Statistical Office
4. The Planning Commission

5. Regional Planning Centers
6. The Institute for Sample Surveys
7. The National Library System
8. Departmental Offices for Planning

With all this paraphernalia, how would it plan? A first task, and one of the most important, is that of identifying problems as to size, scope, location, and trends over time. What conditions prevent growth in this country at this time? The studies that pinpoint the problems depend very heavily upon the library as a basis for profiting from prior experience with related problems elsewhere. These studies tend to get more and more sophisticated as experience accumulates and data from the surveys are made available. Each problem that is pinpointed in this manner is assigned to an action committee which proposes a strategic solution, if any exists at the time; otherwise the issue is held in abeyance.

The problem itself must be put in a form suitable for administrative action. For example, the population problem cannot be posed as a projection of population growth into the next decades, on various assumptions about fertility. This is social science, not planning research. Planners would consider the implications for migration, for rural employment, and for the growth of cities. They would consider methods of family limitation; the respective economic, social, and cultural costs of population controls; how these costs could be minimized; and then finally, perhaps, ask about the possibility of expanding certain programs for spreading the idea of family limitation to couples in the eighteen to twenty-five age bracket.

Once proposals for such program expansion have been worked out, the planners would attach to the project some procedure for systematic appraisal of the changes in attitude and behavior of the population at large. Will such approaches to the population problem, based upon providing information to interested couples, be attractive only to minor subgroups in the population, thus solving only a piece of the problem? Will there be popular protest? Is there a quicker, cheaper approach than has yet been tried? It is easy to see that this proposal for dealing with the population problem would quickly become as complex and elaborate as any river-basin development program. For most countries it is, in fact, more fundamental even than water-resource development.

Once the foreseeable problems have been matched with projects designed to remove or alleviate them, the process of political evaluation of projects and budget making is set in motion. If the political situation, or the foreign exchange, or the government revenues do not permit the crucial projects of this sort to be undertaken, then social and economic growth may be delayed, and planning must be directed toward creating the preconditions for development that have been described earlier. If the budget does cover the essential projects, and can be extended to finance a program which includes other projects judged to make advantageous use of scarce resources, a selection process must be initiated. A small team of experienced planners work out and agree upon *ad hoc* systems of program analysis which seem to be most suited for that country at that time. The systems provide for project-by-project comparisons in the fashion recommended by contemporary economists interested in rational public decisions (Eckstein, 1961).[2] They also take into account the potentialities for reinforcement—the conditions under which the whole contribution of a package of projects will be substantially greater than the sum of the individual contributions. The *ad hoc* systems of analysis are chosen within the framework of a perspective plan that was independently synthesized for the guidance of the national and provincial governments. However, they are much more explicit because the horizons of most projects are much shorter than the fifteen to twenty-five years normally employed in the outlines for growth depicted in perspective plans.

The need for repeated appraisal of programs and projects, as emphasized here, is a technique which allows the government to cut its losses on probable failures while they are still small. In addition, the planning commission needs an index of the overall impact of its programs. For this need the economists would recommend annual income distribution data pieced together from tax receipts, expenditures, savings rate, production levels, etc. When properly adjusted for changes in buying power, the shifts in income distribution strongly suggest who is reaping the benefits from the development. If overall development is successful, large numbers of the population can be expected to move from lower incomes to middle incomes. (This is the well-known "rise of the middle class" that is associated with periods of rapid economic growth.) However, income distribution indexes cannot be used as a suitable appraisal of balance in the complement of ongoing projects, for the reason that the income changes corresponding to general growth tend to lag behind the original action on a planning project by several years (three to five, on the average). The true results of the program are obscured by too many intervening events. *The first responses to projects are almost always found in the social and cultural interactions, and a substantial impact in these directions is a prerequisite for subsequent economic success. Indexes based upon these noneconomic changes should then be the most sensitive.*

In the course of social and economic planning over the next decade it

[2] Otto Eckstein has presented a particularly lucid description of this process in his water-resources analysis, but even it presumes a greater amount of information being available at the time of decision than is ever the case, or is likely to be economical to assemble.

is quite possible that new institutions for information gathering, interpretation, and forecasting will be invented to get development programs
out of the doldrums. The detailed presentation of the most promising
procedures for rationalizing investment in industry and education will
reveal sets of accounts that might well provide the crucial evaluations in
some parts of the world. Therefore the administration for planning recommended here is undoubtedly an incomplete picture of what will be needed
in most countries, and the field offers remarkable opportunities for innovation over the next several decades.

BIBLIOGRAPHY

Backstrom, Charles H., and Gerald D. Hursh: *Survey Research,* Northwestern
University Press, Evanston, Ill., 1963.
> A brief, practical review of the procedures from survey planning to data process-
> ing.

Eckstein, O.: *Water Resources Development: The Economics of Project Evaluation,* Harvard University Press, Cambridge, Mass., 1961.
> An application of the principles of rational decision making to the preparation
> of a program of projects for which the techniques of benefit-cost analysis can be
> applied.

Great Britain Treasury, Organization and Methods Division: *The Design of
Forms,* Her Majesty's Stationery Office, London, 1962.
> Describes how a system of forms for internal government use is linked with the
> compilation of data and its analysis.

Perloff, H. S.: *Education for Planning,* The Johns Hopkins Press, Baltimore,
Md., 1959.
> An evaluation of planning education in English-speaking countries, with pro-
> posals for its further development.

Simon, H. A., et al.: *Public Administration,* Alfred A. Knopf, Inc., New York,
1956.
> A well-known textbook that argues from behavior principles and is therefore
> more general than the American institutions it uses as illustrations. Builds up
> to the strategy of planning and the implementation of plans.

Tugwell, R. G.: "The Place of Planning in Society," rev. ed., Puerto Rico
Planning Board Technical Paper 7, 1958.
> A series of lectures describing the precedents and examples upon which the
> enabling legislation for planning in Puerto Rico was based, and an appraisal of
> the performance of the Planning Board over the first decade of its operations
> as compared to anticipations.

PART TWO

INDUSTRIAL DEVELOPMENT

5

DIRECTIONS AND STRATEGIES
FOR INDUSTRIAL GROWTH

INDUSTRIAL DEVELOPMENT is a term that encompasses a wide range of meanings. Prior to any discussion of paths for promoting industrial development, an effort must be made to distinguish more precisely what is meant. Experience teaches that a good procedure for arriving at an operational definition is to establish first the major existing misconceptions which should *not* be associated with the term. The range of possible meanings and implications can then be narrowed to those that are relevant to developmental planning.

Engineers often mistake the elaboration of the industrial production equipment, the integration of masses of hardware, for industrial development. It will be demonstrated later in Chapter 18 that the monetized value of the production equipment is less than the value of what is built up in the minds of men who operate and reorganize the equipment, when appraised on as nearly an equivalent basis as possible. Technology exists first in the *minds* of men and is expressed initially in specifications, formulas, blueprints, and diagrams; and this is later extended by operating experience. The machinery is only the materialized portion of the industrial system.

Economists have become accustomed to equate industry with manufacturing, and separate it from such primary activities as agriculture, mining, forestry, and fishing on one side and a wide variety of services on the other. However, an infrastructure of transport, communications, and investment services becomes so closely tied to manufacturing that it does not seem worthwhile to disentangle the complex.

The accepted definition of *industry* also contains specialized traditional manufactures produced by artisans which are for the most part incapable of contributing to social and economic growth. Thus most cottage industries in the least developed countries should be excluded from the *planning-oriented* definition of industry as discussed in this study.

A few preconceptions about industry arise also from reading the history of the industrial revolution and reviewing the social protests that resulted from the experience. It must be stated flatly that industrialization no longer necessitates such by-products as smoke, grime, high tuberculosis rates, and blighted vegetation, as it once did. Nor does the machine impose only mind-deadening and degrading routines upon the industrial workers. Industrial jobs today are cleaner and far more interesting than most household work, agricultural tasks, and the traditional service trades.

More explicitly, industry is an organized system of production, including men, equipment, knowledge, and institutional identities. Industrial *development* within a society is judged by an expansion in the *capacity* for the production of goods that are in demand, either within that society or in foreign markets. It differs from economic development in that the per capita concept is missing. Industrial development implies increasing capability of the *production system* only.

This definition suggests that it is quite possible to have an advanced industrial structure supporting a population living largely at subsistence. Such an outcome has not yet occurred, but current population and industrial trends could well result in such an ultimate condition. It could be that the fertilizer, fiber, and structural materials production might be as modern and efficient as any processes known, but the effort required to convert these into enough food, clothing, and shelter would require the participation at peak periods of a predominant share of the population because natural resources would be stretched to their physical limits. The modern techniques of distribution (and salvage) associated with industry would then be used to assure that each household received just enough to survive.

Normally, however, individual consumption and choice are expected to increase during industrial development, and this should happen regardless of the intermediate policies adopted by the state concerning income distribution.

The capacity concept itself also requires definition. It is not a purely technical concept, as is *rated* capacity, but rather an assessment of the ability to produce on short notice without further capital investment. It may be expressed in quantities of standard goods and services produced per unit time, or in index numbers. Nevertheless, as an introduction, we may begin with the calculation of a rated capacity, which is the outcome of a series of agreements between design engineers, industrial engineers, and the various technical specialists.

Every piece of equipment—whether it be a house, machine, or service facility—is designed to perform for its useful lifetime at *rated capacity*. An electric motor, for example, delivers at least a specified amount of horsepower as long as the voltage remains within certain limits and the bearings are lubricated. That is its rated capacity. Most motors will actually perform somewhat better than the rating when they are new. If the line voltage drops noticeably (as in the morning when factories and transport systems all start up), then the motor cannot deliver its rated capacity. The task it fulfills in a factory then cannot require more power than the motor is able to supply under such constraints. If this motor was engaged in grinding and milling cereals into flours and mashes, the drops in voltage will result in less output per installed horsepower than in regions with an adequate electrical supply, and also yield a more variable product (i.e., poorer quality). Under such circumstances the true industrial capacity is then less than the rated capacity. The actual capacity, therefore, could be raised by improving the electric utility system as well as by expanding the flour-mill installations.

Ordinarily a considerable safety factor is embedded in the calculations of rated capacity. Thus, a well-designed plant run by clever managers and experienced foremen may easily reach true capacities 110 to 130 percent of the rated capacity of the production system without extraordinary wear and tear on the machinery or fatigue for the workers.

The most unambiguous means for judging the true capacity of a facility is to refer back to the weeks or months of greatest output. Was there borrowing of internal requirements from the reserves, or drawing from future prospects, in order to reach that level? If so, about how much of the output is accounted for by the borrowing? A true capacity estimate can be achieved by subtracting from the peak output rate the contribution of the extraordinary withdrawals from reserves.

Almost always the true capacity is a level of production which incurs unit costs substantially greater than are experienced at the so-called "efficient production level." Minimum costs per unit of output are generally achieved when operating at 70 to 90 percent of true capacity. An economy that attempts to work all its industry at a level close to 100 percent of capacity should expect upward spiraling costs, and is therefore subject to very strong inflationary forces. Foreign trade relationships are also thrown into imbalance.

THE GOALS AND THE PROGRAMMING

The basic long-run goal of industrialization is to increase, by tenfold or twentyfold in most cases, the total output of consumers' goods that can be distributed to members of the society. Once this capacity-enlarging aim is stated, however, it is hedged immediately by certain conditions which reflect other goals held by the society. For example, because the society is attempting to establish itself as a nation held in respect by other nations in the world, it quickly recognizes that some kinds of industry contribute to the status of a country while other kinds add little. Therefore the speediest methods of building up industrial capacity are rarely the most desirable.

Limitations even more extensive than those stemming from nationalism are usual. Quite a few countries are committed to the maintenance of a given religion, and its taboos may rule out some industries (e.g., leather working, meat packing, etc.). The furtherance of national unity—another common goal—means that the desirable installations need to be distributed more or less equally among various subgroups. In the typical dual society the goals for industry will be exceedingly mixed because the traditional sector would want industry to operate without too much disturbance of the existing order,[1] while the modern sector insists upon facilities that make conspicuous shifts toward standards maintained by the leading industrial societies.

After noting the conditions which impose limits upon industrialization, the process itself must be examined more closely. Industrial development cannot be promoted as an end in itself but only as a means which enables the society to reach its principal goals. Yet, since the process lasts for generations, it will often appear to be an independent goal. Therefore programs of as much as fifteen years duration can be laid out realistically whose principal objectives are balanced industrial capacity of stated dimensions.

Industrial projects lend themselves to programming techniques much better than projects in agriculture, medicine, or even education. Because the internal accounting is more detailed in industry, the quantitative relationships are better known. In addition, the technological requirements per unit of output are very similar throughout the world, whereas traditional manufacturing and agriculture vary considerably from place to place. For that reason economists build their input-output and linear programming models primarily around the modern industrial data.

In theory, the input-output analysis techniques should be adequate for

[1] It is impossible to borrow and incorporate a pure technology. Along with the machinery and engineering advice come some of the less desirable features of modernism which diffuse through the linkages to other facets of society outside of working hours. Typically, new musical themes, the latest dance craze, new coiffures and apparel styles, slang, Coca-Cola and other beverages, and new food tastes are unintentionally introduced. These fads are like the weeds that come free with the purchase of seeds. Some, at least, are inevitable. Their conflict with other programs of development, such as nation building, should be viewed as another of the costs of development which may be minimized.

assessing the impact of a new industry and determining its probable contribution to the chief goal of the society (particularly if that goal can be expressed as income maximization). In a parallel fashion it should be able to assess the interregional effects of a proposed increase in capacity. Similarly, linear programming techniques can take into account many of the constraints imposed by the collateral goals. Industrial capacities for the production of various categories of product provide another set of constraints. There are scores of studies which have elaborated variants of this theory, all of which presume that vast quantities of reliable production data and price information have been collected.[2]

Thus far these techniques for connecting industrial data with the goals for growth and development have been hampered by the lack of data and by the lack of personnel skilled in handling statistics. Since input-output tables reflect conditions several years old, the results of calculations applying to the short run cannot be trusted, and those fitting the long run are too vague. Although the results have been disappointing to date,[3] it seems likely that the improved data collection, which everyone agrees is necessary, will change the outlook. The relatively closed and highly controlled societies, which already have much of the basic information buried in the records required by the various ministries, are in a better position than the open societies which have refrained from controlling important parts of the economy in the past. Thus, it appears that the computations have been most influential in Spain, have not been particularly useful in Sicily and the Mezzogiorno in general (even though industrialization accelerated in those areas), nor in Turkey, where political problems dominated the situation, and were not utilized during the main thrust of Puerto Rican development.

In the recommendations for industrial planning that follow, the procedure endorsed assumes that the assembly of a trustworthy matrix containing usefully defined sectors will require more than a decade of statistical effort. In the meantime the planning must proceed with piecemeal and partial approaches to the evaluation of alternative programs; thus it remains heavily dependent upon sources of political, social, and cultural

---

[2] The simplest presentation of the procedures for collecting data and processing them for such purposes is to be found in *Programming Techniques for Economic Development*, U.N. Economic Commission for Asia and the Far East, Bangkok, 1960.

[3] Alvin Mayne reports that considerable effort has gone into the preparation of input-output matrices for India, Puerto Rico, and the United States without any apparent contribution to the developmental planning. He favors the industrial-complex analysis of Isard, Schooler, Victorisz, and Airov. Cf. W. Isard and J. H. Cumberland, "Designing and Administering a Regional Economic Plan," in *Regional Economic Planning*, Organization for European Economic Cooperation, Paris, 1961, pp. 141–196.

information. The data-gathering developments nevertheless must aim at the comprehensive view that is afforded by input-output and linear programming techniques. It is quite possible that these methods of analysis and synthesis may be used earliest in nonmanufacturing activities, such as message transmission and passenger movements in communications and transport networks, and in the development of education; only later would they be introduced into industrial planning.

THE CHANGE IN OBJECTIVES

Since the society learns as it develops, the conception of what is wanted from the expansion of industry can shift quite markedly over time. This is evident from the emphases taken by the successive five-year plans of India. The evolution of the thinking in Puerto Rico, however, better reflects what changes may be expected in the course of *rapid* growth.

In the instance of Puerto Rican development, it is clear that welfare has been the guiding criterion for industrialization. The Commonwealth of Puerto Rico is too small to entertain aspirations for becoming a politico-economic power with a significant role to play in international affairs. Nor does it seem inclined to erect monuments for posterity to contemplate as reflections of the creative capacities of the contemporary culture. It has been committed neither to magnificent modern factories nor to rural industries as the desired means of production. With the goal of industrialization so sharply delineated, the *value added by manufacture* (a term employed in the census of manufactures which includes the return to labor, capital, and taxes) becomes the truly significant statistic. Out of this sum the workers are expected to obtain higher pay, investments should receive an excellent return, and something should be left over for promoting growth.

The ultimate indicators of increased welfare due to industrialization appear as diminished underemployment, higher national income in real terms, and an increased proportion of families brought up to and beyond the income levels considered sufficient for physiologically adequate and culturally acceptable consumption. In visual terms this will show up as increased health and vigor in the population at large, in new housing, more convenient transport and communications, more education, enhanced social communications, more attention being paid to the arts and to scientific creativity, etc.

Still another element of welfare, so basic that it underlies all these other aspects, must be introduced. It is the increase in the variety of opportunities open to the individual for modifying his life style; this constitutes the major contribution of modern industry to civilization. In preindustrial times the number of roles open to any individual was extremely limited: a peasant could be little else but a peasant, unless he became a soldier or a monk. But now—after some rudimentary education that is universally provided—the choices have been extended to several scores of different occupations. With further education a peasant might move up to almost any of the posts of power and influence which are created by the growth of industry and commerce. This pattern of mobility in society was previously characteristic of periods when old regimes were overturned, but with industrialization, a society can achieve what has been termed "the permanent revolution." It is an important contribution to human freedom, and one that has thus far been only partially effected. Present advances in technology suggest that a further freeing of the worker from odious and routine tasks can be brought about in the next few decades. These advances are as likely to be appropriate for newly developing economies as for the more mature economies where industry has been long established.

Welfare goals for industrialization as discussed above are much too vague for planning industrial development, however. Certain themes must be chosen which provide an index of achievement over time and permit an assessment of the degree of balance. There is always the suspicion that moneymaking by itself is an inadequate representation of welfare improvement; enhancement of the gross national product alone would often aggravate inherent political, social, and cultural difficulties. In the long run such imbalances impose strains which bring industrial growth itself to a halt. Therefore, concrete social goals are chosen which reflect to some extent the indigenous human values which cannot be expressed in pecuniary terms. In Puerto Rico, for instance, the "full employment" theme was adopted in the beginning. The elimination of insecurity and deprivation brought about by widespread unemployment was felt to be a long step toward political and social stability, and a major contribution to human dignity.

Full employment is a theme whose significance had become apparent in the 1930s because of its absence during the Great Depression and the rise of fascism. A considerable amount of critical thinking was devoted to this issue. When these ideas were applied to developing countries, it appeared that the principal role of manufacturing was to provide productive jobs for the unemployed. However, within a few years after the full-employment goal had been adopted in Puerto Rico, it became apparent that an earlier suspicion was being borne out—that, in an underdeveloped country, employment statistics were not a sensitive indicator for improvements in welfare and general social progress. An increasing number of productive jobs in manufacturing seemed to have very little influence upon either the registered unemployment or the number of persons willing to work, who were not otherwise provided opportunities for gainful employment. However, *under*employment did seem to diminish, according to all the indirect indicators available.

At a time when the full-employment goal was still being used, but its effectiveness was waning, a new social goal was introduced. It called for the achievement of a decent level of living for all families. A minimum desirable level of living could be approximated on the basis of studies of consumption and welfare in typical households in Puerto Rican society. All the basic needs for nutrition, health, shelter, education, and other services could be estimated for the average family, and the price of this "basket of goods and services" could be calculated.

The implementation of the new goal, stated in target form as a "minimum family income of $2,000 by 1960," was based upon the previously acquired ability of the economic statisticians to estimate income distributions in that society. The place of industry in an overall program with such objectives was that of generating income in such quantities and in such forms that other institutions could redirect a portion of it to the disadvantaged stratum of the population. It seems quite possible that this goal was achieved for at least 95 percent of the families within a few years of the date set, if the poor family's share of the social services provided free by the government is to be credited to income. The usefulness of this goal for purposes of long-range planning diminished, however, as the likelihood of its achievement in the near future increased. Therefore, while it was still employed in government planning, another social goal with implications for economic planning was being sought.

The most promising formulation explored was that of optimal development of human resources. In this context the prerequisites in human skills for maintaining the society at high productivity are estimated, and then the required investment in education, health, and other services can be calculated. Since these new aims have not yet been reduced to political formulas, many of the implications remain to be elaborated. In general the human resources development criterion requires that industry do its share in providing on-the-job environments that are conducive to growth in knowledge and skill on the part of the employee as well as the management. (The full implications of a goal that embraces optimal development of human resources will be taken up in Part Three.)

ANALYSIS OF COMPETITIVE ADVANTAGES

If a country has been blessed with a major resource or market crop, like petroleum, iron ore, bauxite, cocoa, or fish, the direction which industrialization should take is strongly influenced by the need to maximize the returns to society derived from the resources. The capital required for

launching new industrial activities may be obtained to an important extent by accumulating a small fraction of the returns from the sale of
the mineral or market crop. The trained manpower needed for the first
industrial installations may be borrowed either from the activity of resource exploitation itself or from the services which are created in the
society to make that exploitation more efficient. If political difficulties
arising from past decisions and events in the society do not stand in the
way, and the resources are rich enough, a fairly straightforward program
for industrialization arising out of resource development can be formulated. Several contemporary industrial societies have evolved in this
manner.

To expedite this approach the planners and the politicians will have
to undertake some wide-ranging explorations, and this reconnaissance
will have to be followed by some creative fitting together of possibilities.
Every obstruction to capital accumulation and the establishment of industry should be considered carefully to see whether it cannot be manipulated into an asset. Thus, for example, mountainous terrain, which piles
up forbidding transport costs between prospective industrial centers,
might be made attractive to tourists, who could support much of the
transport system as well as other services necessary for industry. Or
there may be an alien ethnic group that dominates commerce and whose
savings are likely to flee rather than be channeled by government directive. If the climate for business is made more attractive, however, the
foreign connections of this commerce-oriented ethnic contingent may
pump extra capital into the society. A series of incentives would then be
used for directing new capital into high-priority manufacturing and
services.

The thinking that prevailed in Puerto Rico at this stage was systematic
and often ingenious. It is possible to highlight the assets which had been
identified before 1948 thus:

1. Accumulated government revenues which could not be spent during the
   war (roughly $300 million, of which an important part had to be com-
   mitted to specific improvements delayed by wartime shortages).
2. A sugarcane quota for the American market which was only a fourth
   the size of Cuba's but was still an important source of dollars that were
   not tied to any specified program of expenditure.
3. Access to New York so favorable that the trip could be easily negotiated
   by direct air transport, more reasonable in cost than any alternative mode
   of transport.
4. A balmy and comfortable climate, excellent for tourism at least eight
   months a year in the lowlands and twelve months a year in the mountains.

5. A high standard of public health to the extent that the familiar tropical diseases, such as malaria, typhoid, and dysentery, had virtually disappeared over most parts of the Island.

6. Being part of the United States, inside its tariff barrier, yet retaining independence of action; this meant that the largest market in the world was open to Puerto Rican manufacturers (though the output would have to be produced more cheaply than was being done at the time by the most efficient production system in the world).

7. Immediate and unimpeded access of private individuals to the United States, so that if a demand for labor existed there, the Puerto Ricans could move in unrestricted numbers to take advantage of employment opportunities; and vice versa, skilled persons of one type or another (e.g., managers, engineers, consultants, and specialists) could come to Puerto Rico without passports.

8. An apparently limitless pool of unemployed and underemployed workers available for industrial work.

9. Existence of a small group of dedicated young men willing to commit their careers to public service and to the improvement of welfare in their homeland.

10. No evident social and political unrest—despite the impoverishment which existed; the political situation indicated little or no danger of abrupt changes in policy, destruction from rioting, or politically inspired strikes.

These advantages are very special and unique to Puerto Rico. Yet almost any other independent territory could assemble a similar set of special advantages available to it. Indeed, it is debatable whether most of these are "advantages" at all. All but the first of the points can be restated, together with some of their implications, to make them appear as deterrents to industrialization; this was done, in observations made by various outsiders as well as in speeches and letters to the editor all through the postwar period, by the opponents of the program. Almost any facet of a given preindustrial environment can be made to appear either black or white, depending upon one's outlook.

The best-understood relationship between such competitive advantages on the international scene and the industrialization process was introduced in Chapter 1. The classic strategy based upon the exportability of commodities or services derived from a natural resource, as well as the conversion of the credits so obtained into manufacturing facilities, has been a very common one over the past century and is likely to be employed repeatedly in the future. Therefore, before proceeding to explore the other strategies, it is necessary to undertake an up-to-date discussion of the resource-oriented path to industrialization. The object of this strategy is not only to obtain for the society the largest possible share of the "value added in the course of extraction and processing," as revealed by a census of mining and manufactures, but also to take full advantage of all the incidental opportunities provided by the resource development activity, to create a production system with a large, well-balanced capacity.

THE RESOURCE-ORIENTED ORGANIZATION OF SPACE

The principle can be illustrated diagrammatically. Most natural resources, such as a mineral deposit, a forest, a waterfall, or a soil suited to a market crop, may be represented by a point on a map or by a map field. However, the predominant share of the total demand for the ultimate product lies in the rest of the world; therefore, transportation facilities to a harbor on the coast (possibly to an airport, now that air freight costs have been substantially reduced) must be part of the development scheme. Settlements are required at points of transshipment and at the site of the resource extraction. In the case of mining development there will be a company town or camp for the miners; if the project produces cocoa, coffee, or rubber, there must be villages for the growers; and if the resource is waterpower, there will probably be not only electrometallurgical or electrochemical plants but also irrigation districts and market towns. Water developments yield a pattern of transportation and human settlement that is markedly similar to that impressed upon a region by other resources but are far more complex. The simple but typical case of resource development in virgin territory, with people living close to subsistence levels before the development occurs, is shown in Figure 6.

Much history is implicit in the illustration. The resource extraction area shown was served by a construction camp which had been transformed into a typical company town. In it local people and technical assistants combined to operate the facility in the daytime, then separated after working hours according to social class and origin to spend their leisure hours. The airport began as a landing strip to fly in emergency supplies and new personnel, but once operations had begun, a feeder line to the commercial airlines scheduled through the capital was maintained. The railroad and polyglot harbor city, although designed primarily to assist in the export of the commodities derived from the resource, also opened up a considerable area of hinterland. The possibility of extending branch lines in various directions at marginal cost was particularly advantageous. (In recent years roads and bulldozed tracks have been developed as more economical transport routes for small to medium tonnages, while railroads have been reserved for iron ore and large-scale nonferrous metals operations.) Rapid communications and daily plane service have served to diminish the feelings of isolation from civilization that have been common so often in the past in these settlements, and have made it possible to introduce such extra services as printing establishments, banks, and hotels.

Most, but not all, of the additional opportunities created by this typical procedure for resource development are known only in the modern technical culture, with its store of scientific knowledge. Local people can see how to use a bridge in order to expand trading radius, but they are unable to estimate the balance between expected benefits and losses connected with building a railroad branch line or a barge line. They must proceed on faith that local enterprises will spring up to use the extra transport capacity. This faith in the triggering effect that new transportation should have upon a rural economy is frequently justified (in retrospect), perhaps as often as half the time.

It takes these societies somewhat longer to recognize the potentials inherent in the installation of long-distance communications channels.

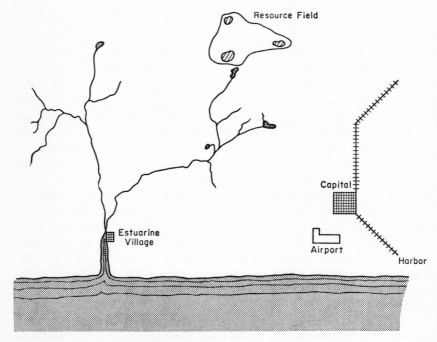

Stage 1. Resource reserves. Resources are prospected and reserves are proved in an undeveloped area with no services. Part of these reserves have high commercial value. The resource may be some mineral complex (e.g., fossil fuels, ferrous or nonferrous ores, etc.), hydroelectric power, some unused fertile soils, or even a stand of forest. (All man-made facilities are represented by figures with straight lines.)

Figure 6. The regional impact

Even Western civilizations, which have used electronic communications the heaviest and the longest, are often at a loss when it comes to deciding what content is worth transmitting. Normally an educated elite is required, with some help from the outside, before the coaxial cables and microwave relays can be utilized intensively. It also takes time to build up the firms which are necessary to supply the needs exhibited in the hinterland that has been opened up by the transport. Ultimately, the communications channels carry data on crop conditions, water flows, freight movements, price levels, operating difficulties, etc.

In the past there have been well-publicized instances where the outsiders removed the resource without leaving any residue of organization or know-how that could be put to work in other directions after the resource was depleted. The profits moved overseas or were spent in luxurious living. The Chilean nitrate case serves as a classic example. There have, of course, been even more instances where the resource development was unsuccessful and the invested capital lost. Since neither

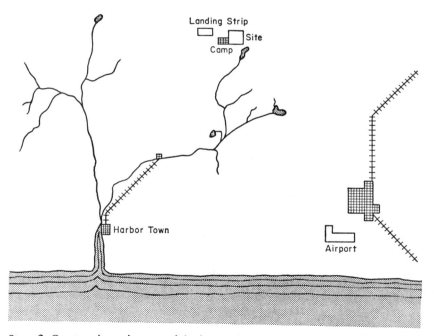

Stage 2. Construction prior to exploitation. An airport is built for bringing workers, materials, and machinery. A railroad (or heavy-duty road) is begun from the village, which expands to a town in the process. Additional growth is registered in the Capital, where many services and governmental offices need to be expanded.

of resource development.

of these extremes is advantageous to the country possessing the resource, rather elaborate measures are now taken to prevent the recurrence of such waste. The capital-importing nations are now concerned to get the highest possible cash return for their natural resources, while the capital-exporting nations are now investigating speculative propositions far more closely than ever before. More of the externalities of a resource-development project are taken into account before the decision is made to proceed.

The major industries that evolve in favorable instances are likely to be sited close to the harbor, but a combination of resources inland, such as coal and iron ore, or hydroelectric power with phosphate and rock salt, could result in the birth of an inland industrial complex. Small plants operated by a single entrepreneur-manager are likely to be set up by local people, and they too would locate mainly in the harbor city. Larger

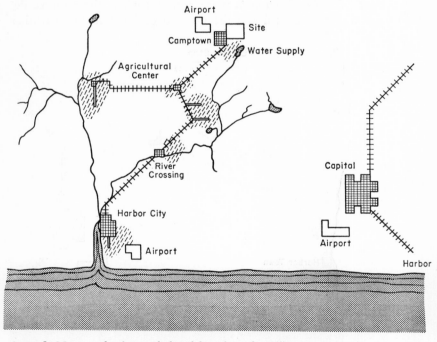

Stage 3. Mass production and the elaboration of ancillary projects. The increasing urbanization and improving transport stimulate commercial agriculture. More of the services are installed in Camptown, making it a relatively permanent community. Harbor City is rapidly developing its capacity to carry on commerce in commodities other than the original natural-resource commodity. The Capital expands further because it must coordinate an increasingly complex development.

Figure 6. The regional impac

factories and related facilities will employ 90 to 95 percent local people, but additionally hundreds of technical experts and managers would be needed.

Perhaps the best suggestion to date for a control policy over resource-based industries which depend upon foreign capital and technical capacities would be to require that a citizen be hired to act as a counterpart for each foreigner brought in with the enterprise. The counterpart would be paid by the firm, but at local civil service rates for that level of responsibility. The counterpart would endeavor to become proficient at the job, and later, should world prices drop and profits be squeezed, there is incentive for the firm to replace the high-salaried outsider with

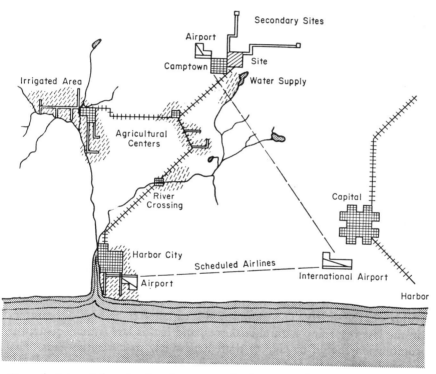

Stage 4. Integrated regional and resources development. The croplands that were opened up by the new transport possibilities are now being irrigated and are producing regularly. Harbor City accumulates a considerable variety of processing facilities. The other communities start installing processing industries that reduce bulk. The harbor development, the bridges, the transport line, the airports, the pure-water supply, and the communications channels, all provide opportunities for external economies which are being exploited to some extent at this stage.

of resource development (continued).

the modest-priced local man. If this is accomplished with reasonable fairness, the company will gain the loyalty of its local staff. At the same time, the firm becomes more sensitive to shifts in sentiments within the country, and more likely to avoid provocation of the extremists.

It would probably take ten to twenty years for local personnel to assume the supervision and management of industrial operations, if the transition were to be effected smoothly (i.e., without wastage of resources or capital). The reason it takes so long is that a great deal must be learned about complex technologies, and there are no formal educational institutions able to teach this know-how. Although a few correspondence and night school courses can be helpful initially, the accumulation of on-the-job experience is the most time-consuming feature in the acquisition of full competence.

Even after local personnel have graduated to top management positions, the government has not actually increased its effective control over the resources. Local people often are the very best *company men,* a term used to suggest total commitment to the current objectives and methods of the bureaucratic private firm. The government must create a countervailing force in the form of a bureau or office which is well informed about markets for the commodities produced from the natural resource. It must know the status of competitive producers in greater detail than appears in trade journals and newspapers. It accomplishes these ends by supporting a commission or agency for the exploration, mapping, and control of natural resources.

This resources-control commission sometimes obtains its powers from the constitutional assignment of ownership of all resources below the surface to the people collectively, and sometimes from the provisions for the control of international trade. The immediate necessity that brings about its formation is the fear that the resources will become the basis of petty politics and personal aggrandizement. Therefore membership on the commission is assigned initially to some of the most trustworthy individuals in the society. The commission is expected to be highly competent in the law regarding natural resources, and if this law is inadequate, the commission should be able to draft a new law to cover the gaps. This capability places the commission (or bureau, or office) in a strong bargaining position with individuals and firms interested in undertaking projects relating to natural resources.

To bargain effectively, the resources commission needs information regarding the actual procedures and rules used for control elsewhere in the world. Because resource development is a highly competitive activity, one nation cannot remain very far out of line from the rest of the world and still have its resources developed. This information is obtained through building up a library and perhaps hiring outside consultants.

The commission must also acquire at least as much information as the firms (if this is possible) about the location and richness of the resource, and prepare the first draft of the development plan, indicating what seems appropriate for the government to do and what the individual or firm expects to accomplish.

A project of this sort almost always has implications for other departments of government. Once a proposal is circulated, they will amend it and add to it. The differences in opinion are often resolved by budget officials and planners. However, many questions of fact arise in this process. If the staff of the resources commission is not able to answer them with its own files, library, and consultants, the responsibility must be met elsewhere, usually by the planning commission.

Often the resources commission will become involved in international attempts to maintain the price of the output. When this occurs, the marketing data that provide the bases for the estimation of future demand will become all-important. When the resources commission sets out to acquire these data, it cannot remain dependent upon the firms to which it has granted concessions. It must either develop a new office of its own or collaborate with other producer nations in some cooperative arrangement. The most persuasive justification for setting up a new statistical bureau is purely practical: the concessionaire may resort to the courts in the event of a dispute with the government, and no government lawyer likes to plead a case where virtually all the data are provided by the other side. Policy makers also favor the creation of an internationally oriented data-collection unit because export markets are known to be fickle and erratic. They wish to have their own appraisals of potential loss (and windfall gain) as quickly as possible so that internal adjustments can be made.[4]

A resources commission is inevitably the object of uninformed criticism from the legislators and the public. It defends itself by conducting studies of the economic returns, direct and indirect, obtained from the resources for which it is responsible. Because many political groups gain their support by exposing policies of inequitable distribution of returns, the commission will also endeavor to estimate in advance what portions of the population benefit at a given selling price and who will be neglected. Conclusive results from such studies require a review of comparative transport costs, the inroads of substitutes, and the standards of quality applied to goods and services. The commission must also be con-

---

[4] It will be recalled by those with experience that the typical resource-development project is initiated in a seller's market when the price of the basic commodity is high and the demand is strong, but a more normal situation exists at the time it gets into full production. Both the government and the concessionary firms may be forced to adjust their original plans as a consequence of this shift.

scious of the need to create opportunities for local subcontractors, and it is well advised if continuing investigations are made toward this end instead of depending upon a law to take effect favoring native enterprises. With such broad terms of reference, a resources commission should become one of the two or three most powerful development agencies in the government.

Curiously enough, most international corporations prefer to deal with a tough and competent commission, one that has the facts and the skill for driving a hard bargain. This is because international corporations with resource development skills prefer continuity of activities to extraordinary profits and obviously feel much more secure when dealing with a commission and staff which must be respected for its comprehension of the task at hand. Because these firms have considerable problems in controlling corruption among their own staff, they very much prefer to deal with honest agencies in the government; a few are coming to realize that it does not pay to descend to bribery, even when it is a "way of life" for business in a given country. The majority among these upright firms are recent entrants into international development, but they represent the most rapidly growing resource-based industries.

The outcome of careful regulation is a resource-based industry that is competitive on the world market and thoroughly integrated into the local economy, with all opportunities for significant external economies taken in hand. The market is as stable as world conditions permit, and growing points are identified for the possible establishment of other export industries. The surplus can be transferred to other portions of the society where institutions are built in such a fashion that they can carry on after the resources are depleted.

THE INSTITUTIONAL FRAMEWORK

The total industrial structure will include, besides the resource-related industries, organizations designed to manufacture and distribute articles for retail markets, and others to supply tools and facilities for the production system. The production of articles for retail markets usually will depend to an important extent upon imported raw materials; therefore such manufacturing tends to be located in cities which have ready access to the world suppliers. The alternative is to be located close to the largest existing urban centers because they represent the important aggregates of consumption that permit the manufacturers to take advantage of the economies of scale if they succeed in capturing a large part of the local market.

Thus far the presence of only two varieties of institutions has been mentioned, the international corporation and the locally organized private firm originating from a family or a partnership. (In the latter, the family members, or partners, often have launched a variety of enterprises.) Obviously another kind of institution which must be considered as appropriate for the initiation and management of industry is the state-owned corporation. Compromises between these forms, usually referred to as *consortiums,* are also becoming increasingly common. The government, the international corporation, and the local interests hold stock in such an enterprise and have come into agreement regarding the management and the policy making.

How is the formation of consortiums and corporations stimulated? Most important for development is the amount of experience that has been acquired in the society toward making complex institutions work as intended. A review of the recent business history of the society is needed to discover precedents which determine how a new industrial firm would be organized. National policy must use whatever bodies of experience are at hand, and it must endeavor to fill whatever gaps become apparent after comparisons are made with countries that have been successful in efforts to industrialize in recent times.

The analysis of advantages and disadvantages as presented earlier in this chapter must be combined with a study of the history of the attempts to develop industrial organizations over the previous decade or two. Instances will be found of abortive attempts to create industry; also some instances where isolated moderate successes were achieved. The study of failures can be extremely instructive, particularly if the investigator is able to identify the crucial environmental factor responsible for bringing about the failure. He should be encouraged to speculate upon the outcome if the government managed to bring that crucial factor under control; very possibly some other factor would have stunted or killed the enterprise at a later date. Whatever they are, the principal hurdles to be overcome by government intervention may be brought into perspective.

It is then possible to synthesize from experience, from the opportunity structure as described above, and from models tested outside the country, at least one institutional framework for the organizations which might successfully promote industrialization. Since each instance must incorporate a highly individual approach, it is difficult to generalize, but five different policy alternatives can be outlined:

1. The government might initiate and itself operate in the public interest a series of key manufacturing activities, adding one after another in order of priority.
2. The government might encourage (through subsidies, credit, guaranteed

markets, and other aids) the local entrepreneurs who wish to enter the manufacturing field or modernize the traditional and obsolete plants they already operate.

3. The government might attract competent industrialists from the outside; with extra incentives it may also attract some outside capital to accompany the imported skills.

4. A politically neutral "development council," either completely independent of government or established as a semiofficial body, might take on the detailed task of information gathering and expediting associated with the establishment of industry within a given territory.

5. A mixed strategy, including several of the above, might be followed, with the creation of widely different instrumentalities by the government and by firms in the private sector.

The first of these was chosen by the U.S.S.R. and Communist China as their sole policy once industrialization had seriously begun.

The second was predominantly employed by Western European countries and by North and South American countries during the nineteenth and early twentieth centuries.

The third is rather new, since almost all the battery of techniques associated with it have been developed since World War II. The fourth has been particularly common as an approach suited for "depressed areas" where a population has been affected by a decline in the value of the resources available to it, or by technological obsolescence of its principal skills.

The multiple approach, represented by the fifth alternative, seems to be more widely applicable than any pure strategy, so that the discussion which follows in the succeeding chapters will be based upon such governmental policy.

BIBLIOGRAPHY

Aubrey, H. G.: "Deliberate Industrialization," *Social Research,* vol. 16, pp. 158–182, 1949.

A historical survey of the means by which various governments have in the past encouraged the establishment of manufacturing. Primarily discusses nineteenth-century techniques as they were employed in the early part of this century.

Baran, Paul: *The Political Economy of Growth,* Monthly Review Press, New York, 1957.

An opposition viewpoint that favors a fully socialist approach to industrialization. Analyzes the planning in Soviet, Indian, and other underdeveloped areas in the light of these views.

Chenery, H. B.: "Patterns of Industrial Growth," *American Economic Review,* vol. 50, pp. 624–654, 1960.

A statistical analysis of the contribution of various sectors related to industry, as well as the various types of industry, to economic growth in about fifty countries during the period 1950–1956.

Meier, Richard L.: *Science and Economic Development: New Patterns of Living,* The Technology Press of the Massachusetts Institute of Technology, Cambridge, Mass., and John Wiley & Sons, Inc., New York, 1956.

Analyzes the contribution of processes still in pilot plant and laboratory and suggests how these may be fitted into plans for achieving adequate levels of living.

6

INITIATING INDUSTRIAL ENTERPRISES

MUCH HAS BEEN WRITTEN in the trade journals and in the economic histories about the function of development banks, industrial promotion groups, Fomentos, and similar organizations. Every developing territory—whether it be a nation, such as Chile, or a region bound with special ethnic and cultural ties, such as Scotland and the Mezzogiorno, a state, such as North Carolina, a metropolitan area, such as Cleveland, or islands, such as Trinidad and Tobago, or even counties and other equivalently small units—must be equipped with one or more such organizations.

For every ten that are formed, however, only one succeeds, and perhaps one or two others achieve their objectives to the extent of meeting expenses. The errors are traceable not so much to improper organization as to poor judgment on the part of the responsible persons. Their image of an industrial society and its requirements is based upon the warped and fragmentary experience of a nonparticipant, rather than upon hardwon experience from creating industrial enterprise. Therefore, rather than starting by considering the proper organizational structures for industrial promotion, we shall first emphasize the task itself, for the successful organization is one that has learned to overcome the special problems posed by that locale and by the governmental form that had previously inhibited the growth of industry.[1]

[1] An elegant analysis of the typical conditions contrasted to the most desirable is found in H. P. Morrison, "Corporation Laws, Taxes, and Customs in Ecuador," *International Development Review,* vol. 4, pp. 18–24, December, 1962. Modern regulation allows wider scope of operations, prevents fraud, and imposes much stricter public accountability.

Wedding information and statistics to the decisions of the business-man before he commits his capital requires the establishment of a body of specialists, who are given different designations in different places in the world: in North America they operate primarily as consultants; else-where they are often called advisers or staff specialists. Their job is the same in any case—they assess the prospects of various enterprises.

The specific proposals for which relevant data must be brought forward originate from diverse sources. They may be categorized as follows:

1. *Local entrepreneurs who combine various inputs of mainly local origin to service local markets.* Most often they are merchants who know the market and are dissatisfied with either the price or the existing quality of the work of the local artisans.

2. *An ethnic group of entrepreneurs living in the society who have family and cultural ties with entrepreneurial groups outside.* The Chinese, Leba-nese, Jews, Greeks, and Hindus have almost worldwide coverage. Also included in this category are the French, Scots, Arabs, and Italians. They are capable of fitting local labor and skills with the opportunities arising in foreign trade.

3. *Agencies of the government which see the need for certain manufactured products in relatively large volume to fill projected demand created in large part by the government.* They have studied the implications of local manu-facture as a substitute for importation.

4. *Multinational firms that are expanding their activities.* They normally pro-pose a branch plant which may be operated as a subsidiary or by an affiliate.

5. *An existing or proposed complex of industries based upon contiguous re-sources, or upon special advantages of location, which repeatedly generate new proposals that take advantage of external economies.* A steel or petro-leum refining complex is the most common, but bulk chemicals, nonferrous metals refining, fertilizers, pharmaceuticals, and bulk food processing are acquiring these characteristics also.

There are, of course, other origins for proposals. They may come from friendly governments, or they may stem from the operations of coopera-tives, to provide two additional examples. In practice, these other forms are rare, and can usually be fitted into procedures developed to handle those listed above.

Proposals originating from the first source above (the local enter-prisers) tend to be naïve about technological requirements, management, and locational principles, but are often sophisticated about marketing arrangements. The second category, the ethnic entrepreneurs, often lack knowledge of local labor management, technology, and ecology, while their grasp of export markets is superior and their experience with various modes of transportation is helpful. The third category, the government agencies, are short on ideas for acquiring competent industrial managers and often show only a superficial understanding of the technology, but they do forecast long-range demand better than the others. The fourth category, in which the multinational affiliate is involved, is perhaps best prepared of all, but these proposals are often vague on such subjects as supervisory personnel, locational requirements, internal transport, and the use of local materials. Proposals in the final category, which includes offshoots of an industrial complex, pose special problems in waste disposal, utilities supply, etc., that must be closely coordinated with other public and private activities. Each instance of this last type is likely to be a complicated special case.

The sources of risk capital and the needs for extra financing make up a separate class of problems which have already been thoroughly studied by economists, since many of them have linked economic growth to capital scarcity and the rate of saving. When the local enterprisers are merchants, they usually have the necessary capital or have previously established credit at a bank; if they are artisans who wish to expand and mechanize, they would need a patron (often a major landowner) to get started if the government did not step in to assist.

The ethnic entrepreneurs usually have some capital, and very often it will be in hard currencies, but the proposals they tender usually require several times the capital they have available. Agencies of the government generally know how to arrange for financing from governmental sources or local savings, but they may have trouble with the hard-currency component. Since the number of sources for international loans is increasing, however, the government requires competence in preparing proposals that will be recognized by an international agency as projects with good development possibilities. Any project that collects charges or tolls for service directly and improves the capacity to export goods and services would certainly be favored by an international financing agency. The last two sources of proposals for industrial projects—the international affiliates and the additions to an industrial complex—have their own sources of credit, but they often search for better terms on loans.

This variety of the financing problems strongly suggests that more than one kind of institution should enter into the financing of economic development. A development bank will not be sufficient. With increasing frequency private capital from inside the country is observed to combine with private capital from the outside and with public capital to form a mixed corporation capable of undertaking major projects. Often the foreign company responsible for the design and construction of the plant facilities will also retain financial interest in the undertaking after it has begun to operate. It is usually to the government's advantage to get extra financial participation of local interests—an example of the consortium arrangement introduced in the previous chapter.

Promotion of such industrial projects also requires a set of incentives to attract the attention of industrialists and guide them into profitable directions. In each case the incentives are calculated to appeal to the economic, social, cultural, and psychological characteristics of the entrepreneurs and managers. They are to be chosen in such a manner that the subsidies, which often may represent a significant cost to the society, act as a trigger for large investments and also for boosting the economy in the direction of goals that have already been agreed upon in the formation of policy. The regulations surrounding the qualifications of a project for incentive payments are exceedingly important, and have been studied by the legal counsel of dozens of governments which are competing for many of the same industrial opportunities.

FORESIGHT IN INDUSTRIAL PROMOTION

Systems of incentives for attracting and guiding industrial enterprises to a developing area are constructed with several criteria in mind. They should include at least the following:

Image Creation. Some salient feature about the place should put it on the "industrial map," so that executives and managers immediately know where it is, what language is spoken, what climate to expect, and have other preconceptions about life there. Luxury tourism is very helpful in creating favorable images in the early stages.

Adjustment to Entrepreneurial Backgrounds. There are several varieties of mobile entrepreneurs, and each brings to a plant quite different experiences. Their personal and family values will often affect the choice of plant sites. Each variety of entrepreneur that can be identified, and promises to be a reasonably good source of prospects, should have provisions made for it in the incentive scheme that attract attention.

Productivity Stimulation. The establishment of a factory is followed by a strenuous effort to organize production so the plant meets market demand with the lowest operating cost. Almost always the challenge is to achieve labor productivity comparable with levels in developed countries. Freedom from traditional constraints (political, governmental, social, and cultural) upon the organization of tasks by the plant manager is regarded as an important incentive.

Sensitivity to Competition. Scores of countries and hundreds of special regions are now competing for the internationally mobile entrepreneur. Each new country entering this competition must match the typical subsidies granted to such firms as well as establish itself as a unique territory with special opportunities for certain classes of firms.

Research on Hazards for Enterprise. Continuous scrutiny of the reasons for failure and lack of further growth will reveal some conditions that can be rectified either through improved governmental coordination or through changes in the law. Such studies are, in effect, concerned with the amelioration of "business climate." The level of optimism about the future, particularly in firms originating from outside, will be weighed very heavily in the calculations of the new prospects.

The most common incentive is tax exemption, and many formulas have been devised. A typical provision forgoes corporation taxes for five to ten years. Its aim is ostensibly that of providing a new firm with some competitive advantage to make up for its inexperience and starting-up costs. In practice, however, it appeals to one variety of entrepreneur—the type that looks for opportunities to pyramid limited capital in get-rich-quick schemes. Such men prefer not to share their gains with the tax collector. Yet even these not-so-admired types of organization builders can be extremely useful in the industrialization process.

The mobile small industrialist from the outside is frequently a member of a marginal ethnic group. He is often assured of a market through his contacts overseas if the price is competitive. Typically he needs credit, a loft or building to rent, assistance in finding suitable labor and, particularly, supervisors. Quite often he is so market-oriented in outlook that he knows little about production organization. He is highly dependent upon the continuous operation of the transport and communication services connecting him with nearby territories and overseas points. Disruption of his foreign contacts causes shutdowns within weeks or days.

The established international corporation has a somewhat different set of priorities. Provisions for clearing away red tape, for currency stabilization, for personal security of managers and technical personnel, and the presence of amenities will attract the international firm that is setting up another branch plant. Therefore such services as a competent, disciplined police force, an effective public health system, and highway access to the prime recreational areas—governmental activities which have hitherto rarely been concerned about promoting industrialization—are very considerable attractions when considering the location of a new plant. These firms appreciate help in the collection of data, they accept assistance in acquiring suitable sites, and their noncitizen employees take advantage of services such as hotels, restaurants, private schools, clubs, private medical dispensaries, and recreational opportunities. The importance of such services is so great the Fomento organization may have to intervene and arrange for setting international standards of service in a select few, and it may have to sponsor the creation of others. International firms also demand a free hand in management; they insist upon a free flow of capital; nevertheless they make greater contributions to industrial development than the less fussy small entrepreneurs. The factory set up by the international firm is better financed, better managed, pays higher wages, and is less likely to fail.

Over the past two decades the world has witnessed a steady migration of mobile industries away from advanced industrial countries toward the metropolitan areas with low wage rates and stable currencies, such as Tokyo, Hong Kong, San Juan, Singapore, Bombay, and Mexico City. The movement was initiated by footloose enterprisers, often refugees, but was quickly followed by many famous names in industry. The number of firms that learned how to operate from scores of decentralized plants in various countries has multiplied by at least a factor of ten during this period, and the educational process is still going on at a rapid rate.

THE CARIBBEAN EXPERIENCE

The range of planning problems associated with industrialization in the Caribbean area is almost as extensive as can be found in the world at large. An illustration of the very large-scale resource development, and the effect it will have in orienting other forms of industrialization, is found in Venezuela. In Mexico a complex of middle-sized and small industries is well established and growing rapidly despite many environmental constraints. Smaller but more elaborate variations on the resource-oriented approach to industry formation are to be found in Jamaica, Colombia, and Trinidad, where modern manufacturing techniques are just beginning to be established. Most interesting of all is the Puerto Rican technique of industrialization, since the pool of resources required was minimal, and the standard forms of infant industry protection were not available to it.

The bases of the Puerto Rican formula are important to examine because it is already imitated widely. Yet only certain portions of it are expected to be relevant elsewhere. Therefore, in the following account, emphasis will be placed on those features which are considered to be transferable to other economies and to other cultures. The evidence of actual transfer will then be analyzed.

The tax-concession incentive was developed by Puerto Rico into an instrument which, because of the special political status evolved by the commonwealth, was superior in some ways to what could be granted to the same firms in the United States. It was used as a primary talking point in intensive promotion by mail, and occasionally by advertisement, in the United States. After the formula was written into law, it was rewritten twice within a decade in order to keep up with the competition, eliminate the loopholes, and construct a truly effective instrument. It received the careful attention of thousands of small mobile entrepreneurs.

Among those contacted a certain proportion, surprisingly constant over the years, made inquiries mainly in the form of requests for information regarding experience with their particular product, and whether it qualified for the special incentives granted to pioneer producers. Among organizations seeking information, a fraction, again surprisingly constant, arranged to have responsible officers make trips to the Island to look over the possibilities in detail. Within the few days normally allowed for these visits, the Fomento strained its facilities to acquire the data needed for assessing the profitability of a proposed plant. As a next step the firm, or individuals who might later form a firm, started negotiations with the Fomento for tax exemption and other subsidies (such as were offered to "core industries," for transport of machinery and equipment, for locating in nonmetropolitan areas, etc.), for factory space, and assistance in recruiting local supervisory personnel.

Other parts of the Americas have some notable opportunities for devising tax-based incentives for industrialists. Personal income taxes in the higher brackets are low in the independent Latin countries. This could be even more attractive for many industrialists. On the other hand, the cost of living in the American or the international style is high, and outsiders often encounter severe handicaps due to foreign exchange difficulties, to political disturbances, and also to a certain amount of chauvinism on the part of the elites in those countries. A program aimed at inviting outside capital to enter an underdeveloped economy must provide reassurances on these matters as well. When combined with some careful advertising of the guarantees that have been made, the tax incentive could attract a great deal of interest in entrepreneurial circles in Europe, America, and Japan. Mexico has become particularly active in this direction, and Venezuela is making a promising new attempt.

British territories can formulate even more interesting tax concessions for American enterprisers than Puerto Rico because these territories do not include a capital gains tax in their personal income tax. Therefore, once appropriate laws have been passed, an effective advertising and promotion program emphasizing capital gains advantages should attract growth enterprises. In Jamaica a rather elaborate formula was arrived at by which a company was permitted to begin depreciating its capital after what is effectively a five-year tax holiday, but the shock of moving from a full rebate on corporation taxes to full payment was moderated by providing stepwise increments in the fifth and sixth years after starting operations. Since Jamaica expected to encounter firms that only partially qualified for incentives, a special category was created which was granted 50 percent exemption.

In the various territories in the West Indies concessions must be provided for firms importing virtually all their raw materials and exporting the output. The most appropriate solution is to grant these firms freedom from duty payments much the same as if they were operating in a free port. This provision breaches the tariff barriers in order to accommodate labor-oriented manufacturing. The special advantages proffered to industries for locating in territories providing these incentives should have considerable effects upon the prospective operations of a sizable number of expanding firms. Other local complications—such as currency controls, insufficient credit, high taxes on personal income, and arbitrary labor union actions, to name a few—may still stand in the way, but these issues reflect basic problems which require special solutions in each territory. An important advantage enjoyed by the British West Indies is that these societies are predominantly English-speaking, so the language barrier is minimized for most entrepreneurs and managers. This cultural advantage overcomes many economic and political disadvantages that prevail.

One of the consequences of the tax-exemption pattern in these semi-independent and independent territories is the increasing reluctance on the part of the industrialist to repatriate profits to advanced countries where he would again be subject to income tax. Thus there is a strong tendency to leave the funds in the country and look for some new investment opportunities. If these profits are not plowed back into the business itself, they may be invested in the local securities, such as the utility and municipal bonds that must be marketed if the environment for industry is to be improved. In addition, the shrewder international firms, which operate subsidiaries and affiliates in various countries, set the prices of the semimanufactures and services transferred from one point to another, so that unusual profits show up in that affiliate where they are most useful or least affected by taxes. Therefore special tax-concession features may easily warp the group profit-and-loss statements, and are sometimes responsible for unanticipated, yet highly welcome, windfalls in capital accumulation in developing territories.

It is important to remember that corporation tax exemption is of very little value to firms which are not able to set up a viable and productive operation. It serves as a lure for the entrepreneur, but its impact is only to concede extra gain to those who already have succeeded. Therefore particularly close attention must be paid to shortening the time between the starting up of the operations and the achievement of a reasonable profit. The bureaucratic delays caused by government should have been foreseen and eliminated, if at all possible. Other deterrents affecting both the probability of staying in business and the achievement of a fair profit are high-priority items on the agenda of the industrial promotion organization.

An excellent example of foresight, aimed at smoothing out obstacles that may impede new industry start-ups, is to be found in the program devised in Puerto Rico. When industrial prospects arrived in Puerto Rico, carefully trained industrial relations officers conducted them about, mainly to talk to managers of existing plants and to view available sites. As described earlier, a channel had previously been cleared through the red tape so that agreement could be quickly reached and settled. If the entrepreneur needed credit, his credit rating had already been looked up and quick decisions could be made. Special technical problems associated with the water supply, the humidity, local materials, transportation, communications, etc., were referred to a consultant who had already become acquainted with the Island's problems and advantages. As a result, when businessmen decided to do business, they found that they could act quickly, occasionally settling the matter within one visit.

Once a factory site was selected and a contract signed, the normal procedure was to send a manager and a few technicians to supervise installation of the machinery. They could not afford to stay long in a luxury hotel but sought housing elsewhere. An important issue in industrial promotion policy was thereby raised. Should the foreigners be settled in an enclave where the housing, clubs, restaurants, cinemas, and schools could be conveniently provided for them, or should the industrial personnel be distributed among the native population so as to accelerate the acculturation process? The Puerto Ricans had experienced a few instances of enclave formation when the sugar industries were modernized in the 1920s, and had traveled enough to see the long-run political consequences of this "solution" elsewhere. They chose to provide the needed services through stimulating a variety of enterprises in commerce with a style which would simultaneously serve the industrial sojourners and attract Puerto Ricans educated overseas. Many catered also to the tourist trade during the winter season. The stimulus resulting from efforts to start industries made it possible for the apartment hotels, restaurants, race tracks, casinos, schools, and supermarkets to show a profit earlier than would otherwise be possible.

It was anticipated that special problems would be encountered by foreign managers and technicians in assembling a work force, so bilingual supervisors were trained. For the additional staffing, a huge file had been built up containing information about persons available for industrial work, describing individual skills and aptitudes. This made it possible to use relatively objective criteria in hiring workers—a service that is appreciated by most foreign entrepreneurs.

It was expected by Fomento that some firms, once in operation, would experience "productivity problems." Preparations were made for trouble shooting in this area, first to conduct on-the-spot investigations and then to make recommendations for changes in work organization. Contrary to the predictions of American economists and technical consultants, it was found that levels of productivity, in physical units per man-day, soon were as high as any in the world for the assembly of ultramodern products, such as instruments and electronic equipment; that they equaled the less efficient American firms in toys, metal products, leather working, and other standard production items. Only the oldest established textiles and needle-trades industries were hard-pressed to exceed half the American production norms. The assistance that was then provided depended upon personal judgments regarding the capabilities of the local management, since the difficulties encountered in production depended almost wholly upon the competence of the management and not deficiencies in the labor force.

For various reasons some businesses reached a point where failure appeared probable. Then a hunt for some new entrepreneurs to buy up the equipment and take over the business became a responsibility of the Fomento. Sometimes extra credit was sufficient to revive the sick enterprise. On rare occasions technical advisers were brought in, or market assistance was given. As argued before, too many failures would have changed the business climate and deterred new prospects who were visiting and exploring the potentialities. Despite its "underdeveloped" character and special business hazards, the foregoing techniques for assistance developed in Puerto Rico reduced the "going out of business" rate there to 6 percent in 1957–1958, as compared with more than 11 percent for the same period in the United States. Considerable quantities of capital were conserved through these efforts.

Each step of this process, and many other of the special decisions affecting new business, must be analyzed by a public relations unit. An industrial promotion agency makes decisions and creates policies that are of considerable interest to many segments of the public it serves, and to many others that are overseas, so that its statements are often front-page news. Any statement that destroys the confidence of the prospective entrepreneurs in the ability or willingness of the society as a whole, and the agency in particular, to carry out its promises of assistance could easily destroy the promotional program. The public relations unit must seek out possible sources of dissension and resistance, and by a process of publishing information or by vetoing programs of action that would unwittingly exacerbate the doubts, should endeavor to prevent any incipient conflict or misunderstanding. This responsibility is as important as the primary intent of the public relations unit, which is to build up an image of a competent, public-spirited, organized effort, succeeding despite many obvious difficulties. Thereafter the unit must insist that this image be maintained with deeds as well as words.

Public relations work requires an extraordinary amount of wisdom and foresight. In Puerto Rico, for instance, it was recognized from the beginning that the use of tax incentives to attract industry away from communities in which they already resided would cause an unfavorable reaction in the region adjacent to the affected community, and the local representatives in Congress would be made very much aware of the feeling. If this should be repeated a hundred times in almost as many places, a formidable bloc of congressmen would be created, willing to sponsor and promote legislation discriminating against Puerto Rico. To avoid this hazard, public relations arguments caused the tax exemption legislation to exclude from incentives those firms that were abandoning communities in which they had previously settled. Only expansions, extensions, branches, or new plants that moved in from the outside were to be accepted for tax exemption. Such a provision may have lost Puerto Rico a dozen or two factories of the less desirable type, but it created an image of "fair play" which enabled the program to survive many crises that would otherwise have been its ruin. As evidence, relationships with both the United States government and the news-reporting services had reached such a level of mutual trust that they even survived an attempted assassination of the President of the United States and an armed assault upon Congress by a fanatic Puerto Rican minority group. Incidents of this type had been foreseen, and preparations had been made in advance to keep the Puerto Rican government and the society as a whole from being associated in the minds of either officials or the public with the acts of extremists claiming to act in the name of Puerto Rico.

The Jamaicans launched in 1957–1958 a similar industrial promotion program in the United States, Canada, and the United Kingdom. Some of the firms first to take advantage of the opportunities Jamaica presented already had plants in Puerto Rico, which they retained, thus illustrating that these programs operating in the Caribbean were likely to be much more complementary than competitive. The kinds of prospective industries developed in Jamaica were very similar in type and composition to those firms that settled in Puerto Rico in the first few years of its program. Jamaica had an opportunity to make a running start because many of the services appropriate to an industrial managerial class were already being provided as an adjunct to its large and rapidly expanding tourist industry. Unfortunately, the government has lately been in a situation where it could not even consider the close coordination of tourism with the promotion of manufacturing and the sale of rum, as in Puerto Rico. Each of these activities must operate with narrowed sights on targets set forth in its own charter.

On the South American continent both Venezuela and Colombia are promoting industry, but Venezuela's program is more advanced. Fronting onto the Caribbean, in Maracaibo, Valencia, Caracas, and along the

Orinoco deep channel, many new industries are rising to fill internal needs; demand has been growing from 7 to 9 percent per year with a few interruptions. Heavy immigration from Southern Europe (until 1960) brought in a supply of technicians and small entrepreneurs. The elaboration of the industrial complexes that process the rich natural resources forms the crux of Venezuela's strategy of industrial development, but as the smaller units are desired to fill out the industrial structure, the industrial promotion program is forced increasingly into the pattern pioneered in Puerto Rico. However, the degree of success will depend much more upon political stabilization, similar to that achieved in Mexico, than any special attraction built into the industry promotion program.

THE MEDITERRANEAN EXPERIENCE

The physical environment, the state of development, and the cultural orientation of the Mediterranean countries greatly resemble the Caribbean area. Indeed, the latter contains a series of transplantations of Mediterranean modes of social organization, some of which matured along the way in the west of Europe and in America. Therefore movements which take place in one of these areas may be expected to have parallels in the other.

The poorer areas of the Mediterranean, being much older than the Caribbean, are endowed with more highly elaborated bureaucratic structures, thus presenting the development-oriented groups with a more entrenched tradition to overcome. There was also the task of reconstruction, since the wartime losses were severe in many of these areas. It was to be expected then that the Mediterranean territories would lag behind, particularly Spain, Sicily, Sardinia, the foot of Italy, Greece, Cyprus, Lebanon, and the Muslim countries. (Israel was an exception; its industrialization with outside sources of capital and technology proceeded rapidly all during the postwar period.) Programs for industrialization began to be organized in the late 1950s, but the coordination was poor, and relatively small amounts of external investment were attracted despite some huge governmental investments in infrastructure, including an expansion of educational opportunity. Not much was accomplished until the 1960s, when the backwash from the spectacular growth of the Common Market group began to spread into the Mediterranean regions.

The Mezzogiorno (southern Italy and Sicily) program represented the most massive attempt to bring an impoverished area up to levels of living consonant with the rest of Europe. Agricultural demonstration units, water resources developments, power plants, and schools were built. The construction of roads was emphasized in particular, so that tourism growing out of a rapidly increasing vehicle population could be promoted. Where the government had the power to direct the location of industries, it strongly favored the Mezzogiorno (and Sardinia).

The response was sluggish but increasingly favorable. When the history of this development is finally written, it seems likely that the lion's share of credit will have to be given to the opportunity to emigrate to Rome and the cities to the north. The rapidly growing industrial firms exhausted their local labor supplies and were forced to look elsewhere for workers. Overemployment developed also in Northern Europe, where the wage minima were markedly higher. Therefore, while hundreds of thousands of Italians from all over Italy emigrated in pursuit of higher wages, millions moved into the cities from the rural areas, particularly from those in the Mezzogiorno. The remittances sent back to the Mezzogiorno appeared in the form of household improvements and also in the mechanization of transport. Attempts to form cooperatives and local enterprises were not successful, except in the provision of services aiding tourism. At a later stage the branch plants began to take advantage of the incentives offered by the national government and discovered, to the surprise of the management, that factories based upon village labor could develop levels of productivity equal to those achieved in the industrial north. This was particularly true in firms hiring women and for the most modern kinds of technology, such as transistor manufacture and calculator subassemblies. After ten years of such development the government could be confident enough of the area to designate it as the locale for the large new steel mills, oil refineries, and other heavy industry. The presumed low quality of local labor no longer increased the risk inherent in starting up these major plants. In other locales a prosperous apparel industry has become established. Over the next decade it seems quite likely that the Mezzogiorno will be transformed in much the same manner as Puerto Rico was in the 1950s, with the countryside being depopulated, the cities bursting their bounds, and many strangers entering to settle in the most pleasant environments. At the same time, the families of those who have become established industrial and service workers in the north will gradually sift out of the south to join them and thereby create small communities of Sicilians and Calabrians all over Western Europe, from Genoa to Hamburg and Zurich to Birmingham.

The same kind of culture existed on the small island of Malta under British hegemony. When its significance as a military base declined owing to technological improvements in weaponry, Malta became politically disturbed. The leaders sought separation with full maintenance because no future seemed to be open to them. They, too, have attempted the industrialization gambit, seeking to make use of their unique location which enables a manufacturer to shift his goods quickly to any market that may open up in the Mediterranean. A small, exceedingly alert population could probably do quite well if the rest of the Mediterranean became prosperous. Malta's formula for promotion remains to be tested, however, and is in any case subject to statistical fluctuations because of Malta's small size.

Spain has had tremendous success with tourism on the Costa Brava and the Balearic Isles; at the same time the government shifted slowly to investments in water resource development and basic industry. Planning by "technocrats" began in the 1960s, coincident with the liberalization of the economy, which included relaxing some of the police controls over labor organization. (The pattern imitates the remarkable French success in planning during the latter part of the 1950s and thereafter—direction of industrial growth by persuading the management of larger firms to undertake carefully coordinated programs of expansion, combined with the control of credit.) Migration to the north has been swelling, but may be cut off in the mid-1960s by a slowdown in Western European industrial expansion. Spain's problems are more severe than those of the Mezzogiorno, and the political uncertainties will probably restrict the influx of international firms. Its natural resources are not rich enough to attract much interest. Nevertheless its prospects for further industrialization are brightening.

In Greece it is possible that the full program of creating an open society attractive to foreign entrepreneurs and capital will be undertaken. It is the nearest analogue in the Mediterranean to Puerto Rico. Greece has gained some industry in the past by combining immigrant labor (mainly refugee) with foreign technology, international capital, and local promoters, but growth was stifled by excessive protectionism. During the 1950s the country managed to modernize transportation and electric power production. It also set up some government-sponsored plants for heavy industry and the development of low-grade mineral resources. This was accomplished with reparations and foreign aid. Toward the end of the 1950s and increasingly during the early 1960s, the emigrants to Western Europe, mainly to Germany and Scandinavia, sent back remittances which eased the foreign exchange difficulties. In 1962 Greece became an associate member of the Common Market and was allowed fourteen years to adjust its tariffs and quotas to the levels that prevail in the European economic community.

Tourism is already playing a significant role in developing the amenities in Greece, although it started later than in most other parts of the Mediterranean area. Its tourist potential is perhaps greater than for any other country in the Mediterranean except Israel's. It attracts an exceptionally educated class of people, many of whom become attached to the country and particularly appreciate its climate. Since the directorates of the international firms operating in Europe tend to be highly cultured, the amenities of the metropolitan Athens region suggest a particularly attractive locale for the industries they manage. The difficulties that stand in the way are distance from the markets and, at present, excessive bureaucratic controls. Also, the government's investment in education has been the lowest in Europe, so the labor force is less well prepared in many ways than even that of the Mezzogiorno. The problem of education has been mitigated to a considerable extent because the middle classes have invested heavily in private studies and have shown great initiative in finding places in universities overseas. A major reform in education was initiated in 1964–1965 which should produce diploma holders equivalent in background to those from elsewhere.

In contrast to a number of other industrially emerging countries, where stresses of social change and political instability are evident, Greece presents a rare picture of social and political stability. For more than a decade Greece retained stable and responsible governments. Individual freedom is highly treasured, the institution of private property has strong roots, and the land-tenure system—a source of unrest in many countries—was modernized before World War II.

In Greece the Ministry of Coordination is in charge of the industrialization effort. In 1962 it had about one thousand proposals under consideration. The underemployment in the Greek economy and the low wage structure seemed to be the most important attractive features for these enterprises. According to the econometric calculations of Papandreou (1962), this condition would change in the early 1970s at the recent rates of economic growth and migration, and much sooner if growth continues at rates experienced in the early 1960s (7 to 8 percent of GNP per year per capita).

If the Greeks score a success, similar programs are likely to be undertaken in Tunisia and Lebanon. The levels of living and urbanization are roughly the same, and similar international propensities are dominant. Turkey has much vaster potentials for industrial growth and trade, but political problems remain unsettled and recurrent outbursts of xenophobia are disturbing. Egypt has similar troubles, and has engaged in many expropriations without adequate compensation while committing itself to an "Arab socialism," using the instruments of national planning reinforced by foreign aid. It has forgone its opportunity for at least a decade. In the rest of Mediterranean Africa, Tunisia has been demonstrating the greatest initiative, but it is still too early to evaluate the strength of that program.

DEALING WITH INTERNATIONAL FIRMS

Thus far the discussion of formulas for promoting industries has centered upon general policies which can be treated with a single body of law. Every contract between the firm and the government which grants the incentives would be made to fit within the framework of that law, the chief purpose of which is to expedite as many small-scale and medium-size proposals as possible so as to minimize the delays that prevent a firm from getting into production. A streamlined administrative apparatus can be created to carry out the intent of the law.

Whenever a multimillion-dollar opportunity comes to hand, however, such law is inadequate by itself because major opportunities almost always involve established international firms that operate in several countries and sell in those and many others. They usually have several alternatives for expansion, and these could be located in as many different countries. Therefore the international firm (it will be called the *company,* as is common in many parts of the world) stands in an excellent bargaining position and expects to obtain assurances from the government which reduce its risks.

If the government is unable to provide adequate police and health services itself to the prospective site, it must grant the company permission to defend itself with company police against brigands and to install its own public health measures (which may range from draining swamps and damming streams to burning brush or setting up quarantine stations). Moreover, when the government defaults on such services, it must grant the company rebates on taxes.

One of the company's major concerns is that of providing an environment suitably attractive as a place to live so that it can recruit families from modern societies who are willing to serve away from home for a period of at least three years. Geologists, mining engineers, public health specialists, and civil engineers have all entered their occupations knowing that they involved working in undeveloped territories. They chose wives and brought up children to be able to accommodate themselves to long separations, but most management personnel expect to make no sacrifices greater than those experienced while living in small industrial cities in modern countries, and rarely will accept less, even if they receive liberal recompense in salary and allowances.

Hence the company is obliged to plan for one or more small communities which are almost wholly dependent upon its operations, or else to locate its manufacturing plant in the largest and most cosmopolitan urban area. In the first case (usually associated with a resource-based industry) the company is inclined to create a small, closed, foreign-language community and a larger "native compound" for the workers. The workers' settlement grows out of the construction camp in most instances. It is almost always to the best interests of the newly industrializing country to resist such exclusivity and insist upon collaborating in the design and location of the community so that it has more of the character of a metropolis within which foreigners can intermingle continuously with the bilingual population, especially the local elites. The international managers, engineers, and scientists can be gradually replaced by local college graduates with much greater ease if the openness of a metropolitan environment is maintained.

The principal point to be made here is that crucial decisions—such as location of settlements, choice of architect, and cost range for dwellings—will be made during negotiations with the company; therefore the government must be informed at an early stage about the issues and their implications. The price of neglect in this area takes the form of bitter strikes and antiforeigner sentiment that show up in greatly reduced labor productivity in the manufacturing unit ten to fifteen years later.

ANTICIPATING POLITICAL REACTIONS

An industrial promotion organization encounters somewhat different problems when dealing with large multinational firms. Then the project planning is likely to be at least as realistic as anything that can be done by a government office, but the accumulation of frictions, suspicions, and animosities that often result from big-company operations may be expected to lead to public demands for government seizure. On the other hand, the company may become a politically entrenched monopoly that fights all attempts to keep up to date and distribute the profits broadly. How can these long-range outcomes, which are all too common around the world, be avoided by action on the part of the industrial development agency?

The newer oil contracts offer a close parallel that serves as useful illustration of suitable policies for this question. Exclusive rights (for exploration and drilling) are granted for a limited territory and a limited set of activities. Then, as knowledge of the true potentials increase, the company designates which half (or some other convenient fraction) of its monopoly rights it is willing to renounce on the date previously agreed upon. After another period (the duration of which might be three to five years) a similar fraction of the monopoly right or subsidy reverts to the government. This allows other firms with competitive interests to enter the country and reduces the likelihood of attempts on the part of the company to obtain the collusion of politicians so as to maintain obsolescent operations at the former levels of return. Under such a policy, the company is obliged to pioneer new industrial efforts and negotiate new contracts for them if it wishes to sustain the flow of incentives and grants made to it. This proposition may be stated another way: few ambitious politicians will hitch their careers to a force with a built-in decay of influence; even more important, they would not find it useful to build up an opposition force intent upon toppling the entrenched interest. It is much to be preferred that the company managers and technologists be replaced eventually by local people, or at least by members of the same culture, and that such people participate in public life according to their personal predilections. They are then accepted as individuals rather than regarded as servants of the company.

It is useful to be more explicit here and apply this illustration to an industrial case. Let us say that any country with a population of more than 5 million people (and many with smaller numbers) will have an opportunity to manufacture its own buses. There are perhaps ten international manufacturers who might ask for the exclusive rights to manufacture. The country itself can obtain considerable savings in bus maintenance and repair if it settles on a single line of buses for intrametropolitan and intercity service. Then it is worthwhile to offer subsidies to the manufacturer who comes in to supply the needs. It would be natural for the government also to eliminate duties on imported engines and parts at the same time it imposed a fairly high duty on finished buses by other manufacturers. It might provide an industrial site and building without cost to the manufacturer, and permit its ownership to revert to the manufacturer after ten years, if the latter was still in the bus-making business. There is good reason for this ownership provision; small machine shops and foundries, closely integrated with bus manufacturing, and successor enterprises, such as medium trucks, are likely to be set up during this interval, so that the site is less useful to the government for other industrial purposes. In conjunction with this policy, the duties on finished buses would be successively dropped so that in about this ten-year period they would reach a negligible level. This would force the entrenched firm to take increasing cognizance of improvements in bus design as the ten-year period passes and very likely the works would be rebuilt upon receipt of property title. It also means that special-purpose vehicles falling under the legal category of "buses" would still be available through payment of duty. This is a better arrangement than granting a strict monopoly, for it encourages the firm to branch out into marine or rail equipment, trucks, irrigation pumps, road-making equipment, mining machinery, and related products on the same terms. It is equally possible that a manufacturer of autos and trucks, coming in initially under independent arrangements, would at the end of the ten-year period initiate a complementary line of buses that was competitive with many of the sizes and models introduced by the first company. The country would profit from such competition.

The first bus-manufacturing plant would probably be established on a site behind the principal harbor because relatively large-size crated components would need to be imported, and many of the harbor services (e.g., welding gases, electroplating shops, diesel-engine repair equipment) would be convenient. Inventory could be kept at lower levels accordingly. In the interim, however, a rolling mill for sheet steel may have been completed elsewhere, with an auto plant located adjacent to it and with good transport links to a harbor. A firm expanding into bus manufacture there could presumably do so at lower cost and at the same time import a smaller proportion of the components. If that should be the case, it would be sensible to write off the first factory and convert it to some other purpose. Thus an alert international firm under such circumstances would have understood well in advance that it would be unable to stay forever in the bus business and would negotiate for new markets in allied fields on similar terms so as to use its management and technical personnel efficiently. It would be less likely to lobby in the parliament to prevent the introduction of what promised to be a more efficient production unit, a reaction which, under present-day concessionary arrangements, is most common.

In summary, special industrial developments of the kind that are initiated with large international firms require first of all the establishment of confidence that the lives of the managers and technologists will be safe and that the funds brought in from the outside will not be expropriated, either directly or indirectly. Second, it is vital to the developing country's interests to prevent the practice whereby in the past a firm has been able to develop a significant political coalition, once it has become established, that allowed it to maintain the concession indefinitely, despite a declining contribution to industrial development. It is proper at the start for the country to negotiate automatic subsidy reductions and franchise limits for the initial enterprise, with important incentives offered for adding related activities leading in the direction of an integrated body of industries. It should be part of such agreements that the managers and technologists do not form an isolated foreign-language enclave, but that the housing and other facilities should foster replacement by local candidates. An atmosphere of polylingual cosmopolitanism should be fostered as much as possible so as to exploit the transfer of the standards of organizational competence introduced by the foreigners to the local elite and expedite the absorption of the foreigners into the social system. The intent is to minimize the friction between the company and the government during the industrialization process and to facilitate the introduction of the most advanced technologies.

STIMULATING LOCAL INDUSTRIES

The foregoing emphasis upon measures for the reduction of conflict and the simplification of the politics of industrialization is not overstated. The granting of subsidies and incentives to a large, successful international firm after lengthy negotiation is political dynamite. Neither the voters nor the normal party politicians are able to understand the kinds of risks which need to be reduced nor the alternatives for investment that are available to the company. One method for removing the political sting from such agreements is to extend the same contractual incentives, subsidies, protection from loss, etc., to a body of local entrepreneurs, most of whose activities fall into the category of small industry. The publicity associated with such a new law will make it appear that a small-industry program has been launched. There are enough possibilities to be explored publicly (i.e., in the newspapers) and enough minor accomplishments to report so that the true potentials of the overall program are often obscured.

The truth is that no one yet knows how to promote local small industries successfully. The costs of administration and the inevitable losses of capital due to business failure combine to make the programs uneconomic users of scarce personnel and capital. A careful examination of the small-industries programs that have claimed success in various parts of the world shows an unwillingness on the part of the claimants to include the considerable governmental costs as additions to the private costs before computing net returns or to add the incidence of private loss in the half or more enterprises that failed.

The strongest and most vociferous effort in many countries goes into programs for assisting cottage industries. In such programs the government provides credit for the producers, encourages the development of new looms, pottery wheels, dyeing and tanning procedures, and similar improvements which enhance quality of output and add to worker productivity. Cooperatives for marketing of cottage industries are also sponsored by the government so as to reduce the number of middlemen between producer and consumer. In more than 90 percent of the instances such measures are inadequate and government subsidies are sought. Since only a few artisans possess skills that cannot be economically displaced by machines, the outcome is an intricate program for the relief of the poor artisan under the pretext of encouraging home manufactures. The process of subsidy is not a bad form of public assistance; it keeps up morale, gets enough production to pay perhaps half the cost of the subsistence, and maintains a pool of labor which can be drawn upon for larger-scale manufacturing enterprise. But it is not in reality a *developmental* measure.

Though the skill of the typical artisan is relatively high, it has little value in modern manufacturing. Indeed, because every trade imposes rules for the proper way to handle tools, differing from those employed in the factory, artisan skills are often a detriment which prevent older workers from ever being employed in factories. (With surprisingly high frequency, women and girls transfer better than men, for reasons to be discussed later.)

It is evident that a cottage-industry program should not be confused with a program for the promotion of small industry that fits into the modern framework. The former is basically a holding operation, a means of disguising unemployment until productive jobs can be provided. The latter is a program for building up capacity for producing a wide range of goods and services appropriate to a modern society. It fills in the interstices between the major enterprises, producing for small to medium-size local markets which are created in the course of growth.

What particular difficulties stand in the way of economic promotion of local industry? The primary problem is their multiplicity. There seem to be no crucial factors that can be researched and resolved by the acquisition of technical or specialized information. A study conducted by the Small Business Administration in the United States concluded: [2]

> Analysis of the case histories confirmed the expectation that adequate causal analysis cannot rely on purely statistical techniques or on a reconstruction of the past experience of either going or defunct concerns. By their nature, both of these approaches cannot take into account a number of intangible factors which become apparent only through direct observation of a business as it moves through the crucial stages of its early development. Repeated contacts with ongoing concerns made it clear that success or failure could not be attributed to single causes but was generally the result of a complex interplay of various factors.

It should be noted in passing that 50 percent of the new firms considered in this SBA study went out of business within two years; that the pay taken out of the businesses by the proprietors was less than the going wage, and the total return on the investment over the first two years was −2 percent. Most of these small businesses were commercial establishments, but the experience is not too different from what is to be expected in small-scale manufacturing. The locale was the state of Rhode Island, an area which was growing slowly in wealth and population. Parallel studies in less developed countries probably could not be carried out successfully because businessmen there are less frank about the scale of investment and the level of turnover than in the United States where many kinds of reporting are customary and income tax evasion is less prevalent.

The major factors believed to affect success of small business in the United States are the same as those reported elsewhere; they seem to be universal. They include *timing* (many businesses are started only because a satisfactory job was lost or was insecure), where the local business con-

[2] B. Mayer and Sidney Goldstein, *The First Two Years: Problems of Small Firms' Growth and Survival,* Small Business Administration, Washington, D.C., 1961.

ditions are an important factor; *location* (many second-class sites were accepted either out of ignorance of the implications or because of the exigencies of timing); *finance* (very small enterprises often lack sufficient capital to expand inventories and provide necessary equipment); *health* (an active business requires the full attention of the owner-manager, especially during the period of initiation); *experience* (many gross blunders are prevented by previous experience in business or in a specialty, but those having the experience are often overoptimistic about the practicality of minor innovations); *business sense* (too often new entrepreneurs do not know how to calculate a profit, set a price, appraise the strength of competition, etc.), and *personality* (an entrepreneur is constructing a new organization and must create patterns of cooperation among employees that are productive, therefore he needs to have a knack for personal relations).

Most newly developing countries have an additional set of factors, associated with obligations to kinfolk, which inhibit the growth and development of a local firm. In the case of the ethnic entrepreneurs mentioned earlier, these relationships can be helpful because much business lore is transmitted from the more experienced members of the family to the less experienced. Financial assistance is often made available through kinship connections if the concern shows promise. However, in families with little background in business, there is a tendency for poor relatives to be parasitic upon those who have visible inventories so that they "eat up his capital." The capital in the family is made available or withheld, not on the basis of experience but upon the whim and fancy of the senior members. Also kinfolk demand, and usually obtain, reduced prices for the goods and services they use, further diminishing the profit margin in the turnover of the firm. Most important, perhaps, is the expectation that the jobs created by the firm be filled with unemployed relatives regardless of their qualifications. If the form of cooperation required between employees is of a kind different from household activities (it is almost certain to be so when producing modern goods and services), then family relationships obstruct efficiency and high productivity. Most families have effective sanctions against cheating and pilfering, one of the great problems for a new firm when setting up its internal controls, but the overall disadvantages of family enterprises usually exceed such particular advantages.

The evolution of the *zaibatsu* in Japan suggests that it is not altogether impossible to evolve a foundation of modern manufacturing and services based upon family ties. They used every device imaginable, from marrying the daughters to promising young foremen and managers to designating the education of the boys being sent off for technical training, in order to achieve growth and balance among a variety of interconnected enterprises. These are schemes worth studying by a man who has ambitions for his family, but there seems to be no way by which these facilitating features of family organization can be expedited by government action. The *zaibatsu* evolved over centuries in a highly competitive environment, and of the tens of thousands that started as small businesses, only a score or so matured into substantial business combines. The Chinese have equivalent family arrangements, but have not been as successful with them as the Japanese.

It might be concluded from these brief observations that families are exceedingly important for the establishment of small businesses, but that there is little that a government can do to assist beyond modernizing the law governing the claims of one relative upon another. Usually family structure is diverse enough within a culture to permit a minority of 2 percent or 5 percent to engage successfully in commerce and then to switch into the provision of manufactures and advanced services. This is the most promising segment of the society for initiating firms, and one which can best be treated in quite another context, to be taken up under human factors in Chapter 9.

The Puerto Ricans have not been successful in local small-business promotion despite the diligent efforts of the Fomento, the prior existence of a commercial middle class of reasonable proportions, and a stable financial environment. Scores of local businesses were successfully established in manufacturing activities; but a much larger fraction of the proposals originating locally were stillborn, the failure rate was higher, and rates of growth slower than for firms established by outside entrepreneurs. There was greater delay in moving from initial proposals to the beginning of production, and therefore greater overhead costs on the part of the promotion agency. Much difficulty was experienced with people who started planning an enterprise enthusiastically and then changed their minds as they began to see the complexities involved.

Yet political necessities are such that the assistance of smaller local entrepreneurs will become the responsibility of the government as part of an overall program of economic development. Given this rather unsatisfactory experience, how then should the government proceed? The following recommendations are based upon the premise that local and internal factors are as significant as the technological knowledge that is required.

1. Review the recent *unplanned* successes. What factors seemed to be at work in yielding the success? Which of these might assist new enterprises?

2. Analyze the typical failures. Could planning have prevented a significant portion of them? Where within the government did the necessary,

but insufficient, information exist? How could it have been communicated to the entrepreneur before he made his commitments?

3. Create a fund for high-risk short-term loans or purchase of equity for enterprises that have run short of capital. This fund should not be considered as an industrial bank but more as a "growth fund," wherein one outstanding success could make up for a dozen losses.

4. Create a cadre of managers and executives who can go into "sick firms" and reorganize them in the hope of rebuilding or salvaging something. This practice is common among the larger investment banks in advanced countries.

5. Develop a list of products and services which are ripe for promotion at the current stage of development. This is done primarily by noting which are ready for rapid growth (owing to governmental plans) and those that are typical of a forthcoming stage of development but not yet produced locally.

6. Develop a list of potential entrepreneurs who might start such firms if freed from present responsibilities and obligations, or who might take on the opportunity as a promising sideline. This proposal means that it should be possible for civil servants, or at least employees of government corporations, universities, schools, etc., to engage in private enterprise while continuing in their jobs as long as no conflict of interest is involved.

7. Connect the opportunities with the entrepreneurs. All sorts of private arrangements may be necessary. The industrial promotion officer then serves as a kind of marriage broker and needs all the finesse and judgment that such a role implies.

8. Diagnose all successes and failures, using methods of identification and analysis that are very similar to those employed in clinical work in medicine.

9. Record and circulate these findings and hypotheses concerning improvement of performance to all interested parties, even though the figures are not likely to look imposing.

10. Continue to experiment with new procedures, incentives, and techniques in such a way that an art of fostering small local business economically may evolve.

BIBLIOGRAPHY

Friedmann, W. G., and G. Kalmanoff: *Joint International Business Ventures*, Columbia University Press, New York, 1961.
   A definitive work on the postwar experience with overseas joint ventures that strongly emphasizes the legal and accounting hurdles. Examples in different parts of the world are systematically evaluated.

Papandreou, Andreas G.: *A Strategy for Greek Economic Development,* Center of Economic Research Monograph 1, Athens, 1962.
A model developed for estimating the economic growth of Greece, based upon the availability of foreign exchange.

Stead, W. H.: *Fomento: The Economic Development of Puerto Rico,* National Planning Association, Washington, D.C., March, 1958.
An enthusiastic description of the history, operations, and performance of the Fomento organizations in Puerto Rico. Contains a brief appraisal of the features transferable to other economies. Drafts of enabling legislation and a series of prior studies are cited.

Yaseen, L. C.: *Plant Location,* American Research Council, New York, 1956.
Primarily a checklist of the factors to be taken into consideration by entrepreneurs when seeking a location for a new plant. Much comparative data are provided. A special chapter is devoted to policy recommendations for industrial development corporations operating within the American system of business relations. Another deals with Puerto Rico as a "new factor in plant location."

7

INDUSTRIAL PLANNING PROCEDURES

AT THE BEGINNING of every program for industrialization a fund of experience has already accumulated which indicates what kinds of procedures are *ineffective*. The same experience may also reveal procedures which have come very close to creating workable industrial organizations in the recent past. The importance of an intimate understanding of the successes and failures in establishing manufacturing and related enterprise over the previous decade or two has already been stressed for the formulation of strategy. It is no less useful in laying out the administrative programs.

In Puerto Rico a great deal has been learned in this area. The processing of local products—other than the rather standard commodities such as rum and sugar, where marketing crises had already led to the creation of an international quota scheme—had encountered major difficulties penetrating into overseas markets and retaining them in the face of competition. The development of local skills through the establishment of handicrafts industries had not worked at all well, if the output was expected to pay off the heavy costs of training in the requisite arts. On the other hand, the extensive home needlework industry, although operated at very low pay and under conditions leading to low productivity, suggested introducing a succession of higher-paying activities in the needle trades which could be taken up by the local labor force as well as by some of the local entrepreneurs.

A series of business failures had been experienced which could be traced to lack of capital, credit, or technical knowledge—a phenomenon that is so discouragingly common in the first attempts to set up manufacturing. This unrewarding experience was matched by equally dismal events in agriculture outside of the sugar industry. Attempts to develop vegetable gardening for shipment north during the off season went bankrupt over and over again, owing to failures in marketing, to the incidence of plant disease, or to improper organization. Citrus fruits met the same fate. There were scores of other examples. In each instance the risks taken appeared unnecessary to an observer from the outside. As a consequence, in the period preceding rapid, induced economic development, the limited number of competent local entrepreneurs that did show up tended to drift to the distributive trades and construction, where detailed knowledge of the local scene gave them advantages over competition from the outside, as well as over the traditional procedures still being employed in these activities. An even larger number of the entrepreneurial "types," that is, persons who would have been in business had the opportunities been better, were to be found holding down government jobs. Thus a small part of the civil service was available which was sympathetic to business and could be trusted to implement procedures aimed at enhancing the profitability of the various industries.

From this prior experience it was possible to deduce the appropriate pattern for allocating responsibility when bringing outside entrepreneurs into the society. When carefully analyzed, the established precedents suggested that the government should take responsibility for the growth of education facilities, health facilities, road systems, electric power, water and sewers, and much of the low-cost housing, while some competent businessmen expanded the remainder of the personal services, wholesaling, retailing, construction, and transport, in accordance with demand. In this way growth remained relatively balanced in the urbanized sector. The activities of the entrepreneurs brought in from the outside of the society fitted rather nicely with those which were already evolving locally.

The administrative procedures for finding and settling industries on the Island were worked out by an informal team made up of civil servants and consultants. If it was found that a change in the direction of industrial development appeared to be desirable, the matter was taken up with the cabinet member responsible, and very often some specific studies were authorized. If changes recommended by these studies could be effected through administrative directives, action was taken promptly; if the change seemed to be a matter of national policy, it was taken up with the governor, and later with legislative committees. Often the search for new directions was initiated by the chief executive himself. There is nothing unusual about this mode of administration. In this case, it was well planned because of very high quality personnel in the key positions, persons who had broad experience and were of like mind.

RELATING LONG-RANGE AND SHORT-RANGE GOALS

A most common mistake is made, once the goals of planning have been agreed upon, a body of relevant data is at hand, and a program for action is to be drawn up. Almost inevitably it is then proposed that the specialist group responsible for constructing the middle- to long-range program should isolate itself from day-to-day affairs and concentrate on constructing the best possible program. Isolation is felt necessary by those who are expected to produce a draft plan, primarily because it would enable them to gain long-run perspective and have time to consider a wide range of opportunities. Their superiors are often sympathetic and their colleagues in universities reinforce them in this viewpoint. The latter often are invited to participate in this stage of planning because some interesting technical problems in optimization are involved. The method sometimes works, especially when physical and structural design is involved and blueprints must be prepared in the next phase, as in roads, water supply, and land use, but with such dynamic activities as industrial development, the experience has not been salutary. As it works out, plans conceived and developed in relative isolation are found to be "unrealistic" when exposed and explained. As a consequence they fail to be implemented. Owing precisely to the isolation, the opportunities that emerged in the preceding months and shifts in political emphasis are almost always left out of account. Then the planners are unable to persuade the hundreds of people who must adapt their actions to the plan so as to obtain superior results.

The alternative procedure is a device frequently called *participative planning* in large, fast-moving business organizations. The planning specialists retain day-to-day responsibilities, preferably of a sort which gives them a view of the operations of the whole organization. Individuals are singled out to look into opportunities that otherwise may be bypassed, and to alert the others. The program is assembled rather hastily, and to those who carry out the task it will appear to be inferior to what could be done if more time were allowed. However, inevitably in participative planning, recent information would not only be taken into account but in general would be weighted a little more heavily in making projections than older information. The resulting program then has the appearance of being sagacious and feasible. In Puerto Rico at least two attempts were made to isolate a planning group for industry and give them the opportunity to prepare technically superior plans. In neither instance were the proposals useful.

Industrial planning often has, in fact, such a short horizon that the latter stages of a five- to six-year capital budget and financial program have virtually no meaning. The attention paid to it would lead to formal entry of figures, but great skepticism would be expressed concerning their significance.

It should be noted, however, that where *heavy* industry is being installed, meaningful projections can be made as much as five years in advance. In those instances an integrated industrial complex is being built up; the construction period averages as much as two to three years, measured from the time of the signing of the contract for the site; thus a five-year projection implies looking ahead only to the production of the next line of new products beyond those for which construction has already been initiated. Horizons for industrial planning are thus seen to be greatly dependent upon the technological character of the industry.

An appropriate form of organization for participative planning seems to be that of making the respective top administrators responsible for it. Each spends a part of his time analyzing, projecting, and reformulating his criteria. Some will depend upon staff for special studies and evaluation. The plans themselves grow out of committee work. Therefore, if the discussions go reasonably well, *education as to the facts* and *achievement of consensus upon specific ends* occur simultaneously. There are, as a consequence, few formal plans, except policy papers which are approved after amendment in conference. Because the policies must change rather frequently if the industrialization program is to be sufficiently opportunistic, only the vaguest and most schematic plans can survive for long periods.

In effect, the staff that draws up policy papers forms an industrial planning team. But its membership is highly variable because of the need for various kinds of background to solve crucial problems. Economic research personnel are usually involved, but the groups assigned to buying land for new industrial estates and laying out blueprints for new "standard" factories are often forced to make analyses that take into account factors applying further into the future. For this reason the technicians responsible for planning electric power production and industrial water supply and familiar with long-term growth in demand may have a key role in working out the directions for industrial expansion.

If these techniques of establishing industry are introduced elsewhere in the world, two kinds of industrial planning may be set in motion. The distant-horizon features would be combined so that natural resources, heavy industry, and agricultural products processing would be studied and programmed together. These categories form a group of fundamental activities with times of preparation reaching two to five years, and therefore, as a whole, have a long-time horizon. A large share of such planning work is conditional because it presumes a certain body of installations yet to be completed and then studies the probable consequences. (In India and elsewhere most of the work of the groups doing perspective planning is of this variety.) There are many disappointments for individuals and teams in this kind of endeavor because most exploratory programs and proposals must of necessity be dropped. The participative planning, arising from fast-shifting committee work among department heads and members of their staffs retaining key administrative responsibilities, would fill out the major part of the needs for the individual sector. In Puerto Rico only about 10 percent of the industrial employment and about one-fifth of the capital investment were of the type that employed long-range programming, while for countries like Venezuela, rich in resources, a major portion of the effort would fall into the long-range category. However, as pointed out in Chapter 1, most countries now struggling to develop possess a relatively small natural-resource base, so the emphasis must be upon the creation of organizations that can conduct participative planning for the short run.

Governments would no doubt assemble a group of long-range industrial planners in an appropriate department. The limited-horizon industrial planning would then be done independently, probably by the industrial promotion agency itself, or possibly by some governmental agency which is closely tied to it. The two programs are knit together into the overall developmental planning when they compete for the same local *in*puts (resources, human or otherwise) that are in scarce supply. In the event of such conflict the elaboration of schemes for integrating the long range with the short range may be worthwhile. Unless or until such competition can be foreseen, there seems to be no reason why the industrial planning should be centralized. The technical skills required for the two different approaches are quite different.

REFERENCE SYSTEMS FOR INDUSTRIAL PLANNING

There is a special kind of risk inherent in the procedures described above when it comes to making decisions based on the short-range analyses. In general each decision is intended to maximize the amount of income added to the economy per unit expended for subsidies and aids. The projects are so drawn up that they represent marginal returns. Continuing in this way may lead into a familiar trap that sometimes occurs when marginal analysis is *used exclusively* for making decisions. For industrial planning this is best illustrated by the following example:

It is easier to induce the needle trades (i.e., garment making) to set up in a newly developing territory than other industries. The mobile firms in the apparel industries tend to have low capitalization and low wages; a dollar spent on promotion may easily gain $10 to $20 in added income for the economy. In higher-capitalized industries, where productivity gains are eventually much sharper but a more complete industrial environment is needed before these gains can be registered, there may be a long period during which the income yield is much less. If all the available plant sites or other scarce factors, such as trained supervisors, should be used up with the needle trades, then the higher-capitalized firms encounter greater difficulties in getting established. The industrial sector could easily reach a plateau where the emphasis on low-wage industries caused a cessation of growth. These fears of premature industrial saturation with low-wage-structure factories warrant a shift in the industrial promotion strategy.

On the other hand, a concentration upon highly capitalized industries with high labor productivity and high wage scales will soon dry up the local sources of credit, while barely affecting the unemployment problem. Thus the other extreme tends to be even riskier, both from a business point of view and from the viewpoint of a politician.

Somewhere in between there should be found an industrial pattern which seems to optimize external economies over the long run and therefore promotes growth. The external economies, unfortunately, are not measurable, but there are various sets of indicators which may be used in the industrial planning. *Reference systems* have been created for this very purpose; they provide a coherent picture of potentially scarce factors related to production. They are constructed so as to be reinforced by scientific, technological, and economic intelligence from other economies.

A reference system provides a natural basis for keeping *nonmonetary accounts,* for demonstrating the degree of dependence of one activity upon another and for obtaining a holistic measure of the pace of change in at least one value dimension. Such systems are particularly useful when the money system is not in equilibrium with the international currencies, so that other indicators of natural limitations and of progress are necessary.

The simplest possible system of this sort is *space,* or land allocation. When land is preempted by one activity, it is not available (with very few exceptions) to others. Thus land of certain categories may be in short supply, with many activities competing for it. In this case careful attention must be paid to location, space, and the distribution of activities. Land use is such a fundamental reference system that it is used universally by urban and agricultural planners without special prompting. For industrial planning, land of itself is rarely crucial, but there are similar sets of accounts for analysis and control which approach land use in their utility but whose statistical and technical properties are quite different. The number of such reference systems maintained by the agencies should be held down to the minimum necessary to cover all the basic needs. The reason for such a stipulation is that each reference system imposes certain overhead costs upon the government to keep them current.

There are four other such systems proposed which are likely to be of central importance to industrial planning:

1. Technological structure of inputs and outputs of installations
2. Human resources—particularly entrepreneurs, managers, and technologists
3. Water and associated climatological resources
4. Soil and mineral resources

Some of the four basic systems mentioned above will also be vital to other phases of developmental planning. The human-resources reference system, for example, provides the backbone of educational planning. In general, these reference systems are defined in the following manner:

Technological structure is built up from the major inputs and outputs of the industrial plants at capacity and must be based upon data acquired by routine methods. (A technique of information gathering suitable for the beginning and intermediate stages of industrialization will be described later in this chapter.) The data should be buttressed by information from the technological literature which describes impending changes in raw materials and product mix, so that prospective technological structures can be projected, and niches for new plants discovered.

Ideally, planners need an accounting model for industrial technology which incorporates (1) the physical capacities of various installations, (2) the flow of various inputs into them in preceding years, and (3) the flow of semimanufactures between them; then (4) the quantities of various categories of outputs, (5) the substitution effects of a marginal unit of input in each category along with the requirements of a marginal unit of output, and lastly (6) a series of linked-growth indices (e.g., having the quality of revealing increasing integration) employing either interfactory flows or other indicators of interdependence of operations.

There is at present no practical statistical system that could encompass this set of requirements, even if the cost of gathering necessary data imposed no limitation. The methods described by Leontieff, Chenery, and coworkers are much too cumbersome to be useful in an underdeveloped area that is short on statistical skills and needs to make quick decisions (a more complete discussion is found in Chapter 5). However, a variety of simplified *ad hoc* models of these flows and interdependencies can be prepared. The choice of the model will depend upon the findings of special studies that have been launched by various decision-making groups for their own needs, and upon models developed elsewhere in the world which can be borrowed.

A brief example will be helpful here. A segment of technological structure oriented toward petroleum can be represented as in Figure 7. It will be noted that while these flows are stated in terms of *capacities,* the actual outputs of the industrial system will average out substantially below capacity.

The diagraming of the flows between the various industrial facilities in a complex puts into another symbolization what is to be inferred from a small input-output table. The complex can expand by adding new

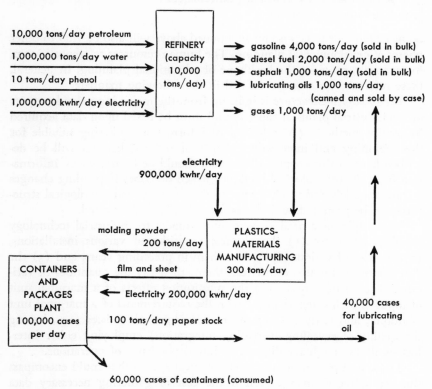

Figure 7. Industrial complex: A petroleum-plastics-packaging combine.

processes at the output side, by using waste products in some of the established processes, or by synthesizing some of the inputs themselves. Sometimes all these can be done at once. For example, the technologist will note that it is possible to take some of the sulfur from the petroleum entering the refinery, reprocess it, and treat a fraction of the gasoline in order to produce phenol—and very likely have some of each product left over to sell on the local market. A competitive process would extract a different component, treat it with air, and produce acetone, a lacquer solvent, as a by-product to the production of phenol.

Each alternative should be drawn up as a project, with costs and marketing prospects evaluated. In much less detail, the subsequent projects that might be added after these, in further elaboration of the complex, should be considered. For example, it might be possible to combine several minor chemical coproducts—like phenol and benzene—with a chlorine plant and produce a series of insecticides and herbicides that could reinforce agricultural development. The rough technological requirements are well enough known and can be drawn from the contemporary literature that would be collected by a good library.

In practice, a new facility is not added to a complex until the principal suppliers have been tested and found to operate up to expectations. Plant addition at a more rapid rate than every two or three years is possible, but failure of a unit to produce the expected quantity or quality would result in embarrassingly large capital write-offs. For one reason or another, the risks of building a facility not able to produce up to expectations seems to be in the neighborhood of one in ten to one in three, based upon experiences over the past decade.

HUMAN AND ENVIRONMENTAL RESOURCES

In the case of *human resources,* the reference system attempts to keep together in one framework the supply and demand for various skills and aptitudes, the evidences for the interchangeability of one skill for others, and the costs for developing and transmitting such skills.

The data to be acquired (again speaking for the ideal case) are:

1. The distribution of natural aptitudes accessible to industry, particularly those associated with higher intelligence (e.g., the I.Q. distribution of children in schools as against those not in school, by age, sex, and location)
2. The labor pools of various districts, by age, sex, occupational experience, years of schooling, and possibly also by language spoken, if that has an important bearing
3. The supplies of various specialist skills, where the types of greatest interest for industry are entrepreneurs, managers, engineers, accountants, technicians, supervisors, and certain kinds of skilled tradesmen
4. The estimated requirements for industry in terms of education and skill, based upon experience elsewhere

The investment in human skills necessary for light and medium manufacturing and its associated services is normally greater than the investment in equipment and facilities, but the heaviest investments in human skills are made many years ahead of the time they are used to the fullest extent. Since it is impossible to foresee the explicit requirements of industry so far in advance, it will often be necessary to convert one kind of skill into another (e.g., chemists into engineers, economists into statisticians, truckdrivers into mechanics) through special training programs at a later stage when the explicit requirements are known. Such transformations are extremely common in developed societies, particularly in manufacturing activities. Therefore, for planning purposes it is useful to group the specialists according to their interchangeability. For example, it is quite common in Latin societies for men with legal training to become industrial managers, whereas in societies influenced by the English tradition it is uncommon, except for a few of the higher executive positions.

The human-resources reference system will be described in much greater detail in Chapter 12 and others that follow. The special problems of creating skills vital to the installation of modern industry is taken up in Chapter 8.

Water and climate are now coming to be understood as a single system, and so a set of accounts for water, with concomitant effects upon temperature and humidity, can now be assembled. Predictions and projections can be made with them. The data needed include:

1. Rainfall, solar radiation, and evaporation rates at various points
2. Stream level and reservoir storage records
3. Underground flows and reserves, including percolation rates through the various top soils
4. Vegetation types and degree of land coverage, enabling an estimate of transpiration rates
5. Water processing and re-use techniques

The accumulation and interpretation of these data can now be made more simply and much more rapidly than in the recent past. Such studies are important even for watersheds with high rainfall where water is seldom scarce prior to industrialization, because there is accumulating evidence that one of the major limits to growth of large metropolitan areas—and therefore to industrialization—is the inability of water supplies to keep up with the growth.

The *soil and mineral resources* reference system has a geological foundation, but it classifies the accessible strata of the earth according to the economic potentials they possess. Geological reconnaissance and exploration, combined with soil analysis, permits a mapping of the territory which becomes increasingly precise over time. The soils categories are oriented toward agriculture, the major user, but in industrial planning they are also important for:

1. Determining suitability for the construction of heavy buildings
2. Designing least cost transport networks

3. Identifying long-term demand for agricultural chemicals and food processing capacity

The geological mapping, as argued earlier in Chapter 5, is useful in the location of settlements and resource-oriented industries, but as most countries remaining to be developed do not have rich natural resources, the findings are not as determinate as they have been in the past.

The soil and mineral data are recorded principally in the form of a map. The chemical constitution of rocks and soils is best understood on a historical basis, that is, the time the rocks were formed and the rate at which they have weathered, eroded away, and been modified by vegetation. The maps are referred to primarily during the course of screening an industrial proposal. Before any commitment is made concerning sites, intensive on-site investigations are in order, including often a few test bores. Findings from these tests are duly entered upon the working maps so that knowledge continues to accumulate.

In some countries the law permits the owner of the land to withhold information about underground structure. In that case, it might pay the government to share the expense of obtaining more samples (which would in any event be needed for a project) in order to assure the accumulation of a body of useful data. The organization of the data seems to be a natural responsibility of a bureau of soil and mineral resources that must be set up at a rather early stage in the governmental push for development.

It may be asked at this point why the foregoing sets of accounts have been chosen, and not others. It has been asserted that *space, technology, human resources, water,* and *minerals* make up the key reference systems for industrialization. Actually, it is presumed that several other similar reference systems will of necessity be maintained by the appropriate ministries, such as the *foreign exchange* accounts, the *national income* accounts, and the *flow of funds* accounts, and further, that the industrialization programs would have to work within limits set by these accounts. The extra systems were selected—and not others, such as, for example, *energy* and *transport*—because associated markets are exceedingly imperfect. When space, technological capacity, water, or soil suddenly becomes scarce, and conflicting demands are made upon the same asset, these particular reference systems can be constructed so as to suggest the best possible substitute. Then projects can be ranked according to benefits and costs within each reference system because a specialized form of valuation has been created to permit a comparison. Proposals that come out poorly when judged within any of these systems will probably need to be discarded, even if they otherwise appear to be profitable. *Shortages in these nonmonetized accounts mean that unit costs will be sharply rising*

in the future—a property usually ignored in project cost calculations.
Experience, much more than logic, justifies the development of these five
independent nonmoney accounts for development at the national level.

INFORMATION-GATHERING TECHNIQUES

None of the foregoing considerations can proceed very far before questions about the *current* state of industry must be answered. Very few
countries today collect adequate information on their industrial structure,
the interrelations of inputs and outputs, and the state of industrial organization in space and over time.

When comprehensive data are required as bench marks for planning,
the organizing of a census instantly comes to mind. In a country which
is primarily dependent upon private rather than public enterprise, the
information provided by a *census of manufactures* tends to be fairly
limited in scope because much of the data cannot be revealed without
affecting the competitive relationships of the firms. In order to understand
why this is so, a brief description of the hierarchical classification of industries by product must be undertaken here.

The industry is subdivided into ten roughly equal categories; each of
these categories is subdivided again, and each subdivision is similarly
subdivided further into conveniently distinguishable classes of manufacturing. A code number is assigned for each level so that the ultimate
classification of the major activity of a factory may be represented by a
three-digit number. The census normally reports totals in each political
unit of territory under each three-digit classification. For most industrial
classifications it is common that there exist only one, two, or three firms;
therefore only the output of much broader categories of firms will be
reported; otherwise competitors in the same category could deduce vital
operating characteristics of individual firms from census reports. For this
reason the standard census information must be supplemented by more
detailed data.

A useful technique for gathering such detailed data is based upon
interviews with the managers of firms. Such data collection could be
combined with the "industrial trouble-shooting" activities which must
exist simultaneously in some portion of the administration. The interview
would seek to obtain all the information which is available to the public,
including the firm's competitors, given the willingness to spend a great
deal of effort in tracking it down. A checklist of such information is
suggested in the appended industrial data sheet (Figure 8). The manager of a factory knows all these facts or can find them out within
a minute or two, unless the plant is very large and elaborate—an unlikely
circumstance in newly developing areas. If the manager is made to under-

stand that he is being asked to divulge only public information, and that the purpose of the information is to enable the government to improve the economic and social climate for industry, and thus aid management's attempts to improve the efficiency of operations, he is likely to respond willingly.

The industrial data sheet provides in brief and readily accessible form the following essential items of information about a factory: (1) the location, (2) physical production data, (3) the manpower situation, (4) the position of the firm in the market and in the economy, (5) the firm's requirements for utilities and services, and (6) the kinds of risks faced by the firm. Such information is quite appropriately based on the firm's expectations, or at least on the publicly stated view of the situation held by the manager or plant supervisor. However, if it is deemed desirable, the figures and opinions can be independently confirmed. Once compiled for the sizable and strategically important installations, if not for all factories in the economy, the collected information can serve a variety of purposes. When combined with the census of manufactures data, it provides a satisfactory overview of the present and prospective modern industrial sector of the economy. If carefully constructed inferences are drawn, a series of disjunctions may be detected. For example, three or four firms may be projecting plant expansions aimed at the same special market which in reality is large enough to accommodate only one. The industrial data sheet will aid in deflecting some of the firms into other markets before commitments are made. Or it may happen that the waste product of one plant could be the raw material for another, but the entrepreneurs and managers responsible had no occasion to discover this.

The industrial data sheet may be drawn up so as to become a folder in a file. All subsequent correspondence, newspaper clippings, publications, etc., related to the factory could be stored in the file. This backlog of information would be reinforced by a similar file of admittedly more sketchy and less trustworthy data for prospective new industrial installations, where the checklist incorporated within the data sheet would be used to prevent mistakes in locational decisions.

For each industrializing country this industrial data sheet would undergo some modification, particularly in the personnel and financial sections, which would take advantage of information-yielding characteristics of local institutions and laws. The time required for the interviews would also vary greatly, according to local custom. (In Puerto Rico, for example, it takes from one to three hours for two professional-level persons to obtain all the available information about typical factories employing 30 to 100 workers, and an equal amount of time to prepare a satisfactory report.) The interview should be repeated after an interval, the length of which would have to be determined by experience and by the rate of

Name of the Plant:
Address:
Telephone:
Cable:

Manager:
Home Address:
Home Telephone:

Photo of the Plant

Map of Locale of the Plant

MATERIAL INPUTS AND PREFABRICATED PARTS

Name and description of materials and parts	Quantity used per operating month	Source or origin	Average price paid during past year	Average cost per operating month

INVENTORY:

Average monthly stock of material inputs, major items:

Average monthly stock of outputs, major items:

Inventory policy:

PRODUCT OUTPUT

Name and description of products	Quantity produced per operating month	Average price during past year	Gross value of output during past year	Sales during past year	Inventory, current value

WASTES: 1.
Method of disposal:
Annual disposal expenditure:
Possibilities of by-products from waste:

2.

UTILITIES:
Monthly water bill:
Monthly gas bill:
Monthly telephone bill:
Other utility costs (per month):

TRANSPORTATION AND COMMUNICATION

Material input weight (monthly average)	Output weight (monthly average)	Origin	Destination	Type of transportation	Packaging types and facilities

Frequency of service required for both the inputs and the outputs:

Transportation facilities inside the plant:

Journey to work for personnel, miles radius from the plant:

Types of transportation employed and time spent in transit:

Most common destination of outputs:

Most common source of supplies:

Most common long-distance telephone connections:

Problems encountered (spoilage, breakage, delays, breakdowns, etc.):

Total number of employees (per operating month):

Breakdown by types:

   1. Number of administrative personnel:

   2. Number of professional technical personnel:

   3. Number of production workers:

Monthly payroll:

Source and availability of various levels of labor:

Employment policies:

Employee pension, health, and insurance plans:

Other fringe benefits:

Unionization conditions and policies:

Recent strikes:

Labor turnover, as a percentage of labor force per operating month:

Provisions for in-service training:

Needs for outside training:

What skills seem to be scarce?

Figure 8. Industrial data sheet obtained by interview at the plant.

STRUCTURES AND EQUIPMENT

	Structure	Equipment
Owners (name and address)		
Insured value		
Rent		
Annual repair and service bills		

Arrangements for repair and maintenance:

Observation about the quality of maintenance and repair services hired:

Average monthly time lost due to breakdowns:

Warehousing and storage facilities (inside and outside):

Capacity:

Periods of full and partial use:

Periods of need beyond capacity:

FINANCIAL SITUATION

Ownership:

Type:

Residence of owners:

Profit or loss:

Last year:

Current year (expected):

Credit rating of the firm:

Source and supply of credit:

Rate of interest paid on money borrowed:

Profit distribution policies:

Government support (subsidies, grants-in-aid, tax or rent rebates, etc.):

CHANGE AND EXPANSION

Expected trend of the market, for labor supply and for material inputs and outputs:

Expected price trends on chief raw materials and products:

Planned production volume for next year:

Planned new products:

Plant expansion programs:

Sales promotion programs:

GENERAL COMMENTS, PROBLEMS, PROSPECTS, ETC.

INFORMATION ON THE PLANT PROVIDED
BY OTHER AGENCIES AT A LATER DATE

Census of manufactures:

Tax receipts:

Labor office:

Utilities installations:

Legal decisions:

Complaints:

Figure 8. Industrial data sheet obtained by interview at the plant (continued).

197

progress of the industrialization. The most active sectors merit a reinterview every two or three years. The reinterview is an excellent occasion for obtaining frank statements from the manager about difficulties standing in the way of expansion and integration.

After the system for data collecting has been used for a while, and perhaps 500 such files have been assembled, some of the data could be reduced to a punch-card code, which would permit more systematic analysis. The importance of this information is that it is relatively current, inaccurate as it might be in detail (managers are inclined to exaggerate some items and understate others). In a rapidly developing and changing economy the value of statistics for purposes of planning and decision making declines precipitately with age. Hence, plant-by-plant information which is only a year or two old at the crucial points would be extremely valuable for all forms of industrial planning.

There is another kind of information assembly which must simultaneously take place. It requires the analysis of relevant developments in the outside world which might yield new opportunities for industrialization. Such data will often not take the form of statistics; rather they will be items from the trade journals published in the United States or Europe for the respective industries. The industrial planning unit would want to have ready access to one or more of the most comprehensive of these sources for each major industry represented in the economy and, in addition, one for each type of industry which is felt to be a reasonably good prospect for the future. A continuous comprehensive survey of foreign industrial trends is hardly feasible because the volume of publication is overwhelming, but a judicious selection of 30 to 50 monthlies and weeklies is likely to be appropriate for planning tasks at the beginning.

Even with this limited number of periodicals the effort required to keep up to date is more than can be afforded when working against deadlines. Further structuring of the technical and economic information coming from outside must be undertaken. There are many ways in which the valuable kernels of information can be separated from the chaff. A technical librarian will know many of these, or quickly be able to discover ways. For example, certain business and technical journals are known to cover specified areas very comprehensively in their reporting of new developments. There are also "abstracting" services to which the industrial development organization can subscribe. Indeed it may easily be found to be the advantage of the industrial planning unit to bring the librarian, or whoever serves as the information specialist, into its regular discussion sessions so that he can direct the scanning of the incoming journals for relevant items into channels which are closely adjusted to the alternatives being analyzed and weighed.

The degree of emphasis to be placed upon acquiring up-to-date information varies to an important extent with the strategy employed for industrialization. A country which depends upon the development of rich local resources would not be quite so interested in data from points outside the economy. Its attention would be concentrated upon the detailed assessment of the location and the extent of its resources, along with optimum modes of exploitation and utilization at these sites. On the other hand, in Puerto Rico, Jamaica, and other densely populated territories, the dependence upon entrepreneurs from outside the society, as well as overseas markets for most manufactured products, implies that the acquisition of technological and marketing information from the outside must play a leading role in the decisions about industry.

BIBLIOGRAPHY

Ackerman, E. A., and G. O. Löf: *Technology in American Water Development,* The Johns Hopkins Press, Baltimore, Md., 1958.
  A comprehensive review of water processing and utilization.

Isard, W., and E. W. Schooler, "Industrial Complex Analysis, Agglomeration Economies and Regional Development," *Journal of Regional Science,* vol. 1, pp. 19–34, 1959.
  Describes how to distinguish between market-oriented and resource-oriented locations for an industrial complex, including the decision whether to split between several locations. Presumes excellent information concerning technology, economies of scale, and markets.

———, ———, and T. Vietorisz: *Industrial Complex Analysis and Regional Development,* The Technology Press of the Massachusetts Institute of Technology, Cambridge, Mass., and John Wiley & Sons, Inc., New York, 1959.
  Describes application of static economic analysis to evaluation of alternative industrial complexes, using data of 1950–1955 on plastics, petrochemicals, and synthetic-fiber technologies.

Krutilla, J. V., and O. Eckstein: *Multiple Purpose River Development,* The Johns Hopkins Press, Baltimore, Md., 1958.
  A review of the analytical thinking that goes into water allocation in major watersheds.

Ross, S. G., and J. B. Christensen: *Tax Incentives for Industry in Mexico,* Harvard Law School International Program in Taxation, Cambridge, Mass., 1959.
  Describes the changes in law, especially tax exemption on new products, coincident with the industrialization of the past twenty years.

The United Nations Scientific Conference on the Conservation and Utilization of Resources (UNSCCUR): vol. IV, *Water Resources,* and vol. VI, *Land Resources,* Columbia University Press, New York, 1951.

A standard source, remarkably thorough, which comprehends the world situation as well as is known.

U.S. Department of Agriculture: *Soil,* Yearbook of Agriculture, 1957.
A readable exposition of soils classification, constitution, origin, and susceptibility to change.

White, Gilbert F.: "Industrial Water Use," *Geographical Review,* vol. 50, pp. 412–430, 1960.
An appraisal of the demands for water by various industries and the reasons for wide variations between plants.

8

THE ADMINISTRATION OF AN
INCENTIVE PROGRAM

NOT ALL OF THE POLICIES AND PROCEDURES that have been outlined so far may be necessary for success in bringing industry from the outside, but reductions in the ensemble introduce increased risk. The policy in any event suffers from certain inherent risks—disturbances of international trade, cyclical trends, hostility of neighboring countries, unfavorable publicity, dock strikes, etc. Taken altogether, these are quite sizable; they should not be enlarged unnecessarily through deference to tradition, niggardliness, or bureaucratic propensities inside the country that has adopted the policies. A Fomento needs most of the measures that have been outlined if it is to remain alert and flexible enough to take advantage of the twists and turns in international relations. There is a critical minimum size for a program for each territory if it is to find enough new industry to repay the overhead costs.

One of the major costs is the maintenance of promotional offices in the world's commercial capitals. Two "foreign" offices capable of working with manufacturers and answering their questions would probably cost $300,000 or more per year. The expense can be reduced, but not by any important amount, by hiring consultants resident in these foreign countries.

Another major expense is that of accumulating internal data such as are needed for the reference systems used in planning, as described in the preceding chapter. These costs will pyramid as time goes on and the more capital-intensive industries become interested enough to start making detailed cost analyses. These costs, too, will amount to hundreds of thousands of dollars per year at a minimum.

Still more expensive will be the cost of constructing standard factory buildings so that they are ready for lessors at the time contracts are signed. They can cost $50,000 to $100,000 each, and many will have to be built because rarely do half of the newly installed industries find private facilities or build their own; in the later stages a larger share will.

In addition to these factors, the special incentives and the services must fit into the budget. Training supervisors, transporting machinery, subsidies for decentralization, and all the rest will cost thousands of dollars per factory started. (In Puerto Rico one-third of the new firms qualified for the extra incentives and received an average of $8,000 to $10,000 apiece in various kinds of assistance.)

Summed up, it seems likely that the *minimum* scale promotion program should aim at a rate of 10 to 30 factories per year within a year or two after it begins and maintain this pace indefinitely. Promoting 20 factories per year with a going-out-of-business rate of 10 percent per year means that an asymptote would be reached around 200 factories. At an average of 80 workers per factory for well-established mobile industries this means a modern industrial labor force of only 16,000 workers, a number that could be easily sustained in a metropolitan area containing 100,000 population. As to costs, taking all factors into account, the minimum industrial promotion program with all its ramifications requires an investment of $2 to $5 million per year. Much depends upon location, educational level of the population, internal salary rates, and the inventory of underused structures.

Not all this sum need appear as the net cost of the industrialization program itself. Water and minerals data collection, for example, is usually the responsibility of a department of the interior or its equivalent. The human-resources data must be covered at least in part by a department of labor. Economic statistics and research are usually the province of the treasury. Overseas offices in major centers of commerce may already be maintained in order to expedite tourism or some major export commodity. The department of education already has responsibility for vocational training. Some measures of economic planning have undoubtedly already been launched, and are probably under direct supervision of the most responsible persons in the government. The factory buildings may be mortgaged to the limit to a development bank, and the expansions in public utilities may be financed by bonds sold overseas. Persons in charge of the program for industrialization must mobilize this collaboration by demanding the attention and cooperation of various kinds of bureaucrats and getting them to assume responsibility for the financial commitments.

Thus opportunities are extremely variable for reallocating the various departmental budgets to an integrated industrial promotion program; indeed it is not unlikely that estimates for the same country at the same time made by local experts may differ by as much as 100 percent from each other. The amount of existing support that can be mobilized depends to a very considerable extent upon the stability of the government, the extent of its majority, and the confidence it has of staying in power through the next election. The greater the confidence and security of the leading political members of the government, the more opportunity they have for reorganizing the governmental structure to facilitate the introduction and growth of industry.

METHODS FOR SCREENING PROPOSALS

The day-to-day action of an industrial promotion agency is concerned with *proposals* to establish industrial plants to expand facilities. First there is the problem of creating bona fide proposals and then of expediting them effectively. These proposals must specify the entrepreneurs, managers, sources of technological expertise, landlords, attorneys, sources of skilled labor force, location, sources of materials, markets, and the approximate time of start-up. Normally a simple balance sheet will have been prepared, illustrating the potential profitability of the proposal.

Once a proposal has been introduced into a smoothly working industrial promotion agency, new alternatives are explored and new balance sheets prepared. The entrepreneurs and managers make counterproposals. The program of special incentives for industry and the prior experience of both the agency and the firm lie behind the recalculation of profitability and risk. The exploration of these alternatives, using all the information at the disposal of the interested parties, assures that the contract finally agreed upon will be a close approximation of what is best for both the society and the firm.

Many of the inquiries that lead ultimately to proposals will merely be indications of interest. For example, a letter from a reputable analyst may suggest simply that "area X is ready for a modern flour mill and a large commercial bakery." At a conference of industrial promotion specialists where this suggestion is brought up, one member may point out that such a mill might fit into a harbor development already underway; another would mention that the by-products would be useful as fish food in commercial ponds. The cost of bread would then be reduced by an amount that can be roughly estimated but the quality would be changed. Would the consumers accept the new product? Obviously many questions are raised, and so a *feasibility study* is likely to be authorized that would consider all the difficulties likely to obstruct the original idea, attempt to devise methods for overcoming them, and then outline the conditions under which the best alternative formulation might succeed. Often a feasibility study will come out with a flat recommendation that the suggestion be dropped; or on the positive side it will indicate which conditions must be met if a promising enterprise is to be established.

On the basis of the feasibility studies the industrial promotion agency might inquire whether entrepreneurs active in bakeries are interested and then, with the assistance of one of them, develop a complete proposal. The analysis of the data thus should generate a hypothesis of the following sort: "If it is at all posible to get this kind of business started, the market situation is such that local output of these manufactures should increase sharply." If further investigation of the data confirms the adequacy of the hypothesis, a *project* can be created. By this manner it is possible to accumulate a variety of such projects—large, medium, and small—with payoffs in the short, middle, and long run, with near certainty or very small possibilities of realization, and involving anything from one factory to a cluster of installations. The overall working plan for industry must be built up from just such an assemblage of projects.

Much broader than a feasibility study is a full-fledged *investment survey* of the kind international corporations make prior to committing themselves to a major project. The investment survey adds to information on the functioning of local political and financial institutions, foreign-exchange restrictions, alternative uses for capital in the country concerned, etc. These comprehensive investment surveys have been encouraged by a subsidy from the United States Agency for International Development. In practice the firm is reimbursed for half the cost of the survey if the results are not used but are then turned over to the agency, thus becoming part of the agency's stock of detailed information about industrialization overseas. By this arrangement the international firms based in the United States are enabled to explore twice as many opportunities in newly developing countries before making a decision regarding investment, thereby reducing the risk of their eventual commitment. Those opportunities declined may well be found advantageous by other firms.

The formulation of projects, followed by the assessing of risks, profitability, location, and timing of each of them, quickly becomes a voluminous operation. In Puerto Rico as many as a hundred projects per year have been put into operation—not all of them involving factories; services related to industry can at times be equally important. For each project which is made a physical reality there are five to ten which fail to make the grade. For a scale of operations like Puerto Rico's, perhaps as many as a thousand such projects in varying stages would be under consideration over the period of a year. The dimensions indicate that a substantial organization must exist for the routine handling of industrial promotion and establishment. It would provide a kind of assembly line

for the routine processing of the bulk of the projects. Under these circumstances the industrial planning unit would consider only the essential
steps in the establishment of industry, and judge how well the administrative routines appeared to be optimizing the total operation. They might
also have to work with the exceptions which, for one reason or another,
cannot be fitted into the routine. Figure 9 shows a diagrammatic presentation of the administrative procedure adapted to the principal strategy
for industrialization. It illustrates the flow of projects or proposals through
a series of filters which tend to sift out the unsuitable proposals. Into each
screening operation is incorporated a series of rules, or criteria, for making
rapid decisions.

Before this routine can begin, however, there must be a prior capacity
to generate the interest of entrepreneurs in undertaking industrial activity within the area being promoted. It operates much like a sales campaign directed at a specialized clientele. The incentive program (see
Chapter 6) is designed so as to elicit interest on the part of this clientele.
Responses and inquiries are followed up with one or more interviews by
an agent of the industrial promotion agency, or a consultant representing
it; the nature of the interest is relayed in as great detail as possible to the
firm's home office, and a visit of some responsible executive to the scene
of the industrialization effort is arranged. This chain of interactions
converts a "contact" into a "prospect." Then as soon as a specific proposal has been submitted (usually after one or more visits have been completed), it is converted into a "project."

The industrial development agency must be willing to use any legiti-
mate technique developed by sales organizations for finding and developing prospects. When one set of approaches seems to yield diminishing returns, another must be created to take its place. Competent selling
must take advantage of short-run opportunities. Manufacturers operate
this way, hence they do not resent this approach and seldom complain
about the attention they receive as a result of it. On the contrary, the
best of them are favorably impressed with a competently run organization, and many feel that if they have to depend heavily upon the cooperation of local agencies in setting up their manufacturing operation,
it is better to lean on a competent administration, despite other disadvantages of the locale, than on one which fumbles and delays. Thus, any
organization whose purpose is to stimulate new proposals for industry
must be quick-acting and extraordinarily flexible. Planning helps most
at the stage where the administrative procedures for processing the proposals are to be improved and perfected.

An illuminating experience can be recounted on this point. In order
to assist in "planning" one such initial industrial promotion, a leading
consulting firm used a team of economists and engineers to appraise the

industrial potentialities of Puerto Rico. They were asked to prepare a list of 100 specific industrial products that appeared—on the basis of prior worldwide experience with industrialization—most likely to be produced successfully. Ten years and more than 500 factories later, 57 products of this list were represented by almost 300 plants. However, more than 200

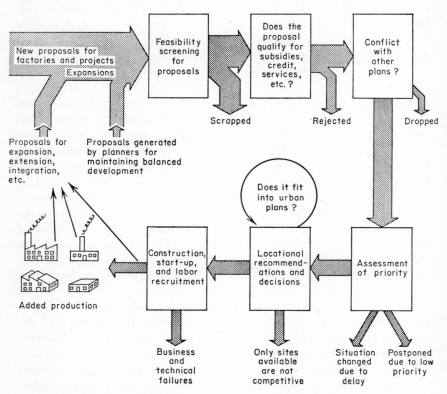

Figure 9. Routine administrative procedure for industrial planning.

products not on the list, considered quite improbable in the beginning, were also represented. The production units that could not be foreseen as suitable turned out to be, as a class, more stable and much more profitable than the others. Their wage scale was notably higher than the average for all industries. One may conclude from a careful analysis of Puerto Rican experience that there is a small chance that virtually *any* product can be manufactured in a newly developing area, and that the results obtained from the "improbable" opportunities, as discovered and developed by diligent salesmanship, are considerably greater than those from industries which can be scheduled and planned five years or so in advance.

The next step, that of screening for technical feasibility, would seek to answer questions of the following type: Are the utility services (such as water, power, fuel, transportation, communication, etc.) available or scheduled to be installed? Will suitable skills in the labor force, especially at the higher technical level, be available at a reasonably appropriate time? Is a regular flow of raw materials available? Would the local weather, corrosion conditions, or other limitations not widely publicized be capable of preventing successful manufacture? Can the proposed equipment and organization meet the competition over the middle run, or is it starting as an obsolescent organization? In case of a breakdown of the machinery would it be possible to obtain repair services quickly enough to keep the enterprise alive and profitable? Does the plant meet the minimum health and safety standards that have been established for the country (or the industry)? An experienced manufacturer is not likely to have overlooked these considerations, but miscalculations are not uncommon. Local entrepreneurs, being less experienced, are likely to make many more mistakes. Frequently the proposals are reformulated and resubmitted as a result of the queries made by the industrial promotion staff at this step.

The next appraisal covers legal and economic aspects. The major questions here are the following: Does the project qualify under the law for tax abatement and other incentives? Will any legal or administrative problems arise from relationships with other firms? Are any special concessions required (example: a waiving of regulations, such as occasional night-shift work for women)? How permanent is the operation in so far as this might be deduced from its capitalization, the markets for the product, or the processes to be used? Does it make unreasonable demands upon special services provided for industry, such as vocational education? If the operation is profitable, will the plant grow? All these factors—and quite a few others—determine the degree to which credit may be extended by the government to the enterprise. The limit might be much less than the enterprise needs to get started.

Following this legal appraisal, it is possible to discover whether or not the proposal conflicts with the programs set forth in the plans for other departments of government, specifically whether it fits into the structure of what the government can afford to provide in the way of services. If the project requires a more rapid development of educational services or health than has been scheduled in the general neighborhood of the proposed sites, this would be discovered in consultation with the planning commission staff. The physical and social plans would normally not affect run-of-the-mill industrial proposals, other than guiding the location decision, but they could affect those which are felt to be borderline cases.

Routine assessment of priority must be made initially on some very simple criterion. It might be based upon whatever is scarcest at the time in the national economy. For a country where the currency is weak, the fundamental criterion might be the number of new jobs created per unit of hard currency extended. (At one time, for Puerto Rico it was the number of new jobs provided per unit of internal public capital committed; later it became the net contribution to national income.) Beyond this basic criterion there may be substrategies for linking industrial installations, for encouraging growth industries to settle, or for providing basic industrial services, such as a dye plant for fabrics or electroplating for stamped metal parts, which would make it easier for entirely new kinds of industry to move into the territory. With relatively detailed information being provided by the firm, and established criteria for judgment supplied by the industrial planning unit, it is not too difficult for an organization to decide what priority should be given to a proposal.

Finally, a specific site must be found for the project. It should fit into the general land-use plans prepared for the regions and the cities. In the initial stages of industrialization there are very few high-priority land uses that could conflict. However, situations can be imagined where a "waterfront" industry discovers that all the metropolitan land in the proximity of the harbor has been allocated to high-valued activities, in which case the alternative locations available are not convenient enough to keep it from establishing elsewhere in the world instead. Similar problems may be encountered with resource-oriented industries. For example, the use of a hardwood forest may be reserved for a growing wood-fabrication industry and denied to a charcoal manufacturer aiming to use the same stand of trees, because the former promises to be a much higher valued use of the resource.

Even if a proposal had met all these tests successfully, there are some chances that it may be stillborn. Experience shows that the entrepreneur may, even while the operation is being set up, lose his prospective market, or his other activities may reduce his resources, or his trusted lieutenant who was to have been charged with starting the new enterprise may unexpectedly resign. These are exigencies which can affect projects of any dimension or priority.

PRODUCTIVITY STIMULI AND PROFITEERING CONTROLS

As has been emphasized earlier, this forced-draft approach to industrialization has a severe political weakness. It can be claimed, with real justification, that through it the government is subsidizing "outsiders." If the latter are successful and remain in business, their profits give the appearance of exploitation of local labor. The loyal opposition, with support from local entrepreneurs and labor unions, is likely to characterize the program as a "sellout" to foreign interests. A special hazard is that in the early stages of a program for industrialization the small population actually employed in new factories—and presumably grateful to an administration which expedited the creation of the jobs—can have little influence upon the way a vote would go, while resentment and suspicion are easily engendered in the population least likely to receive industrial jobs. Therefore the program could be a net political liability for the party in power.

A unique means for countering these natural suspicions was found by the Puerto Ricans. They have created a minimum wage board which investigates evidence regarding profits, costs of living, productivity, and related matters. It is empowered to set differential minimum wages industry by industry, so long as they do not exceed the minimum in the United States ($1.25 per hour at this writing). Since all firms obtaining tax remissions from the government are required to submit full and detailed annual reports, it is relatively easy to discern when an industry is becoming abnormally profitable. If the investigation shows that the high profits are not of a "windfall" nature but may be expected to continue, the board raises the minimum wage to a level for the industry so that the expectation of profit is slightly less than what is earned in the United States. The firms so affected may protest and appeal the decision; a few will threaten to move elsewhere, but the fact is that the new wage level still permits a reasonable profit to the entrepreneur—more than he would obtain elsewhere after subtracting moving costs. The industrial executive's attention is thus turned to improving worker selection and worker productivity as a means of increasing profit. If important increases in productivity are brought about in less than a year or two, the firm is permitted to retain the extra profits. Thus, through superior management, firms can stay ahead of the minimum wage board and make substantially higher profits than would have been made on the United States mainland.

This scheme has many outstanding advantages. It assures a judicial fairness which demolishes the arguments of the political opposition; it concentrates the impact of the industrialization upon working-class levels of living, leading to a broad distribution of the new income; and it encourages good management and techniques for increasing productivity in a way that no amount of editorializing could. Yet it still does not work as well as it might. Its research is occasionally deficient, and many specialists whom the board is forced to use for its varied activities do not have a clear view of its function. When mistakes are made some businesses fail, and new prospects are prematurely discouraged.

In other countries similar devices must be worked out. Most countries are likely to have stronger labor unions than were present in Puerto Rico at the beginning of its industrialization program, and the labor union leaders (who are often also political figures) must be satisfied as to the fairness of any scheme adopted. Where the unions are powerful, there is a tendency to elevate wage demands even more rapidly than labor productivity, so that the manufacturer finds himself in a precarious position, usually depending upon short-range measures and seldom in a position to expand.

Also, each country will have totally different legal, political, and informational requirements for the necessary industrial wage arbitration agency. It is not possible to generalize about the appropriate structure. However, if wage-arbitration machinery is to serve as an adjunct to the industrialization process, whatever the structure, the agency must be preoccupied with the enhancement of labor productivity rather than the meting out of social justice. This is not to say that it should abandon justice as a criterion in its deliberations, but only that the social value of higher incomes be given precedence over the righting of ancient wrongs when making commitments.

One way to tip the scales in favor of growth is to assure that suitable wage data are at hand and widely discussed. Studies of wage differentials within industry reveal that workers themselves feel that the size of the pay packet should reflect the degree of responsibility and skill undertaken by the worker. Skill levels in jobs that can be treated as piecework can be compared to equivalent factories in developed countries. It is not at all unusual for plants with relatively simple technology (although the products themselves may be very modern, such as electronics) to surpass European productivity levels within a year and approach American levels a year or two later, when labor productivity is calculated as physical units of a given standard per unit of work time. Therefore, close attention must be paid to worker productivity in competing parts of the world and the findings should be publicized. This information may offset the tendency toward local comparisons which arouse labor dissatisfaction. Instead of comparing one's wage and responsibilities with those of, say, dock workers, who are often able (owing to their cohesion and crucial role) to gain abnormally high hourly earnings in a developing economy, the unionized industrial worker can make more relevant comparisons. Increased knowledge can reduce the *likelihood* of labor conflicts, but it does not reduce the need for tact and skill in arbitration.

STIMULATING LOCAL INDUSTRY

Certain technologies—such as portland-cement manufacture, electric-power generation, telecommunications, and road hauling—introduce such large economies, or induce such an accelerating demand, that profitable operations can be quickly achieved. Moreover, special features inherent in these technologies force the entrepreneur to innovate continuously in his own market.

These industries are important because their repercussions are extensive. Cement is necessary for low-cost roads, bridges, harbors, and urban dwellings; it revolutionizes the construction industry. Electric power brings with it light in the evenings—an incentive for literacy—also radios, refrigerators, washing machines, and television sets; it is a prerequisite for flexible and efficient factory operation. Telecommunications save time used up by people in moving about and hasten the modernization and urbanization of the society.

Some curious consequences of the introduction of these industries have been observed. They do *not*, for example, increase manufacturing employment; the cottage industries and artisans' workshops in particular will be reduced in number. What they do is effect a *net* transfer of employment to a high-productivity sector. Thus, the introduction of successful locally operated modern industries implies a high rate of going out of business in the technologically obsolescent sector and, what may be equally significant, a reduced rate of small business formation in traditional activities.

The incentives used by governments for promoting locally owned modern industries include protective tariffs, monopoly franchises, technical assistance, credit, subsidies, etc. Because of the political protest that threatens in the event of cancellation, few governments are in a position to reduce the assistance, once the firms have grown to a competitive size. On the other hand, if such enterprises run into difficulty, they ask for more government help. Therefore the government very often becomes a partner, either formally or informally, in the larger local enterprises.

Canning plants and food processors have a different history. As independent units they must bear double risks, those from weather, insects, etc., as they apply to the commercial farmer, as well as changes in taste among consumers, as incurred by marketing organizations. The bankruptcy rate is high, and even when successful, the profits are seldom very high. Occasionally a food product finds a place in the world market and the returns to the industry are very striking for a while. This is more likely to occur when the processing is based upon an export commodity and the stimulus for manufacture comes from the market. Alcoholic beverages, condensed frozen fruit juices, and powdered coffee offer three recent examples where the technology is quickly taken up by local entrepreneurs.

There are a few instances each year, which should come to the attention of the industrial promotion unit, wherein entrepreneurial groups knowing the market overseas can be combined with local groups who know the raw materials, the labor force, and the requisite services at home. The industrial promotion agency may then use its economic research staff, its contacts with credit sources, and all similar capacities to increase the chances that these mutual arrangements will be consummated.

Some proposals have been made repeatedly which have never worked out well in practice during the first stages of industrialization. For example, an overseas marketing organization can be created to develop markets for products in the high-income countries of the world. Designs and product formulations might be found, through working with some local entrepreneurs, which should fill the taste requirements of these overseas markets. For this to be done successfully many of the persons employed by the marketing organizations must be specialists living in the importing countries. These attempts to develop manufactures for export to modern countries have had moderate success in the case of alcoholic beverages, but they have almost uniformly failed in the area of processed food products, clothing, toys, etc.

Multiproduct market development organizations have recently been successfully created for the manufactures of Great Britain, Italy, Japan, and other countries with extensive lines of high-grade and high-volume manufacture. The overhead costs are known to be very large. No one has produced a formula whereby marketing tests can be made on only a few new products per year and still keep unit costs within reasonable limits, although the Philippines has been fortunate enough to have a private agency of this type evolve, and Indian manufacturers appear to be making some headway.

Introducing new manufactured products into North America or Western Europe requires a high degree of sophistication about methods of distribution in these areas, some of which can be learned from industrial promotion, but the remainder must be purchased by retaining specialist firms. It also implies the existence of a series of supporting services close to the point of manufacture. An industrial design center is essential and often also a development laboratory or shop. A pool of master technicians is also required at this phase; otherwise the prototypes and samples produced lack "finish" and are difficult to promote. A source of risk capital must also be available, preferably in the form of a securities market, and economic research of a variety that is able to minimize the risk must also be present. In addition the organizational framework requires a considerable pool of local entrepreneurs eager to "graduate to the major leagues." (The latter condition is hardly evident in Puerto Rico more than a dozen years after its industrialization program began, but the risk of setting up a market development organization has been greatly reduced by the presence of hundreds of imported entrepreneurs who presumably would be encouraged to use its services.) Finally, once a product has gained acceptance in a foreign market, it must be expanded and defended against competition. Constant review is necessary concerning raw material supply, quality control, manufacturing shortcuts, waste utilization, design variations and styling, inventory control, factoring of accounts receivable, advertising programs, labor relations, etc. The more promising local entrepreneurs should be continually prodded and never allowed to rest upon their laurels.

It is often good politics to make a very strong effort at exporting the product of the cottage industries and the traditional work of artisans. Strong nationalists almost always approve of such a policy. At the same time there has been increasing willingness on the part of the buyers for department stores and specialty shops in the world's metropolitan centers to purchase and promote folk arts, as long as the quality control is effective at home and shoddy products do not reach the retailers. The marketing effort usually costs more than the original value of the output from the cottage industries. However, if such an effort is mounted, the additional costs of promoting foreign markets for new factories are quite reasonable, even if they are sold to quite a different set of buyers. This is so because the overhead costs of international travel and maintaining offices in several major cities make up a large share of the total costs. Obviously this kind of marketing is very chancy because fads and fashions shift rapidly in the world's capital cities; if a choice is possible it should be undertaken only at the later stages of industrialization. Risks can be reduced to reasonable levels only when an organization experienced in maintaining and developing international business contacts is available.

ORGANIZATION AND STAFFING

On the basis of the foregoing discussion, the formal organization chart acquires some structure. It may be diagramed initially as on page 214. It is a highly centralized form of organization, since all departments and the consultants report directly to the executive director. This is necessary because the organization must be capable of concerted action on a moment's notice. At the same time it is obvious that the executive director must have the freedom to act, without consultation or review from higher authority, on all matters except those affecting basic policies of the government. On matters concerning expenditure and investment it is advisable that he should be given a discretionary limit larger than would be required for a single routine industrial commitment, say,

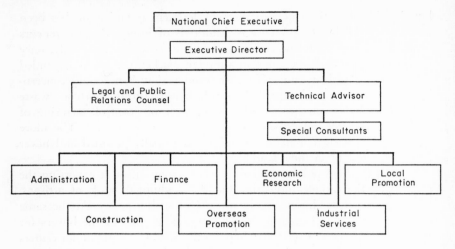

$300,000. The executive director and the corporation would be held accountable, with minor reservations, for the speed and economy with which results are achieved.

As already indicated, the critical appointment is that of the executive director. He should have qualities of integrity, leadership, and dedication—this is a key cabinet-level post which should attract persons with these capacities. His background should be of a sort which would gain the confidence and respect of the business community. More often than not he would be drawn from the ranks of the businessmen. For this job he would need boundless energy and enthusiasm and, along with it, a willingness to persevere despite serious disappointments and reverses.

If the executive director is drawn from business, his technical adviser must have experience in planning and economic analysis; oppositely, if the former were a politician or civil servant, the technical adviser should have a background in industrial organization and promotion. Over the first decade or so of the industrial development program the technical adviser would very likely be a top international consultant, preferably a citizen also. He would be the natural person to take responsibility for relations with other consultants brought in from the outside. Many of these other consultants would be assigned positions as *alter egos* for the division heads or their staff.

The public relations counsel acts as a contact with the foreign public relations firm that is necessary to overseas industry promotion. He must also assemble information on unwanted social changes brought about by the program, based to a large extent upon the nature of the resulting protests. The legal counsel must have at least a background in corporation law, tax law, and contracts. In many societies the public relations role can be joined with the function of legal counsel during the first stages of industrialization.

The director of overseas promotion should have had some practical experience in promotion of new activities. It is difficult to find anyone who has acquired experience in industrial promotion in underdeveloped areas, so that experience in the promotion of almost any kind of organized business-type activity serves as the best possible substitute.

The director of economic research should be a *practicing* economist, as distinct from a theoretician. This man should have had broad government, corporate, or consulting experience before taking the post. If the country has an important resource base or market crop, one of the first additions to the economic research staff would be an economist specializing in such subject matter, because these economic activities could serve as one of the major sources of capital, either immediately or in prospect.

The director of administration must be an expediter. He would handle budgets, accounts, personnel, office building, space allocation, and the various services necessary to speedy action. The first to build up a sizable staff, he would do well to have consultants during the early period when procedures for communication (e.g., accounting, mailing, filing) are worked out, but after that he would operate more independently of outside help than any of the other directors.

These five or six men would constitute the initial team. They would find it necessary to spend their first few months in almost continuous conference while working out a strategy for operations. The particular strategy chosen must be appropriate to the resources available, to the opportunities beckoning, to the expected competition from other countries, and yet one that is compatible with the political situation within the particular country. Once the plan of action has been mapped out, the expansion of the staff can proceed.

Thereafter industrial promotion officers—young men with legal, economics, or business training, who act as liaison men for specific cases—would be selected and trained. From among this crew it is possible that directors for industrial services and local promotion will be found by the time they become necessary. A land-use planner could be retained to identify the most promising factory sites. A contract could be let with an enterprising architectural firm for the design of a standard factory building. The permanent headquarters for the organization could be selected. The advertising program could begin in a modest way.

The director of construction would be hired at about the time that a decision is made to start building factories. He would probably need to be a qualified civil engineer. His first job would be to supervise construction and to introduce measures for the efficient maintenance of the property. Later on he would encounter such varied projects as hotels, harbors, airports, etc.

The director of finance would need to be added to the staff at the same time because it would be his responsibility to supervise financial commitments. As the number of prospects increases, he would be drawn more into the problem of finding alternative means for financing the investments made in the factory buildings, the needed services, and the industries themselves.

The director of local promotion needs to be an alert politician more than anything else. There are many traps for the unwary in this area which would greatly diminish the effectiveness of the industrial development corporation. His appointment might well depend upon his competence for some specific internal projects that required promotion work.

The directors and their staff must be very highly paid, by government standards, if for no other reason than that successfully launched enterprises will often make very liberal offers to the personnel of the industrial development agency in order to attract them to managerial positions in the firm. As discussed earlier, some transfer is desirable so that high standards for management are established, but there must be sufficient flexibility in salary schedules to hold a man if he is critically needed. In many countries this freedom may require that the industrial development corporation operate outside of civil service (in order to escape from salary precedents), or else be willing to classify the key man as a "consultant on long-term contract." The high pay, and the chances for participating in comparatively advance constructive work in the public interest, should attract the most competent young men in the society and assist the industrial development organization in becoming a prestige agency in the government.

BIBLIOGRAPHY

Bryce, Murray D.: *Industrial Development: A Guide for Accelerating Economic Growth,* McGraw-Hill Book Company, New York, 1960.
  Elementary background for the preparation and evaluation of industrial projects that is useful for both multinational firms and civil servants.

Galbraith, J. Kenneth, and R. H. Holton, *Marketing Efficiency in Puerto Rico,* Harvard University Press, Cambridge, Mass., 1955.
  A study of entrepreneurial conditions in the distributive services before industrialization had brought about major changes. The implications of governmental action are analyzed.

Hagen, E. E.: *Handbook for Industry,* The Free Press of Glencoe, New York, 1958.

A handbook for making industry studies, particularly in less developed areas. Contains a checklist of points to be covered that are of interest in various aspects of developmental planning. Intended to prevent the need for repeated studies of the same industries.

"The Mezzogiorno," *Fortune,* vol. 117, pp. 51–74, May, 1963.
A pace-setting advertising portfolio on the Italian south that portrays uncritically the methods employed for promoting its industrialization.

National Planning Association, Studies on Business Performance Abroad: 1, *Sears, Roebuck de México, S.A.,* 1953; 2, *Casa Grace in Peru,* 1954; 3, *The Philippine-American Life Insurance Co.,* 1955; 4, *The Creole Petroleum Corporation in Venezuela,* 1955; 5, *The Firestone Operations in Liberia,* 1956; 6, *Stanvac in Indonesia,* 1957; 7, *The United Fruit Company in Latin America,* 1958; 8, *TWA's Services to Ethiopia,* 1959; 9, *The General Electric Company in Brazil,* 1961; 10, *IBM in France,* 1962, Washington, D.C.
This series of monographs was developed primarily to discover what "enlightened" policies and procedures seem to be effective for the international firms in their operations overseas.

Spengler, J. J.: "Public Bureaucracy, Resource Structure and Economic Development: A Note," *Kyklos,* vol. 11, pp. 459–489, 1958.
A useful evaluation from the point of view of recent economic history.

9

THE HUMAN FACTOR IN
INDUSTRIAL DEVELOPMENT

A NEW ADMINISTRATION for promoting industry spends more time analyzing its failures to attract new industries than it does its successes. The failures being more frequent, they offer fruitful suggestions for action by government.

One of the most common, and also most frustrating, responses of industrialists, upon being asked why they could not set up manufacturing in a given region, is that the "industrial climate" did not exist. Workers were not experienced and communities not conditioned to the kind of discipline that is required to operate modern technology. What can one do to create an industrial climate without first installing industry?

Further discussions with industrialists reveal the specific attitudes and behavior patterns that are needed to compete with enterprises elsewhere in the world. One of these is a respect for the clock, which includes being on time for work and a willingness to keep commitments to complete a task within a given interval of time. Another is the acceptance of responsibility for machines, to oil, grease, clean, and adjust them, and to report to the maintenance men whenever they seem to need other than routine care. Still another is a willingness to take safety precautions when working with machinery. The list could be extended to include many more such items that apply to particular industries.

The history of each industrial revolution shows that complaints about shortcomings in these behaviors have been voiced over and over again, first in the eighteenth century in Scotland and England, again in the nineteenth century in Germany and the United States, and in the twentieth century in Japan and the Soviet Union. They seem to be an inevitable feature of the transition to a modern civilization.

When the industrial development has been initiated, an industrial climate of sorts first takes hold in certain favored suburbs or outlying neighborhoods of the growing metropolitan area. At accessible points around the periphery of the city a series of service institutions spring up, such as machine shops, welding establishments, cartage and drayage firms, docks or railroad sidings, multiple-purpose warehouses, distributors for international firms who either carry spare parts or can get them on short notice, job printers and lithographers, packaging suppliers, etc. These facilities are developed opportunistically, mostly by small local entrepreneurs with very limited capital, so that exceedingly mixed types of structures will coexist in the same neighborhood. The most promising locales will give the appearance of a confused jumble of activities, but more detailed study will show that these industrial slums are important training centers, where apprentices from the poorest classes are taken on informally and the brightest of them move either into higher-status activities (usually after acquiring some extra formal education) or set up in business for themselves.

These urban foci with industrial climate need to be cultivated, and their futures planned. The evolution of such areas in Western countries has shown that they often stifle themselves. Some tend to be strangled by their salvage operations. Collection of old metal is necessary to the establishment and continued operation of foundries, of wastepaper for packaging products, of rags for low-grade weaving operations; worn-out engines are left around to supply spare parts for the repair shops. Over time, however, the lowest-grade junk tends to accumulate and makes the land unavailable for expansions. Other nuisances also multiply. The typical sources of urban blight include the air pollutants, odors, fumes, smoke, and dust. While each operation in itself usually stays within the bounds of human tolerance, the sum of their wastes may easily exceed the limits set by public health requirements or the human senses. Strictly applied land controls are necessary to maintain the health of such communities, but this control is not as simple as it sounds.

City planners find, moreover, that as soon as they designate certain sites in a metropolitan area as suitable places for programs of urban renewal, which involve among other things the removal of nuisance-type activities, the residents almost always voice strong objections. Often a few of the affected landowners have political connections which they use to postpone action on urban renewal.

CREATING THE INDUSTRIAL CLIMATE

Judicious planning of these industrial areas at the start, to prevent overcrowding and junk accumulation, enables the adjoining residential areas to survive and provide an increasingly skilled labor supply. Communities of this sort tend to create their own "uplift movement" as incomes increase and the dwellings are improved. While such foci for smaller industries can never become beautiful, they can at least establish a character which people will respect. To bring this about, the communities request the assistance of various government agencies. Water supply and sewers are common needs, and access for trucks is another. It is one of the duties of an industrial promotion unit to stimulate and coordinate this self-help process and thereby propagate the industrial climate that small entrepreneurs need.

Simultaneously, several neat, orderly industrial estates should be laid out in the more spacious suburban areas. Consistently modern standards for productivity and organization are maintained in these plants. The industrial estates therefore represent a union of two industrial communities: the managerial element with the capital and the market contacts frequently comes from the outside, while the technicians and the skilled operatives more likely than not will be "graduated" from the local industrial communities such as those described above. The industrial estates are responsible for accelerating the spread of the industrial climate that is necessary for the survival of many advanced forms of industry.

Once a number of the residential suburbs have acquired industry and the wage level has begun to rise, it is possible to persuade other factories to move into the countryside without special subsidies. The principal aims of the most venturesome group of industries are to exploit localized resources or to take advantage of lower labor costs. When most of the towns in the immediate hinterland of a city have a factory or two of their own, it may safely be said that an industrial climate has been achieved by that metropolitan area. In Puerto Rico this transformation was compressed into seven to eight years for San Juan, and about ten years for Ponce, a smaller city on the other side of the island.

Part of the industrial climate that is sought must be created in the center of the city where the white-collar specialties abound. Much of the business of such firms is conducted in hotels, clubs, coffee shops, restaurants, and offices. For these activities a few key facilities need to be provided (or guaranteed) initially by the government, but after that the local real estate speculators may be expected to install adequate capacity. The industrial climate in the urban core is really one aspect of the *business* climate, and the affairs of manufacturers are often intermingled with the other aspects (finance, foreign trade, retailing, real estate, publishing, etc.). In the course of industrialization the downtown areas of the city also become a vast training ground. Much of the training is of a formal nature, with diplomas given in recognition of skills acquired up to a specified standard (cost accounting and drafting provide two good examples); most of the training in the marketing of manufactured products, however, goes on inside the firms themselves.

The industrial components of the metropolitan core seldom decentralize of their own volition. As they grow more complex, they induce the creation of more and more small service activities which cannot move out to the suburbs or satellite towns with the head offices. Without them the head offices cannot function at peak efficiency. A common means for reducing the inefficiency in the downtown areas brought about by congestion is to mechanize office services and improve the various communications systems. Mechanization of these activities requires a greater variety of specialists, trained to a higher level of skill and working in relatively comfortable and uncrowded environments. Entrepreneurs can assemble the various factors of production with less delay in a well-serviced central business district.

Various indications of the lack of "industrial climate" are a source of both amusement and annoyance to managers, but the *previous* absence of such an environment has also been shown to be a considerable asset. The lack of a traditional working pace for various jobs means that almost any factory can, within a year or so, reach physical productivity levels higher than the average for any area of Western Europe which has been in that business for half a century, all other things being equal (this is still usually less than for the best by a substantial margin). Furthermore, in any community which has developed a manufacturing specialization over a period of decades, certain work standards and limits to daily production have been set by the workers—often by unspoken agreement; these are passed on from the old workers to the new workers and so become an institutional part of factory life. Whenever factories in the same or similar lines are subsequently located nearby, these work standards tend to be transferred; but if such a factory is established in a different region, using a carefully picked staff for training, quite different work standards will develop. With careful management these workers can be led to a higher productive level than was previously achieved in that industry.

An important feature of the industries that resettle in new regions and countries is that they employ a predominantly female labor force. Women, even in advanced societies, have never been educated to work with machinery, so underdeveloped areas cannot be said to be disadvantaged with respect to labor force experience in these industries. At the same time, the male workers in many areas already have obtained some elementary experience with machines. An important share of commercial agriculture, for example, has been mechanized. Sugar, cocoa, bananas, and copra growing and processing have introduced machinery at key points. Trucks and buses have penetrated to all the market towns and many villages. Radios and jukeboxes have been introduced into most villages. The repair and maintenance of this equipment is mainly done by local men. Schools tend to reinforce these experiences by providing more scientific explanations for mechanical behavior than would otherwise be imparted through apprenticeship. Therefore underdeveloped areas today should be able to take up light manufacturing much more quickly than most of the presently developed countries could at the beginning of their industrial revolution.

The principal difficulty for the industrialization efforts is that the experience with mechanical equipment is neither uniform nor consistent. There are very few clues accessible in a worker's experience which give assurance that he has mastered any specific concept. Certain elementary principles seem to have been overlooked at the same time that surprisingly advanced concepts have taken hold. The employer cannot depend upon a customary standard of comprehension and experience in a given class of workers, as in North America or Europe, because the institutions which instill these qualifications are still new, incomplete, and in the process of transformation themselves. In any sample of the labor force that a factory manager is likely to encounter, he will discover instances of surprisingly high competence mixed with ordinary and incredibly ineffectual capacities. (He is likely to consider finding the few extraordinarily good people to be a matter of good luck, and to complain about the poor quality of the remainder of his work force.) Once the workers are screened through personnel tests, school records, and previous work experience, a factory organizer can plan his work more carefully and achieve much higher productivity.

ROLE OF MANAGEMENT COMPETENCE AND TRAINING

In general, successful competition in the international market will depend very little upon workers' backgrounds as long as they have had six to ten years of schooling, but will depend almost entirely upon the skill of the manager. These plants in Puerto Rico, Mexico, the Mezzogiorno, and elsewhere have managed to exceed United States productivity levels (on a physical-units-per-day basis) by using the same careful considerations of worker convenience and morale as are used in industrially advanced areas. This happens despite the fact that their workers are drawn from the same sources, and work in the same locales, as other managers in other industries who feel lucky to reach 60 percent of United States productivity norms.

By changing the emphasis from the experience of the worker with machinery to the experience of the manager with the worker-machine relationship, the problem of pushing up productivity is made more tractable. It would take a full generation before many of the cultural programs intended to promote an "industrial climate" (such as science-and-industry museums, construction toys, tool kits, build-it-yourself projects, and general science films) could be felt. But managers are in a position to respond more quickly—particularly if, by their own standards, their initial efforts are only partially successful. Furthermore, providing a general background education for all potential industrial workers is an expensive and haphazard procedure as compared with the development of a cadre of professional managers. Such a group could learn quickly how to make allowances for the deficiencies of the local labor force while at the same time utilizing to best advantage its diligence and willingness to learn. By this change in focus of attention, a mountain has not been transformed into a molehill, but at least the barriers to industrial development are made easier to negotiate.

For every 1,000 industrial workers anticipated a generation hence, about 50 managers will be required. This does not include foremen, group leaders, supervisors, or other responsible persons who work on the fringe of managerial circles. The proportion of managers is high because it is expected that most of the new industry will take the form of many branch firms and scattered small factories.

A predominant share of the managers will eventually need college training. This educational requirement will probably be more important in countries employing programs similar to the Puerto Rican technique for industrialization than it has been in the past in the older manufacturing areas. The manager and his staff must act as a bridge between a technology which is 99 percent recorded in technical English (or some other European language) and work patterns which are organized in the local idiom. These circumstances require a greater facility for communication on the part of the manager than in developed countries. The acquisition of communication skills, especially for technical subject matter, is probably the most important single contribution of a college education.

If they are to compete successfully in the international market, the managers will need more than a college training in accounting, engineering, industrial psychology, labor relations, or business administration. They will need also a readily accessible reservoir of information (based on accumulating local experience) which would provide leads on how to deal with various management problems. All the minor *innovations* which, taken singly, have a barely perceptible effect upon improving worker productivity, stability of employment, or quality of product must be brought together and made readily available to the managers and to the "trouble shooters," who, as consultants, diagnose production difficulties and try to find solutions. Such information must also be fitted into teaching materials for special training courses which would be offered to managers due for promotion. In other words, there must be a *center* for propagating the "lore" of management, as it pertains particularly to the local environment. This center would also encourage experiments which would endeavor to confirm and extend studies done elsewhere on managerial problems.

A great deal of attention must be paid to the channels of recruitment for managers. Their jobs require a high level of intelligence; hence recruitment in its earliest stages depends heavily upon the educational system, first for discovering youngsters with good minds, and then for the training which is provided for them. The cadre of managerial talent cannot be drawn from any one division of the university, or of the business world, or from any one stratum of society, because of the variety of the tasks to be performed and the large number of managers required.

Managers in the more technical industries (such as electronics, vehicles, and chemical processing) are likely to be drawn from the engineering staffs of the international firms. Another important source of managers is to be found among the locally trained technicians and engineering aides. They might be developed first into foremen, and then later into managers, usually for small firms. These men, like the engineers, are likely to gain from formal training in successful management methods.

The business administration, labor relations, and other specialists from the local colleges that are trained for business, if they are at all available, tend to gravitate to the larger firms and government corporations. Once in such firms, they need management courses less, because improved methods of handling the labor force are already part of the established company policy, and the company executives make sure that the policies are understood and implemented.

Perhaps the most surprising source of managers is the law profession. In Puerto Rico, as in many nonindustrial countries, a large fraction of the ambitious and intelligent young men choose law, even if there is known to be a surplus of law graduates. Because politics always offers an interesting alternative to a desultory law practice, the law profession continues to attract a stream of excellent minds. In the course of economic development, it is not unexpected that some of these would be diverted to the establishment of new industry and to the higher-salaried jobs in those firms, often transferring from government operating agencies.

In Puerto Rico a very common intermediate step in the career line to management has been the post of industrial promotion officer with the Fomento. Several years' experience working with entrepreneurs, with whom the industrial promotion office is collaborating for the establishment of new industry, seems to be excellent training for management. It does one other thing which can be invaluable to the society: as an industrial promotion officer the recent university graduate is trained to compute in economic and social terms what kinds of action are best suited to the public interest. After he becomes a manager, there is evidence to show that these lessons are not forgotten—he continues to act with wisdom in the public interest wherever the interests of his firm are neutral. *Under these circumstances a high degree of cooperation between government and private enterprise can be maintained.*

The problem of managers has been reviewed in a matter-of-fact fashion. Actually it is the greatest barrier of all which is likely to stand in the way of industrialization. For the first generation at least, managers are going to be so scarce that they will have to be steadily imported from the developed countries—where they are also scarce. The availability of managers is likely, in fact, to be rate-determining in economic development once the requisite capital is at hand. (Indeed, there probably will never be a surplus of managers in Puerto Rico, for example, because of the tremendous unsatisfied demand that exists in Latin America. The high salaries available elsewhere, in closely related cultures, for managers of proved competence will probably drain off an important number of them as the supply increases. This is not wholly disadvantageous because new markets are opened up by these managers, and thereby trade is not only increased but also diversified.)

Despite the shortages of key personnel, it is rather remarkable how rapidly local personnel can take over the posts of chief officers in charge of industrial installations in a society committed to mass education. After a decade of accelerated growth in Puerto Rico, about half the installations were run by Puerto Ricans. A few are actually executives, but the great majority function as plant managers. It is true that the larger factories, judged either by employment or capitalization, are more frequently operated by persons brought in from the outside, but even among them perhaps a quarter are run by Puerto Ricans. This is a strikingly rapid transition, considering that 90 percent of the enterprises were started with the aid of outside know-how and overseas capital, and no laws had been passed discriminating against foreign managers.

ENLISTING ENTREPRENEURS

The initiators of enterprises, being founders of new organizations, are frequently viewed as "first causes" in social and economic growth, and they have thus excited a considerable amount of attention on the part of investigators over the past several decades. Often, it is claimed, the crucial limitation upon development is a shortage of risk-taking organizers of new social units independent of the household. If that is the case, one asks how entrepreneurs may be created, discovered, or identified before they have actually succeeded.

An educational system has never been established which produces entrepreneurs in a manner similar to engineers or schoolteachers. Nor are there any well-founded claims that entrepreneurs can be trained, in the way that managers and executives are trained. Indeed, many members of business college faculties are convinced that formal education inhibits individual enterprise; it reduces willingness to take calculated risks. Therefore no set of practices for developing industrial entrepreneurs, or any other type of entrepreneur, can be said to exist. A national policy that calls for more entrepreneurial activity must draw upon observation, plausible argument, and the new hypotheses that merit investigation.

Entrepreneurs, it appears, are created by family background more than anything else. Childhood development in an environment where proposals for enterprise are continually discussed and analyzed is likely to lead to some sophistication in identifying opportunities and exploiting their possibilities. When the first earnings of the individual so brought up are obtained from a small unit, where the factors affecting its survival are visible to all employees, the early susceptibilities are likely to be confirmed. Most of the ethnic entrepreneurs that have already been mentioned—the Chinese, the Levantines, the Jews, the Greeks, the Arabs, the overseas Hindus, and others—appear to produce a high frequency of entrepreneurial personalities for this reason. The number of shopkeepers, small businessmen, scroungers, and manipulators in a few locales, therefore, is in oversupply, and the resultant cutthroat competition can be as detrimental to economic development as an insufficiency. In Athens, for example, being in business for oneself carries so much prestige that many people will accept cuts in hourly earnings of a third or more, plus risk of family capital, in order to operate a firm of their own. As a result, it is rarely possible for any business to achieve a size which enables it to employ the technologies with marked economies of scale. Therefore costs of distribution remain high.

In any society where the scarcity of entrepreneurs becomes an issue for governmental consideration, the amount of social change must already be great enough to be evident to everyone in the society. A plural society has come into existence, and at least one modern culture is included in the mix. Thus the transitional society introduced in Chapter 2 provides the most suitable background for discussing a search for entrepreneurs.

In the transitional society the founders of new enterprise—the *de facto* entrepreneurs who must be differentiated from the potential variety—are found in all social classes. Those in the lowest strata have little to lose beyond their own time; entrepreneurship for them involves producing or finding things that may be disposed of in the marketplace. Most of the organizations created by such people, outside of marginal farms and fishing, are concerned with the distribution of goods and services. The peddlers who establish their own routes, for instance, are entrepreneurs who come from households very close to the bottom of the social ladder. Their organizations seldom exceed four people.

At intermediate status levels in such societies one finds entrepreneurial artisans as well as white-collar workers. Artisans start up in the traditional sector, but are most likely to meet with success when supplying a need that has multiplied as a consequence of the rapid growth of the modern sector. White-collar types have acquired the biases of modern society; they often adapt a modern product or service to the local needs; their ideas about the proper means for hiring employees, acquiring raw materials, and maintaining relationships with clients will often break with tradition. A successful artisan entrepreneur finds it very difficult to assemble more than ten apprentices, journeymen, and unskilled helpers because the traditional social obligations become so burdensome, while the white-collar type not infrequently builds up organizations including scores, even hundreds, of individuals. The capacity to spend more of his time communicating enables even the poor but hardworking white-collar organization builder to create sizable enterprises.

At the upper-middle level in social status one finds proprietors, merchants, and the lesser professions, such as teachers, accountants, and engineers, who sometimes begin modern industrial enterprises. They are the kind most influenced by the measures aimed at promoting locally owned and operated industries discussed at the end of Chapter 6.

In the upper classes, it seems, one can often identify a few figures who have made the transition from major landholder, or a leading merchant, to becoming a large-scale enterpriser in manufacturing, or modern merchandising. Very often the entrepreneur starts as a rebellious young man from a wealthy tradition-oriented family who could make a leap into the modern technologies because through his family he was able to obtain a university education outside his own country. He is intent upon being his own boss and has the financial resources which permit him to think in large terms.

This *post hoc* viewing of entrepreneurs who succeeded suggests quite another influence of family upon the choice of activity and the scale of operations. Again we can draw upon Puerto Rico for examples, and demonstrate explicitly the role that such persons can play in industrialization.

Families which start with a well-run enterprise, and also have many sons, tend to branch out into new growth opportunities until each son has an activity of his own. Their home-nurtured insights are made more effective when a technological education is added. Integrated industrial and commercial complexes can be formed more easily when undertaken by such families. Spin-offs from the complex may be entrusted to sons-in-law, cousins, and trusted lieutenants.

At a relatively late stage in the promotion of industry, it may be possible to create a corporate organization with sufficient controls to prevent striving young employees from accumulating some capital from rebates and other questionable practices and then taking some of the best customers with them as they go into business themselves. This organization does not depend upon the discipline exerted through family ties, but creates group loyalties and professional standards in its responsible members that parallel those developed in the international corporation. This challenging opportunity requires an entrepreneur with tremendous drive who worked up to an executive position in an international firm before setting out on his own. Such individuals are readily identified and deserve wholehearted support of the industrial promotion agency. They are indispensable persons but not very lovable. It is to be hoped that they would accept the image of the millionaire that has been established by Carnegie, Rockefeller, and Nuffield, so that their capacity for creating organization could spill over into the support of new cultural and welfare schemes in areas where government is ineffective.

To conclude this analysis, it appears that *the industrial promotion agency needs to keep a file on promising promoters and entrepreneurs.* How many close relatives do they have in and out of business? For what scale of operations are they best suited? What kinds of experience have they acquired thus far? As each opportunity for new enterprise comes to the attention of the agency, it should be able to enlist one of them and provide suitable assistance. Without such an active file the small- to medium-size opportunities would often go to outsiders by default or disappear altogether without benefiting the economy.

RECRUITING TECHNICAL PERSONNEL

In the estimation of the operator-owners, obtaining credit seems to be the gravest difficulty for small factories. From the standpoint of an outside analyst, however, the gravest deficiency in enterprises originating from within the developing society is the lack of technical personnel. Local firms seem to be far more vulnerable to technological change than equivalent-sized immigrant firms.

A supply of technologists is indispensable to the modernization process. If the developed section of the industrializing economy is to expand steadily by 10 to 20 percent per year—a range that is quite feasible for the period of exponential growth—the number of persons admitted to the skilled trades (electricians, machinists, toolmakers, etc.) and the supply of technicians (draftsmen, engineering aides, chemical analysts, cost accountants, etc.) must increase almost as rapidly. Thus over a decade the quantity of technical personnel must be increased by two to five times. These rough approximations are introduced mainly to indicate the amount of pressure placed upon the institutions responsible for their training. Perhaps 20 percent of the industrial labor force in the long run must fit into these categories, a fraction smaller than that in Western Europe mainly because the earlier scarcities force a choice of technologies which economize on these skills.

Rough estimates of the technicians needed in the next few years can be prepared by comparing the enrollment at the colleges with the "help wanted" advertisements and the list of industries negotiating for plants. The severest shortages in Puerto Rican development, for instance, appeared to be as follows:

Electronics and television operating engineers
Surveyors
Refrigeration and air-conditioning engineers
Engineering draftsmen
Aircraft maintenance specialists
Internal combustion engine operating engineers
Chemical analysts
Communications-instruments technicians

Total cost to the society for providing such specialized skill and training will run from $1,000 to $5,000 per person trained. At the present time this cost is borne partly by parents who provide board, room, and incidentals; partly by the learners themselves, particularly if they take night courses; partly by the firms that pay more in wages than the trainee's labor is worth; and the largest portion by the government. As more and more children of the very poor are being brought into the higher ranks of the labor force, the expense ordinarily borne by parents usually will fall upon the government. As time goes on, therefore, fewer of the costs will be hidden and more will show up in the governmental and industrial accounting. Vocational education can become a major drain upon development funds.

A more feasible and equitable means for financing vocational education would be one where the cost would be charged to the individual who increases his earnings as a consequence of it. He would assign a certain fraction of his subsequent income, beyond subsistence, in repayment for his education. Accordingly, for anyone who does very well as a result of his education, his repayment is at least proportional to his gains. Paying for one's own education is taken for granted in commerce, for typists, business-machine operators, secretaries, etc. It is only justice that this tradition be extended to industry for at least the equivalent skills. Such a system of financing education would be extremely useful in training the poor but bright youngsters for the very essential trades and specialties, and it could even be extended later on to university-level education, particularly for scientists and engineers. (This scheme will be discussed in detail in Chapter 18.)

FIGURING THE NEEDS FOR SCIENCE

A newly industrializing area does not need the same proportion of engineers and scientists in its working population as is found in North America and Western Europe. This is because it is economical for the new society to engage in only the most practical forms of research and development. The only exception to this rule would be in those very rare instances where the appropriate studies are being neglected elsewhere in the world. The primary need for higher scientific and technical skills is for getting production started, and for maintaining output and quality levels once the plants are operating. Thus the resident scientists and engineers serve mostly as top-level "trouble shooters" in the more advanced technologies.

An industrial program that emphasizes a combination of light and medium industry in small establishments, with a subsequent admixture of some heavy industry, should plan for no more than two to three professional grade scientists and engineers per thousand industrial workers. This ratio is to be compared with 10 to 15 per thousand in North America. In developing regions, scientists and engineers are much more likely to work closely with nonprofessionals, and they often assume administrative, teaching, and other responsibilities as well. The suggested ratio assumes that the resource development problems are not unique, and the products scheduled for manufacturing are not based on local innovations.

The exceptional problems in industrialization associated with resource development, however, will merit some research effort, both at home and abroad. Research for agricultural industries, as for agriculture itself, will often have to be carried out in the heart of the regions specializing in food production and export crops. On the other hand, the exploration for mineral deposits and petroleum can be best done by contract with outside firms that are equipped to move ahead quickly with this work. Very little of the contingent work can then be done locally. Only if large quantities of low-grade reserves are discovered will much of the development-type investigations have to be carried on locally, either by government or interested firms, with close contacts being instituted with leading research centers in the world. These contacts would be equally necessary in development work being done for agricultural industries.

The need for international specialization, and the kinds of strategy involved in the choice of the specialization, will be taken up in Chapter 11. However, the impact of the research and development needs of these specializations upon the supply and demand for engineers and scientists cannot be overlooked here. In order to resolve the planning issues, it is necessary to pose the leading question: *What kinds of institutions can be created that will assure—within a decade—research and development in these specializations that is at least as advanced as any in the world?* Any aim less than this would be a waste of effort.

These institutions take many forms. The British, for example, have perfected a technique of government-industry collaboration in a series of "research associations," each with a laboratory of its own. In other countries it is common practice to set up an institute or department in a university which would endeavor to carry on work at the scientific level, while most of its trainees get jobs in the developmental stage production in the firms. This system works only when an extremely unusual man is available for the university post and has most of his career ahead of him. A third approach would use a research committee, staffed with liaison officers, making grants and contracts both at home and abroad to individuals and institutions. All approaches may be combined into a single program, and in larger countries it is probably best that the plan should be comprehensive in its attack on the research problem.

Note that at no point is the suggestion made that the government should assume complete responsibility for the research in a prestige specialization. Government-conducted research, in the United States and Europe at least, very often fails to get its findings utilized. Private industry is not inclined to use opportunities developed in government laboratories. This is partly because it is too difficult to get details which might make the difference between profit and loss, but in most instances it is because politics make it impossible to get a temporary monopoly—equivalent to the granting of patent rights—which the firm needs to reduce the risk inherent in innovation. Industry is different from agriculture, fisheries, and forestry in this respect. Although governments are very active in enterprises in most developing countries, it is difficult to find a single international specialization in manufacturing that was created by government initiative. Governments are usually drawn into business when existing enterprises are facing bankruptcy. Specialties, however, are usually created during economic upswings, when the economy is experiencing surges of private investment.

It is already apparent that much more money and effort will need to be expended upon pilot plant work, market research, and market development than upon the original scientific research. These developmental activities must be closely attached to production, preferably in the same firm or organization. The ability to compete successfully in the world market will depend much more upon the capacity to take advantage of new ideas quickly than upon the capacity to generate the ideas in the first place.

Another important reason can be advanced for starting up applied research in each area in which the economy specializes. Whatever the product, there will be substitutes or alternatives arising from research in the rest of the world which threaten to make the specialization obsolete. The first hints of these threats appear in the international engineering and scientific literature, and the only persons who can appraise the nature of the threat are technical people working on similar problems. Early recognition of the potential threat may lead to a reorientation of local research so as to prepare the local industry for the new source of competition. By such use of research, it is possible to remain for a long time a leader in a field of specialization.

In long-range industrial planning, the number of scientists and engineers required for research effort will have to be estimated each time a specialization is adopted. The principle to be followed here is that enough engineers should be provided to cover all the growing points in the technology that are relevant to the developing economy. On the other hand, a research establishment should not be so large that there is not enough capital to exploit its proposals. For example, if knitting were to be chosen as an international specialization, the applied research group might include machine designers, fiber and filament specialists, a mathematician, several librarians, and perhaps some product designers and home economists. As an organization they would try out the latest ideas detected elsewhere, test those suggested by people connected with the local industry, and occasionally develop some innovations on their own. The group would naturally be located somewhere close to the geographical center of the industry. If the research nucleus fails to stimulate and advance innovations that are respected in older centers of the industry (New Jersey, Nottingham, Switzerland, Scotland, etc.), the enterprise will decline and most of the markets will be captured by new underdeveloped areas offering still cheaper labor.

AN ALTERNATIVE FORMULA

At the beginning of its program Puerto Rico had about 10,000 students enrolled in college from among 2 million people. A decade later there were 25,000 students from a population only 10 percent larger. This number is to be compared with 1,000 to 2,000 persons studying at a similar level drawn from a population almost twice as large in the British West Indies (and having roughly the same literacy levels). Regardless of the debates about relative educational standards, it is evident that the Puerto Rican formula for industrialization requires at least ten times the skills created by higher education than are available in most of the underdeveloped societies. As a consequence the reformulation of the Puerto Rican techniques to make them applicable to some other economic and cultural environment calls for an investigation of the best possible substitutes for professional-quality services.

Fortunately, since World War II the expanding activities of the North American, British, and other Western European governments have created a cadre of professionals whose principal interest is the stimulation of modern industry. The United Nations agencies have recruited thousands of persons for their missions. The International Bank for Reconstruction and Development has been particularly interested in industrialization programs; UNESCO, the FAO, the ILO, and other such agencies also sponsored relevant programs.

Many persons with experience in laying the foundations for industry have drifted into private consulting groups, and others have returned to the faculties of universities from which they were drawn for overseas service. Some of the international engineering firms and the research institutes associated with colleges and universities have collected staff with background in this work. Thus it is becoming possible to contract privately for many of the essential skills.

Nevertheless, for every hired consultant the developing society must provide either an understudy with reasonably good qualifications or an administrator capable of supervising the contributions of consultants. The reason for this relationship is obvious. There is always some initial mistrust of consultants (they may hold prejudices against the local mores, or could be acting in self-interest, etc.) which can only be dispelled by persons who are working very closely with them. A communications channel must be established between the fund of knowledge brought in by the consultant and the organizations inside the economy, for which face-to-face contacts are necessary.

Moreover, one of the major tasks undertaken by the hired consultant is the training of local people to take his place when he leaves. Owing to language difficulties and family problems, consultants on extended tours of duty tend to form a small society of their own. If local people are not selected and encouraged to move socially in these same circles, much of the cultural lore associated with the operations or the manufacturing facilities will not be transmitted.

A large share of the technical analysis and economic research which precedes the completion of an industrial proposal can be carried on in North America and Western Europe so that considerable savings can be achieved in the demands upon local technical manpower. Therefore the consultant firms make possible a net reduction in the requirements for local professionals, if the country is able to pay the price.

The overall shortage of college-trained persons leads to the conclusion that technicians, works engineers, statisticians, accountants, personnel specialists, and even most of the factory managers must get their training by some other means than attendance at a university. It may be obtained from commercial colleges, through released-time training, night school, correspondence courses, and the like. Much more of the training needed must come from experience acquired on the job. Instead of being engaged with textbooks and seminars in administrative science and technology, the prospective managerial class would be shuffled about from job to job so as to gain practical experience. Instead of absorbing general principles and mathematical equations, the men who run industry and its associated services would learn about "whom to see, when, where, and for what purpose." Much of the necessary basic skills and formal knowledge could be provided by programmed instruction, as described in Chapter 15.

It will be noted that this study has taken pains to make quantitative estimates of the number of technically trained persons needed for industry in developing economies. The industrial development agency must have an even more precise estimate of supply for that place and period, and thus be able to gauge the shortage. The industrial development agency is then faced with the task of identifying and encouraging talent. This effort is much larger and more varied than that of assembling a cadre of entrepreneurs, but nevertheless it can be conducted in much the same manner. *A list of names of people must be built up to include all persons who seem able to overcome the lack of higher education and thus show promise for filling the technical and administrative positions effectively.* Then, as posts open up in new businesses, the agency is able to nominate someone with relevant experience and nominate others to take the place that was vacated.

The development of personnel demands a great deal of experience, both with the local society and with the personnel requirements of various industries. Obviously an outside consultant is needed who is familiar with industrial experience, but his knowledge alone is not enough. Several people are required who know intimately the influences of the origin of a prospective technologist and manager, his family, village, tribe, region, prior connections, and political inclinations as they can affect the kind of work to be performed. One would normally look for such talent scouts within government where the best organization already existed, most likely in the army or the majority political party.

It is virtually impossible to work this scheme when manufacturing is done in a plethora of small and independent factories, as in Puerto Rico. There the government could develop some of the bright youngsters, but its service is not flexible enough, and many persons are reluctant to leave the government service for the confusions and risks of manufacturing, even if their income should increase by 50 percent or more. Therefore this pattern for promoting new manufacturing talent is more appropriate to the stage of development commonly found in Japan, Italy, and elsewhere.

In this pattern all new ventures requiring substantial capital and competent management would be regarded as *participations*. Local family firms, government corporations, international corporations, and firms hitherto localized in foreign countries, in all possible combinations, contribute to the financing, the tooling up, and the marketing. Each also makes nominations for the responsible positions in management and on the board of directors. A network of such participating enterprises permits the small circle of executives most concerned with growth to move talented managers and technicians to those posts where they are most needed. The government agency is a source of nominees from *outside* the group of participating companies, to which they turn when a real shortage exists.

This alternative opens up some severe political problems, however. Governments stay in power through their ability to attract support, usually in the form of votes. Labor-union support is in most instances essential to the party in power, and labor unions have an ingrained suspicion of the motives and the aims of employers. Since this procedure of government participation implies close cooperation with employers *at the confidential level,* it would certainly appear to union leaders that the government was dominated by an increasingly powerful industrial bloc. These feelings would not be controverted in the least by the annual reports of the firms. Profit and loss statements would show—if manufacturing is to expand rapidly—higher profits than in other countries, and higher also than those obtained in other sectors of the economy.

Thus, it is again necessary to find a device that satisfies industrial labor but which nevertheless postpones consumption, including the extension of welfare measures, until after the productivity increases have been achieved. As noted earlier, the predominant dependence of the new industries upon female labor, which is slower to organize and vote as a bloc, makes the task of synthesizing a formula somewhat easier than it has been for countries which have already industrialized.

Were it not for these political difficulties, accelerated programs of industrialization would very likely have been worked out more frequently in the past. Therefore, it may be safely asserted that the primary innovations necessary to trigger off the transition to modern industry are political in nature, and almost certainly indigenous. Such formulas cannot be borrowed. The enterprising politicians must precede the industrial entrepreneurs, and the political task has so far proved to be too much of an art to describe exhaustively. The creative aspects elude simple elaboration, so this study establishes political synthesis as a precondition to industrialization (Chapter 2).

BIBLIOGRAPHY

Berliner, J. H.: *Factory and Manager in the U.S.S.R.*, Harvard University Press, Cambridge, Mass., 1957.
>   A study of managerial behavior in Russian industry, particularly during the period of growth prior to World War II.

Galenson, Walter: *Labor Productivity in Soviet and American Industry*, Columbia University Press, New York, 1955.
>   Traces the improvements in labor productivity in Soviet industries, particularly mining, iron and steel, machinery, textiles, shoes, and sugar. Discusses the policies responsible for these changes.

Harbison, Frederick, and Charles A. Myers, *Management in the Industrial World: An International Analysis*, McGraw-Hill Book Company, New York, 1959.
>   Chaps. V and VI are especially recommended. Illuminates the crucial role that managerial resources play in the development process.

Jaques, Elliot: *The Changing Culture of a Factory*, Holt, Rinehart and Winston, Inc., New York, 1952, and *Equitable Payment: A General Theory of Work, of Differential Payments, and Individual Progress*, William Heinemann, Ltd., London, 1961.
>   Extremely insightful reports on the effects of innovations on the work culture, attitude toward responsibility, concepts of justice, and the problems of management.

Miller, Bruce H.: *The Political Role of Labor in Developing Countries,* The Brookings Institution, Washington, D.C., 1963.
> A survey of the evolution of unionism in Africa and Asia, emphasizing the basis for a cooperative role between unions and government.

Scott, J. E., and R. P. Lynton: *The Community Factor in Modern Technology,* UNESCO, Paris, 1952.
> Investigates the relationship between industry and the community within which it operates. Primarily dependent upon European examples, and concerned with a malaise that is more easily prevented than cured.

Stepanek, J. E.: *Managers for Small Industry,* The Free Press of Glencoe, New York, 1960.
> Traces the sources of managers and entrepreneurs in various cultures, mainly the South Asian.

Whyte, W. F. (ed.): *Industry and Society,* McGraw-Hill Book Company, New York, 1946.
> A remarkable selection of reports showing the interaction of industry with social behavior. It serves as an illustration of how this area can be usefully studied without the elaborate tools social science has since developed.

10

INDUSTRIAL LOCATION

THE THEORY OF INDUSTRIAL LOCATION in the past has been dominated by economic analysis. Accordingly, the recommended location was that point on the map which provided adequate labor force and minimized transport costs between resources and markets. When such analysis is carried out in greater detail and takes into account the cost of holding inventories, including losses in perishables, the places in the transport network that require change of carrier assume importance in industrial locations.

Economic factors clearly control the locational decisions in the development of lower-grade, large-volume resources. Into this category fall the refining of ores, the processing of agricultural products, the fabrication of heavy machinery, and the manufacture of materials used in construction work.

In underdeveloped areas the modern market-oriented industries (where delivery to the user becomes the major cost subject to reduction) are much less significant because of the low incomes that exist. The sizes of the markets are sufficient to justify only a few of these industries, and then only those with plant sizes and equipment which supply products at higher unit costs than in developed countries.

The theory and practice of plant location and site location according to economic principles have been analyzed in detail elsewhere (cf. Isard, Yaseen). Normally, these methods aim at the maximization of profit to the firm, although the more sophisticated analyses (for which real data never seem to be available) aim to maximize the sum of internal and external economies. (By the latter is meant the reductions in cost and the generation of new opportunities attributable solely to the increases in efficiency caused by the proximity of one economic activity to another.) There are also external *dis*economies—e.g., congestion in the transport system—which may ensue in the event of poor metropolitan planning. The reference system encompassing technological structure, the interchange of physical inputs and outputs, provides partial evidence of integration and conflict among industries. The judgments of probable optima are gained from the *ad hoc* models of the industrial economy.

Historians and human geographers who have studied the origins of industry in various parts of the world during the nineteenth and early twentieth centuries have inferred from their work that another highly significant factor influences industrial location. Innovating entrepreneurs —the inventors who set up firms to exploit their own ideas—usually started their operations close to home. Then, if the novel process yielded markedly reduced costs, or the new product found widespread acceptance, the profits were very large and were plowed back into the factory. The operations sometimes expanded to the point where thousands of workers were employed before it became necessary to decentralize further additions to production. Thus places where innovation was combined with entrepreneurship have been industrialized, despite some serious economic disadvantages in location.

When the same innovation appeared almost simultaneously in several different locales, the economic forces affecting industrial location played a more significant part because those firms which were blessed with the lowest transportation costs tended to survive ensuing cutthroat competition and were able to expand most rapidly.

Today, however, the possibilities of successfully combining technological innovation with entrepreneurship are rare in the developing countries. If the occasion should arise, and a promising market does develop, there is a body of internationally active firms, with all the accumulated techniques of twentieth-century science behind them, ready to move in and skim off a large share of the profits. Thus the spontaneous springing up of small centers of industrial activity in odd places is now much less likely than heretofore. Where the phenomenon does occur, as in the vicinity of Tokyo, São Paulo (Brazil), Medellín (Colombia), and Bangalore (India), to take a few frequently discussed but still unexplained examples, it should be assisted and carefully nurtured by planners. The difficulties and diseconomies standing in the way of rapid expansion should be identified, and the communications and transport plans adjusted to improve their chances.

Since so little is known about the stimuli responsible for the generation of innovating entrepreneurs, this factor cannot be usefully manipulated by planners charged with laying out an industrialization program.

The appearance of the phenomenon can be treated as an unexpected opportunity that adds significantly to the potentials for industrial integration.

PSYCHOLOGICAL FACTORS

Industrial planners for underdeveloped areas quickly discover that, according to *strictly economic* principles of industrial location, their own territories are disadvantaged. There are far from a sufficient number of firms that may be expected to settle and accumulate a surplus large enough to enable them to grow. The principal opportunities open to the planners involve adding psychological features in the form of special incentives so as to attract the most mobile entrepreneurs to the industrializing areas. Once they have been tempted and start actively considering the choice of a new site for manufacturing, many surprising elements enter into the calculations of the "feasibility" of various sites. Most of these elements are concerned with enhancing the likelihood of survival of the firm. The critical features in modern transportation, for example, are much more related to the *dependability* of the service (vulnerability to cancellation of trips, interruptions due to strikes, availability of substitute services or routes, etc.) than to freight rates charged, which enter into economic calculations.

The dominant factors in determining location must relate to the crucial elements for the profitability of manufacturing in developing territories. For a program of forced-draft industrialization the point has already been made (Chapter 9) that more depends upon the managerial capacities of the resident factory heads than upon anything else. It follows then that a social, cultural, and physical environment needs to be provided which will attract and hold competent managers. The more complete the social services, the recreational attractions, and the pleasantness of environment in a given location, the greater the chances will be for finding and keeping good-caliber persons from overseas. Such factors restrict the locations of plants to daily commuting distances from residences outside a metropolis.

For the "footloose" manufacturing industries the standard analysis of economic factors in location may typically rule out 95 percent of all the relevant areas, but the number of possible locations remaining may still be numbered in the hundreds. The choice then depends rather heavily on sociopsychological arguments. One important criterion is the degree to which a community looks after its own welfare problems, rather than waiting for assistance from the central government. The openness of the business class stratum, particularly evidence of their willingness to accept new factory managers, is almost as important. The community's familiarity with the characteristics of a special labor force (e.g., women and girls with coffee-culture backgrounds) will also be helpful to the entrepreneurs when deciding.

Some firms wish to postpone unionization as long as possible, since it tends to reduce their control over operations. On the other hand, international corporations that have already been completely unionized in their older plants may select sites which ensure early unionization, but of a kind that minimizes jurisdictional problems. All firms will be alert to the problem of spontaneous, unauthorized strikes which so often reflect low morale, community disorganization, and the social dynamics of a "depressed area."

Even with such criteria taken into account, 20 to 40 percent of the prospective factories started by entrepreneurs from a highly developed country may still be located in any of a handful of communities. Amenities are even more important in these circumstances. The hobby, or some other special enthusiasm of the owner or manager, may become the final basis of choice. The accessibility of good salmon fishing or a small-craft harbor or skin-diving opportunities may give one area a substantial advantage over another in attracting new industries in this footloose category.

If the industrial planning incorporates the procedure described earlier for constructing standard factory buildings ahead of the demand, then some of these psychological influences as well as the economic factors must be taken into account by the industrial planners themselves in the site-selection process. Mistakes in this phase will show up in the form of higher vacancy rates, and perhaps also the loss of industrial opportunities whose locational requirements could not be met in time. The industrial planners must get the information they need about the psychological factors from careful observation of the location decision process employed by entrepreneurs interested in the territory for which they are planning. Some of this information can be acquired from consulting firms who are continuously engaged by business interests looking for industrial sites. Still more can be obtained when discussing the housing requirements and the leisure-time interests of the executives and top managers and their families.

METROPOLITAN AREA DEVELOPMENT

Since much of the localization and an even larger part of the siting of factories must be done long before the arrival of the occupants themselves, a few additional considerations need to be introduced. Factory location patterns can be quite influential in establishing the growth pattern of the metropolis. Consequently the city planners and the transport planners are extremely interested in integrating industrial land use with other land use in the metropolis. Their concern is for the maintenance and improvement of the quality of services to the people affected by the plant. In particular, they wish to minimize losses due to overcrowding and congestion.

New plants may first be divided into two groups—those moving into the hinterland owing to resource orientation or various psychological reasons, and those needing metropolitan services. The latter may be expected to make up the bulk of the new industry.

Within the metropolitan area at least three patterns of site selection may be noted. (1) Heavy manufacturing and various portside industries quickly develop close interrelationships with each other; increasing smoke, dust, odors, and freight traffic tend to reduce the quality of housing and other services in the vicinity. (2) Many new firms will rent lofts, warehouses, store fronts, or whatever accommodation is available in order to test out the operation over a year or two; then they will expand into new quarters in a nearby industrial estate, where most of the newly trained urban labor force can be retained. (3) Industrial estates may be planned for the periphery of the metropolitan area so that the firm has sufficient room to expand, if it appears desirable, without paying moving costs. These estates are located far enough out from the city so that some underemployed rural labor can be recruited.

Early experience in Puerto Rico led to the setting of certain land-use standards for industrial sites. Prime industrial land was flat, well drained, serviced with utilities, adjacent to a labor supply, and convenient to public transportation. With a few exceptions its alternative use would be no more intensive than two-story residential buildings, its prior use normally having been agricultural. Industrial land was bought up in advance by a government corporation which was guided by the following standards:

	Lot Size	Employees	Employee Density
Heavy industry	30 acres	150	5 per acre
Medium industry	4 acres	80	24 per acre
Light industry	2 acres	80	40 per acre

The average investment in a standard factory for light industry (in 1960 dollars) was about $600,000. About 3 percent of this amount was expended for land purchase, 7 percent for land improvement, 20 percent for factory construction, and the remainder left for machinery and working capital. Medium and heavy industries are much more variable in their costs.

An additional category of plant which was labeled a "local industrial center" was included in later plans. These were simple concrete facilities of about 3,000 square feet, located in the more isolated communities.

The intention was to provide modern facilities for the local cottage industries which would enable them to compete more effectively. It will take some years yet to discover the major advantages and disadvantages inherent in this kind of program, but it already appears that the political advantages are perhaps most significant: it can be pointed out to any of the politicians who demand that the Fomento bring a factory into their locality that the industrial centers among his constituents are not used up to their capacities.

Experience accumulated over the first decade of Puerto Rico's factory-building program has shown that the initial space standards are too generous. They were designed to accommodate a 100 percent expansion of the firm at a later date. It now appears that only 10 to 20 percent of the firms can be expected to expand operations on the original site to the point where floor space is doubled. A government corporation holding the property can make substantial economies by providing only a nominal amount of space for expansion on the site, and then guarantee moving expenses to those few firms that grow out of the original site.

An aspect of the site selection that has seldom been emphasized in the past arises from the detailed analysis of human resources. The predominance of females in the industrial labor force raises the question of the kinds of sites suited to their needs and convenience. Accessibility is very important; hence factories that are close to pools of unemployed female labor should exhibit less absenteeism. Absence from work occurs at a rate which often detracts from productivity because most working women continue to function as homemakers and many emergencies at home require their presence. Being able to get home within a few minutes when called should diminish the workers' absenteeism and ease their worries. Therefore the provision of factory sites in all major low-cost housing projects seems to be as logical as the provisions already made for schools, shopping, and recreation. Since the requirements for transportation are little different from those of the shopping area, factory buildings for light industry (at a rate of one for every 200 to 300 families) may be most profitable for society when made an adjunct of the shopping center.

DECENTRALIZATION

Once an industrialization program is underway, the political pressures upon it begin to mount. Each parliamentary district plots and schemes to get a symbol of industrialization in its own territory. It is virtually impossible for the government to explain that a factory in every district represents an uneconomic approach; just enough of the early plants elect to go to the hinterland and thereby unwittingly encourage the agitation.

One of the methods for assuaging local jealousies (and the politicians'

demands for reelection purposes) is to lump together all the developments aimed at improving economic efficiency. One district might use
an agricultural market, another an improved road, another a tourism
development, another a commercial refrigeration installation for fisher-
men, and others factories. Even then some capital losses may need to
be sustained in order to forge a political majority that would continue
to support the development program. A good share of this unavoidable
expense might easily take the form of building factory structures in unlikely territories—and the justification of such policy is likely to go under
the heading of "decentralized industrial development."

The arguments for and against decentralization are normally put in
a nonstatistical form. Under these conditions the administration will proceed to do whatever is expedient in the short run. The weighting of the
arguments in costs versus benefits has seldom been possible, but in Puerto
Rico it has been feasible to assemble some crude accounts. The logic
underlying a cost-benefit analysis of decentralization is worth a brief
exploration.

Puerto Rico acceded to the political demands some years after the
industrialization program had begun. Therefore the localization pattern
prior to the onset of decentralization was quite well established and could
be projected into the future. Special incentives were granted to firms,
ranging up to $25,000 for locating in a community with no other modern
factory, and $15,000 in towns where less than 150 persons were employed
in factories. In addition factory rentals were reduced as much as 45 percent in the less accessible communities. Assistance was also given to firms
using indigenous materials. Altogether this set of subsidies enabled the
remote communities to increase their share of new jobs created from 12
percent just prior to the subsidy program to 25 percent once it was in
operation.

The special incentive grants and the rent subsidy, added to rental
losses on vacant factory buildings, were estimated at $1.8 million; they led
to a shift of about 3,100 new jobs to points outside the principal metropolitan area. Thus a capital loss of $500 per new job was implied in the
decentralization program.

More people than just the industrial workers move in the course of
migration. At least another one-half job is created in the service trades in
the metropolis to accommodate one extra industrial worker. Both job-
holders bring dependents to the city with them as quickly as they can
afford to do so. As a result of this decentralization policy, altogether about
five persons did *not* migrate who might otherwise have done so, for each
job created.

Also to be taken into account was an income loss on the part of the
worker. In Puerto Rico, as elsewhere, the wage differentials between the

chief metropolitan area and the remoter areas show a reduction of 20 to 35 percent. Some of this differential is due to transport and communication costs, some to the lower productivity, and the remainder to the labor-supply surpluses in the hinterland. If the real loss in income to the society is set at ten cents per hour (about 15 percent of wages), the overall income loss to the wage-earning class as a whole amounts to $300 per year per job.

It appears that, aside from earning power, the workers and their families were at least as well off staying close to home. Although the range of governmental services was poorer at home, particularly educational and health facilities, the housing in the city would, on the average, be much more crowded and poorer in quality. The worker and his family moving to the city also give up the social contacts which assure them of assistance in times of adversity. One may therefore conclude that, for the marginal job, the industrial position that could be displaced to the hinterland, the worker and his family should be relatively indifferent as to whether the job appeared close to home at a lower-wage rate or in the city where his expenses were higher (roughly the amount of his rent).

The advantages and disadvantages of decentralization strongly affect the program of social and economic development at the government level. In Puerto Rico the metropolitan communities were engaged in slum clearance, replacing the highly congested shack towns and dilapidated tenements with hygienic housing. An estimated 15,000 to 16,000 persons were kept out of the shack towns (which would have pushed farther out on the fringes of the urban area and pressed still further over the lagoons), and this represented about 25 percent of the metropolitan growth for the period. Experience with slum clearance suggested that the metropolitan authorities would have to spend about $500 to remove a slum dwelling housing five people. Thus $500 capital loss to the industrial development fund, as was calculated above for creating a decentralized industrial job, was offset by $500 capital saving in the program for improving health and welfare in the overcrowded cities.

Decentralization has an additional effect upon the rate of investment in urban services. It postpones the visible need for approximately $6,000 more investment per industrial job in good-quality housing, school buildings, streets, and associated services. This is the amount that would be used to raise the consumptive level of the urban population by improving the standards of the services. It represents a considerable quantity of capital that might otherwise be used in further industrial development.

It may then be inferred that, if capital was truly scarce, the Puerto Rican government would favor continuing a decentralization policy such as had been instituted. However, by this time the society could obtain large amounts of external capital at reasonable interest rates, for housing and some of the related urban facilities, while that part of the budget from which the decentralization subsidy was drawn had to be justified before the legislature each year, and the formal procedures of budget making would not permit this subsidy to be considered as an offset to slum clearance expenditures or as a means of conserving external credits.

The conclusion that follows from the foregoing analysis of costs and benefits is that shortages and surpluses in the various earmarked funds will determine whether decentralization or centralization is the best policy for advancing growth and development. For Puerto Rico there was no clear economic and social advantage either way, so this was an issue that rightfully belonged in the political arena. The decisive issue then becomes one of determining the effect upon party organization and the value of the subsidy program as a bargaining point in acquiring more support for the government. If a clear gain for a policy of centralization could have been demonstrated, the publication of a carefully argued report would have helped greatly in getting the proper policies accepted in the budget-making process and in the legislature. Much of the effort expended in industrial planning must be put into the preparation of appraisals of this kind that incorporate economic, social, cultural, and political elements.

REORGANIZING TRANSPORTATION

Transportation problems make up a relatively technical and complicated sector of developmental planning. Only a few of the relevant issues will be taken up here—those that relate directly to industrial location. A systematic approach to transportation planning would require a section by itself.

Prior to the institution of a program for accelerated industrialization, transportation systems in a country are oriented primarily to resource development (see Chapter 5). Market crops and minerals must be delivered to the ports. The docks themselves are organized to handle the kinds of bulk products that originate in the economy, whether it be oil, ore, sugar, bananas, coffee, cocoa, or rice, and to receive general cargo in return. Some small additions to the routes in the export-oriented transport system may be aimed at improving the efficiency of movement of persons and thereby ease the chores of administrators.

With the onset of industrialization the transportation facilities must now connect factory with raw materials and market. At the very beginning factories are located to make use of existing transport facilities operating well under capacity, but as the number of factories increases, certain expansions and reorganizations are made necessary by the marginal contributions of new factories to the traffic pattern.

Manufactured products from mobile industries usually have low tonnage requirements as compared with resource development. Their raw materials, in the form of wire, sheet metal, plastics, leather, cloth, paper, dyestuffs, chemicals, and manufactured components, are valued in the neighborhood of $300 to $1,000 per ton. Therefore these industries depend upon a bonded express service using trucks for delivery to the site and for hauling away the output. (A typical factory with 100 workers may use up two tons of raw materials per day, and produce one ton of product, the remainder being discarded or burned; it makes weekly shipments but accepts inputs at irregular intervals. Perhaps two-thirds of the factories entering Puerto Rico have these approximate characteristics, while the other third deviate widely from the pattern.) Manufacturers prefer frequent and dependable transport service because it reduces the amount of capital tied up in inventory.

The trends in freight-rate differentials in the past decade have encouraged an increasing proportion of manufacturers to use air freight. Firms engaged in manufacturing quality apparel, electronics, instrumentation, pharmaceuticals, plastic toys, embroidery, and similar products where the value approaches $2 per pound have been particularly interested. One of the major justifications for organizing operations in conjunction with airfreight service is the convenience of shipping direct to retailers. Another reason is the reduction of vulnerability to dock strikes. Export-oriented manufacturers overseas depend upon the simultaneous operation of three harbors or more and know from experience that dock strikes and slowdowns are not infrequent and that their consequences can be disastrous for a small business.

Manufacturers are also understandably concerned about travel to work. Regular passenger movements are greatly increased by the presence of industry. Dependable bus or pickup service for workers is absolutely essential and constitutes a leading consideration in site selection. Thus the development of a metropolitan mass transportation system is closely linked with the rate at which industrial sites are taken up by manufacturers. In the hinterland a small local entrepreneur encouraged by the manufacturer may purchase a superannuated bus which moves people to their jobs and children to schools, and is available for chartering on evenings and weekends. The predominantly female employment in the new industry encourages the use of buses instead of bicycles.

The combined emphasis upon trucking and vehicular passenger movement means that industrialization emphasizing light and medium industries stimulates the development of the road system and the airports.

The railroads tend to be neglected and allowed to decline. Harbors are essential, but very little extra in the way of warehousing and docks is required; however, unloading equipment may need to be modernized in order to reduce the turn-around time of ships.

In densely populated countries, which are likely to develop metropolitan areas greatly in excess of 1 million persons, this emphasis upon improving the street and highway system at the expense of railroads may later be regretted. Larger metropolitan areas are capable of generating intense congestion at many points which can be "solved" only by creating freeways at the expense of several million dollars per mile. Experience shows that the existence of a freeway generates so much new traffic that still other freeways are soon required. This pattern is extremely wasteful of capital at a time when capital is scarce.

At least two strategies seem to be open. If a low residential density is possible, it may be appropriate to set aside the land for the freeways prior to the growth of the metropolis. By this means the most expensive feature of urban road building—that of land acquisition and the removal of structures—may be reduced in cost by 70 to 90 percent. An alternative is the construction of a good road into the hinterland; it introduces a new set of attractive industrial sites and provides one of the best means of further decentralizing the growing manufacturing activity.

Where higher population densities are necessary, it is better to plan on the electrification of existing railways and subsequent conversion of some bus lines into rail routes. Bus and light vehicle traffic would be reorganized so as to integrate with this plan. The large factories, expecting to employ thousands of workers, would tend to seek favorable locations on the prospective rail grid. Others of average size or smaller could function effectively using secondary and tertiary routes. There are recent innovations in land transport equipment (the "land cruisers," new trolley buses, etc.) which can smooth the transition from roads to railways, but they have not yet been tested on an important scale.

Too often different transportation systems are administered and regulated by different agencies of the government. Rail transport, road transport, shipping, and airlines are granted altogether different forms of charters, and the legal requirements put upon them regarding their financing, taxation, and operations tend to preclude integration of services. In most underdeveloped countries a network of subsidies, both direct and indirect, supports the respective transport systems and disguises the true costs. The imbalance in the subsidies, combined with obsolescent regulations, often leads to the dependence of a new manufacturer upon an uneconomic route.

To avoid these difficulties *a plan for integrated transport development should be set in motion at the same time as the plan for promoting indus-*

tries. An accelerated program for industrialization requires first the assembly of a great amount of detailed information about transport, much of it even more specific than the data required for coordinated metropolitan transport planning. At a later stage, as the industrial complexes evolve step by step, additions to the transport facilities become an integral feature of the industrial-capacity expansion program. If, on the other hand, the modern small industries are allowed to be distributed in space in response to short-run factors alone, the growth of transport capacity is likely to be lumpy. Periodically, then, each next step in the expansion of capacity would require huge amounts of capital, or foreign exchange, at a time when the funds can be used to advantage elsewhere in the economy. Delays are introduced because of lags in financing. When this is the case, the industrialization program will lose valuable momentum for lack of suitable sites.

BIBLIOGRAPHY

Greenhut, M. L.: *Plant Location in Theory and Practice,* The University of North Carolina Press, Chapel Hill, N.C., 1956.
> A treatment that provides the classical economic background, several detailed case studies, and the present theory stated in relatively nonmathematical terms. Literature cited primarily precedes 1951.

Isard, W.: *Methods of Regional Analysis: An Introduction to Regional Science,* John Wiley & Sons, Inc., New York, 1960.
> An elaborate, relatively mathematical approach to location theory, external economies, and programming that can be undertaken when statistics are excellent.

Meyer, John R.: "Regional Economics: A Survey," *American Economic Review,* vol. 53, pp. 19–54, 1963.
> A systematic assessment of the current work, both pure and applied, on the subject of regional economics.

Richards, Glenn C.: "A Guide to Transportation Planning," *Traffic Quarterly,* vol. 12, pp. 227–241, 1958.
> Outlines the methods that may presently be employed for coordinated planning of land transportation systems in metropolitan areas. Provides references to current handbook and general data sources and sets forth the plan for their extension.

Yaseen, L. C.: *Plant Location,* rev. ed., American Research Council, New York, 1960.
> A guide used by industries and area development agencies for the economic rationalization of industry.

11

INTERNATIONAL SPECIALIZATION

EACH COUNTRY PLAYS a specialized role in international affairs. It maintains certain recognized relationships with other countries over the long run. The economic specializations of the various countries are almost always inextricably intertwined with political and cultural relationships. Thus colonial countries are usually oriented toward the mother country in their trade, educational, and political systems, no matter what the geographic separation may be, while contacts with neighbors are left undeveloped. Quite a different relationship exists between countries bordering each other which have had a history of suspicion and conflict. In such cases a part of the international role of each is to stand opposed to each other, often with borders closed and minimal commercial and cultural contacts. The total role that a nation plays in the international scene is defined by the bonds it maintains with the hundred or so other societies in the world. A program of economic development is intended, among other things, to change this role, and the industrial planning, through its requirements and its consequences, is perhaps the most important feature of the development program that exerts long-term effects upon international relations.

In the strategy for industrialization that has been outlined here, it was emphasized that the technology to be used in the early stages of the growth of manufacturing must be imported from the outside. Therefore contacts with some highly industrialized countries need to be expanded so as to include the transfer of know-how, of information about markets for semimanufactured and ready-for-sale products, and some venture capital, if at all possible. Thus the growing economy necessarily becomes *more dependent* upon other economies, even though at many points it becomes materially "independent" by producing goods for its own consumption which had been previously imported.

In the preceding chapters the bonds between nations were treated primarily as a resource—a reservoir of economic opportunity—which contributed to the formulation of short-run and local projects. There remain some long-range implications of international relations which require careful study before internal strategies take final shape.

A review of the history of industrialization reveals that military pressures have been markedly influential in determining both the type of industry initiated and the places it was located. The strategy of a defense against potential aggressors has been paramount in establishing national industrial policy. Several countries tried to establish a self-sustaining economy capable of producing its own supply of armaments, so that the pattern became fairly well established before World War II. These autarchic features of industrial policy became obsolete with the development of nuclear weapons and the establishment of the United Nations. International conflicts remain with us, but they have assumed a different character—one that is relatively independent of the industrialization program. Arms are obtained by negotiating with the great powers, or by purchase on an international black market. Issues are likely to be settled too quickly to allow converting one's own heavy industries. The exception to this assertion exists where nations have borders with nonnuclear states that can be defended by infantry, but even then most of the decisive weapons are obtainable through making agreements with the major powers. The conclusion to be drawn from these arguments is that the long-term implications of international relations cannot be illuminated merely by a study of history, but require an analysis of contemporary forces on the international stage.

More often than not, henceforth, the march of events will tend to introduce some kind of a planning crisis in which both international relations and the development program are involved. It may have to do with a shortage of hard currencies, or some explosive international incident, or changes in the terms of trade; whatever the issue, the directions that industry may take will depend upon the decisions arrived at on these other questions. Sometimes a revaluation of international status will be sparked by internal events, such as a shift of control from one dominant party to another. In any of these events some hard choices are necessary, and the following questions are almost sure to be asked in those circles which are free from political dogma: What new roles could this nation play on the international scene, once some progress has been made in improving the level of living and the indigenous manufacturing has begun to expand rapidly? What would be the respective effects of the new roles upon the pattern of internal industrial growth? Which of the possible roles is preferable, given the local tradition, the geographical location, the resource structure, the internal politics, and the new aspirations?

Each alternative national role carries with it a bundle of subsidiary options which make the subject difficult to discuss in the abstract. For the sake of clarity and brevity, various means are sought here for describing or cataloguing the national roles. Since even at the research stage they are usually characterized by locally expressive catchwords and slogans, it is necessary here to use parallels and partial analogies. In order to be more explicit, the example of Puerto Rico is again used.

During the period 1900–1940 Puerto Rico became one of a series of *colonial sugar economies*. This category also included Cuba, Hawaii, Barbados, and Mauritius, with Java, Jamaica, the Philippines, and British Guiana showing many of the same characteristics in special regions. As in the larger colonial areas everywhere during this period, the primary goal of Puerto Rican society was independence, or at least political self-determination. The foremost desire was to become a member of the company of nations.

At the beginning of World War II political self-determination was granted Puerto Rico, pending the end of hostilities. During the long wait a few foresighted people began to consider the further implications of independence, including the problem of international relations. It was then felt that the resource structure of the Island limited its population to intensive farming as the primary source of income, so that the best future it could hope for seemed to be that of a "tropical Ireland"—an agricultural society that managed to maintain itself somewhat above subsistence levels by engaging in trade with richer industrial societies nearby.

The early success of Operation Bootstrap brought forward more ambitious visions. It became evident that the proximity to large economies provided more than one kind of opportunity, but then the implications of a highly industrialized future had to be considered. The simplest image to convey this possibility was that of a "tropical Switzerland." Switzerland, as observed from a distance, was perceived to have achieved the highest level of living on the continent of Europe by combining tourism with an alert, flexible industrial establishment and to have accomplished all this without the aid of large quantities of natural resources. Similarly, it was believed, Puerto Rico might specialize in various kinds of light assembly and a different style of tourism. The Swiss banking interests might be paralleled by encouraging Puerto Ricans to serve as agents for the American organizations dealing with Latin America, using bilingual San Juan as a natural base of operations.

Such a way of viewing the future can be immensely helpful in suggesting appropriate balance in the capital budget and the long-range projections of land use that are associated with transport and water development. It helps also in the development of higher education by indicating the priorities according to which new departments should be established in colleges and universities. However, upon careful study the analogy broke down; Puerto Rico could not hope to institute watch manufacture, for example, or heavy electrical engineering. A hotel was built in the mountains (the principal justification for it, incidentally, was not based upon experience in Switzerland, but in Jamaica, where climatic conditions are very similar), but the attractions seemed far less appealing to tourists than those associated with the shoreline, so the hotel was not an economic success.

What changed Puerto Rico's aspirations was the unexpected acquisition of heavy industry in the form of petroleum refining, petrochemicals, fertilizers, etc. Furthermore, the large migration of Puerto Ricans to North American cities had begun to create a much closer bond to American culture than had been anticipated because a significant fraction returned to the Island bringing newly acquired tastes with them. Now, barring major setbacks, the concept of an international role represented by the term *tropical Switzerland* is actually too modest. The Puerto Rican society not only has potentialities for greater affluence than Switzerland, but opportunities coming into view in the cultural area have much wider implications. Yet, even when obsolescent, this image of the future nature has utility. It provides a coherent view of otherwise disparate activities (e.g., light-assembly manufacturing, pharmaceuticals, overseas services, and tourism), which make up one facet of the future society; these activities draw upon complementary portions of the labor force and so may be said to be "balanced." It provides a basis for sectoral optimization in national policy making which may be valid for one or two decades longer.

INDUSTRIAL SPECIALIZATION

The formula for industrialization developed in this study requires a heavy dependence upon foreign trade. Those societies that have relied upon the sale of a market crop or a bulk natural resource (ores, petroleum, lumber, etc.) realize from rather bitter experience that the world market is an unstable crutch. Owing to wide swings in prices and major variations in supplies, it is difficult to get the firm leverage from world markets that is needed for long-range planning. Larger economies, such as Brazil and India, will often find that the best opportunities for investment are of the type that represent import substitutions. The middle-sized and smaller economies are more likely to find that, despite the risk, the best chances for accumulating capital lie in catering to the world market. In addition, they would supply those manufactured products which to some extent complement the internal effects induced by variations in the market crop or mineral exports; that is, if the participation in the world market tends to be cyclical, the manufactured products may have a competitive advantage when contracyclical; if the present activities make unbalanced demands upon the labor force, the unutilized portion can be allocated to the kind of manufacturing suitable to the remainder of the labor force and to the world market.

These principles are, however, far too general for purposes of industrial planning. What each country would like to establish is a set of relatively permanent specialties. Thus, if anyone in the world wished to sell watches, he could not afford to overlook the Swiss industry; if he wished to sell cameras, he could not pass up the opportunities provided by Japanese manufacturers; if he wished to sell men's cotton shirts, he would be unwise to ignore Hong Kong as a source. This list could be extended to hundreds of items.

An example helpful at this point will also introduce a conclusion that is based upon experience rather than theory. Sugar refining was an activity that logically could be expanded in a sugar economy, but quota restrictions and unused capacity in the United States prevented its expansion. One of the loopholes afforded was the manufacturing of chewing gum, candy, and soft-drink syrups for the world market, particularly the portion represented by North America. On paper one could construct the possibility of an industrial specialty in the hundred-million-dollar-a-year category manufacturing a variety of candies ranging from lollipops, cough drops, and dime-store bulk varieties, through candy bars, candy-coated chewing gum, and other products at the candy counter, to white chocolates and other fancy delicacies bought as gifts from luxury candy stores. The refined syrups need not be crystallized in a sugar-producing economy before the blend of flavorants is added. Moreover, there appeared to be a considerable amount of competitive advantage in the scheme that would overcome transport costs. The establishment of such an industry would require the acquisition of several scores of artisans, the setting up of a trade school, and the importation of knowledgeable entrepreneurs. All these things were considered in Puerto Rico, but the first factories established were not very successful. Apparently the industry is largely of a regional nature, because of differences in tastes and markets, and therefore less mobile than was anticipated. Also, because the health problems of overweight and tooth decay in North America were blamed upon sweets, the market was not expanding as rapidly as food consumption in general. It was fortunate that the Fomento had not moved quickly at this early stage to establish this specialty. Chances are very high that it would have been a fiasco. Graduates from the trade schools would not have found suitable employment, and the optimism necessary for a favorable industrial climate would have been much more severely diminished.

Clearly, the potentials for industrial specialization are discovered only through detailed industry study. One or more consultants can be hired to review the range of possibilities. However, the commitment to an international specialization, where the government assists by making available special institutions which service the industry, should not be made before at least *two* independent members of the industry have been established and are apparently able to operate successfully regardless of the assistance. (Businessmen reason that if there is only one firm which merited such attention, there could easily be government favoritism, and they would hesitate to set up a new factory in the face of hidden risks of this type.)

Even if a proposal for specialization is turned down after careful study, owing to excessive risk, the prospects should be reviewed every few years. Timeliness of entry is a major factor contributing to success in industrialization. Thus it is quite possible that, after all, the confectionery industry will take root in Puerto Rico in the not-too-distant future. The government there knows much better now how to promote the necessary service institutions for such industries, and it has also been reorganizing the local distribution system so that significant markets are being created at home for such products. Also, it is easier now for a few firms to make early profits in a small but growing market that is protected by substantial transport cost barrier.

Several principles need to be observed in choosing an international specialization in which the developing country would attempt to reach the frontier in technological developments. The first of these refers to the absolute growth rate of the industry in the world. Electronics manufacture, for example, is growing at an exceedingly rapid rate everywhere in the world, while shoe manufacture is barely staying ahead of population growth, and fine needlework is declining in importance. Obviously, it is preferable to find a secure niche in a rapidly growing industry. If it is impossible to find a suitable specialty that is growing rapidly in absolute terms, the next best choice is to find one for which international trade promises to grow steadily over the long run. Thus the manufacture of apparel cannot be considered a growth industry; nevertheless, the more standard items are increasingly successful in crossing tariff barriers.

A second principle has already been referred to in this chapter. It is obviously helpful to encourage industries which use low-grade resources such as silica sand, limestone, clay, salts, etc. Cement consumption can be stimulated by designing and demonstrating how people can build their own houses out of cement block and slab and achieve good quality results. Cement, glass, tiles, and similar products in excess of local consumption can be exported to smaller economies in the vicinity and may even take advantage of temporary shortages in major economies. Contractors may follow the product overseas and make bids. Reinforcing rods, prestressed beams and shells, frames, finishes, forms, etc., may also be developed for export.

Some specializations in industry require a high proportion of effort in research and development. Normally such a prerequisite would make it impossible to establish that specialization in an underdeveloped country on account of the shortage of high-grade personnel and the appropriate services needed during the initial stages of industrialization. It is possible, however, to negotiate for the transfer of information derived from research and design by using the international connections of the plants already established in that specialty. With few exceptions, it is cheaper to pay royalties than to innovate. Nevertheless, a research and development laboratory needs to be created, and government cosponsorship is almost always required. One major reason for small-scale research effort is that it develops within one's own society persons who can identify a useful discovery while it is still in the laboratory stage, plus the fact that the experience involved in carrying through the development phase greatly improves the technical capacity of the indigenous management. Research makes a contribution also in assisting adaptations of the industry to local opportunities. A small research group in an industrial specialization will pay for its maintenance merely through preventing mistakes in major investments and in the location of facilities. The demands for consultation and for laboratory checks are often so great that research is a misnomer. Yet truly competent people cannot be attracted unless the opportunity to do research is promised and the facilities are provided. Some modern and technically complex industries can be established with the help of only a handful of good scientists and technologists.

A fourth important principle is to be aware of what other countries in the same predicament are doing. If, for example, a half dozen countries in the same part of the world seem to be making commitments according to the principles just outlined, then the best policy would be to do just the opposite. For example, dying industries in developed countries frequently are afflicted with high labor costs, low productivity, and poor managements. It is usually possible to attract a few entrepreneurs with the requisite know-how, so that facilities with much lower production costs can be created. The sharply reduced costs reflected in lower prices are often able to open up altogether new markets. The chances for expansion may then be better than finding a highly competitive niche in a growth industry that must be shared with other countries. Similarly, the opportunity to import cement and construction services from developing countries nearby, at prices that are little above marginal cost, may suggest an important saving. The rather large amounts of capital that need to be invested in these industries can then be committed elsewhere. Specialization in international markets has the characteristics of a many-person game where most of the cards are showing and individual strategies can be deduced, so a competent player devises a strategy complementary to those that have already been chosen by the others.

A final principle hardly needs to be stated because leaders of developing countries appear to be most conscious of it. Nevertheless this account would be incomplete without considering political and cultural assets. The political and cultural ties a nation has, mostly residual from various stages of its history, can be exploited on various occasions for establishing an industrial nucleus. In the relations between nations there are circumstances regarding some industrial specialties where it is of mutual advantage to the richer nation and the poorer nation that the latter should develop a strong foundation in production techniques. This is the way the British Commonwealth connections have been used to bolster the export industries (many of them basically agricultural, but some derived from minerals) and to draw upon personnel elsewhere in the Commonwealth for the initial university departments and research institutes. Likewise in the plastics, electronics, and pharmaceutical industries, Japan has been drawing heavily upon the international firms based in the United States. Israel has perhaps been most proficient in this borrowing process, but it has had difficulties at the marketing stage for the new products.

CULTURAL INTERACTION

One of the reasons for seeking international specializations for the developing economies in industry and elsewhere is the need for the expression of cultural style. As industry gains a foothold and foreign contacts multiply, a wave of imitation is likely to be set off. The growing middle classes are particularly willing to experiment in public with the tastes and styles of the established modern societies. The artisan class finds it profitable to cater to these whims. Both groups are more conservative in the home, but even there, when people graduate to higher status in house construction, foreign styles begin to intrude.

The educated classes in an emerging society tend to become very disturbed by the sight of this "imitative" behavior. Many of them are sophisticates of the traditional culture which is being set aside and grossly neglected. Most of them have been taught enough about the foreign cultures to appreciate that the imported new styles are very bad imitations, and the artifacts which bear these distasteful forms and patterns are shoddy. Movements are set into motion which call for a return to the old virtues. Still other factions seek to create a new formulation of the old themes which will enable them to compete with the new imports. The industrialization program cannot expect to escape the friction between these two sets of cultural interests and those of the new bourgeoisie. Out of this conflict a synthesis can be expected, a style that is definitely a hybrid of the old with the new, the native with the foreign. The younger members of the educated classes can accept it, and foreign visitors respect it. The themes may be expected to appear first in the universities, trade schools, and art circles.

The first place in industry to reflect the new unity in style should be within the international specialties, if the services have been organized suitably. The characteristic imprint, or "signature," is put tentatively upon certain experimental models; when these are quickly accepted by buyers from New York, London, and Paris, who are avidly seeking novelty, a period of hectic industrial expansion may be predicted. If the creative flair has cultural roots, the theme will spread to other products and services. Italian industry has profited immensely during the decade of the 1950s from its discovery of an indigenous but internationally respected style. Japan shows strong signs of reaching equally high standards in the future. In Puerto Rico is seen self-conscious groping for such a style with enough hopeful developments to suggest that the synthesis sought may be achieved.

Style is even more evident in cultural activities. Hitherto it dominated only clothing, furniture, literature, and drama. Now it is reflected also in films, recordings, magazines, advertising, and television programs. Although predominantly cultural in character, these activities are superimposed upon industries of a highly technical nature. The evolution of a style, or a family of styles, can by itself result in a large-scale industry which fills the communications channels opened up by television, radio, and high-fidelity phonographs. Other countries are willing to pay for films, tapes, and printed materials that have more vitality than the content created at home. Thus international specialization in manufacturing need not rest with a set of "products," such as might be identified in a catalog of manufactures. It may just as easily be a class of images or ideas that is being sold. The solid artifacts that convey them are not irrelevant, but they are nonetheless trivial. The transfer of meaningful symbols across national boundaries appears to be one of the most rapidly growing activities of all. The pioneer in this direction in the Caribbean area has been Mexico where a film industry and a publishing industry are outcomes of the intense cultural activity in the vicinity of the capital. In Europe, Italy and Greece have been increasingly successful in the export of cultural materials.

It seems unlikely now that highly industrial societies of the future will allocate as much as 40 to 50 percent of the urban labor force to manufacturing. Even if manufacturing far outdistances agriculture, mining, forestry, and fishing as a source of income for developing societies, the "services" as they are presently defined will require a larger share of the labor force. Some of these additional services are needed to collect, process, analyze, and report on the data required for accelerated economic development, but an even larger portion is likely to be devoted to the manipulation of symbols for internal consumption. They constitute at the same time an enormous system for adult education and a market for the consumption of the ideas that float by on the stream of symbols transmitted by the mass media. Only the better quality output can be retailed profitably outside the boundary of the society.

The principal point to be made is that a single-minded approach to industrialization, which concentrates wholly upon the economic and technological factors in the founding and nurturing of manufacturing activities, is likely to lead to a misallocation of scarce resources.

Cultural factors play an increasingly important role. It will be seen also that during these early stages of industrialization a greater investment needs to be made in education for the improvement of human resources than in machinery and factory structures.

To recapitulate: The planning of a set of international specializations requires a sensitivity to international trends that is rarely found anywhere in the world, and cool judgment about risk taking as well. If public servants with these attributes do not exist, a group must be given the opportunity through service abroad, including participation on the international secretariats, to develop the necessary talents. It must be presumed that at least one such strategist for industrial development would be available. He would, as a matter of course, (1) review the world's growth industries, (2) investigate the industries in which world trade is growing, (3) consider exports from industries using low grade resources previously focused on local markets, (4) evaluate the technologies that depend heavily upon research and development, (5) assess the growth of competition in these areas, and finally (6) discover what can be installed by exploiting historical, political, and cultural relationships with the technically more advanced countries. In setting up a specialty the government must assist in the creation of specialist schools, in the establishment of foreign artisans and technologists in well-equipped workshops and laboratories, and in the provision of ancillary services. The specialty would go beyond imitation of designs; it must improvise a new style. More often than not the style will be a hybrid that draws upon the traditions of the society but also borrows from abroad, and it may be expected to appear earliest in the intellectual circles. Many of the expressions of this style are in activities that are not strictly manufacturing, such as tourism, film making, music, etc. This style must be encouraged to evolve and advance, rather than be allowed to stand still and become purist.

BIBLIOGRAPHY

Tinbergen, Jan: *Shaping the World Economy,* Twentieth Century Fund, New York, 1962.
   A revaluation of world trade and capital flows with recommendations for new approaches to integrating the various development programs.

Weiss, H. K.: "Some Growth Considerations of Research and Development and the National Economy," *Management Science,* vol. 11, pp. 368–394, 1965.
   Presents a mathematical model for the interaction between R & D and GNP, with quantitative comparisons between national economies.

PART THREE

EDUCATIONAL DEVELOPMENT

12

THE EDUCATIONAL FUNCTION
IN DEVELOPMENTAL SOCIETIES

AT ANY MOMENT in its course, every human society possesses a fund of knowledge which is the residue of accumulated experience of prior generations in that society, as well as of other societies from which it may have learned or borrowed. This fund of knowledge has the property of growing and increasing over time as long as the society maintains itself. It is lost or reduced only by catastrophe. The knowledge itself deals with both a comprehension of environmental forces and an understanding of interpersonal relationships within a framework of customs that have been mutually accepted. The application of this collective wisdom tends to maintain the unity of the society and reduce the risks of disaster.

It is not surprising, then, that every society should be deeply concerned about the transmission of its accumulated wisdom to future generations. In the distant past much of this transmission was accomplished in long, absorbing sessions of storytelling by the elder members, but much else remained to be depicted in the ritual occasions which were repeated with little variation each calendar year. In contemporary societies children are carefully guided into a world which becomes increasingly complex, and are introduced to it with the aid of more and more elaborate descriptions and explanations.

For thousands of years this function of instructing the young has been specialized. Quite early in human history certain persons were assigned these duties as their prime responsibilities. At first such tasks were delegated to slaves who taught the manual of arms, master craftsmen who trained apprentices, scholars who interpreted the classics, priests the religion, etc. All transfers of cultural experience make up education in its broadest sense, even though the term *education* now usually refers to the formal aspect of the process carried on through organized instruction in schools. It is this *broadest* concept of education with which planning for education must be concerned.

A society that has undertaken economic and social development is faced with unique educational problems. The wisdom of past generations is no longer sufficient to meet the crises encountered. Beyond the society's boundaries, on the world scene, is a rapidly expanding body of social thought, political action, technology, science, and philosophy which must be comprehended. Within these concepts, especially those having worldwide applicability, lie the principal opportunities for improving the level of living. *Therefore the developing society must draw upon a worldwide fund of knowledge, much of which is intrinsically alien to traditional ways of thinking.*

It has already been pointed out repeatedly that the developmental effort tends to exploit foreign ideas, combining them with local ideas, in order to improve welfare at home. Thus the function of education expands greatly beyond that required of a society in equilibrium. The educational system must teach individuals enough about world culture to enable the society to grasp opportunities available to it and still provide continuity with the past. It must prepare for action in the midst of rapid social change and provide key insights which permit ready adjustment to a new way of living. When the scope of education is expanded in this manner, each individual will be making many more personal contacts, he will be dealing with a variety of new social institutions, and encountering new and unexpected value systems. The education system designed for the transition cannot solve the problems of each person passing through it, nor can it transmit generalized rules for behavior in the new age, but it can give *a foretaste of some of the new situations that will be encountered*. It can reduce the confusion experienced by so many young people who are living through the transition period.

Educational systems have their beginnings in a subsistence level economy several decades preceding the "takeoff" or "breakout" stage in economic development. The rudiments of an educational system get established through the initiative of a few forward-looking nationals who managed by one means or another to seize an opportunity for themselves to study at one or more of the world's advanced centers of learning. It takes only a few dedicated persons with such backgrounds to plant the seeds by starting schools and other institutions, whereupon contacts with better-educated societies create niches in the environment which enable the schools to take root and grow. The prestige and status everywhere attributed to literacy and classical scholarship are sufficient to attract an increasing enrollment.

The first schools anywhere have almost always been private—they were by-products of ecclesiastical instruction or business enterprises—but the example of the institution of free public schools in Western countries has been followed elsewhere with great rapidity, so that local governments and the state in our times very early undertake the tasks of expanding the educational system.

Prior to the sustained spurt in economic growth an investment in education is seldom recovered in the form of increased real income. The outlay for education is viewed as a means of acquiring social status, and as such serves as a substitute for the acquisition of land or honorific titles. In many societies it is a means to becoming an officer in the army or a government official. Families with property or commercial interests wish to have some of their children receive formal education as a means of defending what they possess. In a subsistence-level economy, public investment in education confers few short-run advantages. The education is used in a very few vocations that the comparatively few privileged people take up.

Over the long run, however, many classrooms full of students are exposed to pedagogues and thousands of persons in the towns and cities will have acquired extra skills in communication. Once that supply of competence is available, it is possible to create the institutions that are so necessary to economic development—the banks, markets, transportation systems, communications network, a civil service, a responsible political leadership, a judiciary, cooperatives, entrepreneurial organizations, etc. Then, some time after this burst of organization has begun, the growth in production may result. *Investment in education, therefore, is a prerequisite for economic development.* It must begin well before the reorganization of the institutions of the society, a process which necessarily precedes the takeoff.

Once the prospects for economic growth appear promising, expanded investments in education become a paying proposition. Persons with communications skills and technical training suddenly become scarce, so that they command a relatively high wage. The expected income of persons who have been educated is so large that it would pay the costs of the education and yield a profit that in most instances is greater than might be expected from a business investment of the same size. During the growth phase of the American economy for which there are data (*ca.* 1900 to the present) there is evidence that, despite the huge outlays made for education during that period, the rate of return from secondary and higher education of all kinds was in the range of 10 to 20 percent before taxes, as compared to a return of about 10 percent before taxes on other capital investment. These figures suggest that economic growth in the United States would have been more rapid if the outlays for education had increased more rapidly in the 1900–1940 period than they actually did, and if greater attention had been paid to the kinds of education supplied.

Of course, not all investments in education turn out to be so advantageous. One of the explanations given for the rise of Nazism in Germany during the 1920s and early 1930s was the unemployment of a large fraction of the graduates of universities and technical high schools. In India at the present time there is a tremendous increase in the production of higher certificates and university degrees despite the observation that unemployment seems to be correlated with the amount of education. In both societies, nevertheless, there were shortages of trained people in some trades and professions. The oversupply occurred because more prestige was attached to classical education per se. Thus a blind emphasis upon education for education's sake can be self-defeating.

In the developmental society there needs to be a balanced introduction to ways of life that had been experienced thus far by only a minor fraction of the population. These new life patterns are public-oriented rather than family-centered. There must be some education for rural life if the production of food and fiber is to be made more efficient and dependable, but the heaviest emphasis must be placed upon the concepts that are useful in *urban* life.

These requirements lead to a definition of a *general education* that is suited to conditions of continuous social and economic growth. If the introductions to the new way of life succeed, one would expect to see fewer victims of the rapid social change. The half-educated, unemployed white-collar and subprofessional groups that live from hand to mouth and shift from one extreme philosophy to another would then hardly exist. Most individuals would regard social change not as a threat to their way of life but as an exhilarating adventure in self-improvement and a source of personal and collective opportunity.

EDUCATION AND CULTURAL DEVELOPMENT

The task of development is at the same time also a struggle to become a new and independent cultural and political entity. Increased wealth and increasing international contacts bring with them the need for identity; a cultural system must be created that befits the new rank among nations that is being achieved.

In earlier times, when a nation represented a relatively homogenous linguistic and ethnic population aggregate dominating a territory, the educational system was designed to propagate nationalism. The curriculum inculcated a set of patriotic symbols and an ideology that were calculated to make the state a cohesive, single-minded unit. The work of scholars in comparative education (e.g., Kandel, Hans, etc.) shows that the principal justification for constructing the first comprehensive school systems was the need to extend the standards of good citizenship and the tenets of the official ideology. The economic contributions of education were assigned secondary or even lesser importance.

These early school systems imprinted many ideological and linguistic myths in the minds of the educated. When nationalisms came into conflict with one another, compromise in some cases was found to be impossible, and a series of disastrous wars occurred. Thus today, through UNESCO and other agencies, attention is paid to the curricula of educational systems to see if the pathological features cannot be removed. The promotion of national loyalty and unity should be possible without generating dangerously chauvinistic ideology.

Viewed in the perspective of decades, the development of the political system and the development of the educational system—comprising equipment, trained personnel, tested curricula, and experienced administration —are mutually interdependent programs directed to the same end. When considered on a budget-to-budget basis, however, they are relatively self-sufficient activities whose common efforts overlap at only a few points. The use of education as a means for adjusting to social change brought about by economic development is certainly necessary, but education may also be employed as a directive agent, pointing the younger members particularly to niches in an overall social structure of a type that is believed to be most desirable by contemporary social philosophers.

For the typical Anglo-Saxon mind of today, the implications of the preceding assertions have a rather shocking quality, whereas leaders in rapidly developing territories will accept them more or less as a matter of fact. In the American tradition the ideal society is seen as one which tolerates, indeed often encourages, widely different cultural norms. Thus cultural choice, including career choice, is held to be one of the basic freedoms that is to a large extent left open to the individual. Americans have tended to make a virtue of necessity for blending a broad diversity of regional and ethnic types. Elsewhere the philosophers have propounded that cultural integration, brought about primarily by government-supported educational institutions, provides a kind of intellectual home by offering a measure of personal security and participation not otherwise available.

The seeking of a new cultural unity, a national character, is not entirely incompatible with the emphasis upon adaptation and adjustment. Most Anglo-Saxons concerned with educational policy are reluctant to set the total configuration of a society for fear of some mistake which would cast it inflexibly into the wrong mold. They emphasize *process* rather than *outcome*. Social philosophers in developing countries are more willing to prescribe some structure or pattern, still of necessity incompletely defined, for the "good society." Normally the latter will insist upon free expression of private opinion and attitude but allow that the government should subsidize and propagate the preferred cultural views and creations. The Latins fit within the orbit of both traditions, and the examples drawn from the Puerto Rican scene must take both into account. Each society must work out its own compromise between the imposition of a standard character, or style of life, and the toleration of divergent patterns that take over important segments of the education of youth.

The decisions regarding the kind and the content of long-range cultural *goals,* where the educational system is to be the primary instrument for attaining them, cannot be made by planners. Together these proposed goals constitute some of the "givens" of the planning situation. If the decision as arrived at is not internally consistent, or is not operable within the resources available, then much of the programming of educational development becomes fragmentary and uncoordinated and loses meaning. The staff work associated with long-range planning may be used to illuminate the problems of implementation and thus bring about more realistic political and cultural choices, but it does not have the power to *make* the choices and demand their acceptance. In a democratic society the planners may have influence, but not authority.

Educational planning is much more difficult when cultural directions are not established by the government. Lacking this direction, plans must rest upon general agreements as to the preferred cultural framework for the long run that already exist in implicit form as embodied in the constitution, the judicial decisions which interpret it, and the various institutions which continue to receive general approval. When these agreements and concurrences become more explicit over time, educational planning can be made more coherent.

The relation of cultural goals to educational planning can be illustrated in part by referring again to our prime example. When Puerto Rico was annexed to the United States it was presumed by Congress that its cultural future was that of assimilation—just one more ingredient for the American melting pot. The schools, accordingly, were to be the principal instrument for bringing about the transformation of Puerto Ricans into typical Americans. The curriculum in the early schools was modeled after the American, and the language of instruction in public schools was English. The teacher-training staff in the school of education of the college that later became the university were Americans, and many of the early classroom teachers themselves were imported from the mainland. The response in Puerto Rico was not enthusiastic, since few persons were convinced of the superiority of the American culture over their own. Criticism and conflict centered around "the language of instruction," and the arguments simmered for four decades. The issue was eventually resolved by teaching English as a second language, with a curriculum which was borrowed in part from the American schools but which had been translated into proper Spanish. A bilingual Spanish culture was to be propagated which could maintain close relationships with the United States. (With the establishment of commonwealth status a decade later, the aims of education became more explicit, but those developments are reserved for discussion at a later stage.)

History was kind to Puerto Rico in one respect, in that it came into the twentieth century without strong cultural divisions within its own boundaries. In much of Latin America, and almost all of Africa and Asia, there are two or more coherent ethnic groups within the respective nations. When that is the case the educational system must be designed so as to build a bridge between the two communities that will foster communication and assist in the integration of political and economic activities. In many instances cooperation between the respective ethnic communities is a prerequisite for economic development—indeed for survival of the state as a self-governing unit—and so merits a very high priority over a span of several decades. Education has usually misfired when used as an instrument for unifying cultures, especially when a special form of teaching (including language of instructions, methods, curriculum, philosophy, etc.) is imposed by a central government with little consideration of local needs; nevertheless it has contributed greatly to cohesion in Canada, Israel, and Yugoslavia, to mention three recent examples.

THE SCOPE OF EDUCATIONAL PLANNING

From this discussion it should be evident that the meaning of education as employed here—which should in all cases be employed in developmental planning for education—includes not only the elementary and high schools, the colleges and professional schools, but also the trade schools and business colleges, all the arrangements for evening classes, community educational work in rural and urban areas, much of the agricultural extension, some of the public health work, and special features of the mass media, including radio, television, films, and pamphlets.

The scope of the function is so broad it cannot be planned in detail. If all the possibilities inherent in the educational process are to be realized, teachers, writers, commentators, executives, community school boards, and civil servants must be granted a high degree of discretion. Most countries have already developed many institutions and procedures which safeguard the freedom of the educator from central domination. Planners are obliged to assess—from estimates and measurements made within the society—those approaches which seem to be the most suitable for solving the problems of the immediate and foreseeable future. When funds are scarce (a condition that exists almost universally), planners must search for criteria that determine which educational programs deserve increased allocations. These criteria will, for the most part, be provided by the educators themselves, but they are expected to coincide to an important extent with judgments derived from such reference systems as the *human resources* analysis (already introduced in Chapter 7) and the principles of *lifelong education,* which are taken up in detail in Chapter 13. Planning for education must rest as far as possible upon an expert appraisal of the situation, and the decisions must be arrived at by the established democratic processes. In addition, the implementation of decisions must be administratively simple and effective.

In the past, education has normally been split up into a department of public instruction, or some similar agency, which is expected to cope with formal instruction in the elementary and secondary schools and may also be given responsibility for urban vocational instruction and teacher training. A commission for higher education, responsible for colleges and universities, operates as a separate body. Various regulatory bodies for television, radio, the press, and other services will also exist. In addition, each department of government invariably finds that some feature of education is vital to *its* operations. The departments therefore budget for it and maintain control over the teaching process. Obviously, each unit is jealous of its prerogatives, and challenges regarding the competence of the others occur not infrequently in public.

Under such circumstances the strategic planning in education is accomplished in the office of the executive. It is implemented by allocating funds in the budget to explicit programs. The principal difficulty such planning has met in the past is that the performance of an agency, or program, could not be measured in terms of some generally applicable criterion, except perhaps by the number of degrees, diplomas, and certificates of an established standard that were produced. The reference systems mentioned above provide sets of accounts for making such appraisals across administrative divisions.

Economists usually speak of education as an aspect of "welfare." In their way of thinking, it is a service and an item of consumption. Such a definition will work tolerably well in a society maintained at equilibrium, but it fails very seriously under conditions of economic growth. Then, a part of education—that part most related to fostering economic and social growth—becomes an investment, and is commonly denoted as an *investment in human productive agents.* When such outlays are made, the work subsequently performed should result in greater outputs than would be anticipated in the stationary society. If economic growth occurs, the extra value obtained is considerably larger than the investment. This observation suggests that educational goals can be separated into (1) those which are needed to *maintain* society in its condition and (2) those which contribute to rapid economic and social *improvements*.

Goals are expressed here in a way that is quite different from the way they appear in the voluminous literature on educational philosophy. The latter body of thought holds that the educational system must assist the student to achieve *self-realization*, defined as step-by-step progress toward the potentials that are inherent in the makeup of his own personality. The education process is oriented to the interaction between teacher and student, once the decision has been made that there shall be teachers and institutional situations where teaching is expected. The huge body of discussion among leading educators about the proper goals of education is of little value in making the decision as to how much support should be given to education, and of not much more help on the problem of deciding how to allocate effort among the various forms of education. The budgeting process requires criteria and specific aims that are less psychologically oriented than the concurrences between educators and more directed to social, political, and cultural ends. Perhaps this deficiency in educational philosophy should be anticipated because there is a similar gap in medical philosophy concerning how much effort should be spent upon health and what is a reasonable basis for subdividing the effort. The philosophizing for the professions seems to be more concerned with ethics than with welfare maximization.

THE AIMS OF EDUCATION

Among educators it is generally agreed that the school and community must inculcate certain social values if society is to be maintained. These are human kindness, honesty, sincerity, individual responsibility, fair play, an appreciation of beauty and truth, together with equable relations between the sexes, the age levels, social classes, and ethnic groups. These things indeed are required for the survival of the society; but other objectives equally important are those that will contribute more to social and economic growth, namely, greater skills in communication; skills in reasoning and computation; skills with machines and in the fabrication of materials; an appreciation for organization and the seeking of improved understanding, orderliness, precision, etc. In this discussion of developmental planning for education, attention will be concentrated upon this second set of objectives, but it must always be kept in mind that the first cannot be dismissed. On the contrary, as the society grows, more effort must be allocated to the *maintenance* features of education if the more advanced position is to be retained.

It should be remembered that there is a greater time lag separating the expenditure of effort from the outcomes in educational planning than in any other type of planning, except some forms of conservation of natural resources. Any planning done now would first affect the operating structure of the educational system two to five years after the plans have been accepted; but some five to fifty years will elapse before the young people, upon whom most of this money and time is expended, would show their response to the changes. The major impact would probably show up in the period two to three decades hence. Therefore the objectives for education planning must be based upon the needs and conditions visualized for a date a quarter century hence, rather than for the near future. In underdeveloped societies, where changes are now as rapid as almost any place in the world, a future so distant is more obscure than in the relatively advanced countries in North America and Western Europe.

Demands upon the educational system will arise also from plans being made in other sectors of the government. The dependency of *industry* upon the skills and attitudes brought into being through formal education has already been emphasized. Improvements in *agriculture* are even more difficult to bring about because there are rarely any community institutions which provide the equivalent of "in-plant" training in industry, so that the modernization of agriculture will require an elaborate system of education ranging from the training of agricultural technologists to the supervision of demonstration plots in each locality. The plans for *urbanization* must establish a new style of life. It is therefore expected that most of the residents will be trained to understand the uses of the facilities and institutions in the urban environment; otherwise the costs of misuse and underuse pile up prohibitively. The plans outlined for *communications* (telephone, radio, television, films, printing and publishing, postal system, etc.) will have considerable influence upon the media that are to be employed for education. The plan for improvement of *public health* will depend heavily upon the teaching of nutrition and hygiene in the schools and of family limitation through adult education techniques.

Certain of the aims of education in a rapidly developing country can be deduced logically from the definition of education itself. Thus, when setting down the general goals, a plan for education might be expected to include the following (among others):

1. *To transmit to the new generations the wisdom of human relations which has evolved in the specific culture.* This wisdom exists as a set of ideals. Often the ideals cannot be carried out in practice to the extent that people would wish because of extreme poverty and overcrowding—conditions which should eventually improve in the course of development.

Many relationships between production-oriented social roles, which are often transmitted along with the ideals, may become obsolete and virtually useless because of the remarkable efficiency of the technology being imported from the outside. Yet it is not easy to disentangle traditional techniques from the ideals. In addition, there may be a few of the ideals which constitute a grave hindrance to progress (a common example might be the tendency for responsible officials to grant special favors to relatives—a traditional practice which, incidentally, has been largely eradicated in Puerto Rico only after decades of special indoctrination). Under these circumstances, the tradition of the society is usually rich enough in alternative standards of conduct so that one feature of the tradition can now be emphasized at the expense of the other. The undesirable consequences of conflict between the old and the new are thereby partly avoided. This is a strategy well understood by pedagogues who are alert to the changes going on in their own society.

2. *To provide seeds for new understanding, new capacities to adapt, and new sources of leadership, looking toward the continuation and progressive improvement of the society.* This may take the form of transmitting through the educational system an introduction to scientific outlook, an emphasis on achievement, the highlighting of new roles in social action, and ideas of progress, together with ethnic, spiritual, and moral values. In the first stages of development, this aim may need to be limited to a small fraction or class of the population, but in the later stages it must be extended to all the population accessible to the educational institutions.

3. *To propagate the necessary skills needed to carry out the successive stages of economic development.* Preliminary estimates are needed of the quantities of various skills required by the economy at various stages, ranging from five to twenty years into the future. From such estimates some specific educational priority assignments can be derived, such as those concerning the education of women to carry out a certain number of industrial and commercial activities, or firm targets of the type which, for example, might specify that there should be at least a stipulated number of qualified engineers by the year 1970. Some of the requisite skills, generally those at the advanced technical or professional level, must be acquired overseas, and for that purpose some persons must be trained to a point where they can successfully extract from the education outside what will be useful at home.

These aims all are consonant with other goals of socioeconomic development. The people rightly assume that it is the duty of the government officials to do everything in their power to further them.

HANDLING OF CONFLICTING AIMS

The gravest problems facing the educational planners, those that be-devil them at every turn and cannot be ignored, have been hinted at but have not yet been squarely faced here. How do planners establish which way some aspect of education should be decided, if the people are divided or uninterested? These attitudes are two separate problems, but both are likely to lead to conflict. The first represents a fundamental cleavage in the thinking of the society. Most often it is an inability to agree upon a principle or criterion for setting priorities. The second will frequently lead to disagreements between various schools of thought among the leaders, where arguments will often become too abstruse and theoretical for popular participation.

At the time of the founding of the United States, religious education was an issue which could not be settled by consensus. Too many incompatible sects existed. The solution arrived at is typical: nobody's religion was to be taught in public schools, but opportunities were granted to all to teach their own doctrines in their own institutions. Sometimes the issue is compromised, *quid pro quo,* while at other times the decision can be postponed. Often it can be left to local option, where consensus may be more easily achieved. In some places a judicial decision will be respected. The method by which an appropriate means for resolution and accommodation comes into play depends upon political finesse. Thus education and politics cannot be divorced. The basic problem is that of finding short-run political solutions which, if perpetuated, do not destroy the beneficial features of the plans for education.

A conflict of the other variety may be posed as follows: *What should be the place of the society among the world cultures, in the long run?* This is a question of ultimate direction, a favorite ground for debate among intellectuals, and one which has already been introduced. A matter like this is weighed differently according to economic class, occupational status, and prior education. Thus views can be expected to change as levels of living increase and as the economy takes on certain attributes of development. One thing is certain: arguments concerning cultural direction and of "national character" cannot be removed from the circumstances of how people make a living, how they communicate, and how they move about. One kind of situation prevails if large numbers of citizens emigrate every year; another, if the number is small. If the territory should become an important holiday center, the services to the tourists will do much to mold the cultural environment. Similarly, the cultural question is strongly influenced by the exchange of experts and technicians with neighbors and with the technologically advanced sectors of the world. Consequently, a question must be raised from the start concerning the extent that cultural views should give direction to economic activities, as well as to educational activities, and how the society can develop a modern cultural base within the limits of the growth which the economy exhibits.

PRIORITIES IN EDUCATION PLANNING

The success of income-generating programs relies heavily on the creation of a pool of well-trained, skilled workers who have a firm grasp of modern industrial and agricultural techniques. It is generally accepted that a degree of literacy up to the sixth grade or its equivalent is a minimum essential for educational programs. Once such a minimum level of education has become universal, the modern media of mass communication (books, pamphlets, magazines, newspapers, radio, television, recordings) become visibly effective as tools for educating individuals in every phase of modern living.

Another type of priority deserves consideration, the need for developing top-quality "public servants" in the broadest sense of the term. Whenever a society has started to change its social and economic structure, it needs many more problems solved than when it remains static. So it is most essential that as many as possible of particularly good minds are found early and developed into competent public servants.

The special priority that comes out of this latter consideration of higher education is a systematic search for the top 1 or 2 percent of the youth. This does not mean that scholarships should be routinely provided for that fraction of all the youngsters in school; it means that strong efforts should be made so that virtually *none of this top fraction will arbitrarily be deprived of education.* These youngsters would then be assured of thorough college preparation, either by direct or indirect means. The cost of such a program of precollege development is likely to be rather small; it need not affect the allocations of funds to priority programs designated in the plan for industrial development, but it should yield a potential return out of all proportion to cost.

BIBLIOGRAPHY

Carnegie Endowment Study Group: "Needs and Resources for Social Investment," *International Social Science Journal,* vol. 12, pp. 409–433, 1960.
 An admirable review of opinion and technique for measuring and judging social outlays, including education.

Hans, Nicholas: *Comparative Education,* 3d ed., Routledge & Kegan Paul, Ltd., London, 1958.
 An analysis of the factors that have shaped educational systems up to the 1950s, primarily from a European point of view.

Kandel, I. L.: *Comparative Education,* Houghton Mifflin Company, Boston, 1933.
A classic description of the mode of organization and operations of six different educational systems—American, English, French, Italian, German, and Russian—as they had evolved from quite different historical origins and were shaped by nationalistic ideologies.

Miles, Matthew B.: "Educational Innovation: Resources, Strategies, and Unanswered Questions," *American Behavioral Scientist,* vol. 7, pp. 10–14, February, 1964.
A trenchant evaluation of what is known concerning the use of education for achieving planned social change.

Vaizey, John: *The Costs of Education,* George Allen & Unwin, Ltd., London, 1958.
The trends in school expenditures in England and Wales from 1920 to 1955, with estimates of the benefits accruing to the respective social classes.

Walton, John: *Administration and Policy Making in Education,* The Johns Hopkins Press, Baltimore, Md., 1959.
A series of philosophical discussions in the American public administration tradition that involve a few comparisons with British administrative procedures.

World Confederation of Organizations of the Teaching Profession: *Conditions of Work for Quality Teaching,* 1963 theme study, Rio de Janeiro Conference, August, 1963.
International contrasts between what appears to teachers is most needed for the improvement of quality of formal education.

13

LINKAGES FOR EDUCATIONAL PLANNING

Despite the fact that education requires funds normally in excess of those allocated to any other single governmental service, it is a governmental activity which tends to get separated from the main stream of budgeting and programming. The reasons for this separation may vary from one society to another. In some places the basic budgetary and curriculum decisions are made by local boards and commissions, with a portion of the funds being supplied by central governments. In other instances the decisions are made by professional educators whose primary concern is to keep the educational system from becoming the servant of petty political interests. The separation of the budgeting and programming exists in the most developed countries as well as in those in the earlier stages of development. Therefore the kinds of linkages that join educational programs with other major programs for the purpose of optimizing economic development are still in an exceedingly rudimentary state. Fortunately, relatively new and economical means for collecting data offer opportunities for rationalizing the educational planning process and tying it to the overall program.

As with any other government activity, the needs in education can be brought into perspective when considered as elements in a system which is larger than education itself but still much smaller in scale than the whole. Because these extremes are brought together for comparison, measurement, and analysis, the frameworks for accounting are called *reference systems.* The two reference systems most useful in a developing society for accumulating data and comparison proposals are *human re-*

sources and *lifelong adaptation*. The first links education with many programs affecting health, urbanization, and industry. The second links education with welfare administration, the maintenance of law and order, and community organization.

Education is the major tool available to a society for developing its human resources in that, through education, the kinds of human understanding and human skills that are so necessary for progress are brought into existence. But if the society faces a specific problem of known dimensions which must be resolved within a few years (e.g., the development of a new irrigation district, the elimination of malaria in a given region, the operation of a marine transport system) and its solution requires a number of persons with given levels of understanding and skill, education is not the *only* procedure for satisfying the needs. A department of labor, for example, may seek out the needed characteristics in the existing labor force, arrange for substitutes to be found for the jobs these persons are now holding, and recruit the key people for the more essential task. Or a research organization may be able to recast the problem so that the distributions of skills in the labor force already on the scene would be able to handle the situation; this procedure is in effect a substitution of research personnel for the specialized skills. Or a health department might be able to reduce the amount of time lost on account of sickness and disability among persons already in this activity, and thus make the needed additional labor available. Usually one of these possibilities, or some combination of them, is less expensive than another, measured in money or time. Other things being equal, the less expensive program would then be adopted.

Lifelong adaptation is a catchall label which refers to the provisions by which institutions, programs, and activities of various sorts are able, despite the rapidity of social change, to maintain *participation of all ages and for all personality types*. No section of the population should be excluded by prejudice, oversight, or lack of foresight; nor should they be handed a dole, or pensioned off, and then forgotten. Poor societies cannot provide "cradle to grave" security for their members because of the cost, but they can do a great deal to assure that opportunity for constructive effort is presented to all ages and all groups.

The existence of a reference system based upon lifelong adaptation and the use of readily available knowledge regarding population according to age, sex, and residential location, and further combined with an inventory of the coverage of public and private social institutions, would alert the planner to the existence of special needs some years before they become critical. Given that time in advance for preparation, some very economical solutions can be worked out. The adaptation to change may well be achieved by a minor modification of the school curriculum, or it may be incorporated into the programs of the voluntary associations that tend to spring up in developing communities. Because a human population is so diverse, the proposals and adjustments resulting from needs for lifelong adaptation tend to be relatively small in scale but extremely varied.

ANALYSIS OF HUMAN RESOURCES

In contrast, proposals deriving from human-resources analysis must be the basis for huge investments. If information gathering has been initiated along the lines recommended in Chapter 4, there should very early be a sufficient basis for estimating the human resources available in the society. Then the amounts of human resources required for achieving given targets can be estimated when the existing technologies and organizational procedures are expressed quantitatively.

Data concerning population, labor force, employment, and location are most essential. Human resources may be considered first as *fractions of the total population which meet certain standards of proficiency.* That the persons being counted actually meet such standards can be judged by examination of individuals, interview, observation of them at work, measurement of their output, or records of their past performance. However, it is inordinately expensive to collect useful data concerning *each* adult in the society in this direct manner. This direct approach has value only when information is desired regarding the supply of specific, scarce professional-level skills. Therefore the aggregate picture of human resources for the developing society must be based upon inferred and indirect evidence.

Some of this information may be obtained from answers to questions that have been included in the census questionnaire. Perhaps the most important of these questions are: "How many grades of school have you completed?" and "What is your present occupation?"

Quick surveys can be made of the membership of unions, crafts, guilds, and professional societies. Such organizations are usually quite careful in their scrutiny of the qualifications of candidates, and they reject individuals who fall below a given competence. The existence of a few scandalous exceptions does not really invalidate the overall statistics, so the rosters of membership are a meaningful indicator of the existence of skill in a population.

Other indicators of competence are based upon self-selected participation. For example, the number of persons using a library and purchasing books will indicate the proportion who are actively literate. The question also may be asked, "How many persons listen to the radio regularly, see television, read a newspaper, and subscribe for magazines and other periodicals?" It is surprising how much of this information can be obtained at negligible cost.

In many democratic societies there are constitutional safeguards which prevent the collection of detailed information on the membership either of the unions or customers of private enterprises if the organizations object. In that case brief social surveys can be instituted that cover all these questions, along with many others, which will provide a preliminary estimate of the degree to which human resources have been developed. The classification should take the following form:

Educational Level	Skill Level	Social Characteristics
Little or no schooling	Unskilled	Tradition-bound
Elementary school diploma	Semiskilled	Aware-passive
High school diploma	Skilled	Self-starting
College level training	Supervisory	Group leaders
College graduates	Administrative and professional	Community leaders
Professional school graduates	Top professional	State leaders

The first column utilizes standards within a formal educational system and probably correlates most closely with proficiencies in communication. The second makes assessments based upon performances in the production side of the economy. The third reflects the extent of participation in social and political institutions.

Behind all these breakdowns are important limitations. Not everyone has the capacity to acquire college level training or fill a supervisor's job. A minimum level of intelligence and a satisfactory state of both physical and mental health are required. These requirements become more restrictive as increasingly higher standards are established within a developing society. Thus, underlying all these developed human resources is a limit, or more accurately, a *potential*, which is set by levels of intelligence and health. These factors too can be measured in a crude fashion.

Education, in a human-resources context, represents the investment of time, money, and effort whereby the human potential is transformed into a competence. The approximate quantities of special competences required to achieve the aims of the society may be deduced from the series of targets which have been set in the development plans. From this point of view education is a means to a specified end, i.e., development.

Studies on human resources are now becoming highly important in developed countries. Special emphasis is placed upon those talents and skills which are found to be scarce in the existing society. The studies usually endeavor to describe the extent to which the intellectually gifted persons are available, the degree to which these individuals find their way to responsible positions requiring such talents, and the kinds of wastage of talent which are observed to exist. There are other talents sought at least as avidly, such as those which yield the most competent pilots for high-speed aircraft, or make possible a success in the creative arts, or would do well in the Olympic games or in professional athletics.

The shortages in human resources experienced by modern societies in the course of their growth have only recently resulted in quantitative assessments of the supply of specialized talent. The first relatively comprehensive analysis was offered in the report of the Commission on Human Resources and Advanced Training in the United States (1954). Since then, each time a new and apparently long-term shortage appeared, investigations were undertaken to discover the supply and demand of the scarce skills and to formulate policies that might improve the prospects for the long run. These studies prepared the way for decisions regarding the development and allocation of human resources at the national level. Thus far attention has been drawn particularly to scientists, engineers, and teachers.

Again it is useful to refer to the experience in Puerto Rico, where such studies were more closely related to comprehensive social and economic planning. A special committee on human resources was created there by the Planning Board and the Department of Labor. It undertook an analysis of manpower needs and supply for the same period that projections were made for the population and the growth of the economy. The committee first reviewed historical trends and current commitments to education and from this information was able to estimate the future supply of educated manpower. In consequence it was able to assert with some persuasive force that the commitments to education were inadequate and might easily obstruct achievement of the economic targets that had been set. The analysis of human resources strongly suggested that the planned 5 to 7 percent annual growth in real per capita income required an increased allocation to education, even though the educational effort, expressed as a fraction of gross product, was already close to being the highest, if not the highest, in the world.

It is worthwhile to outline how such data may be employed in arriving at conclusions which can be the basis for important changes in budgeting allocations. The projection of proved programs for industrialization and the reorganization of agriculture and commerce led to the expectation that Puerto Rico could reach a per capita output by 1975 essentially the same as that achieved by the United States, as an average, in 1950. Since detailed statistics were available for the American economy of that period, it could then be assumed that the proportions of specialized skills needed to reach those levels of productivity (i.e., the United States in 1950) would be the same as in the North American economy. This assumption is quite reasonable because most Puerto Rican manufactures would be made by machines brought from the United States and would be sold in the American market, and even the banks, retailing centers, and other commercial institutions were increasingly modeled after the American counterparts.[1]

The committee on human resources reasoned that the structure of the Puerto Rican economy of the future must be quite different from that of the United States in 1950 because Puerto Rico does not have the resources to sustain the heavy industry that is so important to the United States. The target economy for 1975 in Puerto Rico must necessarily be biased toward light manufacturing and tropical agriculture. Thus the appropriate distribution of the labor force between professionals, managers, clerical workers, sales workers, craftsmen, operatives, service workers, private household workers, farm managers, laborers, and farm laborers would need to be shifted somewhat. A model was created of what the United States labor force would probably have been if most of its heavy industry were operated immediately outside. This model epitomized in broad strokes and large dimensions what Puerto Rico was trying to achieve on a small scale.

Then for each occupational group an estimate was made of the amount of education required (see Table 3). The review of the programs of the Department of Education, combined with an analysis of the effects of migration, made possible an estimate of the expected supply in the labor

Table 3. Employment by Occupational Group and Sex, 1975 (in thousands)

Occupational group	Both sexes	Male	Female
Total	798	585	213
Professionals	55	33	22
Managers	67	58	9
Clerical workers	100	38	62
Sales workers	50	34	16
Craftsmen	90	85	5
Operatives	192	140	52
Service workers	54	30	24
Private household workers	13	1	12
Farm owners and managers	39	38	1
Laborers	40	39	1
Farm laborers	98	89	9

[1] It will be argued later that this assumption may easily be too conservative; that a still more efficient allocation of human resources is possible than was employed by the American economy in 1950, and that the targets within education derived from these other considerations would be more easily achieved by the Puerto Rican educational system.

Table 4. Education Level of the Population, 1950–1975 (in thousands)

Educational level	1950	1955	1960	1965	1970	1975
Population (15 and over)	1,249	1,294	1,374	1,438	1,494	1,500
College	17	21	25	34	42	53
Senior high school	68	101	161	212	278	341
Junior high school	103	105	145	150	198	190
Elementary school	282	290	300	335	330	331
5 years or less	779	777	743	707	646	585

SOURCE: *Puerto Rico's Manpower Needs and Supply*, Commonwealth of Puerto Rico, 1957.

force (Table 4). In this instance a significant shortfall was demonstrated which could only be modified by:

1. A sharp increase in educational effort
2. A radical change in migration patterns
3. A radical increase in labor force participation

The second and third possibilities are least amenable to government action and control in a democratic society.

REALLOCATION OF HUMAN RESOURCES

A crude estimate arrived at by using a model in the manner described above serves to illuminate the dimensions of the shortfall (or surplus). It can also designate the portion of the school system which would be most seriously affected. It can say relatively little, however, about what kinds of skills need to be imparted to the next generation. Much more explicit suggestions regarding the demand for specific skills would arise from a study of the anticipated changes in the developing economy, when taken sector by sector, checking the established responsibilities and special programs of each department of government. Some of the most typical situations encountered in the developing economies are worth reviewing at this point.

1. The exploitation of natural resources—soils, forests, minerals, waterpower—normally begins long before the period of sustained growth. The *foundations of the educational system are laid down when commodity export is established*. Basic facilities for transportation and communication also are installed during this period. The need for the integration of extensive operations introduces a demand for trained persons in local enterprises and an even larger number for governmental activities.

2. By the time the takeoff in economic development occurs, the needs for manufacturing are most evident. Manufactured exports to developed

countries must meet certain quality standards if the market is to be retained. This means that careful controls of the manufacturing must be instituted which enable it to adjust to variable quality in the local raw materials and to changing markets. At this point industrial workers need preliminary training—literacy, a sense of responsibility, a capacity for disciplined work, vocational skills, an understanding of machinery, etc. In many cases a predominant share of the industrial employment will be female; some special measures for training women may have to be adopted because often in these same societies they have received little or no education. In addition, industry will require a large number of persons able to write letters and handle simple accounts. A somewhat smaller number must be able to write comprehensive reports, while a few must be educated to the point where they can draw up written evaluations suitable for policy making. At least a few should acquire a background which enables them to draft the plans, directives, and regulations that are employed for executive action. The top officers for the enterprises tend to be selected from this most highly trained class.

3. Industrial expansion depends to an important extent upon the grasping of opportunities in specific locales, but it is not possible to concentrate education solely in those regions in which the plans for industrialization call for special emphasis. Most of the labor force getting its first job in manufacturing will have left school some time earlier. The workers will also have come from other places. For them *there must be created a coherent program of vocational courses, night classes, and on-the-job training.* Most of the curriculum for vocational training for industry will be dictated by the shortages in trained persons felt by enterprises already in existence and the demands of others just being formed.

4. Agriculture presents a vastly different picture. For one thing a prosperous agriculture must get along with *fewer* workers. In a period of rapid economic development the emphasis is laid upon increasing the productivity of labor, particularly on a per-man-per-year basis, but also on an areal (per-acre or per-hectare) basis. Although illiteracy may be a grave difficulty for many rural communities, *the main educational task is that of introducing new techniques* of cultivation, fertilizer use, new seeds and crops, and machine-operating skills. The manpower requirements most difficult to meet here are for demonstrators, teachers, community organizers, and nurses. They work with the agricultural extension service, the schools, the cooperatives, and the clinics.

5. In commerce it is not so much the numbers employed which change during the course of development as it is the quality of the services. In the traditional society, a person could be virtually illiterate and still become a good trader, but the period now being described is when people have the extra income with which to purchase such staples as ice cream

and antibiotics. These new products require knowledge of equipment and conformance to a strict health code, or they demand technical servicing of some kind. Bicycles and automobiles, for example, demand knowledge of mechanics. *The new services are much more elaborate and so require personnel to have, on the average, four to six years more schooling for their maintenance than did the old.* Most of the schooling must be in the area of general education—reading, writing, arithmetic, hygiene—but a year or so would be required for the mastery of certain specialized skills and the use of up-to-date business methods. Much of the responsibility for creating these specialized skills can be left to commercial enterprises, some of them with international connections, which will enter the business of selling courses of training in typing, business-machine operation, bookkeeping, inventory control, etc. The principal governmental task is then one of supervising and guiding these businesses so as to minimize waste.

6. The construction industry can be a crucial sector in a rapidly growing economy. It is frequently retarded by a lack of plumbers, glaziers, riggers, sheet-metal workers, stonemasons, plastics fabricators, and the like. Each of these crafts is likely to have its own program for apprenticeship and training, but many of them will be rendered inadequate because of the change in the character of buildings required for urban development and the tremendous volume of new construction induced by economic development. Resorting to subdivision of tasks and small assembly lines will make it possible to complete the simpler mass construction projects on schedule, but hotels, terminals, office buildings, factory buildings, hospitals, and similar structures tend to encounter long and costly delays if undertaken without outside assistance. *Vocational-education courses seem to offer a partial solution, but careful study of the allocation of the scarce skills may reveal other contributions that can be made by an analysis of human resources.* For example, in some climates a strong seasonality exists in the construction industry; the labor for the more complex structures then can be scheduled for the beginning of the slack season.

7. The social services sector, represented in the government by such departments as health, defense, welfare, pension services, transportation, etc., each can be scrutinized for the changes in operations which must be expected to occur in the course of economic growth. It may be found that some extraordinary demands will be made upon the human resources available. For example, public health services are normally assigned the task of introducing information to the public relating to opportunities for family limitation. As soon as effective methods have been worked out, these programs should have high priority. It is then that shortages will appear in social workers, nurses, pharmacists, etc.

New channels of training would have to be provided to upgrade persons with experience in low-priority occupations. Some of the women, for instance, who would otherwise become competent household servants might, with training, become practical nurses; clerks might be transformed into pharmacists with reasonable technical proficiency. In each instance there would be a precedent in the society for such transformations which can be seized upon, publicized, and expanded. A feeling that this is a "proper" approach to modernization of the society is most necessary; otherwise the persons who fill these new and more responsible roles will not know quite how to behave, nor will the persons who use the services understand how to accept them. By means of textbooks, posters, and perhaps radio and television talks by leaders, it is necessary to provide prototypes for acceptable behavior which permit the newly taught persons to practice what they have learned.

Up to this point the human-resources needs for education itself have not been discussed. During the early evolutionary stages, education proceeds with a teacher leading a class with the help of a few worn, outdated textbooks. Then the teacher is given more equipment, better training in teaching methods, and a wider range of books. Minimum standards are enforced through the preparation of standard examinations and the appointment of a staff of inspectors. School lunch programs are initiated, and after that a visiting nurse or traveling clinic is added. Classroom teaching is coordinated with programs on radio and television. Summer courses are prepared which inform the teacher about new materials and techniques, and regular circulars are sent out to reinforce and add to the teachers' background training. As soon as schools are available to all children in a province or region, heavy emphasis must be given to improving the quality of education. This means more training for teachers, a better-organized curriculum, flexible school structures, a variety of associated services, and increased emphasis upon administration. Many educational specialists must be created and fitted into the structure of the educational system.

Once all the sectors of the economy have been surveyed, a different kind of demand schedule for manpower can be worked out. When the needs for persons with basic education up to certain standards, and for practitioners of various occupations, are matched against the current supply, the *gap* becomes the target for the educational system.

The planning for education cannot use these estimates directly, however, because in a developing society there is a rapid diffusion of skill out of the occupations for which training is given into other rewarding activities. Female schoolteachers usually marry two or three years after they begin to teach. Craftsmen may go into business or commercial agriculture, and factory workers may go back to the rural areas. Thus, for every modern job that must be filled, two or three persons must be trained. On the surface this pattern seems to be excessively wasteful, but in most instances the indirect effects of the training bring about a number of innovations and adaptive changes in society that repay the investment in education within a decade or two. Instances of this sort are generated almost as frequently by vocational education as by more general studies.

Skill shortages are not the only problem. Warnings have already been introduced that there may be an oversupply of lawyers and architects, alongside a grave deficiency in the supply of accountants and engineers. In some societies mastery of the classics was once the surest path into the civil service, but under conditions of growth the concepts of efficient organization, of justice, and of beauty undergo a radical change, so that the greatest surplus arises, paradoxically enough, among the humanists.[2]

Once this first set of approximations has been completed, a very important planning decision must be made.

It must be ascertained whether any component of human resources may be a serious limit to socioeconomic growth. Many developing societies assume that their growth is limited by lack of capital, when what is really constraining development is the shortage of some segment of human resources, making the investment of capital too risky. This limit will appear (after close inspection of the supply-demand relationship) as an inability to develop local measures for making up a critical deficiency in human skills. It is important to note that a country may be limited by lack of capital at the moment, but upon receiving only a moderate flow of investment from the outside, it will often discover that *the development of its human resources is too rudimentary to maintain even that rate of investment.*

A grave deficiency of engineers, for example, will require quite drastic measures. Promising young men might be sent off to the best schools overseas to acquire the necessary training. The principal objection to this is that it is time-consuming; instead then, for a moderate cost, engineers might be imported from areas of local surplus in Europe and Japan. Still other vital skills may have been acquired by migrants, some of whom

---

[2] Whenever families are responsible for the investment in education, rather than the student himself, there is a strong tendency for the career choice to be oriented to the past rather than the future. Families are extraordinarily conservative in educational matters. The proper investment in education requires a knowledgeable assessment of the future demand for skills, a body of facts which heads of families do not ordinarily possess during periods of rapid economic growth. The decisions made with insufficient knowledge of the trends are most likely to lead to the embarrassing oversupply of some kinds of trained individuals. See also Chapter 2 concerning education practices in traditional societies.

can be attracted back to their country of origin. A wide variety of alternatives are open; all that each first requires is some imagination for generating a proposal that introduces an opportunity for action. A decision may be based upon an analysis which establishes comparison costs and returns of the respective proposals; or the government may find it advisable to use all the proposals at once—then the decision must be the allocation of funds among them.

The central theme of *human resources* as a reference system coordinates the planning of education with the remainder of the developmental program. Through it, any new claimant for manpower and special skills comes immediately to the attention of the education authorities. Educational measures, as well as other stratagems for meeting this need, can be reviewed, and it is expected that whichever is most economic or most politic would be adopted. This procedure seems eminently reasonable to all concerned and is quite simple to organize with the present state of knowledge.

METHODS FOR LIFELONG ADAPTATION

In the course of modernization the whole society changes. Many people will have received education good enough for the traditional society, but that environment is being gradually undermined and replaced; at mid-career they are faced with becoming superfluous. If there has not been careful planning, this discovery comes as a shock, and it may cause a flash of violence or sabotage. The kind of action needed to prevent these sudden jerks and spasms so costly to the development process is to establish effective channels of communication between the modern sector and all members of the population. It is essential for the whole population, not merely those attending school, to be able to make adjustments to continuous change. The content of each channel, therefore, must be adapted to the particular segment of the population it can reach. Popular culture may predominate, but indicators of change and news of opportunity are also conveyed continually.

It is logical, therefore, to propose that every medium for the transfer of information and training be considered as an educational channel. What do the youth, middle-aged, and older people feel they ought to know? What range of opportunities for improving their personal condition and position would they welcome? From which persons or agencies would they accept such assistance? What media for the transmission of information do they trust? How much of their own effort are they willing and able to expend in order to get such educational assistance? It can be seen readily that the population can be divided into hundreds of special "publics" according to their respective interests and needs. Ways and means can be found for serving each one of them as economically and effectively as possible. Inevitably this reference system tends to emphasize education conducted *outside* the schools.

Lifelong adaptation is good educational practice in any society, but it is much more necessary in a developing society. If development is to proceed with reasonable rapidity, a society must depend very heavily upon the willingness of its adults, who have been out of school for many years, to carry out new tasks requiring new skills. Because the tasks are novel, the skills must be acquired in a learning situation which exists outside the school system. The tasks cannot wait until appropriate classes are given in the schools and their graduates pour out into the community. Fundamental individual adjustments have to be promoted, and various forms of education are the principal means for aiding these adjustments.

The basic viewpoint involved here came to be very well understood in Puerto Rico. The whole island was converted into a "class" for studying the mechanics of a democratic political system. For twenty years almost every medium for the transmission of knowledge played some role. The purpose was to make political responsibility on the part of the individual voter and his representatives a feature of the established way of life. Citizens should no longer think of themselves as colonial dependents, but persons who decide for themselves, as a body, the future of their commonwealth.

The educational planner can survey any given set of educational programs with the principle of lifelong adaptation in mind. In many instances it will be administratively convenient to prepare and continue such programs of education under auspices other than those of the Department of Education. For example, in the childhood stage, an effort might be made to introduce new kinds of books and toys, those which develop finger skills, mechanical skills, and communication skills more appropriate to future activities. This may require only an encouragement of publishers, toy manufacturers, and the like, by a system of prizes and awards. At the elementary school stage this may involve organized recreation, radio and television programs, and some initial experimentation in the arts. For teen-agers there may be science clubs, boy scouts, sports, and apprenticeships and arrangements for part-time employment of those still in school. For adults there might be literacy campaigns, agricultural extension services, evening classes, cooperative activities, libraries, museums, and many kinds of programs using radio and television. Older people will respond to discussion groups, to programs on radio and television, the availability of workshops, and chances to visit old friends who have moved elsewhere.

Wherever such education is conceived as a consumption item, a matter of personal pleasure, the individual can be expected to meet the cost either in whole or in large part. This would be reflected in his attitude toward radio and television, sports, toys, and the like. The general problem of determining when it pays to undertake the programs which must be more heavily subsidized by the government will be discussed later, in Chapter 18.

Another way of viewing lifelong adaptation is to consider occasions in a lifetime for which a person may need preparation. These might be courtship, marriage, and parenthood; or they could be job finding, job holding, and promotion; or obeying, cooperating, and leading, and a great many others. The original relationships in the society, providing for all ordinary contingencies which are met with at different stages of life, in many instances have become ineffective. New ways must be found, and it is the function of education to disseminate such wisdom, once it is agreed upon that the new ways are worthwhile. Schools have been very important in disseminating ideas about nutrition and personal hygiene. Radio and television dramas have been used to illustrate polite and responsible behavior in urban environments.

Methodologically, then, the reference system for lifelong adaptation comprises:

1. A detailed list of channels for social communications and of structured situations (e.g., games, clubs, buying at a market, etc.)
2. A designation of the public for each of these by age, sex, and location
3. Identification of the neglected segments of the population, again by age, sex, and location
4. Identification of the possible interests and the institutional memberships of the neglected segments

The potentials for lifelong adaptation, positive and negative, can be presented in map form, where certain prospectively backward or depressed areas can be outlined, or in the form of population pyramids for the respective localities. It will probably be far too expensive to employ the more sophisticated statistical techniques because the greatest concern is for a residual population that cannot easily be characterized.

The life prospects revealed by such a reference system may come as a surprise to many policy makers. The cultural environment for the elite in a developing country may not be as rich and varied as in the advanced countries, but it still tends to operate the communications systems in the interests of a tiny fraction of the population. The elite tends to see others as pale images of itself. Societies based upon a Latin tradition, and most of their former colonies as well, concentrate their culture in the capital, so that the outlying areas are greatly neglected. Societies influenced by the British institutions often neglect ethnic groups which are not forceful or dominating. Such biases are seldom evident to the people that hold them until the data point them out; not infrequently the data are disbelieved for a long time.

These two reference systems—human resources and lifelong adaptation —cannot by themselves solve problems, but they provide a basis for collecting information and statistics about a mass of interrelated problems and processes. They suggest reasonable and economic means for being comprehensive—for not neglecting some parts of the society—and for seeing a single program in relation to the whole. They permit planners to talk specifically rather than vaguely. Arguments drawn from these reference systems may be used as reasonable justifications for modifying budgetary allocations. They make arbitrary, malicious, and ordinary mistaken judgments less likely.

BIBLIOGRAPHY

Brameld, Theodore: *The Remaking of a Culture,* Harper & Row, Publishers, Incorporated, New York, 1959.
> A study of the educational system that is being constructed in Puerto Rico. The human resources are surveyed with the most advanced anthropological techniques.

Halsey, A. H., et al.: *Education, Economy, and Society,* The Free Press of Glencoe, New York, 1961.
> Contains more than forty well-selected articles on changes in social structure and institutional change wrought by the growth of education in Western societies.

Harbison, Frederick, and Charles A. Myers: *Education, Manpower, and Economic Growth: Strategies of Human Resource Development,* McGraw-Hill Book Company, New York, 1964.
> Contains a quantitative internation comparison of levels of human-resource development which permits a scale of four degrees of development, and the strategies applicable at each level are elaborated separately as sets of general policies.

Office for European Economic Cooperation (Office for Scientific and Technical Personnel): *Forecasting Manpower Needs for the Age of Science,* Paris, 1960.
> A comprehensive study of the supply and demand for technical manpower in Western Europe, with policy recommendations.

Pressey, S. L., and R. G. Kuhlen: *Psychological Development through the Life Span,* Harper & Row, Publishers, Incorporated, New York, 1957.
> A thorough review of the data accumulated on the changes in human behavior and capacity as a function of age.

Russell Sage Foundation: *Socialization through the Life Cycle,* New York, 1964.
> Different kinds of social bonds are needed at successive stages in the life of an individual. A review of present thinking.

Schramm, W. (ed.): *Mass Communication,* The University of Illinois Press, Urbana, Ill., 1960.

A modern survey of the effects of the use of advanced forms of the mass media, with primary emphasis upon measurement rather than speculation.

Wolfe, Dael: *America's Resources of Specialized Talent,* Harper & Row, Publishers, Incorporated, New York, 1954.

An analysis that is based to an important extent upon achievement tests and criteria of professional competence developed in the United States over the two preceding decades.

14

ELEMENTARY EDUCATION

IN MOST PARTS OF THE WORLD elementary education includes the first six years of schooling a child obtains, but in some regions it may extend to seven, eight, or even nine years. Children are admitted to school at ages five to seven, depending upon maturity, and continue to ages twelve to fourteen. Puberty represents a natural breaking point in an educational system either for entry into the adult world or for advancement to schools allowing more options on the part of the student. The elementary curriculum covers the handling of language, especially reading and writing, calculation and the use of numbers, and an introduction first to the structure of the community and the immediate environment, and then to the national scene and the outside world, in the guise of history, civics, geography, sometimes agriculture or science, some classics of literature, art, or folk culture.

The techniques of planning for the elementary educational system must be fitted to the governmental level that has been assigned responsibility for the elementary school. In societies where communities have assumed, or been assigned, responsibility for the provision of schools and teachers, the task of predicting future enrollment and building enough classrooms in convenient locations rests with the community. The province or state is then left with the responsibility for outlining a standard curriculum, training the teachers, arranging for the publication of textbooks and other teaching materials, working out minimum standards for structures and equipment, and developing a system of inspection and examinations which will assure that education of a respectable quality is being provided by the communities. The variation in the quality of the teaching will be very great during the period an educational system is being founded, but the outcome of this kind of planning is an equalization of educational opportunity for the bulk of the population. It can accomplish very little toward the accelerated training suited to the unusually gifted children, a problem which will be taken up later. The best the state can do in its regulation of locally managed elementary education is to introduce a mechanism which brings a high proportion of these gifted children to the attention of persons other than their teachers and fellow students.

Too often communities in developing countries are governed by cliques representing traditional interests which resist most of the modern ideas. A state intent upon economic development is then tempted to take control of the whole apparatus of formal education. Whether it does or not is a political problem which cannot be generalized upon and so will not be discussed here. Full state operation of the schools may leave too few important decisions to local leaders, and thus induce apathy in the leadership of the towns and villages, but it can also introduce a modern style of life to a part of the next generation that might otherwise not have been able to make the transition.

COLLECTION OF DATA

Education planning can become comprehensive and detailed when a majority of the schools are administered within the same system. Under these conditions the census data, particularly the age-sex breakdowns by locale, are exceedingly valuable. With this information available, it is possible to make many of the necessary projections of demand. For example, how many children may be expected to enter school five years hence, district by district? Ten years? Fifteen years? In the past how many persons in these districts had completed their elementary education? To what extent is education for children being provided beyond what was obtained by their parents?

The planner quickly realizes that a comprehensive approach requires more data than can be deduced from the census. The prime sources stem from the operations of the school system itself. Examples of the kind of data that can be provided with reasonable accuracy are:

Enrollment
  Names of students
  Language(s) spoken in the home
  Residence
  Distance from school
  Physical defect or disability

Attendance
    Seasonality
    Reasons for dropouts
Inventory
    School buildings (including age and condition)
    Classrooms
    Equipment
    Playgrounds (by size)
Staffing
    Teachers (number and level of training)
    Administrators
    Clerks
    Janitors and maintenance
Special services
    School lunches
    Clinics
    Extracurricular activities
    Polling places in elections

In the developing countries there is a tendency for this operating information to be unreliable unless special measures are taken. Teachers, administrators, and clerks are not accustomed to filling out official government forms. They do not understand the precise meaning of the terms employed, nor do they know how to report the special cases that come up too frequently. Therefore, if these operating reports are to be used for comprehensive planning, care must be taken to establish and maintain procedures which assure the reliability of the statistics. The needs of the planners are more stringent than those of the administrator, who is most often worrying about filling next year's classrooms with teachers. Therefore the planner may insist on a small statistical unit to train clerks in keeping school records and to investigate the instances where major inconsistencies turn up.

A different set of records may be used at a later stage in the economic development. By then it should be possible to work out a set of examinations that could measure to a reasonable extent the achievement of the students in the respective parts of the school system. Such examinations are indicators that a year of schooling can be equated to a certain amount of progress by the average student, and that this quantity will be constant from one year to the next. The planner may be convinced from the statistical techniques employed by the educational psychologists in developing the tests that the measures are reproducible, but he must discover for himself whether the "progress" is toward the kind of developmental society he visualizes or in some other direction that is irrelevant or incompatible. When adequate devices for measuring achievement in school work exist, a true performance budget can be set up which will point the way to efficient allocations. It can be said then how much education is being produced per teacher or per unit of expenditure, and this calculation may lead to the consolidation or reorganization of the least productive schools. Until that time, the planner and budgeteer must be satisfied with certain superficial indicators of improvement or retrogression, such as the amount of double and triple enrollment in the school system (i.e., use of the classrooms for more than one shift of students), the frequency of repeated grades, the number of hours of teaching per teacher, the number of books circulated for outside reading, changes in pupil-teacher ratio, changes in educational level reached by teachers in their own education, etc. These qualitative indicators, when applied with judgment, would enable a professional educator and an experienced planner to predict which schools would promote the greatest achievement when achievement can be measured independently. They also indicate crudely what immediate efforts may be taken to improve the quality of elementary education.

PROJECTION OF ENROLLMENT

At the foundation of every education plan is the enrollment program. When census statistics and some operating experience are available, it can be carried five to ten years in advance. The following set of procedures should work reasonably well for statewide systems of elementary education embracing six years of schooling when projecting enrollment for the next year:

1. Estimate the number of live births for the calendar year six years before the given date.
2. Subtract deaths and other losses in the preschool ages based upon age-specific mortality estimates obtained from the census. (Most of this loss is incorporated in the infant mortality data that are now independently estimated by almost all public health services.)
3. Adjust for nonattendance factors, such as disability and isolation (based upon comparing past operating statistics with census data).
4. Add previous schoolgoers (from operating data).
5. Subtract an expected number of school leavers who are dropping out before matriculation (based upon extrapolations of past experience as revealed by the records).
6. Subtract deaths in the six to eleven age bracket (based upon census information).
7. Subtract graduates (from school records).

The resultant figure is an expected enrollment for the next year. This set of procedures may be repeated, using the calculated figure instead of school records, to get an estimate of enrollment the following year. The procedure may be repeated until the full five or ten years has been reached.

The calculation methods described above are quite simple and routine, but laborious. It will be proposed, in many different parts of the world, that this programming of future enrollment be carried out in the office of the department of education by a computer. The enrollment in the various school districts can be superimposed upon an inventory of school-rooms and other facilities available. The time of appearance of the deficiencies can be quickly discovered by such means. The principal advantage of computerized school calculations is that after a year or two of tests and trials of the data-processing effort, the conclusions affecting budgets can be made available earlier and more explicitly than before. The data that lie behind the decisions about new facilities will be more nearly current.

A computer-systems group will often be convinced that they can also find a least-cost solution for the school-enrollment and school-facilities budgeting problem. That contention is probably correct only in a theoretical sense because the development of an educational system quickly encounters complexities that are not observed in the developed economies which are the primary source of experience with educational data. The principal shifts which disturb calculations stem from the urbanization process, the partial breakup of the traditional family structure, and the enhanced geographic mobility of a segment of the population. The increased flux forces the planning in most parts of the world to be conducted in a decentralized fashion and with shorter horizons. The problems encountered are worth more extended discussion.

When there are several states or provinces in a developing society, one may be richer than the others, and is then the target for migration. Persons who make the first moves in migration are not seeking elementary education, but they bring spouses, children, and relatives as soon as they get established. Thus some of the children born in poorer states tend to show up in the schools of the richer ones. If the quality of education is high in one state when compared with the others, there is then also a tendency for children of other states to come in and live with relatives while attending school in the better system. These propensities for moving about in search of opportunity may change strikingly within a single decennial census period and may thus modify the longer-range projections for enrollment.

In Puerto Rican planning this migration factor became crucial for estimating the capital budget for education. The whole natural increase of the island (about 2½ percent of the population per year) had been moving to the continent, and the various departments of the government saw no good reason for discouraging the flow. The enrollment projections, when carefully corrected for migration effects, led to strikingly different conclusions from those that would be adopted by administrators who make their allocations by extrapolating the recent past into the near future.

All through its history prior to 1956 the section of the Department of Education responsible for elementary education in Puerto Rico was pressed to the limit to find schoolrooms and teachers to supply the increasing demand for education. Some kind of facilities had to be provided. The whole department was oriented toward building, teacher recruitment, and expansion. Then suddenly the pressure was off and there was nothing to look forward to but steady shrinkage in the size of classes. Obviously this should be a period for concentrating upon improving the quality of the education provided. It required altogether different skills in administration.

The downward trend of elementary enrollment hid an even more striking decline in rural enrollment. More than half of the rural schools being used at or beyond their physical capacity in 1955–1956 would probably have to be abandoned by 1970 for lack of sufficient students! These remarkable changes were brought about largely by the external and internal migrations coincident with industrialization and economic development. The Puerto Ricans were fortunate in having thorough studies available covering the characteristics of the major movement—demographic, economic, and sociological—but they found it exceedingly difficult to estimate trends in internal changes of address, where the moves involved distances requiring the transfer of children from one school district to another.

Most other developing countries will not experience such an abrupt shift from the scramble to provide teachers and buildings for children who need the rudiments of education to the phase where emphasis must be placed upon raising the standards of that education. For them there is less risk of waste of social overhead capital invested in school buildings and school equipment. But the need for collecting current data on internal population movements is evident. It is best carried out, perhaps, in conjunction with other government departments whose work is affected by migration, such as the labor department and the departments responsible for housing and social welfare. They may find it convenient to take monthly samples in the respective labor-housing markets, each of which would normally comprise a number of elementary school districts. Following migration through changes of postal address, or through starts and stops in the use of electricity, tends to be misleading because the poorer people, and those with the largest families, tend to be left out of such statistics. Food rationing, if it is carried out in those metropolitan areas with scarce supplies, may provide the most dependable source of data.

The enrollment projection of the secondary schools is based upon the data and estimates prepared previously for the elementary schools. In a period of continuous economic growth an increasing proportion of the children finishing elementary school will go on to the secondary schools. Therefore the cessation of growth of enrollment was less evident in the secondary systems and the transition to the period where administrators must concentrate almost entirely upon quality is delayed six to nine years, or longer, after it is experienced in the elementary school system. This means that some of the excess teachers in the elementary schools can be retrained for work in the secondary schools. *It also means that the elementary school system must be in the vanguard of the educational planning.*

NOTES ON PROGRAMMING FOR SCHOOLS

It is still necessary to convert expected enrollment into budgetary estimates. Since the major operating cost in education is that of teachers' salaries, the students-per-teacher ratio becomes a crucial statistic. Almost all improvements in the quality of education (providing teachers for handicapped children, supervising practice in writing short papers, administering tests to measure achievement, adding extracurricular projects, expanding the school libraries, etc.) require an increase in the number of trained teachers per thousand students, which means a decline in the students-per-teacher ratio.

Policies for improving quality in the elementary school system, then, must be studied for their effects upon this ratio. Thus, it is possible to divide by the ratio (which may be as high as fifty initially and then gradually decline over time to thirty or less) to obtain the demand for teachers. Knowing the resignation rate of teachers from past operating statistics makes it possible to estimate also the need for additional teachers. Often the estimate of teacher demand is complicated by differences between urban and rural schools.

During a period of rapid growth in enrollment the supply of teachers cannot be built up fast enough, particularly of those who are fully qualified and willing to teach in rural areas. This means that many teaching posts will be filled by persons who have little training beyond high school. They are given temporary, or "substitute," teaching certificates. Temporary teachers tend to remain in teaching an even shorter period than those who have received full training.

This situation is useful when planning for the transition to quality improvement mentioned above. It is not necessary to reduce abruptly the enrollment of students intending to become elementary school teachers several years *prior* to the transition in order to prevent a surplus. There would instead be a strong pressure for replacing the resignations of those holding temporary teaching certificates with new, fully qualified teachers. Those temporary certificate holders who wish to remain in teaching would be encouraged to go to teacher-training institutions to complete work for their diplomas. Very rapidly, then, even the rural elementary schools would be staffed with teachers having two to three years training beyond secondary school, almost always in teachers' institutes (otherwise called normal schools or teachers' colleges). The introduction of measures of achievement becomes much simpler and more trustworthy when the teaching is carried out by trained professionals, even though the majority have not yet received training and education up to the levels reached in the most affluent countries.

A few observations about the sociology of the scholastic professions are needed to explain in another light the emphases adopted throughout this study. Otherwise many of the recommendations will appear to be illogical and arbitrary.

Teaching is a profession that was once delegated to males. The schoolmaster had an ancient and honorable role in the community, and in many societies still in the first stages of economic development, he continues to dominate the teaching profession. Once development gets under way the general scarcity of men with communications skills draws them into the new productive activities and other departments of government service. Their places are taken largely by young women with middle-class orientations.

Most societies severely limit the occupations open to respectable young women with education. They are not encouraged to start enterprises, to become engineers, managers, civil servants, and the like, but are limited to welfare work, some clerical and secretarial work, nursing (in some cultures), and teaching. Thus the supply tends to be sizable compared with the demand, and the wages tend to be set at a very low level as compared with the other professions. A majority of the female teachers will marry after a few years in the classroom. The schoolmasters, holdovers from an older era, are elevated to the posts of principal and other higher administrative positions.

Filling the ranks of the teaching profession with young women converts the elementary school into a matriarchal institution. The school draws its charges from a locale and inculcates them with the values and proprieties accepted by middle-class women. These proprieties are not always consonant with the existing values of the community, but are usually quite compatible with the new institutions that will have been created to bring about economic growth. Such an arrangement is quite stable, once it has been achieved, so that new recruits to the teaching staff are soon indoctrinated. It can evolve rapidly into a fully modern educational organization because there are few lifetime positions that are worth defending. It is true that much of the subsidy granted by the state for teacher training is lost because of early marriage and ensuing pregnancies, but in most instances this loss is likely to be recouped by the low salary scale that prevails for a relatively high-grade skill and by the adaptability of the system to measures for elevating the standards of instruction.

In each society there should be a transition to a steady state where virtually all children in the six- to eleven-year age bracket are provided opportunities for education. Then the demand for teachers can be calculated from birthrates, net migration rates, and resignation and retirement rates. The annual requirement becomes fairly stable. However, the enrollment in teacher-training institutions and schools of education in the colleges must be scheduled at substantially greater rate than the annual requirement. In most countries perhaps 50 to 100 percent more should be enrolled in order to compensate for the fraction of those enrolled who change their minds about a teaching career.

The second largest item in the education budget is for school buildings and equipment, together with their maintenance. During the period of rapid expansion of the elementary school system there are calls for blueprints for standard school structures and standards for site planning. Prefabrication of standard structures may be justified in many areas. However, as the transition to the steady state of full enrollment is approached, there is a great possibility of building an excess capacity of schools in rural areas and the central districts of large cities. In the preparation of the capital budget it will then be necessary to determine, by studying a series of typical cases in detail, whether it is not more economical to accept double registration (two shifts) in some schools for six years or so. This means that at the peak, the demand for schoolrooms would be somewhat less than for classroom teachers. The calculation of the number of classrooms required parallels the calculation made earlier for teachers but is reduced by the amount of double enrollment that seems advisable.

A certain amount of lead time is needed for adding to the supply of schoolrooms. Construction may require one or two years after signing the contract, and land acquisition may take a year or more prior to the letting of contracts. Thus *expansion of the supply of teachers by increasing the capacity of teacher training in institutions must be paralleled by simultaneous action yielding a roughly equivalent increase in the supply of classrooms.*

The transition in the educational system which is followed by a strong movement to improve the quality of instruction has strong effects upon the construction program. The new schoolrooms are expected to be better equipped, more soundproofed, more secure against heavy rainstorms and against vandalism, more flexible so as to cope with the needs of special projects, and more durable. The cost per schoolroom may easily double or treble, disregarding any effects of inflation.

School planning at this stage must match expectations of rapid increases in enrollment with a more carefully considered plan for locating and building schools. To be considered, for example, is whether in the new growing economy the elementary school becomes the cornerstone of the neighborhood and if a group of such neighborhoods will supply students for the secondary schools. The neighborhood unit built around an elementary school has been considered an optimal approach to the design of housing for new communities in Western countries. As was indicated in the discussion of industrial planning in Chapters 9 and 10, communities with light manufacturing might find a somewhat different plan more suitable. It is suspected that in sections of the cities made up of low-cost self-built houses, the threat of double enrollment will encourage a variety of other solutions, ranging from decentralized "cottage" and "store-front" schools to school "parks" that serve a whole ward or sector.[1] The site selection for schools may then shift to the agencies responsible for urban planning, since about 90 percent of the new schools during this period would serve urban populations; the school planning left to the department of education would become more a matter of school *design*. The design of the structures in any case must fit the new, improved techniques of instruction and the curriculum. In fact, the mere occupation of a well-designed, new building is often sufficient stimulus for bringing about a sudden and substantial improvement in instruction.

The remaining budgetary provisions for elementary school have to do with the content of the curriculum. What educators have discovered from their experience is that the rate of learning is profoundly affected by the *order* in which the respective concepts are presented. They also recognize that the best order is not the same from one culture to another. In fact, it is seldom constant even when moving from one subculture to another within the same society. Therefore research has to be carried out from the start which aims to discover the proper order of exposure for terms, symbols, operations, and concepts. These findings must be relayed to teachers in the course of their professional training, and translated into textbooks, extracurricular reading, and other teaching materials. Curricu-

[1] The "cottage school" holds classes in a building that can be converted to dwellings when the school demand is reduced. It is used for primary grades and rarely combines more than four rooms. The "store-front" type presumes increasing population or wealth in the community, which can then use extra commercial space to advantage. School "parks" are provided in the nearest open space, and students are transported to them by bus.

lum development is best carried out in a school of education with an experimental atmosphere. Professors and research associates will be applying what has been learned about child psychology and elementary education elsewhere in the world to problems of teaching children who are growing up in this culture at this time. Prospective teachers catch some of the flavor of experimentalism, in contrast to the dogma which had been presented to them only a few years earlier, and are more likely to modify their methods later when the innovations are being spread throughout the school system.

It will be recalled also that social change is accelerated by progress in economic development. As a result, teaching methods and materials found appropriate for one decade become obsolete for some parts of the society by the next. Studies of the social and cultural changes must be linked with the ongoing educational research programs. The institutes for higher education which train teaching staff and the publishing houses which produce materials for the school system are kept busy adapting to the environmental change and to the needs for improving the quality of education being provided. The transition to the steady state in enrollment does not affect the growth in requirements for research, advanced training, or the production of teaching materials. Their budgets must expand for at least a generation longer.

The planning for secondary education, particularly of the nonvocational or general type, must follow much the same patterns as those established for elementary education, and so it need not be discussed as a wholly separate matter. Some differing features in secondary education planning can be summarized as follows:

At the secondary level dependence upon operating statistics obtained from the educational system as a whole increases, while the utilization of census data for the programming of teachers and classrooms diminishes.

The setting of achievement standards seems to contribute even more to the efficiency of teaching in the academic secondary schools than at the elementary level because the tests enable the teachers to place students in classes having roughly the same background and ability.

Teachers need more background in content and less in methods, while the demands for a variety of teaching materials may easily exceed the means for producing them. It should be possible to borrow more heavily from the richer societies for textbooks and equipment because children in the secondary schools are beginning to participate in an international culture that comprises science, technology, the arts, and even common political systems.

Architectural design problems are almost always more complicated in secondary schools; the design of a standard structure may never be achieved.

Nevertheless, the basic principles are sufficiently similar so that techniques of integrated planning evolved to handle elementary education structures can be developed further over succeeding years to accommodate the same students when they reach the secondary level.

Those features of planning for secondary education that are most seriously modified will be taken up in the discussions on vocational education and higher education in the following chapters.

BIBLIOGRAPHY

Engelhardt, N. L., et al.: *School Planning and Building Handbook,* F. W. Dodge Company, a Division of McGraw-Hill, Inc., New York, 1956.
 Devoted to planning, layout, and construction of school buildings. Covers checklists, standards, specifications, cost estimates, construction problems, timetables.

Featherstone, W. B.: *A Functional Curriculum for Youth,* American Book Company, New York, 1950.
 A discussion of the kinds of content that should be included in schooling, particularly at the secondary level, with emphasis upon educational planning.

Gwynn, J. M.: *Curriculum Principles and Social Trends,* The Macmillan Company, New York, 1950.
 Traces the evolution of the curriculum in the United States with an analysis of the social forces that shaped its content.

15

THE VOCATIONAL EDUCATION SYSTEM

THE HUMAN-RESOURCES REFERENCE SYSTEM provides a most useful guide to the planning of vocational education. In most developing societies it is found that youngsters, even after six years of education, are relatively homogenous and undifferentiated from the standpoint of the tasks which need to be carried out. Teachers would be unwilling and unable to say which student at this level would make a competent plumber or a good factory worker or a capable farmer. They *are* able to ascertain which ones are unusually bright and therefore suited for further education and which are unusually slow, but little else is certain. Requirements for entry into the most productive sector of the labor force make it necessary to add extra training directed to those jobs which are expected to be available. Vocational education is usually the quickest and most economical means available for converting unskilled individuals into the journeymen craftsmen and maintenance specialists needed by the expanding economy.

The set of institutions fulfilling this function can be called the *vocational education system*. It will include those courses in agriculture, homemaking, commerce, and mechanic arts taught in the public schools which are not, however, an explicit part of *general* education. In addition it will also include the special vocational schools, the privately operated "colleges of commerce," the training courses instituted by business-machine and appliance makers, the apprenticeship courses sponsored by the craft unions, on-the-job training, etc.

In principle, of course, the professional schools, which prepare individuals for careers in medicine, law, teaching, engineering, accountancy, etc., are primarily vocational. They are, however, normally incorporated within the colleges and universities as part of the *system of higher education*. These professions are the highest prestige vocations; they are very salient, and as such serve to attract the educational motivation and vocational choices of a large number of persons whose training falls short of these professional levels.

Most administrators will sense at once that the assignment of jobs to persons is much too complex a function to be subject to centralized and detailed planning. Furthermore, the conscious direction of the development of individual careers could involve undesirable constraints upon individual freedom of choice. Certainly, a democratic society is better advised to let the existing local and private institutions counsel the youths regarding an occupation or career. When certain of these institutions (especially the family) are unable to keep up with the growing needs of the economy, they then may be given an assist from the responsible governmental agencies in the form of a guidance program, such as will be taken up shortly. Thus, quick conversions of "raw manpower" into useful *competences* are best left to the free play of rather small interacting and competing firms, offices, apprenticeship systems, installations, etc. These media are able to adjust to the short-range opportunities to which much of vocational education is attuned. Meanwhile, aggregate statistics must be assembled which highlight any significant shortages or surpluses a year or two prior to their occurrence. Then government, through providing information and perhaps some special incentives, would act to attract persons into the unfilled occupations. (As will be seen later, it is more difficult to reduce the ranks of the occupations in surplus.) This procedure is not detailed planning; it might be referred to as "lubrication" of the institutional mechanisms underlying the labor market.

STEPS IN PLANNING

In most developmental societies the respective vocational schools are supervised by independent government agencies. Some of the agencies are part of the national government, but more of them operate on a state and community level. Many are financed by churches, international corporations, and private endowments. Under these circumstances good planning requires that a strong effort be made to develop standardized statistics comprehending all institutions and then to prepare a licensing scheme aimed at eliminating fraud in the private sector and a waste of resources in government agencies owing to unnecessary and overlapping services.

The information should be collected first by professional statisticians, or their nearest equivalent, and then by persons they have trained, until a comprehensive inventory has been accumulated. The following information should be obtained from *all* vocational educational institutions, while for the larger institutions extra information may be acquired that can be exceedingly useful:

Number of staff, qualifications of staff, number of classrooms and workshops available, special equipment and facilities employed

Previous year's intake of students, estimated capacity, previous education of students

Courses of study offered, time required for completion of courses, tests of competence employed at time of completion

Previous year's output of trainees, estimated capacity, type of employment upon completion

Previous year's budget, source of funds, market value of physical capital employed

It can be seen that the chances of collecting homogenous statistics are poor when it is remembered that vocational training includes the teaching of such trades as those of undertakers, waiters, evangelists, and gardeners, as well as those of the building craftsmen, truck drivers, skilled machinists, typists, bookkeepers, and technicians—trades normally in mind when using the term "vocational training." Statistics obtainable are least adequate for the lower grades of training and the shortest courses. Therefore it may be decided that some convenient cutoff point should be used, and educational investments below that point would be considered too small to be counted. The cutoff point may be set somewhere in the neighborhood of $20 per person being trained. The sum should include the sacrifice of income on the student's part, since he will be taking time from work while being taught the new skill. In a poor society this figure may represent at most a month of full-time study on the part of one person, or about four months at the normal part-time study rate. As development proceeds these costs increase, primarily because the salary scale of teachers must be raised and because the cutoff point encompasses more of the miscellaneous forms of vocational training. It is more feasible to be comprehensive at this later stage because most of the short courses are sponsored by larger organizations which keep better records.

The next step requires the grouping of this inventory of vocational training into some set of grades or levels, preferably according to the degree of skill to be found in the finished trainees. A system of certificates and diplomas can be instituted if it does not already exist. Over time a set of standard examinations can be prepared by responsible members of the respective trades. In a few instances the employers of the output of the schools will take the trouble to prepare the tests themselves. The examinations would be used to determine whether a certificate or diploma should be granted to the individual for the degree of skill he acquired. In quite a few instances the examinations can be borrowed unchanged except for translation from the United States, Great Britain, France, Scandinavia, and elsewhere, but more often the borrowing process requires more substantial revisions.

Quite consistently a peculiar problem is encountered in borrowing a standard set of examinations. The original examinations were set for conditions in the trade existing in the country for which they were prepared. They are not only less relevant, but also more difficult for trainees in newly developing countries, and so are an improper and unjust test. Nevertheless, almost any effort to rectify these disparities is strongly opposed by the students and the certificate holders alike; they suspect a conspiracy, though the objections are seldom consistent. Some protest that the trade will be deluged with second-rate entrants; others claim that the new tests are used to restrict competition; others point out, quite rightly, that any changes may be used as a pretext to prevent the worker from obtaining a work permit in the trade if he should migrate to more developed countries. Thus the transfer of the standards of performance, and appropriate tests for maintaining the standards, is seldom a smooth and uncomplicated process.

The succeeding steps required in planning for vocational education are much less clear-cut. In societies where a large fraction of the population has been engaged in cottage industries, a strong effort would undoubtedly be made to transfer breadwinners from trades with low incomes to others with better prospects. Many highly skilled trades are rendered obsolete by the introduction of modern factory methods of production. The social costs of economic development are borne most heavily by those persons who were engaging in cottage industry. Introducing special forms of vocational education for the obsolescent trades may enable these individuals to salvage a part of the skill. It is more likely, however, that some form of community education, as is described later, may be more appropriate in most of these situations.

A STRATEGY FOR GUIDANCE

Inextricably connected with the expansion of vocational education is the guidance of young people into appropriate careers. In a developing society a son no longer follows the occupation of his father, nor does a daughter continue in the pattern set by her mother. The choice of a career is a new freedom opened up to a relatively large section of the population, and it naturally results in a great deal of indecision and confusion at first. It seems quite plausible to ask that the potential ability and self-discipline of the individual be fitted to the needs of the new jobs that are being created, thus achieving the optimum harmony between job and worker; but in practice this policy would require detailed information about both the worker and the job which neither the schools nor the employers are able to provide. Some kind of compromise must be found which demands relatively little effort on the part of the educational system, since it is handicapped by a shortage of trained personnel. The most promising solution to the problem of collecting and transmitting guidance information arises from a study of the *sociology* of the various occupations and the professions. The relative prestige accorded to the respective occupations and professions remains quite stable during the earlier stages of the development process, so that the structure need not be repeatedly reviewed.

Once observations have been made upon the special preference for occupations inherent in the traditional culture and their consequences upon the flow of talented youngsters through the educational system have been understood, plans for redressing the bias can be drawn up. In most instances the plans turn out to be quite simple and inexpensive. This is so because the student whose aspirations are set so high has a mortal fear of failure. When he sees a relatively clear and attainable path to higher social status, even if in a somewhat different direction than he had first chosen, there is a fair chance that he will switch goals.

A Puerto Rican physics professor has described this phenomenon as follows:

> Until recently there were only one or two persons a year who would major in physics. With few exceptions the degree was used as a means for obtaining entry into medical school. Quite a few students taking their first course in physics became interested in the subject matter but had no background for visualizing what a career in physics would be like. Assurance that it is now the highest paying of the sciences in the United States is helping some, but the knowledge that electronics and instrument-making firms are now settling in Puerto Rico and would be very anxious to hire native scientists and engineers apparently is sufficient to persuade a much larger number to major in physics and to dissuade some of those who complete their studies from later undertaking medicine as a lifetime profession. (Personal interview, 1952.)

The most important part of a plan concerned with career directions is that of bringing information about opportunities opening up in a developing society to the individuals who are about ready to make personal commitments to a career. Still another is a series of scholarships and fellowships in technical, subprofessional, and professional specializations which other planning units find to be essential to meeting the targets which have been set. Thus the physics graduate referred to in the quotation above might best take a year's course in instrument design overseas before accepting a responsible position in a firm. The system of external scholarships is already highly developed in most countries, and the educational planner needs only to guide the various scholarship programs into the most productive channels. Some of the economic criteria for designing such programs are discussed again in Chapter 18.

For every person who achieves subprofessional or professional status, there are five or ten (perhaps more) who had imagined themselves playing such a role but lost out in the early stages because of imperfect preparation. Such persons have the drive and the imagination to make a success in other occupations. The medically oriented man whose general education stopped at the elementary level could, for example, become a hospital cook or an ambulance driver after a year or two of vocational training combined with experience. If his education stopped short of high school graduation, he might become a drugstore clerk and eventually a businessman servicing the medical profession. A high school graduate might add some night school courses and become a dental technician or a chemical analyst. This redirection enables such persons to satisfy their desire to be in the healing profession, but at less responsible tasks. Thus, plans for vocational education should be constructed so as to reinforce this personal identification with the service rendered wherever the cultural heritage makes this possible. Any institution which manages to assemble this sympathy of vocational interests at all levels of the organization can become extraordinarily effective in carrying out its mission.

Vocational-education authorities may also make rather long-range plans in conjunction with the plans of other units concerned with increasing productivity in agriculture, construction, marketing, etc. Systems of schools and curricula may be established in order to meet the needs for the modernization of such activities which have long existed in the economy. Here programming is important. For example, there might be the long-term need for hundreds of demonstrators in agricultural extension and an equally large number of nutritionists and inspectors, but they could not be used productively if they were made available all at one time. In general, training provisions for these kinds of vocations can be programmed in easy stages, so that improvements in the organization of production are brought about in an economic and orderly fashion.

The principles involved in lifelong adaptation have not been mentioned in this discussion of vocational education because they add very little to the argument. Some of the content of vocational education (e.g., workshop experience, machine repair, mapping and drawing, cooking, nursing, etc.) would interest persons at almost any age and might be of value to them in their households or leisure-time interests. Once a complete program has been set up, however, the reference system based upon lifelong adaptation would suggest few changes, if any, because all age levels and all stations of life can be handled as a matter of routine.

With the achievement of universal education the spirit of much vocational education tends to shift. The enrollment transition described in Chapter 14 leads to the inclusion of many students with low motivation to learn. Because they retard the progress of the majority, their presence in classes becomes a severe problem to the teacher who is intent upon improving the quality of education. The normal solution in the schools is to introduce a program of "practical studies," which include agriculture, manual arts, homemaking, and drawing. Whether this streamlined education for those children lacking academic aptitudes or interests can be called "vocational" is doubtful, but that is the euphemism applied. The strong, progressive, self-help features of the training in the manual skills characteristic of the early stages tend to become diluted with a flow of lackadaisical enrollees at the lower levels. An observer would normally conclude that a decline in the quality of vocational education had set in, but the change should be ascribed instead to a drop in the quality of the incoming classes. The vocational schools supported by the public are much more susceptible to such change after the transition than those operating in the private sector.

Vocational education has an extremely practical function in development because it transforms members of the traditional society into a cadre of service workers for the modern society and thereby enables the latter to grow more rapidly than its own reproduction rate and control of resources would warrant. A heavy burden is thus placed upon those responsible for vocational education. Yet despite its importance the field has remained a kind of stepchild in education ever since national educational systems have been formed. Even where the national ideology insists that all honest occupations are equally honorable, and all students are required to do some manual work in school, vocational education has remained less respectable than the purely academic type. This is reflected in the fact that it has been impossible to find truly relevant discussions in the literature on the subject. The primary emphasis in current publications has been placed upon methods for creating interest and motivation in students, intended to prevent premature dropouts in compulsory educational systems. Systematic evaluations, based upon the function of vocational education for social and economic growth, are missing.

PROGRAMMED INSTRUCTION

Nevertheless, vocational education is currently undergoing a major technological revolution—under the guise of a new slogan—which promises to be far more important in the long run for the newly developing countries than for the developed. *Programmed instruction* is a technique that has been applied much more broadly than in vocational education alone. Indeed the initial effort was devoted to teaching reading, mathematics, and foreign languages. A large share of the ultimate applications, however, will be directed to the teaching of relatively simple technical courses, many of them to workers while on the job.

Programmed instruction involves a step-by-step question-and-answer process that enables a person to acquire knowledge of new informational material. It is important that the answer be available immediately, so that the student is encouraged by discovering that he is capable of obtaining a correct result, and can then proceed to the next question. It is also important that the steps be made so simple that the learner will make relatively few errors and therefore not become discouraged. The materials may be presented in any of a variety of *teaching machines* or, more often, in a modified textbook. When the course is completed, the student is able to demonstrate his capacities by passing the same kind of examination normally given by teachers or accrediting institutions, or he may be able to carry out some standard task with acceptable efficiency. The primary advantage of programmed instruction is that the student can set his own pace. His learning is independent of the others in the class.

This harbinger of revolution in educational techniques began as a series of applications of modern learning theory in psychology in the middle 1950s in several American universities. By 1960 several business firms saw the usefulness of applying teaching machines to special problems in teaching and were producing both equipment and programs. Almost from the beginning it was clear that the *program* was far more important than the equipment. The student must be led by the program through the complexities of nomenclature and specialized operations to the point where his mastery is sufficient to be able to "think for himself" in the new subject.

The program usually consists of *frames* (the number may be in the thousands), each of which contains some additional information and includes questions which relate this information to what was previously known. When the program is tested out on a sample population of students, and all the errors on the respective frames are tabulated, it is possible to deduce what parts of the program may be defective and which parts are unnecessary. The program then may have to be rewritten, perhaps expanded in the difficult parts and shortened elsewhere, before it is used in educational work.

In programmed instruction, failure of students to understand materials presented to them is blamed upon the educator-programmer rather than the student! Many methods for improving programs are coming to be known, so that educators in this field are confident that anyone can be taught who can learn to read, but some will be able to complete a program as much as three times faster than the laggards.

Teaching machines take many forms. Basically, they are simple mechanical mediums for presenting the program to the learner. The most elaborate teaching machines are those which use a computer to observe the pattern of success and vary the path the program takes so as to suit the needs of the student. In the long run it will be possible to adjust longer and more difficult programs, such as might be needed to undertake the repair of advanced electronic equipment, to individual styles of learning rather than to the typical student. However, computerized techniques seem to be appropriate only for the highest priority educational tasks.

The largest single effort in programmed instruction up to the present time that has been conducted in the United States was launched in the Air Training Command for the U.S. Air Force. Persons with at least high school and often some college education were taught by teams of consultants over the period of a year to write programs. They then spent about a year of apprenticeship, programming representative courses that were needed by the military. No program for instruction was to be accepted until 90 percent of the students were able to make a 90 percent or higher score on the final examination. This is to be compared with prior methods of instruction where typically only 30 to 40 percent of students taking a course would reach the 90 percent score.

The significance of programmed instruction for developing countries is now more understandable. This technique, better than any other, assures that students will reach a given level of competence despite the relatively poor selection methods that are employed. *It is not dependent upon the technical competence and skill of the teacher.* Inherent in it, also, is a procedure for continually improving the performance in a given industrial environment by changing a few frames at a time. Moreover, there is a body of tested programs being accumulated in the English language and the American culture which can be drawn upon rapidly by the rest of the world. Even students whose English is mediocre can learn from these programs; their language deficiency merely slows down their progress; it does not detract from ultimate performance. It is apparent already that it is much easier to translate programmed instruction into new languages and cultural contexts than textbooks.

The programs that will be available after 1965 are most applicable to tasks associated with modern technology—machine assembly and repair, electrical circuitry, accounting, business-machine operation, quality control, transport scheduling, etc. Hundreds of elementary courses in foreign languages, mathematics, and the physical sciences should also be on hand. These are courses also taught in a vocational secondary school.

How is programmed instruction to be introduced into a developing country? The procedure is very similar to that employed for other major changes in education. At least the following steps appear to be necessary before a self-sustaining effort can be established within the country:

1. A specialist in educational technology would be invited to work with the Minister of Education in a survey of the institutions for educational research, libraries, publishing houses, teachers' colleges, and on-the-job training. He would attempt to discover the relevant sources for trainees and the resources that could fit into a full-scale effort.

2. A commitment to speeded-up education must be obtained at the top political level, preferably with the concurrence of opposition parties or factions.

3. The minister of education with key aides should tour installations which produce and use programmed instruction. His office would have prepared a tentative list of high-priority applications to educational problems that suggest themselves, and these would be tested for feasibility during the trip. Arrangements could also be made at that time for sending the first wave of trainees to centers for programmed instruction.

4. A group of young teachers and technical writers would be dispatched to several of the centers for programmed instructions. There they would be accompanied by an even larger number of supervisors who would take a short course in the applications and use of programmed instruction and return to prepare the way for the newly trained programmers and the readily borrowed programs. The best supervisors could add to the present state of knowledge about educational programming by conducting small studies of the applicability of certain existing programs in cultural contexts that would be unusual as compared with those in which the programs were first developed. Such work would gain the respect of educators all over the world.

5. Several new university departments and service institutes should be formed in various parts of the government which produce the trained programmers who would return after one to two years' training, so that the latter may get at the high-priority educational tasks.

6. Publishing and printing facilities would be contracted for or imported at the same time. They could begin work on the translations and continue with the new programs specifically directed to internal educational needs.

7. A self-financing system of distribution of programs must be worked out. Programmed texts are likely to be two or three times as expensive as their predecessors and therefore will strain the book budgets of the school system. If state enterprise is likely to profit from the training, it should finance the use. If trainees qualify for a higher salary as a result of the increased competence, it is reasonable that they should pay for the texts.

8. The central institute carrying on the research and training in programmed instruction (presumably in connection with a leading university) should

start new institutes in technical colleges, teachers' colleges, and government departments, intended to produce the specialized programmed courses needed to expedite production or to improve the quality of the public services.

Experience in the United States has shown that the body of professional programmers for programmed instruction who are working at their craft can be expanded in size quite rapidly. In 1963 it was estimated that 300 to 400 such persons were so engaged, and this number had been doubling in size about every two years, despite serious losses to other activities that were often somewhat related.

This growth rate suggests that there will soon be a substantial capability for training foreign students in the United States. A large-scale transfer of the technique to the developing countries should be possible in the late 1960s.

Refinements in programmed learning are already beginning to appear on the scene. Almost all of them involve more elaborate equipment for measuring the learning achieved and an accounting of the process by which complex concepts are mastered. Some of these findings are likely to be valuable in developing countries also. Therefore a channel will have to be created with very little lag due to cultural barriers in order to transfer the newest findings about instruction into the educational systems of the developing countries. Technical forms of vocational education should profit most.

Within a decade it must be anticipated that each purchase of new technological equipment by developing countries (such as aircraft, electric power plants, medical instruments, machine tools, etc.) will have associated with it a complete series of programmed instruction training courses in the local languages which should speed up on-the-job training. The series would also reduce the frequency of expensive errors in plant operations and accounting. Thus every piece of advanced hardware would have associated with it not just an operating manual, as at present, but much more elaborate instructions. A complete contract may on the average assign 10 to 30 percent of the expenditure to "software" components; already one category—computers—promises to exceed 50 percent. The information associated with machines is coming to be relatively highly significant as compared with the cost of the materials that go into the machines. Henceforth much more knowledge must be exported with the machine and acquired by the receiving society. Newly developed countries expect to make the simpler machines themselves, but cannot expect to do more than become proficient in the use of advanced machines and thereby reduce the "cultural lag" that separates the first application anywhere in the world and successful utilization by the developing society.

BIBLIOGRAPHY

Cotgrove, S. F.: *Technical Education and Social Change,* George Allen & Unwin, Ltd., London, 1958.

A discussion of the evolution and operation of the vocational and technical schools in the English social system.

De Cesco, J. P.: *Educational Technology: Readings in Programmed Instruction,* Holt, Rinehart and Winston, Inc., New York, 1964.

A collection of recent publications central to the development of programmed instruction and related technologies of education, including a glossary of the new terms.

Grazia, A. de (ed.): "The New Educational Technology," *American Behavioral Scientist,* spec. issue, vol. 6, no. 3, pp. 5–77.

A lively collection of twenty varied articles on programmed instruction, new library and school design, and educational measurements.

Hughes, J. L.: *Programmed Instruction for Schools and Industry,* Science Research Associates, Chicago, 1962.

Instructs in the writing of programmed teaching materials and the use of programmed learning techniques, including recommendations on the use of consultants.

16

PLANNING FOR HIGHER EDUCATION

OVER THE PAST TWENTY YEARS a considerable body of widely diffused and not very well coordinated experience has been accumulated which points to the desirable relationship between the institutions of higher learning and the preparation for economic development. Unfortunately this experience has not yet been put together in a monograph where the conclusions are readily accessible. The picture presented below is the typical evolution of higher education in a society as it becomes involved in economic development, as gleaned from the accounts of educators and the reports of students of educational problems.

Initially the colleges and universities, if they exist at all, are likely to be quite inflexible and their curricula extremely classical. The kinds of persons trained are likely to be priests, lawyers, teachers, and perhaps doctors. Their studies are adapted to a relatively static society ruled by a small, privileged elite. Often the educational institutions themselves have strong traditions which keep them from adapting to the needs of commerce and industry (this has been particularly true of the Moslem world, but other cultures derived from the Mediterranean area have also demonstrated great conservatism in their educational institutions). Under such circumstances it is often necessary to establish wholly new institutions of higher learning which have built into them the desired adaptability and can thus fill the needs of a developing society.

The first of these needs is introduced by the literacy campaigns. At the very beginning, teachers of the primary grades will have no more than secondary school training, but as the secondary schools must become greatly expanded to fill the requirements for ordinary teachers, there ensues a demand for secondary school teachers who normally are trained at colleges and universities. Later some college training is extended directly to the elementary school teachers in the manner of the "normal school" arrangement in the United States and the teachers' institutes elsewhere. A successful program for removing the barrier of illiteracy would require normal schools and colleges with an enrollment capacity of one to three students in teacher training per thousand population.

Superimposed upon the demand for elementary and secondary school teachers are the needs reflected by projects for increasing the magnitude and the efficiency of resource use. Faculties are imported from the outside, or created by sending local young men overseas, for training the specialists and technicians needed. In Puerto Rico this took the form of establishing a school of agriculture and mechanic arts because of the prominence of the sugar industry; in other countries mining, forestry, fishing, or tourism might become principal emphases.

Associated with economic development is a great deal of construction. Accordingly, departments of civil engineering and architecture are needed to enable local contractors to erect modern bridges, buildings, piers, dams, airports, etc.

The new projects for transportation, communication, power production, manufacturing, and trade also require modern methods of administration and management. Therefore, under one name or another, schools of business and public administration are established. Initially, accountants and executives seem to be the most needed skilled persons, but later the usefulness of many other skills that can be taught in colleges is appreciated. Other forms of engineering also, such as electrical, mechanical, and chemical, become necessary. The number of personnel required in each skill depends upon the kinds of projects undertaken and the pace of the development. Within a decade or two after the new departments and schools have been created, it can be expected that the demand for resource-use specialists, engineers, and professional administrators would exceed that for teachers and would continue to expand with development.

Health problems often stand in the way of specific projects for resource development so that a demand is generated for medical specialists. The demand is greatly increased by health problems associated with urbanization. Thus medical instruction is given a new emphasis—that of public health. This is strongly reinforced by the popular association of the ends of economic development with the full-fledged welfare state, a cornerstone of which is medical treatment that is free and accessible to all. In many societies a large share of the first increases in real personal income is expended upon medical services. The high value which people put upon health and the provision of a public service which promotes medical assistance makes it economically desirable to stress preventive medicine.

ESTABLISHING NEW TRAINING PROGRAMS FOR SPECIALISTS

In any long-term development plan it is possible to foresee some time in advance what kinds of specialists will be required, as well as their approximate numbers. It is clear, then, that the appropriate college departments can be established five to fifteen years prior to the time of need. This gives the departments time to establish channels of recruitment which assure a satisfactory flow of students immediately prior to the period of greatest need for their ultimate services. In appraising the plans being made at some intermediate stage of economic development, higher education should be reviewed in the light of what has been done to meet these needs; then it is possible to fill the gaps that might be revealed.

In the efforts to set up new departments in higher education one feature is encountered which did not exist a generation ago. The standards of competence set as acceptable by the various professional associations (such as the American Chemical Society or the American Medical Association) or the accrediting organizations (such as the North Central Association of Colleges and Secondary Schools) are now widely recognized. In the period after World War II these standards have been informally extended so as to apply to colleges and senior high schools elsewhere in the world. The British and French standards are less formal but equally rigid. The standards set make it difficult for beginning institutions to evolve and grow, so that over time a competent faculty emerges. Professors do not like to take positions in an unaccredited department, nor do good students choose to study in them. Therefore, if it is to succeed, each new school and each new subject must be introduced at a standard and of a quality which receive respect in the most developed countries. This means that very elaborate long-range planning must be undertaken by the university administration so that each new activity is introduced at a level which ensures creditable performance from the beginning. Any lower level results in a damaging loss of prestige that often takes decades to overcome.

The efforts to achieve and maintain an accredited status reveal very quickly an important difficulty encountered in a rapidly developing society. This is the rather poor and improperly oriented training given in the secondary schools. The painfully assembled, competent young faculties in the reorganized university find that the majority of students in their classes do not have the background expected of them, a background which is provided almost routinely in the most developed countries. This gap complicates their teaching and greatly reduces the quality of the skill transmitted to the most promising students. Thus, one of the functions of higher education in a developing society is that of reforming the hastily constructed secondary school system so that it actually provides the general education which fits the student not only to the prospective future of the society but also to the disciplined course of studies presented at a modern university.

The content of such high-quality general education courses may be developed to start with in the first year or two of the present university and then, when the requisite teachers have been trained, brought into the secondary school level. The total process would very likely take two or three decades to carry through comprehensively, but with each step the quality of higher education, as measured by objective standards, would surely improve. It is also certain to improve the utilization of human resources since a stimulating program of general education is likely to discover and recruit for professional work a higher proportion of good minds than would the holdovers of classical and formal education that would be displaced.

Ideas about what constitutes general education for a modern society are again in flux. They had crystallized once in the nineteenth century around a course of humanistic studies based upon the classics. In North America, and less strongly in Europe, this core was displaced by a liberal arts emphasis in what became known as *progressive education*. Now it is not only the content of the liberal arts that is being criticized but also the methods. The critics propose that more mathematics be taught, and more foreign languages; that twentieth-century science be emphasized, and that approaches to rational policy making in national and international institutions ("modern politics") cannot be ignored. The classroom lecture is highly inefficient and should be displaced to a large extent by library studies, programmed instruction, workshops treating existing problems, studio practice with newly acquired techniques, and the manipulation of systems that simulate important economic, social, and political institutions (e.g., mock courts, business games, etc.). The transformation of education is barely underway, and it will be a generation before a major number of colleges and universities are reorganized, but it is apparent already that one of the aims is to bridge the chasm between the "two cultures" (referring to the hypothesis publicized by C. P. Snow) [1] of humanists and natural scientists; the other aim is to produce graduates with greater skill in communications and analysis as well as ability to use the recently accumulated bodies of knowledge.

[1] C. P. Snow, *The Two Cultures and the Scientific Revolution*, Cambridge University Press, New York, 1959.

An example of a change that is highly relevant to planning is the proposal to introduce statistics and modern mathematics to replace the usual compulsory geometry course. Programmed-instruction approaches to statistics have already been developed which produce levels of understanding at a speed equal to the best classroom teaching (which is rarely available). Also, as explained in the previous chapter, the new programmed textbooks and teaching methods are likely to be more easily transferred to the context of a developing society than the materials and techniques previously available. They will be most applicable in the advanced secondary and the early years of higher education.

This "institution building" process, which uses the higher education system as an instrument for raising standards throughout the educational system as a whole, can be expedited through exchange relationships with universities in the developed countries. University-to-university exchanges have now become quite standard, and a great deal of experience has been accumulated. Usually the more advanced university uses the relationship to develop a department or institute of specialized language and cultural studies in the area served by its partner, so that the graduates of the former may enter the diplomatic corps and international business firms operating in that general region. Under this arrangement the exchange can greatly benefit both parties to the agreement.

SOCIAL GOALS AND RESEARCH

In a developing society the university has a higher function beyond the task of training competent professionals. It must have both the freedom and the capacity to explore the possibilities which remain open to the society in the future. In a university it is possible to harbor widely diverging philosophies of life and therefore quite different outlooks upon what social goals may be held desirable. Here the possibilities of taking on new goals and dropping some which previously had been accepted may be argued among the experts. The panel of judges would be the collection of future teachers, executives, bureaucrats, and legislators to be found in the student body, plus that part of the public which participates in the high culture and the open debates which keep the neighborhood of a university alive and exciting. The verdict may be delayed by a decade or two while the implications are being sorted out and evaluated, but in the course of these discussions studies can be made of the methods employed elsewhere in solving social problems and philosophical paradoxes.

Occasionally some quite new hypothesis may emerge which could conceivably be applicable to the future of the educational system, the socioeconomic system, or the legal system. It must be tested for internal consistency, for realism, and for harmonious relationships with other important institutions and ideals. The realization comes quickly that exploration of these issues is a necessary function for higher education if it is to play a decisive role in shaping the intellectual future of the nation. Therefore some of the most imaginative and best-trained faculty members must be granted time and money in order to retain contacts with the vanguard of thinking in the world at large and to make small contributions themselves whenever the local environment provides them with special advantages over other investigators in the parts of the world where academic research can be more richly subsidized.

In order to reduce to a reasonable and nonviolent level the bombast and special pleading that can result from the exchange of views regarding social goals, it is evident that an emphasis on fact finding is necessary. Without relevant facts, or understanding of the complex interrelationship of various social and economic forces, the presentation of views becomes an exercise in the manipulation of the emotions of a literate and often romantically inclined audience. The kinds of studies that might be encouraged at a university include analyses of the potential for overseas commerce, the long-range social effects of migration, problems of achieving higher productivity in manufacturing, the possible specialist roles the society might assume in the hemisphere or the world scene, desirable patterns of community organization for a time when levels of living are more adequate, cultural relations with the major international blocs, investigations of various remedies for internal social problems such as juvenile delinquency or rural poverty, and others of this type. The "White Papers" that are treated with so much respect in the countries associated with the British Commonwealth of Nations draw very heavily upon university staff for the investigations. It is evident that this higher function of the university, making of it a key institution in the goal-changing mechanism within a society engaged in developmental planning, fits the patterns being adopted by most Western and neutral societies.

The research facilities in the universities are often extremely useful to the planning agencies in their regular operations as well because frequently special information of a character not adapted to the census or other operating departments of the government may be required to complete a satisfactory plan. The flexibility of the university makes it an obvious place to turn to for assistance. However, this kind of applied research on the part of the university should be discouraged the moment it appears likely to become routine. While universities are well suited to do the pioneering work and pilot studies, the scarce research personnel should not be permitted to incur responsibilities for more than a two- or three-year span unless—as in the case of forestry and oceanography—the exploratory studies themselves are inherently long-term propositions. Universities seem best fitted to operate on the frontier of knowledge, working with new methods as well as new data; on the other hand, standardized studies, using well-known methods to generate new data, are best suited to commercial firms or special sections of the bureaucracy. (The Bureau of Standards and the Federal Reserve Board in the United States government operate in this capacity.)

DEMANDS FOR COLLEGE TRAINING

The rate of growth of higher education is dependent mainly upon the growth of the secondary schools and the increasing numbers of qualified youth completing senior high school. As pointed out earlier, the flow of secondary school graduates is limited to an important degree by a shortage of university-trained teachers in high schools, as well as the shortage of funds for new facilities. Probably no more than half the high school graduates have a level of intelligence and study habits suited to college work. Under these circumstances a not unreasonable approximation is a rate of growth of enrollment of 50 to 100 percent per decade, the rate achieved or exceeded in the past when making allowances for the war and for a heavy load of remedial teaching.

To assist in visualizing what the demand might be for college training, the following procedure might be applied. In order to be explicit, arguments will be used that are drawn from the Puerto Rican situation around 1950 to 1952.

The Puerto Rican government, because of its accrediting relationships and cultural ties, wished to achieve very rapidly the levels of college attendance that are common in at least the poorer parts of the United States. For this purpose the states of Alabama, Louisiana, and Mississippi were chosen as comparable. The proportion of the age group from eighteen to twenty-two years attending college in these states was calculated, using data given in the U.S. Statistical Abstracts. This proportion was applied to the same age group in Puerto Rico for the year 1960, with rough corrections for prior migration. Such an extrapolation gives a college population of 10 to 11 per thousand inhabitants (the overall age distribution in the two areas is quite similar), or about 23,000 to 26,000 students by 1960. If Puerto Rico should attempt to achieve by 1970 the 1950 United States level for college attendance, the number of students would reach a point somewhere between 35,000 and 45,000. (The target for 1960 was reached, but only with the assistance of colleges and universities supported by churches with some outside funds.)

While such comparisons are illuminating, somewhat more fundamental approaches are now being made available. Referring back to the premise that the educational system should establish conditions which improve the utilization of human resources, the problem is to develop suitable indexes or measurements which will indicate improvement. To do this a system of examinations can be prepared which screen out the less competent and unprepared candidates for college entrance. Considering, however, that examinations per se always are an imperfect instrument, excellent academic performance in a high school of good standard should also qualify the candidate for entrance. Those students who fall below the line would be encouraged to take up extension or extramural studies, or to attend junior and technical colleges. Room should be made for the transfer of the most promising students from these courses of study into the universities, using their performance as evidence of competence. It would be most surprising to find any single technique of selection which would predict performance in higher studies with a correlation coefficient greater than .40, but a combination of techniques such as described might assure that eventually three quarters or more of the most promising talents emerging from the high schools are developed via the university.

The preceding arguments hold without reservation for the higher education of males. The policy for the education of women will depend upon the social roles that are being opened to middle-class women in the developing society. If they are restricted to office work and teaching, as is common in many Latin societies, then teacher training and post–high school commercial training may provide a solution that is both economic and socially acceptable. Nevertheless, high-quality minds are found in roughly the same frequency among women as among men, so that when the scarcity of needed talents is felt (and it is likely to be experienced in practically all societies after takeoff), new roles must be opened up for women. The changes can be made first on the civil service; the growing industries are likely to follow very quickly in opening up placements. The absence of most women from the labor force for ten to fifteen years during the child-rearing ages fits them to rapidly changing departments of government and to jobs that do not fit neatly into the promotional ladder.

A metropolitan university should develop an advanced program of short courses and extramural or extension courses. Most of these attract enrollment of ambitious individuals who hope to qualify for a more responsible job demanding a different combination of skills than they acquired in the course of their formal education and work experience. A really productive university is active from early morning until late at night, seven days a week, and fifty-two weeks a year (a little time is needed for maintaining and renewing the facilities). This bustling atmosphere should be transmitted to the junior civil service, manufacturing, and commerce and help develop the talent even after it is fully employed.

Locating universities in the pleasant countryside greatly reduces their stimulus, and thus it is, with few exceptions, highly uneconomic.

A JUNIOR COLLEGE SYSTEM

The junior college is primarily an American invention. It has many incomplete analogues in such institutions as technical colleges in British Commonwealth countries, polytechnic schools in Latin countries, and the early forms of the technical high schools in central European countries. Yet as these other institutions are being adapted to contemporary needs in rapidly developing regions, their function and curriculum seem to be moving in the same direction as the junior college, which is itself a product of a social environment experiencing unusually rapid economic growth.

A junior college normally provides two years of training beyond the completion of secondary education, but it is flexible enough to accommodate courses of instruction both longer and shorter than two years. At its inception it is designed to provide technical and subprofessional training. As income increases in the region it services, the teaching emphasis shifts to general education and the improvement of widely used skills, such as home economics. Still later it becomes a focus for the cultural and economic development of the country or city region it serves.

Experience to date suggests that it is probably not worthwhile to set up a junior college in any community which could not rapidly supply at least four hundred students with the prerequisite background. It is also taken for granted that because of the extra expense involved, very few students would be living away from the home of their parents or close relatives; therefore the site must be expected to serve an area which at its limits is only an hour or so removed from the home by bus or other available daily transport. This provision makes it probable that the junior college will evolve in time into a community or city college adapted to the means of livelihood of the people living within its range, and will serve their special cultural interests.

The character and history of junior college systems puts them into an embarrassing intermediate position between the local secondary schools and the universities. This predicament has never been resolved neatly, and so it is not possible to say from a distance whether the junior college should be a direct responsibility of the city or a larger administrative unit embracing the region, or of the department of education, or a junior branch of the university. The decision will depend to a large degree upon the methods by which education is financed at these respective levels and upon the conditions which must be provided in order to guarantee competent instruction.

The educational task of the junior college would be (1) training of subprofessional technicians, (2) training for transfer to the university (teaching general studies and less specialized courses), (3) training persons for middle administrative jobs in commerce, industry, and civil service, and (4) training preschool and elementary school teachers. The smaller junior colleges located in the less densely populated areas would offer limited curriculum, but the larger ones would provide a complete curriculum and might also conduct miscellaneous additional educational activities in the vocational and adult education fields. To put it another way, the smaller schools might train only two or three different kinds of specialists, most of whom are likely to find employment close to home, while the larger schools would train dozens. Both would also provide a sound course of studies in general education for those students who would move on to the university at the end of their two years' work. A substantial proportion of the classes would be given in the evening so as to enable day workers to attend.

FACTORS IN THE PREPARATION OF PLANS

Since much of the physical and operational planning for higher education relies upon the judgments of university administrators, it should be remarked here, first, that this discussion covers only those aspects which are related to developmental planning *in general*. Every top-level university administrator must take into account as well the *special* restrictions of sites already built upon, the faculty that has hitherto been assembled, the alumni who retain their loyalties, and the particular arrangements that have been worked out for cooperation with other institutions, both public and private. These are the resources with which the university or college administrator must work. He must also take into account the prospective demands for instruction in the humanities, fine arts, athletics, and many other consumption-oriented activities associated with higher education because these aspects have much to do with the acceptance of the institution by the community in which it resides and among the strata of society which it serves.

Above all, a construction program for higher education must avoid building monuments to national figures and famous architects. It might start more functionally from what local university administrators believe can be accomplished at their sites over the succeeding five to ten years. The sum of these proposals needs to be matched against the prospective structure of enrollment in that period. In a promotion-oriented society there tends to be an overoptimistic representation of what individual institutions can accomplish in a given time span, with the result that the sum of the proposals will exceed the supply of suitable entrants. Such a

Planning for Higher Education 327

case must be scaled down, primarily according to a criterion of *marginal cost per student*. Under these circumstances the aim of the planner would be to allocate increased enrollment to those institutions of higher learning which promise to provide a competent level of instruction for the least overall cost to the student and his family as well as to the state. Quite often the opposite situation prevails—then university faculties and administrations tend to be too conservative in their approach to the problem and assert that they are unable to cope with anticipated expansion in enrollment being thrust upon them without actually trying very hard to use their installations and staff efficiently. Then the planners are faced with sponsoring the analyses and justifications for allocations themselves.

What happens when institutions of higher learning are actually pressed to the limit of their capacity to provide for students, and an unfulfilled demand is left? The junior and technical college system can take on an academic program of studies and thereby provide a quick, inexpensive, but not altogether suitable substitute for the first years at the university. It can fill the gap if the difficulties lie primarily in the lack of teaching space or of dormitories, but not if the shortage lies in the supply of teaching staff. The shortage of adequately trained teachers demands the exploration of other possible solutions.

Normally the establishment of a new college or university would require ten to twenty years from the time of its founding before it could make a substantial contribution to the national capacity. Several exceptions come to mind, and they are worth exploring. A university may be able to make arrangements to engage the top professionals in the society and persuade them to use part of their time for teaching. For that it needs a location in the heart of the metropolis, possibly even renting the back rooms of downtown office buildings. Another opportunity arises from the international mobility of scholars, which enables them to escape persecution and neglect elsewhere and teach in those societies which respect and encourage their efforts. The universities of many developing countries today have been enriched by the presence of refugee scholars. A third possibility is that of effecting exchanges with universities elsewhere in the world, aimed at filling the gaps in the staff.

Thus far the discussion has revolved around what may be called strategic planning, which, for higher education, is dependent upon the opportunities and challenges present. The major items in the capital budget for higher education are justified on these bases, but the arguments are bolstered by projections made from operating data. The data collected most easily include quite a few categories that are already familiar:

Number of staff; categories and qualifications of staff; number of accredited departments; special institutes and programs supported

Previous year's admission of students; estimated capacity; previous education
of students (including transfers from other institutions of higher education); principal means of support of students; library use; number living
in dormitories and supervised lodgings

Degree programs offered; time required for completion; library size; tests of
competence employed at time of completion

Degrees and diplomas granted previous year; estimated annual capacity; categories of employment obtained

Previous year's operating budget; sources of funds; endowments; physical
equipment available (floor space for classrooms, laboratories, residence,
maintenance, administration, etc.)

Practically all the information given above is included in the annual
reports, catalogues, calendars, reports to trustees, and reports to accrediting agencies in the more highly developed areas, but even there the standards of reporting are far from uniform. If allocations are to be made from
a central budget (as exemplified by the University Grants Committees
in the British Commonwealth countries), there will be strong pressures
for standardizing reporting procedures so as to enable comparisons to
be made for budgetary review.

The inputs for research include (1) personnel (about 40 to 60 percent
of the expenditure when staff and advanced students are employed part-
time); (2) library, laboratory, and computing facilities (about 15 to 25
percent of the expenditure should go into these categories); (3) travel,
fieldwork, collections (about 5 to 10 percent in established universities
but a larger proportion in those that are just beginning to organize research); (4) administrative work, including accounting, secretarial work,
office space, police protection, personnel supervision, etc. (about 20 to
35 percent, depending upon the extent to which these responsibilities are
not undertaken by the investigator himself). There are also extraordinary
pieces of equipment associated with research that are commonly located
in the vicinity of universities—astronomical observatories, cyclotrons,
nuclear reactors, engineering experiment stations, agricultural experiment
stations, meteorological stations, botanical gardens, phytotrons, museums,
clinics, studios, printing and photographic establishments. Only when
the information produced is foreseeably significant to the society can
fundamental research be justified.[2]

[2] As an example of what is meant by "significant," India is faced with increasing
difficulties in water allocation as economic development progresses. The monsoon
cycle is responsible for most of its rainfall. Other countries are as dependent upon
the monsoon as India, but none is in the position to do fundamental research on the
subject. Therefore climatological research at the fundamental and applied levels will
have to be undertaken by the Indian government if technical possibilities for breaking bottlenecks in water-resource development are to be available at all. The most

Financial planning for higher education in developing countries is in a particularly chaotic state. It is recognized universally that private sources of funds, such as were depended upon very heavily in the nineteenth century by countries going through the development process, are far from adequate. Instead various patchwork and makeshift arrangements have been worked out for bringing in metropolitan, state, national, and more recently international sources of funds. The amount of subsidies to be granted to the recipients of higher education is very difficult to assess under these circumstances, although it is known to be large in comparison with the investment made by the recipient and his family. The returns from this investment are potentially very large, but they are deferred for a decade or two. If income taxes cannot be conveniently levied, it is difficult to recapture the returns for further public investment. Thus, with only one or two exceptions, *higher education tends to be undercapitalized in developing countries.* The capital is committed to projects which yield more immediate returns that are more easily recaptured. The complexity of the calculations prevents a satisfactory justification for any policy that leads to greater allocations to higher education.

BIBLIOGRAPHY

Allen, Herman R.: *Open Door to Learning,* The University of Illinois Press, Urbana, Ill., 1963.
> The evolution of the land-grant college in the United States as a means for "promoting the liberal and practical education of the industrial classes," together with recommendations for reorganization and extension into the international arena.

Carmichael, C. C.: *Universities: Commonwealth and American,* Harper & Row, Publishers, Incorporated, New York, 1959.
> A composite picture of seven university systems in English-speaking countries.

Myint, Hla: "The Universities of Southeast Asia and Economic Development," *Pacific Affairs,* vol. 35, pp. 116–127, 1962.
> A frank comparison of universities in Burma, Thailand, Indonesia, and the Philippines which recommends a commercial approach for the provision of the middle levels of higher education.

Ward, Phebe: *Terminal Education in the Junior College,* Harper & Row, Publishers, Incorporated, New York, 1947.
> Reviews curriculum, community functions, and vocational education in the junior colleges, emphasizing the requirements for vocational guidance.

worthwhile research and development problems that can be associated with institutions of higher learning are concerned with unique natural resources and health problems.

Weidner, Edward W.: *The World Role of Universities,* McGraw-Hill Book Company, New York, 1962.

Analyzes the exchanges between American universities and overseas universities, assessing the impact that the recent programs have had on both sides, with proposals for reorganization and reform.

White, R. Clyde: *These Will Go to College,* The Press of Western Reserve University, Cleveland, 1952.

An analysis of the demand for college education in an industrial state.

17

COMMUNITY AND ADULT EDUCATION

To a very large extent economic development is a cumulative program of self-improvement on the part of communities. If given some encouragement and reinforcement from the outside, most people can do much better with the meager resources available to them than they have done in the past. If, in addition, they are continuously provided with useful items of information, they can improve themselves still more.

But all this needs "doing," and the process of organizing a group to do things it has not been accustomed to doing requires new leadership. The new leaders will be persons in the community who recognize better than the traditional leaders how to draw upon experiences that some of the members of the community had acquired in the outside world, and also how to use information obtained externally by one means or the other.

Educators have come to understand the properties of this "bootstrap" approach to collective self-improvement. They can specify most of the prerequisite conditions for getting the process started, and they have become aware of the special kinds of information which ought to be delivered to the community, stage by stage, if progress is to be maintained. They have studied the methods for presenting this information so that it becomes understandable to rural people. They have found methods for selecting and training rural representatives who can gain the confidence of the various communities and serve as contact men with the whole array of government services, religious institutions, and large commercial enterprises that may develop interests in the communities.

In each region different patterns will arise, but after a decade or so of experience of this kind, educators have very skillfully put together organizations which can stimulate and service large numbers of these self-help programs. The recognizable achievements most commonly are (1) improved sanitation, (2) improved convenience of water supply, (3) a road connecting with the basic network provided by the central government, (4) a school, (5) organized recreation, (6) a health center or clinic, (7) improved agricultural practices, and (8) the organization of credit unions and cooperatives.

In the earlier stages of economic development one dollar spent on a competently organized program of community education may well yield as much as 10 to 100 dollars of welfare gain. The principal limitation is that of finding and training suitable personnel.

However, current thinking about community education and "village development" seldom has gone beyond the improvements listed above. What should people do *next?* How can they be assisted in the *further* stages? Historically the path of economic development lay in the development of a local specialty, often a craft, the products from which could be exchanged for useful articles in a regional market. The crafts led gradually into manufacturing and urbanization. After many economic and social reforms were effected to deal with the changed structure of society, the transition to a modern industrial economy was assured. Therefore it is not unexpected that in countries aspiring to economic growth many attempts have been made to introduce crafts, usually as part of broader village improvement programs. They have been almost uniformly unsuccessful because the visible returns have been too uncertain and too small. Almost every time a success is scored in the market, a machine will be invented or adapted, and a factory will be set up somewhere which will undercut the handicrafts and take away their customers.

The conclusion is inescapable that the historical process of economic development is no longer feasible for any society which maintains commercial contact with advanced economies. Community education must find another set of interests upon which it can focus.

Before proceeding further it is necessary to underline the urgency for discovering a technique for a transition from community improvement to a stable industrial society which fits into world conditions likely to exist in the latter half of the twentieth century, rather than those which have existed in the recent past. Current successes with sanitation and the health centers bring about a marked drop in the death rate and an improvement in the physical stamina of the adults. Initially this means more land cultivated, more crops harvested, and greater returns from local effort, especially after roads are completed. However, it also means a sharply reduced infant mortality rate, an increasing number of dependents, and a net growth in population of 2 to 3 percent per year. The subsistence needs of the extra population catch up with increases in production even in the more favorable instances. Any program which follows after community education must be prepared to deal in one way or another with the problems posed by the limits to local resources and the increase in the population. It is not too much to expect that the program of community education itself should serve to ease these inherent difficulties.

POSSIBLE DIRECTIONS FOR COMMUNITY EDUCATION

Given such complications, what are suitable ends for community education? Keeping in mind that the overall aim is to raise the level of living to adequacy or better, several ends come to mind which have hitherto seldom been considered in community education programs. One is the preparation for migration. Industrial societies need their workers in urban aggregations; even societies that make their living from agriculture, such as New Zealand, need more than two-thirds of the population in the urban communities if they are to maintain a good level of living. Under such circumstances, community education programs may aid in providing reliable information about opportunities in cities and may do much to reduce the risks taken in the transition.

In most instances population growth in rural areas tends to be so rapid that the cities cannot expand fast enough to accommodate the migrants from the countryside. In Puerto Rico, after public health measures eliminating malaria and purifying the drinking water had taken effect, the population growth went far beyond what could be supported in its cities. Fortunately, a safety valve was available to it which is open to practically no other rapidly developing area—the cities of a highly industrialized area. Even with the 800,000 or so Puerto Ricans removed to the United States, and a Federal-subsidized housing program in Puerto Rican cities, the slums at the periphery of the insular cities grew steadily during the first fifteen years of development. For Puerto Rico, the use of community education to encourage selected movement out of areas with limited resources may be in the right direction; but migration by itself is still not an adequate solution to the population problem even there.

One alternative would be to introduce family-limitation and family-planning techniques into community education. This program would attempt to get at the crux of the whole problem directly rather than at its undesirable aftereffects. It would try to maintain stability in numbers of the community during the period when the new ideas are being introduced. There is some hope that this can be done because in those underdeveloped areas which have been surveyed carefully it has been found that the *desired* size of family among the poorer classes is two, three, or four children, although after health conditions have been improved five or more are likely to survive. These extra children quickly use up the gains achieved in the first enthusiastic stages of self-improvement, and the resulting depressing effect is not overly difficult to convey to the members of the community.

The problems and implications of building a nationwide educational program around the central issue of family limitation and population control have been taken up in some detail elsewhere.[1] In brief, it was noted that present educational programs employing public health nurses on home visits, reinforced by meetings of groups for discussions and the showing of films, costs hundreds of dollars per birth prevented, as calculated from extrapolations of the previous fertility of the population given access to the education. The best programs to date are able to achieve a 10 to 20 percent reduction in fertility in communities where the need was for a 50 to 60 percent reduction.

In Japan the near solution to the population problem was achieved through the efforts of the mass media (newspapers and magazines), an acceptance of abortion in its cultural tradition, and an extremely high literacy rate among even the very poorest people. These conditions may be duplicated in parts of Formosa and Korea in the near future, but not elsewhere. The rest of the developing areas must work out programs which start from a much lower educational base.

The reorganization of community education in this direction is controversial because it violates the religious dicta accepted by many educated people (including those of Catholics, many Moslems, and certain Protestant sects). Because it is controversial, a government may find it politically impossible to proceed with a generally accepted course of action which implements a balanced program of community education. It may have to choose between an unbalanced program or none at all. Many enthusiasts for community education may even reject both migration and family limitation as additional aims (either for nationalistic or ideological reasons). They are unwilling to face the population problem, but maintain a faith that somehow, in a manner not predictable, a resolution of the difficulties will be found. At the same time, other claimants for funds can point to well-defined operations by which their objectives can be reached. The budgeting process, with its careful scrutiny of justifications for expenditures, is much less likely to allocate funds to programs about which there is grave doubt that they will be able to achieve the ends sought, especially when there is confidence that funds applied elsewhere

[1] R. L. Meier, *Modern Science and the Human Fertility Problem,* John Wiley & Sons, Inc., New York, 1959.

will almost certainly yield a *net* improvement in welfare in the long run as well as the short run.

Other strong proponents of community education hold that a third alternative exists. A community that has picked itself up by its own bootstraps could acquire a modern enterprise and by this means jump directly into the middle of the twentieth century. For a few rare spots in the world that have been richly endowed by nature so that it is possible that mines, oil fields, forests, grasslands, or sites for big dams can be developed, this viewpoint may have value, but most areas have a paucity of natural resources; there are extremely few communities that can look forward to such a transition. The main hope for these communities is that a factory or two can be located close at hand. Yet studies of industry show that the best locations for the predominant share of manufacturing are close to existing cities, whereas the techniques for community education were developed for locales so far from cities that the urbanizing influence was not strongly felt. Therefore the employment of community education, *as it now exists,* for the quick transition to manufacturing and modern resource use, seems doomed to failure *if used as a general policy.* It misses the mark mainly because of the rather special requirements for efficiency that exist in modern industry. However, out of the quickly changing patterns of economic development may come new tasks for community education. In Puerto Rico one finds a society sufficiently advanced to suggest how the industrializing process may lead to a redefinition of at least some part of community education plans and programs.

It appears that what is needed in this area of community and adult education is a great deal more institutional efficiency. Relevant information about coordinated participation must be brought to unlettered people in sufficient amounts to bring about distinct behavioral changes. Some of these changes are small, as in the case of fertility limitation, but they are crucial to economic development. The cost of transmitting meaningful messages needs to be reduced by a factor of five or so over what it costs today. Very likely this efficiency can only be achieved through mechanization and reorganization.

COMMUNITY EDUCATION AS ADULT EDUCATION

The locus of community education might change in part; instead of focusing entirely on the rural community, education might shift some of its efforts to the urban areas, and specifically to the urban slum or near-slum. A formula for collective self-help then is likely to be replaced by another which builds up individual *self-reliance*—a special personal initiative which is helpful in maintaining one's identity and survival in a complex world. By self-reliance is meant an enhancement of McClelland's achievement motive at the same time that the need for affiliation is diminished (see Chapter 3). In this way the objectives of community education would appear to merge with another form of education carried on simultaneously in the rural areas, that of agricultural extension work.

The agricultural extension system was created to bring information about improved methods of cultivation, animal breeding, homemaking, and marketing to those people who otherwise have no occasion to find out about such possibilities. It has been designed for regions which are cultivated by independent farmers tilling land for their own account, so that the extra returns go predominantly to them rather than to landlords or tax collectors. In many ways this emphasis upon self-reliance—the grasping of personal opportunities—serves as a fair introduction to life under city conditions. However, it too can be improved considerably by taking into account the opportunities for urbanization.

The greatest educational hurdle in the urban areas comes under the heading of vocational education, which has already been discussed in Chapter 16. However, vocational education is not enough by itself. Competent observers do not concede that the smooth and speedy conversion of country girls into factory workers or boys into construction hands solves the general educational problems of these young in-migrants. They also need to know how best to live in the new environment and something about the unexpected variety of opportunities now being opened to them. Above all, this reorientation has to be done economically, at a total cost of no more than a few pennies per capita per day.

Again in Puerto Rico, some excellent solutions have been discovered. Among the most important is a government-operated radio and television-station network which transmits trustworthy information, music, and reports on sports events. The private stations evolve serial dramas ("soap operas") that explore the facets of city life—melodramatically, to be sure, and with a heavy interspersal of "singing commercials," but in a fashion that attracts new immigrants and old residents alike and teaches much about alternative ways of life that would otherwise not be grasped. The impact upon living patterns is most remarkable, despite extremely limited resources for programs. When techniques of connecting content with viewer needs have been developed further, television should become the most effective force in the education of lower-middle- to middle-income groups.

The mass media may introduce people to the existence of a new idea or a concept, but study and review are necessary for its retention and application. In many societies the library can provide a foundation for adult education. Whenever the mother tongue is one that supports a flourishing book publishing industry, the library system becomes the cheapest and most effective means for reaching the serious education-seeking adult. If the vernacular is not one of the European languages or Arabic, the library must be built around the language employed for secondary and higher education, and as a result, it tends to become more an adjunct of the school system, with commerce quickly developing into a strong user.

The creation of a system of libraries (see Chapter 4 for detailed recommendations) encounters many special and unexpected organizational problems which are now being met with the assistance of international agencies (especially UNESCO) and private foundations. Most newly developing countries, for example, are located in the humid tropics, whereas most of the books printed are designed for storage in temperate environments with moderate humidity. This means that mildew, termites, cockroaches, and other pests must be kept under control. Special buildings and technically trained librarians are required. The circulation of books requires promotion; books cannot be allowed to stand on the shelves but need to be distributed through book carts or bookmobiles, lending societies, schools, and professional groups. Librarians report that newspapers and radio do not displace books but have instead been major stimuli for specific book requests. On the whole, libraries are essential for completing the transition into the modern culture and so far have no substitute.

DETERMINING PRIORITIES

The needs for community and adult education are highlighted particularly by the reference system of lifelong adaptation (Chapter 13). Wherever economic development requires social change on the part of an age group, an ethnic group, the residents of a particular area, or the practitioners of a trade, there should be means for transferring information to these groups about the implications of the change and about the new opportunities being opened up. Preferably there should be more than one channel of communication with the groups so that individuals can check their impressions from one against another. There must be a way for the groups concerned to ask questions and receive answers, and therefore person-to-person contacts are absolutely necessary. The bulk of the information, however, may be carried by audio-visual channels, by magazines and pamphlets, and by vocational training.

Radio channels are presently the cheapest means for reaching the large masses of barely literate population. The new inexpensive transistorized radios overcome the problems of finding links to electric power lines or to a supply for batteries. What is needed are messages that have meaning for the listener. The population might easily be subdivided into hundreds of publics, each having a different complement of interests and a convenient time in which they can be served.

The use of television as a medium for adult education is hindered by the cost of developing constructive programs that will appeal to the illiterate and barely literate population. The initial dependence of television programming upon the low-cost films exported from the few countries with cinema industries, combined with a scarcity of programs produced by the stations themselves, leads to a superficial assessment of its potentials; a lowbrow eclecticism is fostered in the viewing public. Despite these undesirable effects, the increases in the repertoire of images brought about by television are sufficient to justify rapid expansion of the medium in both commercial and educational directions.

Television and other audio-visual techniques may serve as an economical substitute for an accelerated literacy campaign that would be prerequisite in education for family limitation. After a year or two of viewing occasional programs on the subject, the *possibility* of limiting the size of family should become real to members of the urban public, and the *value* of doing so may become clear. Highly personal discussions are set into motion between women friends and likewise between men, so that the specific information of more informed persons spreads through the community. Many parents then would be induced to apply for help in family limitation at a clinic or public health center in the vicinity. Extensive studies of this process within the Puerto Rican and Jamaican cultures have been reported; [2] this work needs to be extended into the community and adult education program and into the era of television in developing societies. It is apparent already that any program for expanding the public health aspects of adult education must be highly organized for the long run even though it requires only a small fraction of the overall audio-visual output. Fertility control is one aspect of education which has been grossly neglected in Western societies, so that there are no earlier formulas for the newly developing societies to adapt to their own needs, as with textbooks, nutrition programs, and the like. The ingenuity and initiative required for linking family limitation with hopes for improving general welfare will have to come from within the circle of adult education specialists of the country undertaking development.

Priorities for the content of community and adult education may be separated into those with short-range and long-range effects. The short range might emphasize the following:

1. Consumption efficiency (savings obtainable at markets)
2. Short-term employment opportunities (harvests, construction, etc.)

[2] R. Hill, K. Back, and J. M. Stycos, *The Family and Population Control,* The University of North Carolina Press, Chapel Hill, N.C., 1959.

3. Civic duties
4. Exploration of the urban environment
5. Interpretation of political and social events

For the long range:

1. Accustoming residents to industrial and urban requirements
2. Providing background for fertility limitation
3. Creating understanding between ethnic groups, social classes, and various communities of interest
4. Developing the self-help theme for housing, gardening, and community services
5. Establishing a dependence upon libraries and the written record

The opportunities in the field of community and adult education are so vast it seems likely that the proportion of resources devoted to it needs to be increased. At the same time great care must be exercised to assure that the goals are indeed being met. The evaluations of the effectiveness of the programs must go on, coincident with their development. These take the form of sample surveys instead of the tests and examinations used in the other parts of the educational system.

BIBLIOGRAPHY

Adrian, C. R. (ed.): *Social Science and Community Action,* Institute for Community Development, The Michigan State University, Lansing, Mich., 1960.
  A set of papers which introduces the application of modern concepts in economics, sociology, political science, and community planning.

Beaty, W. W. (ed.): "Community Education," Yearbook of the National Society for the Study of Education, 1958, pt. 1, 1959.
  Includes a series of descriptions and critiques of methods in community education by such specialists as Margaret Mead, Harlan Cleveland, and Richard Poston.

Butts, R. Freeman: *American Education in International Development,* Harper & Row, Publishers, Incorporated, New York, 1963.
  Emphasizes the roles that educators overseas must take in creating "communities of modernizers." The concept of *educational development* is formulated, but more as a series of challenges than as a set of procedures. Finally a report is made upon successes and failures in educational assistance programs toward creating a self-sustaining program of educational development.

Holmberg, A. R.: "The Research and Development Approach to the Study of Change," *Human Organization,* vol. 17, pp. 12–16, 1958.
  A classic study which depicts new ways of obtaining information needed for community development.

Lund, Ragnar: *Scandinavian Adult Education,* 2d ed., Det Danske Farlag, Copenhagen, 1952.

A description of the development of folk schools, libraries, workers' circles, and radio programming in four Scandinavian countries.

Plumbe, W. J. (ed.): Current Trends in Newly Developing Countries, *Library Trends,* vol. 8, pp. 125–341, 1959.

A review of the programs that have been undertaken in developing countries, with some hints for improvement.

18

WHEN IT PAYS TO EDUCATE

THERE HAS BEEN no educational or administrative theory which suggests *how much* of the public funds should be devoted to education as a whole. This issue has been settled in large part by the political process. Some kind of compromise had to be found between education and the other competitors for government funds. The resultant outlay for education was an outcome of the interaction of the preconceptions of the politicians and bureaucrats with the special interests of lobbyists and pressure groups. The various biases and special interests are often embedded in precedent and tradition, but they are also stimulated by comparisons with other countries. Any government that greatly misjudges the demand for education should expect to lose support from the public after the mistakes based upon such comparative analysis become evident.

But is the public, or even the politically active portion of it, the best judge of the appropriate allocation to education? More specifically, if the public says emphatically that economic development should be given highest priority, will the choices it makes via the political process regarding education be at all compatible with the other programs needed for growth? The likelihood of finding the proper emphasis to be put upon education as compared with the other sectors is not at all high. Voters recognize their lack of experience in the area of education and so are willing to entrust, within rather wide limits, the crucial judgments to the experts. Thus the planner and administrator must face the problem of discovering criteria by which the total budget for education may be set.

The planner would like to know what economic criteria enable him to determine when it is best to invest in education rather than projects in other sectors of government activity. Thus far educators have not judged such expenditures as investment; educational planning has been primarily directed toward reducing the gap that existed between public aspirations for the acquisition of knowledge and skill and the present output. The educational administrators prepare a program that eliminates the gross discrepancies in educational opportunity. Thus the aim has been consistency rather than maximum output.

Most budgetary practice begins by assigning a share of government revenue to education and then adjusts at the fringes of this figure in order to accommodate high-priority programs dependent upon education. The 30 percent proportion in Puerto Rico cannot be used elsewhere because only a negligible allocation had been made to military defense, a large item in many countries. A better approach is to take the fraction of national income given to education, but even such a figure depends heavily upon the supply of teachers, the relative birthrates, the amount of urbanization, etc. Then it is possible to argue that the allocation to education should grow rapidly until it reaches a level between 6 to 12 percent of gross national product, the actual target being set by comparison with countries which have similar cultures and have been growing rapidly for more than a decade. Such arguments are good only up to a point; they are unable to show by any logic acceptable to unbiased observers what the planned budget should be within a considerable range of any reasonable figure.

It is apparent upon careful inspection of an education budget that the bulk of the educational program under way cannot be quickly cut or expanded. If it should be cut back strongly, the continuance and survival of the nation as a single cohesive unit over the long run is in peril. If it should suddenly be expanded by half, the money may get spent, but very little extra educational achievement would result.

Normally, planning and budgetary efforts are used throughout an educational system as measures for adjusting local facilities and staff to local needs. It cannot be expected that improved budgetary controls and reviews will result in a saving of funds, since the surplus discovered in one sector is almost always needed to make up for the deficiencies toward meeting even the minimum standards discovered in another. The best strategy for directing growth and development is to concentrate attention upon the fringes and margins of overall programs. What *new* activities can be added which will achieve greater returns than the average for the whole system? What features could be *removed* without affecting balance and consistency and without appreciably reducing educational standards?

There are also new projects and proposals which employ education as a means of producing direct increases in income. Examples appear frequently in industrial plans, where programs of apprenticeship and on-the-job training are proposed, in agriculture, where education is needed for the introduction of a profitable new crop, and in other resource-use activities where people must learn to use new equipment and materials. Then the cost of education becomes part of the investment program and its productivity can be evaluated. Presumably such "investment in the human agent" is equalized at the margin with the other factors of production. Present evidence (Svennilson et al., 1961) is that education can be remarkably productive when considered purely in its income-generating sense, and prior societywide investments in education lie behind most of the remarkable bursts of economic development experienced in Europe, America, and Japan.

Two analytical devices for judging the economic yield of education have emerged thus far. One attempts to create an institution which recaptures a share of the returns from education so as to pay its costs and perhaps even make a profit. Educational institutions would then be expected to expand until their profitability was in equilibrium with other corporate enterprises. If these hypothetical enterprises (so far none have been formed) could promote in a free market a larger volume of education than at present, then the evidence is strong that the society is underinvesting in education. The reverse argument, concerning overinvestment, is more difficult to assert because accounting procedures do not yet permit clear distinctions between the investment component and the consumption component.

The other approach would analyze national economic aggregates and attempt to isolate the effect of education upon the returns to capital over the long run. The proper methods of analysis, particularly what categories of items should be included as costs of education, are still hotly debated. Nevertheless it appears that even the most conservative formulation will grant that the net returns to society from education have been roughly equal to those from physical wealth (about 10 percent per year). If the knowledge transmitted remains relevant to the challenges posed by resource scarcities, it might be expected that education should remain profitable for the society.

THE VALUE OF GENERAL EDUCATION

It is relatively easy to trace the immediate economic consequences of an investment in *specialized* education because the rewards granted to competence in the specialty are usually quite explicit. There is much greater challenge involved in identifying the consequences of investment in general education, where the effects are largely indirect and become widely diffused throughout the economy. The major outlays for general education take place in elementary and secondary schooling, but they can become substantial also in programs for adult education.

Before any calculations can be undertaken, data (or private estimates based upon close observation) of the following types need to be available:

1. The average governmental costs per year of schooling for the respective grades in the school (see Figure 10)
2. The anticipated costs involved in proposals for expanding elementary and secondary schools (expressed in the same units)

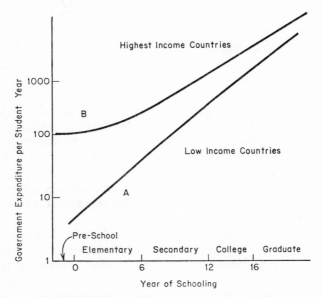

Figure 10. Governmental costs per year of schooling.

3. A survey of the extra household expenditures associated with school attendance at the respective levels
4. A survey of the earnings of school-age juveniles, comparing the part-time wages of those who are in school with those who have dropped out
5. Reports on the size of classes for the respective grades
6. A survey of lifetime incomes as a function of the years of schooling completed (see Figure 11)

By combining all but the last of these categories of information, it is possible to estimate the overall costs of education as a function of the grade being taught. UNESCO (1955, 1958) has supplied a world review of budgetary commitments to elementary education so that some approximate figures can be used in an example. These tables show that govern-ments spend $8 to $15 per student per year in countries with per capita incomes in the neighborhood of $100, and that the extra expenditures in the household for clothes and supplies may run to $2 to $5 per student year. Thus, in a six-year elementary school system, the total costs prob-ably range between $10 to $20 per year per student. In this kind of society there is a tendency for the size of class taught by a teacher to diminish as the level of education increases, so that the normal load may be fifty

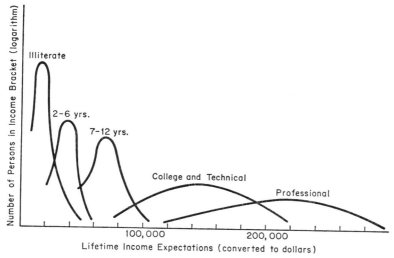

Figure 11. Typical income expectations according to amount of education completed in developing societies.

students in the first year and perhaps thirty in the sixth. Since salaries make up the major share of educational costs, and the proportion is rela-tively constant within a given region, the increase in cost of a student year as one progresses up the educational ladder can be calculated.

Typical government expenses have been computed for an economy having a per capita income of about $100 per year during the 1950s (see the curve for population A in Figure 10). Such a society may be expected to have 20 to 50 percent literacy, so the opportunities for extending ele-mentary education are quite large. For purposes of comparison, a similar curve is presented that is typical of a society with a per capita income of approximately $250 per year (see curve for population B in Figure 10). Such a society may be expected to provide education for most children of elementary school age, and the literacy rate would be 40 to 80 percent, depending upon the length of time that this emphasis upon general education had been maintained.

The lifetime income data are most likely to be derived from figures available in the treasury department from studies concerned with taxation. It is difficult to predict the exact form such information would take because much depends upon the quality of data regarding income distribution. What is wanted is the average income of respective ages received by heads of families having given amounts of education. In most instances it is impossible to segregate general education from full-time vocational education, so that these two categories may need to be combined when collecting data. The lifetime incomes associated with the acquisition of a given level of schooling should constitute a range of expectations for persons obtaining that amount of education at that time. A typical relationship is shown in Figure 11. The first ten years of schooling are devoted almost exclusively to general education in all countries, but the proportion in further education is quite variable from one country to the next, so that more sophisticated techniques may be necessary to identify the selective impact of more advanced general education upon the incomes.

Now, referring to proposals for expanding elementary and secondary education which have had their costs analyzed in this way, consider the investment in a group of persons which converts them from illiterates to graduates of a six-year elementary school. Their expectations of income gain are very considerable. With a bit of calculation an estimate of gross return can be obtained. In typical cases it will appear to run 30 to 70 percent per year on the investment in education, sometimes even higher. This is a very high return indeed, but there are some qualifications which tend to reduce it.

The major factor left out of the crude calculations described above is the education of women. The crucial need for literacy and further education among women was emphasized in the discussions relating to the role of family limitation and adult education in the process of economic development (see Chapter 17). Thus, the education of women is necessary for sustained economic growth, but the effects of such education do not appear in the form of markedly increased earnings accruing to their personal efforts. The effects show up in the form of reduced family size, improved educability of children, less waste in the household, as well as higher productivity on the job when the women do get an opportunity to work.

Another missing factor is the loss of educated persons, due to death or injury, before their educational expense has been repaid. This correction is normally minor because the death rate is small between the ages of ten and forty years in any country with a rudimentary public health service.

Still another factor must be considered, namely, that any notable increase in the supply of persons with elementary education could depress the relative wages of the sector of the population possessing elementary education. There are three methods available for preventing the reduction of income to levels below expectations. One is to invest in manufacturing, transportation, and communications equipment to such an extent that sufficient new opportunities are created. Another would carry the surplus graduates on through to the higher levels of education so that they might join the ranks of the skilled workers and the professionals, occupations in which shortages take much longer to overcome. The third method would encourage the emigration of partially educated persons to more industrialized areas. The labor market is very imperfect, and so it is not at all simple on the basis of past performance to predict many years ahead the effects of changing supply and demand upon wage levels. The most effective development plans would make sure that all three of the above-mentioned policies were available to the government in the event of need.

After such factors as those above are taken into account and adjusted for population growth and inflation, it is possible to compute an apparent rate of return to be expected from an allocation to general education. Before the decision becomes a firm one, however, it is worthwhile trying to detect what level of investment in education would be *too great* and therefore lead to waste. This consideration will be taken up after first considering an approach that is best applied to vocational and higher education.

SELF-FINANCING SCHEMES

Recently arguments related to this approach have been advanced, which start by asking the question, "Who profits from specific educational expenditures?" If a class of persons exists who can convert the skills acquired at government expense into substantial personal profit, then perhaps some means should be found for returning some of their profits back to the financing of this education. For many forms of trade school training and advanced clerical skills the principle is well established that the trainee should assume responsibility for the total cost of the specialized training. If the trainee appears to be a reasonable risk, he can borrow the money, and thus is enabled to mortgage his anticipated earnings. But this question asks whether there exist some equivalent areas in the publicly supported areas of education, where the public support serves as a subsidy to special classes of persons.

A glance at the pay scales advertised in a developing territory reveals that there is an excellent chance that the scarcer technicians and the professional classes may be able to demand salaries which run 70 to 90 percent of what would be obtained with the same education in the developed countries. Oppositely, should these same persons *not* have obtained this education and were thereby held down to semiskilled and craft occupations, their annual wages would amount to only 20 to 50 percent of those in equivalent activities in developed countries. A major discrepancy in pay scales has evolved. Closer scrutiny will reveal that this is another facet of the dual society. The modern, internationally oriented jobs are well-paying, while the traditional occupations pay poorly, even for highly skilled work.

In part this differential exists as a holdover from colonialism, particularly when it applies to governmental posts, but there is a "brain drain" of significant dimensions for developing countries which forces them to meet salaries offered in developed countries for engineers, applied scientists, draftsmen, statisticians, linguists, managers, etc. The low level of pay in the traditional sector can be attributed to a general oversupply of labor and a nontransferability of the skill to another cultural environment. Wherever these circumstances exist, higher education—even advanced secondary education—almost automatically results in a huge increase in earning power for the individual.

Universal concepts of justice do not accept such preferential treatment. If the education is publicly supported, the material benefits should be spread widely. In most countries the Soviet policies of selection and reward will be cited by educational reformers (even though the outcome has so far not been very different). An alternative is to develop an institution which would at least pay for the needed higher education by siphoning off a portion of the extraordinary gains in personal income that derive from the education.

It is feasible in any country to prepare a series of estimates of expectation of lifetime earnings according to occupation and educational level. In most countries there will be considerably less variance than indicated in Table 5; but if, as in Puerto Rico, the college-educated stream can

Table 5. Educational Level and Expectations of Earnings, Puerto Rico, 1960

Level	Total cost of education	Annual earnings expected	Normal lifetime earnings
Illiterate	$ 0	$ 100–600	$10,000–25,000
Six years' schooling	500	300–1,200	20,000–50,000
Ten years	1,000	800–2,500	30,000–100,000
Twelve to thirteen years	1,500	1,000–4,000	40,000–150,000
College training (14–16 years)	2,000–5,000	1,200–10,000	50,000–250,000
Professional (17–22 years)	4,000–10,000	1,500–25,000	80,000–500,000

migrate to other locales, then expectations spread out almost to the extent indicated. It is also relatively easy to estimate from life tables, and medical statistics, the proportion likely to be lost to the profession through death and injury before reaching the age of retirement. As a consequence, one may compute the purely selfish returns anticipated from a college education or a technician's training. It can be seen that the $2,000 to $5,000 invested altogether by the state, combined with smaller amounts by the individual and his family, can yield 10 to 50 percent per annum in the long run, depending upon the profession chosen. This gain accrues to the person educated; it does not count the special benefits to the community and society at large that may be generated by the application of the skill acquired.

It would be theoretically ideal if some investment trust or insurance company lent money to promising students in return for a portion of their subsequent earnings beyond subsistence. It is important that the return be calculated as a share of income and not a lump sum. Then, if some students decided to become artists, or poets, or schoolteachers (all of which are relatively poor-paying professions), it would not matter because the insurance company would have also financed doctors, businessmen, and electronic engineers whose share would no doubt more than make up for the former group. This way no person would have a specific debt hanging over his head that restricted his personal freedom of choice as to a career, but merely a tithe upon his earnings over his exemptions when he pays his income tax, no matter which society he lived in at the time. Such a scheme has the merit that it would then reduce the losses incurred to developing societies by the migration of home-trained talent. It would, over time, hasten the equilibration of the use of human resources because personal and family financial barriers to college attendance would be removed.

An investment in human resources along these lines has some highly appealing features for local investors. The returns, in the form of amortization and interest, remain a relatively constant proportion of national income. Thus, if inflation had occurred in the interval between the investment and the payout, the returns are in inflated currency. This form of investment can be rendered virtually proof against inflation. Because it offers the kind of security that is much sought after by conservative investors in a developing economy, they would be willing to accept a relatively low interest rate. Indeed, should the possibility present itself, it seems likely that an institutionalized fund along these lines would reduce the bidding up of the price of land, property, and even gold because in many ways it would constitute a superior hedge against inflation.

A description of such an operation will help answer many questions on this point:

A mutual fund could be created by insurance companies and banks. It would lend sums to students after they were accepted at technical schools and universities. These sums would be used for tuition, supplies, and subsistence. For each sum obtained, the student contracts to return a proportion of his income above subsistence (a quantity defined in the contract), including capital gains. Thus $1,000 on the basis of existing wage and salary structures might require 2 to 3 percent of future income lying above subsistence (roughly equivalent to taxable income in countries with income tax). This would be enough to repay capital and perhaps 5 to 8 percent interest. The debt arrangement should be a personal and professional obligation so that it operates across international boundaries. The fund would insure borrowers against death and injury at least up to the level of indebtedness. If real wages increased at a planned 2 percent or 3 percent rate per annum, a sizable surplus should accumulate. This surplus could be split, half going as rebate to the borrower and the other half as bonus to the lender. An investor in a cross section of human resources would possess the nearest thing to a share in the society itself.

As long as there are standards for admission to institutions of learning, the administrative costs of this funding would be relatively low. Any student having capital initially would, of course, not participate because he would be committing himself to pay a fraction of unearned income to the fund. Poor students would benefit the most. Educational institutions could expand as rapidly as qualified entrants appear because tuition costs reflect total operating costs. Budgetary control over advanced secondary and higher education by government is ordinarily minimal in order to guarantee academic freedom; here it would virtually disappear and would have to be replaced by some kind of regulation of educational standards. Scholarship and bursary programs would be virtually meaningless because cash gifts would no longer be necessary for assuring that the brighter students would be able to continue their education. Part-time work in college would still be advantageous to the individual if it were available in subprofessional categories of work and at those rates of pay.

Legal and administrative difficulties standing in the way of creation of such a fund are substantial but not insoluble. The gravest problem seems to be that of establishing a standard computation for income. Developing countries are able after some effort to collect income taxes from the professional classes and larger entrepreneurs on a relatively just basis, but the middle-income group poses greater difficulties. Another problem is that education has been ruled as consumption, not investment, and so the income devoted to repayment of education loans is taxed, as the laws presently stand in most countries. A serious complication arises in the financing of education for women: when they marry, should the lien on their income be transferred to their husbands? Or should a higher rate apply for women, limited to a share of their own earnings? (Cf. E. Shapiro, "Long Term Student Loans," *Harvard Educational Review,* vol. 33, pp. 186–207, 1962; R. L. Meier, "La théorie économique des sociétés en voie de développement," *Économie appliquée,* vol. 26, pp. 401–424, November, 1960.

BALANCING THE GROWTH

Education should be encouraged to come into equilibrium with other uses for capital through a variety of different measures. This will certainly occur within families who are in a position to pay educational expenses for their children. Also, the enterprise system in vocational education may be regulated so that equilibrium is approached in the private sector. Special schools can be organized as private firms for introducing scarce skills into the economy—a much easier task when no subsidies are required and tuition-with-subsistence loans are available. (In the Philippine Republic much of the higher education for dentists, engineers, and other medium-grade professionals is provided by private universities.) Correspondence schools, commercial colleges, and advanced trade schools are most likely to operate as private enterprises. Only universal general education seems to have a predominantly public function and falls outside the scope of commercial institutions.

The government and other large employers may find it necessary to make financial guarantees to the educational institutions (whether private or public) for specific educational services rendered. The creation of a sufficient supply of elementary school teachers, for example, might require public subsidies; similarly, training of nurses to accompany a hospital expansion program. Governments have already devised many methods for obligating citizens for such investment in their personal development. A common procedure is to obtain promises in writing that a stated amount of time will be put into some designated service (e.g., teaching, nursing). Usually it calls for a year of service for each year of subsidized education, but the formula has many variations. In such arrangements the person who received the training is obliged to give up part of his freedom of choice, particularly when, how, and where he may employ his newly acquired skill. These schemes are less flexible than the self-financing approach and less well suited to rapid rates of economic development.

In the foregoing paragraphs education has been treated as an activity suited for regulated enterprise in the development of human resources. The purpose has been primarily that of clarifying the issues and relationships. Most educational systems are irrevocably committed to other modes of financing, and so they are faced with a more complex procedure for bringing education into balance, but the following procedure for collecting and analyzing data can usually be employed:

1. Collect information from a suitably constructed sample of persons who have received education and specialized training, regarding their earnings and capital gains.

2. Review the marginal costs for additions to different levels of the educational system, subdivided so as to show average estimated costs to the individual, the family, the community, and the state.

3. Construct tables reflecting lifetime earnings as a function of education for such categories as medicine, law, engineering, teaching, civil service, business.

4. Make estimates of income distribution in the important categories. (It is probably too expensive to set up comprehensive surveys for this purpose, but in many instances professional societies collect data which may be used after some verification and analysis.)

5. Consider cost versus prospective gain in lifetime income when persons are moved from the upper levels of the general education group, preceding specialization, to a higher educational level. What is the discounted value of the increase in income, using realistic rates of interest? How does it compare with the government subsidy involved in the education? Does it exceed the total cost of the education?

6. Consider the fraction of the extra income that is recaptured in the form of taxes. Are the amounts sufficient to repay the costs? Are they collected by the same levels of government that make the outlays? (Often states, provinces, and communities are authorized to invest in specialized and higher education but then are unable to expand the facilities in accord with need because the taxes are generated on the national or federal level. Tax reform then is almost always prerequisite for the balanced expansion of education.)

7. Repeatedly review data on the placement and earnings of graduates over the five years immediately following completion of studies. If a noticeable slump should ever occur, this tabulation is a signal for a review of policy in those categories of education. Perhaps more careful analyses of expectation of earnings and recapture in the form of taxes may be in order, and these changes should then result in budgetary reallocations.

8. When additions to the investment in specialized and higher education no longer yield a return in the form of private income superior to that obtained elsewhere in the economy (as calculated in step 5), a thoroughgoing review of the *noneconomic* returns from education needs to be undertaken. It is quite possible that the psychological and cultural by-products are valued highly enough to justify continuing as before, but that the nonprofitable

outlays should be considered a form of *consumption*. This form of consumption should be encouraged in heavily populated areas if it exacts a minimal drain upon scarce natural resources and replaces other kinds of consumption which strain such resources.[1]

It is worth taking time here to ponder the consequences of the rationalization spelled out in the preceding steps. If education and tax authorities act according to these recommendations, the government in effect will have taken over the functions of the mutual fund for the finance of education, described earlier. Repayment of government investment in the education of individuals then would not come out of increased earnings of the individuals themselves (who profited from their own education), but from increased earnings in the population as a whole, and the overall investment would be guided by the market value of skills. While freedom of choice by the individual being educated is reduced somewhat when the government monopolizes education, the responsiveness of the schools to government planning controls is increased.

Many governments are handicapped by the wide gulf that separates tax policy and education policy. It is virtually impossible to get concerted administrative effort that will make tax reforms coincide with changes in the structure of the educational system. Under these circumstances governments might do better by adopting a mixed public and cooperative (mutual) method for financing education. Such a device can be made still more advantageous if it is possible to induce a transfer of private savings from relatively nonproductive investments into education. It would work particularly well in the universities of South Asia and Africa, where diploma holders achieve high social status and economic opportunities merely by qualifying for the degree.

One administrative reform that could be made without great difficulty is the creation of two capital accounts for education in the capital budget. One would list programmed expenditures for land and physical equipment as before, while the outlay for education itself could be restated as another kind of investment. Annual operating costs, including salaries, maintenance, and amortization, should be compared with the same figures for twenty-five or thirty years earlier, appropriately corrected for changes in the value of the currency and population size, to discover whether losses due to disability, death, and migration are being replaced. At our present state of knowledge the important point to make is that *the difference between these outlays is the estimated government educa-*

---

[1] Here, as in preceding paragraphs, the situation is argued in terms of the *typical* imperfections of the market, the tax structure, and income distributions in newly developing countries, and not with all the caveats and provisos of rigorous economic distinctions.

tional investment in human resources, and its magnitude should be visible. Over time the linkages with other investment decisions should become clearer.

COLLATERAL COSTS AND BENEFITS

One of the uses of education that is repeatedly referred to in one or another context elsewhere in this book is its contribution to national unity. Education up to the college level displaces some of the allegiance directed to family, tribe, or community and transfers it to an unseen abstraction— the nation. When the education reaches the lofty peaks of postgraduate study, the symbols of nationalism have less appeal; advanced higher education fosters identification of an individual with still more abstract concepts of "the true, the beautiful, and the good" that transcend national boundaries. Thus the political effects of educational policies also need to be appraised.

Some indication of the political consequences of elementary education may be obtained from comparative studies already made. UNESCO's *World Survey of Education* (vol. II) has plotted the rate of increase in elementary enrollment in various countries for the two-decade period 1930–1934 and 1950–1954. This past investment is just now in the 1960s having a maximum effect upon social and political organization. The countries which experienced the greatest enrollment gain are, in order of decreasing rate, Ghana, Belgian Congo (including Ruanda-Urundi), Iraq, Nigeria, Kenya, El Salvador, Turkey, Thailand, the Philippines, Formosa, and Malta. It is interesting to note how many of these territories emerged from colonial status during this period and that others, far down on the list (such as Angola, Mozambique, Liberia, Ethiopia, etc.) have thus far not provided enough education to create a strong following for nationalist or revolutionary leaders.

Governments find it difficult to maintain internal order during the period when the new loyalties are being created. Many countries build up military expenditures to dimensions comparable with the education budget, even if they are not threatened by neighbors but only by internal dissension. The increases in elementary education are also followed by increases in urbanization, the growth of the capital cities and commercial centers being the most spectacular. In the city the authority for maintaining order is given to the police, who must be backed by militia or the regular army when quelling major riots. The presence of a large number of literate but not really educated persons enables the charismatic leader to build up within a few years a disciplined following capable of carrying out written orders and therefore also capable of effective resistance to government.

There are costs and hazards also associated with secondary and higher education. If the output of diploma holders accelerates beyond the white-collar intake of the civil service and large businesses, there is a tendency for political extremism to develop among the unemployed members of this class. To put oneself above physical labor, once such educational levels are reached, is quite common. To blame the government for not providing a job directly appropriate to the diploma held, regardless of experience or competence, is even more common. Leaders of the new semieducated masses can be drawn from the ranks of these embittered, underemployed intellectuals. Rifts and splits on ideological issues are common.

On the positive side it is necessary to point out that innovations can spread much more rapidly through a society that can read and inquire. Many new ideas are continually produced, but only a few are practical successes and only a fraction of these can be disseminated successfully. Organized research and investigation are carried out predominantly in advanced societies, and the results, both theoretical and practical, are conveyed through scientific and engineering journals, catalogues, and exhibitions, so that today the government technical groups and the universities in developing countries are most aware of the details and the potentials. The basic information is highly concentrated in the major cities and among the upper classes. Elementary education reduces the cost of communicating this information down and away from the bureaucratic hierarchy and improves the quality, or level of abstraction, of the concepts that can be successfully conveyed. Thereby more diffusion is permitted from the stores of the internationally held accumulation of technical knowledge. With more information of greater reliability at hand, better decisions are reached at the level of the industrial worker and the small entrepreneur in various businesses. Better decisions mean less waste and more product per unit of input to the process. So it is apparent that research and invention on the one hand and education on the other represent two separately organized social activities that must merge before their impact upon economic growth can be felt.

FACTOR PROPORTIONS

The machinery for introducing into a society the knowledge and information which permit it to achieve greater efficiency is administered in various parts of the government. Research and development are scattered over many agencies, but with a particularly heavy component in those with responsibilities for the exploitation of natural resources. The educational divisions have already been described. Mention has been made also of the private efforts in education, publication, libraries, etc. The contacts with the stock of knowledge accumulating on the international scene outside of the society have been referred to briefly. How much of the national income should be spent for all these efforts? Is there any opinion on the proportions that should be spent upon the *different features* of this machinery?

Perhaps the most advanced quantitative analysis to date of the need for education and the programming of the relationships between expansion in primary, secondary, and higher education is provided by Nigeria.[2] It began with a manpower survey and forecast which revealed considerable misuse of the existing skilled manpower and inappropriate salary structures. It then established balances in the degree of skill (semiskilled, skilled, clerical, technical, professional) and worked out an enrollment expansion program up to the year 1970. It envisaged an increase in the public allocation to formal education from 2.5 percent to 4.0 percent of the gross national product. Private expenditures are likely to increase greatly but still remain small in comparison. Unfortunately, the benchmark data on overall supply were rather shaky, probably understated, so that the plans face major revisions.

Comprehensive statistics for allocations to education are collected by UNESCO. They show that the highest rate of expenditure upon education, expressed as percent of national income, is to be found in Puerto Rico and Japan. Comparable figures are not available for the Soviet Union, but it is believed to be not far behind. These societies are also those that have exhibited the highest rates of economic growth in recent times. Governmental outlays for education after the "takeoff" stage has been passed can reach 6 percent of the national income. To this must be added substantial outlays by private groups for vocational education, adult education, libraries, etc. Also to be added are the costs of education to the family, especially the income forgone in order to undertake full-time education beyond the age of fourteen.[3] Then the total expenditure upon education in these rapidly expanding societies reaches 8 to 9 percent of the income. Since in both Japan and Puerto Rico there is evidence of a continuing shortage of many kinds of trained personnel to the extent that the shortages exceed the surpluses, this sum does not represent an overcommitment.

In advanced countries the allocation to research and development activities now approaches 2 to 3 percent of the national income, although approximately half of it is devoted to military objectives and has minimal

---

[2] Federal Ministry of Education of Nigeria, *Investment in Education,* Lagos, 1960.

[3] It is recognized that the inclusion of the "opportunity costs" does violence to the "proportion of GNP" concept. In most cases it can be neglected without changing the social policy implications, but overlooking it could lead to overinvestment in education.

relevance to the goals of economic growth. These expenditures produce the seeds for innovations that can be exploited elsewhere in the society. In newly developing territories much of this effort is better spent on the creation of efficient borrowing procedures. A constant review can be maintained of the technical problems arising at home and the developments abroad. On many occasions it will be seen that international correspondence, the acquisition of books and periodicals, education abroad, purchase of prototypes, or acceptance of technical assistance from the outside would enable the adaptation or use of the knowledge generated by worldwide research and development. The initiation of innovation by all these techniques that are not labeled "education" may easily require 1 to 2 percent of the national income.

Thus, in a period of rapid, continuous economic growth where gross investment rates in physical equipment are reported to be 15 percent of GNP or higher, the allocation to education and the spread of new knowledge—a special form of investment in the human agent—that seems to be in rough balance should be about 10 percent of GNP. These relative proportions, when using the best technology and institutional structures known to work in newly developing territories, seem to generate economic growth at a rate of 3 to 7 percent per year on a per capita basis, although for considerable periods the rate may be even higher (Svennilson et al., 1961).[4] This is, of course, no guarantee that other nations following in the wake of the leaders will find these proportions equally productive, but at the moment it is not possible to identify serious objections to the pattern of development they imply. If there is any long-run trend that can be detected, it appears that the investments in human resources (which should include some of the expenditures upon public health where they are relevant to production) are steadily increasing in significance as compared with the investments in physical equipment. Quantitative data are too fragmentary and unreliable to be able to assert how rapidly this trend is moving.

BIBLIOGRAPHY

Bowman, M. J.: "Schultz, Denison, and the Contribution of 'Eds' to National Income Growth," *Journal of Political Economy,* vol. 72, pp. 450–464, 1964.
A thorough critique of the macroeconomic methods for measuring the value of education.

[4] Svennilson et al. have shown that the ratio is quite different for relatively well developed countries such as those in Western Europe, where gross investment rates in physical equipment and inventories average 20 percent of GNP and education plus research only about 5 percent. The stock of human capital in those countries is already very high and can be used more efficiently.

358   Educational Development

Keezer, D. M. (ed.): *Financing Higher Education, 1960–1970,* McGraw-Hill Book Company, New York, 1959.
A report upon the organization and financing of higher education in the United States, including some estimates of the demand for the skills produced, with emphasis upon rationalization of the system.

Machlup, F.: *The Production and Distribution of Knowledge in the United States,* Princeton University Press, Princeton, N.J., 1962.
The first thoroughgoing attempt to create categories of research, education, and communication suited to macroeconomic analysis.

Martin, L. R.: "Research Needed on the Contribution of Human, Social, and Community Capital to Economic Growth," *Journal of Farm Economics,* vol. 45, pp. 73–94, 1963.
Introduces for the first time a clear distinction between the human resources embedded in the individual (learning), in the organization (know-how), and in the society (knowledge) and points the way to measurement.

Schramm, Wilbur: *Mass Media and National Development,* Stanford University Press and UNESCO, Stanford, Calif., and Paris, 1964.
A marvelously clear, simple, and systematic presentation of manner in which mass communications are being used to bring about economic and social development all over the world.

Schultz, T. W. (ed.): "Investment in Human Beings," *Journal of Political Economy,* vol. 70, October, 1962, suppl., with contributions by G. S. Becker, J. Mincer, L. A. Sjastaad, G. J. Stigler, B. A. Weissbrod, E. F. Denison, and S. J. Mushkin.
This is the most thoroughgoing theoretical and technical treatment available to date, which sorts out, in measurable form, the economic effects of investment in education and health. The data, however, cover only the United States, and only a few citations apply to conditions outside the United States.

Svennilson, I., et al., *Targets for Education in Europe: A Study of Policy Considerations Related to Economic Growth,* working paper for Policy Conference on Economic Growth and Investments in Education, Washington, D.C., October, 1961, Organization for European Economic Cooperation.
A statistical evaluation of the role of education in the economic growth of Europe and the implications of programming an expansion in the allocations to education.

UNESCO: 1, "World Survey of Education," 1955, 2, "Primary Education," 1958, Handbook of Educational Organization and Statistics, Evans Bros., London.

Vaizey, J.: *The Economics of Education,* Faber & Faber, Ltd., London, 1962.
An introduction to economic policy for education in developed and underdeveloped areas. Excellent bibliography.

19

THE DISTRIBUTION OF FACILITIES
OVER SPACE

In the earlier stages of economic development in most parts of the world, the two great competitors for funds are education and transportation. Schools are needed to introduce participation in the national life; they provide mutual experience for the respective communities which permits them to identify their interests with those of the larger cultural entity. In short, education, when publicly supported, unifies. Likewise, the improvement of transportation annihilates the barriers of lost time and effort which separate human settlements. Better roads link together the economies of villages and towns into a regional framework. Thus transportation also contributes strongly to political unity.

Although the departments responsible, respectively, for transportation and education may vie with each other for support, the one trying to expand at the expense of the other, both are engaged in bringing about economic and cultural integration of the society. True, they constitute strikingly different ways of approaching the same high-priority, long-range goals; but it will be seen that because the "journey to school" rapidly becomes such an important element in the planning of educational facilities, the evolution of the transportation and educational systems is interlocked. In the very early stages of economic development, schools tend to follow roads, while in later stages the needs of the school buses often justify road improvement. The *location* of schools, then, is always a function of the stage of the transportation system.

What are the principles for locating school facilities in order to achieve maximum social return?

In the early stages of development when there exists a vast pool of unschooled children and general illiteracy upon which to work, the decisions are relatively easy. Teacher training is emphasized, and the teachers are sent wherever the villages and towns will build schools for them. If given a choice, the teacher will almost always go to the community "on the road" in preference to one "in the bush" because he retains the chance to see newspapers, attend meetings, and keep in touch with groups progressing at higher and more intellectual levels as well as at the village level. His sense of isolation is alleviated. In this period, it should be remembered, whatever educational facilities are available are quickly used up to and beyond their rated capacity. A teacher is sometimes expected to struggle with fifty or more students in the morning and an equal number of others in the afternoon. Therefore little attention is paid to the accessibility of the school for the population of eligible students.

The next stage is that of converting the educational system which grew up in response to local demands into one which is comprehensive, so that each child now is physically able to get to a school. This process takes much more planning. The central educational authorities must resort to the census to make reasonable allocations of school building funds. The recruitment of teachers has to be better organized, and institutions for training them expanded. School buses are purchased for secondary schools, too, in order to obtain the higher standards and greater efficiencies usually possible in schools that operate with more than two hundred students.

There follows a period when the struggle is no longer one of getting schools to children, or vice versa, but one of providing education of satisfactory quality and duration. At this point the economic calculations regarding the sizes of schools and their locations become more elaborate. Important amounts of money can be wasted by adhering to tradition because the capital invested per school-age child in educational facilities ranging from kindergartens to colleges, including such equipment as school buses and playing fields, increases by a factor of five to ten times over the previous periods.

SITE SELECTION

One basic decision is that of site selection. In virtually every modernizing society the government has been granted the unlimited right to take over private property if the land or the structures are to be used for educational purposes. Therefore the choice of potential sites is a very wide one.

The start is made with the rough dimensions of an economic unit for a modern school (say, six to thirteen rooms for an elementary facility) and a set of preliminary architectural specifications adapted to the climate and the culture of the people, and thus designed to keep maintenance costs at a low level for at least the first few decades of use. Then a map can be consulted which shows those areas for which satisfactory schooling has already been provided. Such a map should also show areas that have populations so diffuse that the standard structure cannot be used; these too can be ruled out of the initial decisions because they must be taken up as special cases. Within the territory remaining, other departments of the government are planning projects of importance to economic development which may be reinforced by the location of schools in the neighborhood. Therefore a set of priorities for the location of schools may be generated in part by the geographical impact of other programs.

Elementary school organization is also importantly affected by the existence of different language groups in the same locale. Usually literacy is achieved in the mother tongue in the primary grades, while the language or languages used for the integration of the state and national affairs are taught intensively somewhat later. The location of classrooms for the primary grades, therefore, may be strongly influenced by the division of land and labor among ethnic groups living in the vicinity of each other, as well as by the acculturative policies in general. The location of schools, in turn, may well be influential in building a bridge of understanding between such groups, whereas if it is left to local option, the choice of site would tend to reinforce the *status quo*. Location of facilities thus becomes a key issue in a pluralistic society.

The system of socioeconomic and political priorities establishes a locale, but not a *site*. An appropriate site could be selected first on the basis of journey-to-school costs as measured in time, hazards, and money. Traffic engineers are quite familiar with these calculations; they serve to establish what is a "central" location for a school. Inquiry must also be made as to whether any of the suitable sites are likely to be necessary to industry or commerce over the next decade or so. Because of the tremendous emphasis which must be given to increasing the productivity of capital and labor in the income-producing activities, industry and closely related activities must be given priority for land use. This leaves a quite restricted number of sites to be investigated in detail.

Once planning work has been brought to this point, the education authorities are then ready to consult the community about its wishes and to inform it as to what the alternatives are and the reasons why they are limited. This will involve considerable discussion on the part of the community since schools, once they are well established, often serve as community centers and may take on other functions also, such as being headquarters for a mobile clinic or library. A school may also become a recreational focus for the community. Some features of the locational decision may even be submitted to a local referendum so that individuals may vote on the issues. In the process of discussion the local community formulates ideas and plans for using the facility, so that the structure becomes not so much a monument to education as an active institution affecting many strands of life in the community.

It is not difficult to find economic locations in regions where the population density exceeds 1,000 persons per square mile (about 2,500 per hectare). Economic size units can be sited well within walking distance of the prospective students. It is when the density amounts to only a few hundred per square mile and the settlement pattern is disperse that locational choice becomes problematical. Then the operation of a standard-size school may require a school bus and improved roads, or it may be necessary to settle for many temporary two-room and four-room buildings so as to enable the journey to school to be undertaken on foot. Wherever population falls below 100 persons per square mile, the schools must either be scattered about in small and uneconomic sizes or consolidated in villages and towns served by a well-organized transport system. In all instances the changes due to migration tend to be so large that many initial sites for schools will become obsolete within a decade after the schools are built.

This consultative process for planning the economic distribution of elementary educational facilities over territory may be applied to the secondary schools with only a few modifications. Decisions regarding the number and size of the secondary schools, however, will depend much more on the policies which are established with regard to human resources. Some societies will decide that they most need persons who are highly trained. In this case the secondary schools will be small and selective. Other states will decide that a full complement of skills should be distributed as widely as possible through the population. The logical procedure then would be to build each school incrementally. It might start modestly, but additions would be constructed every five years or so until the facilities could handle the bulk of the population in that age bracket. The need to expand in stages places special requirements upon the design of a structure and the choice of its site.

Somewhat different problems are associated with the location of a university. Here the journey-to-school provisions are overshadowed by the functions which are more or less independent of attendance at lectures and examinations. A university contributes the most to economic and cultural development when it becomes a pacemaker in the introduction and synthesis of ideas. If it is isolated in some country estate it cannot do this; nor is it likely to do so if it is geographically surrounded by a sea of illiterates. Normally, one expects to find a zone in each of the principal urban centers which already serves as the focus of intellectual life. Locating the university on the periphery of such a neighborhood tends to bring about continuous diffusion of new persons and novel ideas into the old circles. Since the university is simultaneously a convenient repository for knowledge accumulated by other countries as well as for much of the world's technical information, it should also be within "consulting distance" of the national or provincial governmental centers. Any country dependent upon foreign trade and commerce would require that its commercial center, usually a port city, also have a university—if it is not already provided for by these other requirements.

Of very great value in choosing the original site for an institution of higher education is the provision of room for expansion in at least one direction. The organizations and services dependent in some way upon universities tend to establish a variety of permanent structures at the periphery of a university over a span of only a few decades. Hospitals, apartment houses, seminaries, theaters, stadia, passenger depots, and research institutes congregate there and inevitably become relatively permanent barriers to physical growth. They should be allowed to settle on no more than three sides of the university's principal quadrangle or campus. On the other hand, any university which is built as a collection of colleges distributed throughout a rapidly growing metropolitan area as small "groves of academe" finds that there is insufficient coherence of interests among the faculty, and this lack of contact leads to sluggishness in taking on new responsibilities so necessary to industrialization and overall development. Also, the academically oriented institutions ordinarily found in a university are scattered about and sometimes not built up at all. They are not able to reinforce each other in influencing the urban environment.

The locational decisions for the major universities, both public and private, have already been made irrevocably for the majority of the other nations which are currently preparing comprehensive development plans. Therefore there is little value in discussing in greater detail the problem of finding appropriate sites. Henceforth the principal locational choices will be those which make the best adaptations to decisions which have already been made.

Locational decisions regarding special facilities of higher education, such as teachers' institutes and junior colleges, are not quite so vexing. The usual procedure is to establish another new unit once the first site has become overcrowded or extra demand has appeared elsewhere. There are fewer political and cultural commitments made to the site, so it often becomes quite possible to move the institution after a few decades to a new location, bringing to the abandoned site some use or purpose that is more appropriate to its dimensions and environment. The procedure for locating vocational schools, training centers, and similar institutions follows the same pattern.

The preferred practice for each of these would entail making a survey of the access to future users of the facility, preparing a tentative set of specifications for efficiently pursuing the intended educational activity, and then examining what geographical alternatives remain open. Once a site has been chosen, the preliminary design of the structures and equipment would be carefully reorganized so as to achieve maximum utility from the land. This last step is commonly referred to as *site planning*. Such practices are already well accepted, though far from universally applied, in developing countries.

Site planning must be concerned with such aspects as the isolation of the school grounds from traffic, the use of existing mature trees for shelter, surface drainage, orientation to the sun and the prevailing winds, control of noise, layout of play space, sidewalks, landscaping, etc. As soon as the building of schools becomes an important activity, there will be several architects, engineers, and construction firms specializing in schools. If the education department inspectors are conscientious, economic techniques for site planning and school construction that apply to the respective climatic and economic regions can be speedily developed. The detailed specifications are shared by the firms and the supervising architects, along with planners employed by the government.

DIFFERENTIATION BY AREA

When funds for education are scarce and the social services need to be concentrated in specific areas (principally at the sites for large scale exploitation of natural resources and the growing industrial centers), it may be necessary to establish two different quality standards for education. One would cope with the exigencies as best it could in rural areas (on account of the scarcity of buildings, equipment, and teacher training, such schools must depend upon local improvisation). The other would attempt to maintain modern standards in the principal cities and lay the foundation for the future system of universal elementary education. The limited amount of planning that is possible to undertake under these circumstances would be devoted almost entirely to the *urban* program. *Education must precede the crucial resource developments and the establishment of modern industry;* therefore the specialization of education according to geographical areas must reflect the development *potentials* of the various subregions. There may have to be one set of standards for the education intended to bring about a ferment in the traditional society, and another that is intended to expand the modern sector.

The key data affecting school location are those that are also the concern of the urban planners. However, in the past—and most likely in the future, too—the decisions regarding school locations have had to be made before the planning for metropolitan development has really begun. The educational planners may be forced to sketch out the future of the metropolis five, ten, and even twenty years ahead, including its future population, the new land likely to be occupied, the evolution of the transportation system, the redevelopment of central areas, etc. Within this framework, then, it is possible to lay out school districts with roughly equal school populations, many of the districts already being fixed by the presence of existing schools. Somewhere near the center of each district, measured in terms of journey-to-school convenience, a site needs to be chosen and cleared of existing structures. Normally two or three levels of the hierarchy of school types must be planned simultaneously so that students move from a set of primary schools to a designated intermediate school—unless they are deflected into private schools—with several intermediate schools channeling their graduates into a high school.

The first sketch plans are likely to be drawn up at a time when perhaps no more than 10 to 20 percent of the schools scheduled for construction have been put into place. The plans must therefore be subjected to continuous revision. One of the major sources of corrections, outside of the operating data compiled by the state or metropolitan school administration, should come from changes in the migration patterns.

The regionalization of new facilities for higher education, particularly for universities, requires more sophisticated analysis. A university is a national asset of unique significance as well as constituting a state and metropolitan responsibility. Its integration with government, commercial, residential, and transportation facilities calls for careful study by specialists. The growth of the institutions in terms of students, staff, structures, extension services, and curricula needs to be assessed for as many as three decades in advance. The placing of colleges and universities calls into play some of the higher strategies regarding the place of education in developmental planning. Many of these were discussed earlier, but some have been reserved for the closing arguments in chapters following.

20

THE OVERVIEW FOR PLANNING
STRATEGY IN EDUCATION

BY THE TIME developmental planning is no longer merely talked about but has begun in earnest, and planning for education is consciously linked with the planning in other departments, the inherited educational system has been so firmly entrenched, it cannot be scrapped. Very likely it is so constituted that it cannot even be thoroughly remodeled. How, then, is it possible to bring about all the striking changes in intellectual skills and viewpoints that are so necessary to economic and social development?

From the beginning of the planning effort it seems necessary to involve a small group of educational philosophers who have gained a breadth of understanding which permits them to see education at home as relatively sophisticated outsiders would see it. They would have the freedom from immediate pressures and local biases which would allow them to make cross-cultural comparisons. Such people would not arrive at judgments of the kind which assert that system A is bad, B is mediocre, and C is superb, but would point out that A emphasizes certain techniques and values in its teaching methods and as a consequence obtains a certain set of results, whereas B, using a different assortment in a context which is not quite the same, gets more or less analogous results. With the perspective gained from comparing and analyzing various national systems of education, it is possible to understand the limitations (and advantages) of one's own system more realistically. By viewing the total educational system inherited from the past both from the inside and from the outside, it is possible to develop some reasonable hypotheses concerning alternative grand strategies for the elaboration of that system.

One of the major discoveries that one makes in carrying out this cross-cultural analysis for developing areas is that three distinct philosophies of education have been transmitted to these territories. Each philosophy evolved in a different part of the world, and each yields a remarkably different allocation pattern for the funds devoted to the respective institutions. Their respective impacts are illustrated in Figure 12. The amount and type of training for each age class which the authorities on education feel to be appropriate can be demonstrated quite easily in a visual form. This type of diagram constitutes a simple means of portraying the idealized, long-range goals for educational investments in human resources. If sex roles are greatly differentiated, the diagram should indicate this by becoming a "pyramid," analogous to those used by demographers.

A few words should be added about the methods and outcomes of these representative systems. The typical American approach, for instance, tends to place a high priority upon widespread public education and upon public participation in educational management. It will also be liberal in its employment of modern mass-media techniques, ranging from illustrated pulp magazines to radio and the documentary and educational film. It aims at creating a modern mass culture, no matter how lowbrow and infantile initially, and then at every level of sophistication in the system introducing the various ideas necessary to cultural and economic improvement. The tasks of development become a matter of popular concern. The respective programs can obtain evidence of the degree of popular acceptance from elections, from the markets, and from the climate of opinion generated. The normal response to such an educational system seems to include a high degree of occupational mobility, great geographic mobility, and a very fluid, adaptable society in most other respects. Political continuity is difficult in this kind of atmosphere; good-quality politicians are needed to press the development program.

It is interesting to note that if a similar diagram were drawn up based upon the available fragments of recommendations of Soviet experts to underdeveloped satellites, it would probably appear not too different from that normally suggested by the Americans. However, the contrast between the respective curricula designated "general education" is extreme because the basic premises regarding the place of the individual in society are so far apart. The Soviets have tried to instill conformity to authority in order to make central controls workable, even while attempting to achieve the mobility and flexibility in the social order that are so necessary for effective resource development. Their idealized system is a reworking of the Central European pattern, adapted to rapid urbanization and industrialization.

1. The most common outcome of American thinking about education:

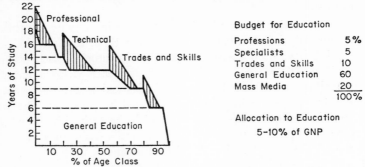

Budget for Education

Professions	5%
Specialists	5
Trades and Skills	10
General Education	60
Mass Media	20
	100%

Allocation to Education
5–10% of GNP

2. Similarly for the British mode of organizing education:

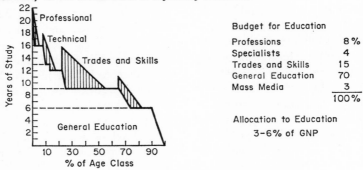

Budget for Education

Professions	8%
Specialists	4
Trades and Skills	15
General Education	70
Mass Media	3
	100%

Allocation to Education
3–6% of GNP

3. An alternative program based upon an advanced peasant economy:

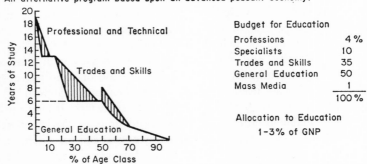

Budget for Education

Professions	4%
Specialists	10
Trades and Skills	35
General Education	50
Mass Media	1
	100%

Allocation to Education
1–3% of GNP

Figure 12. Apparent goal of contemporary overall educational systems in educational development.

In contrast to the American approach, the thinking in other English-speaking countries emphasizes the creation of an elite culture within which a restricted number of better-educated persons will circulate. Popular culture, they reason, will exist, and it ought to be permitted to mutate freely from one pattern to another, but it is relatively trivial and unimportant. They feel it is essential that an honest, highly competent, and stable administration be created and maintained. The civil service that can be brought into being by such a system ought to stand in the best position to take advantage of the opportunities for development that present themselves to the society. This model seems well suited for circumstances where social change can be gradual and smooth rather than rapid and bumpy. However, it suffers from an inability to implement massive efforts once agreement has been reached that a given objective is worthwhile.

The third pattern belongs to a different context. It visualized development proceeding only up to the level of a peasant society, such as exhibited by nonindustrial Europe around 1900. In such a society general education is not important. Even literacy is not essential. Decisions must be made by an elite which is in general quite well educated, but along classical lines. The ranks of the tradesmen and specialists need to be built up, mainly to establish essential services and maintain public order at a decent level—the prerequisites for a prosperous peasantry. The proponents of this system are to be found among administrators and educators in Spain, Portugal, other Latin areas, and a few Moslem areas.

Each of these patterns, it must be emphasized, represents an ideal. In a given territory, each will be modified according to what is possible to achieve immediately and what must be postponed. In many governments adhering more or less to the second pattern (most of them associated with British educational activities), the posts originally created for training technical specialists are only 30 to 70 percent filled at the same time that those for general education at the college level are 90 to 100 percent filled. Thus the supply of technicians in the future may be expected to be woefully meager.

In some countries the cultural and linguistic diversity will hinder the growth of a system, and in others it may be some political element which must be appeased. Therefore the emphasis actually given to the respective features of the system in a ten-year plan may be quite different from the ideal structure.

RECONSTRUCTING EDUCATIONAL SYSTEMS

Since, as already has been pointed out, the education planner cannot turn in his outmoded system for a new one, for the most part he is limited to patching, mending, and letting out seams. However, it is often possible to introduce new subsystems, planned so as to be independent of the worst restrictions and so as to expand and fill some gap or deficiency in the traditional system.

There are several ways of analyzing education in terms of subsystems. One of the most important of these is the distinction between the public system, normally supported by taxes, and various private systems. The private systems may include religious groups, cooperatives, endowed institutions, corporations (most provide organized in-service training for their own employees, but also those operating as a business), labor unions, publishers, radio and television networks, producers and distributors of films and recordings, etc. The important distinction between public and private is that the government has only *indirect control* over the decisions regarding growth and expansion in the private sector. It can set certain standards of performance in each activity, but these are almost of necessity minimum expectations. It can assure comprehensiveness either by filling the gaps itself or by providing an often wasteful set of subsidies to the respective private organizations. The disadvantages of such incentives are balanced by the remarkable flexibility which is obtained and the number of experiments and innovations which it is possible to carry through. The allocation of responsibilities in education between the public and various private systems of limited scope presents very nearly an infinite set of possibilities, so the real task of the planner is to suggest a few which appear to be best suited to the particular territory with which he is concerned.

Referring again to our principal example, planning for education in Puerto Rico has been faced with a variety of private organizations in education and related activities almost as extensive as that found in long-established states. It must take into account in its projections and plans the following subsystems:

1. A school system leading from kindergarten to college, operated by various orders of the Catholic Church
2. Some relatively unconnected educational institutions linked in one manner or another to other churches which altogether cover eighteen grades of schooling
3. Schools of commerce and other vocational schools functioning on a non-profit basis, sometimes endowed, sometimes subsidized by companies or craft unions
4. Other schools in the vocational field which are operated for profit
5. A public library system that extends the use of published materials to persons who cannot purchase them
6. Publishing activities in newspapers, newsletters, magazines, pamphlets, books, and advertising which are operated primarily for profit
7. Radio and television networks and individual stations which are operated primarily for profit
8. Producers, distributors, and exhibitors of films and recordings who operate primarily for profit

All these institutions may be expected to play a useful role in the extension of education. Licensing and other regulations will require them to submit certain basic statistics, such as enrollment, units of output, etc. Publishers deposit copies of their output in designated libraries as a matter of record.

In a developing society, performance standards for the operation of private institutions of this kind do not exist as a matter of tradition. Nor can they be introduced effectively merely by licensing and regulation because the latter tend to require only the minimum standards of honesty and decency, and even then require an efficient enforcement staff. When standards are lacking, many excesses and even scandals must be expected; also, the contributions of the private organizations to national education goals are not very dependable. In Puerto Rico a valuable principle has been used which has a much greater effect upon improving the performance. In any really important operation, ranging from newspaper publishing to the making of film documentaries and radio programming, the government has created units for which personnel have been selected who can be expected to achieve high-quality performance and operate wholly in the public service. It sometimes takes a decade or more for the influence of these high-quality standards to trickle down to the level of public appreciation and acceptance by the businessmen, but a review of recent history and an analysis of the flow of key personnel in the respective trades reveal that on the whole this influence has been strikingly effective. The output is not consistently improved, but the spectrum is broadened so that the output is not of uniformly low quality, aimed at the barely literate masses, but will achieve a moderate amount of depth in a fair share of the work and occasionally reach the level of artistic accomplishment. Sometimes, as in the case of the newspaper published by the government, the quality of the competing publications in the private sector may improve to the extent that interest lags, so the government enterprise may be dropped without loss to the overall education and the public communications system.

There are also subsystems which may come into being as important features of developmental planning that are basically not educational at all, but they can be carried out more cheaply when grafted upon the general educational system. For example, the task of improving the nutrition and general health of children is greatly eased in Puerto Rico and most other places by the school lunch program. In a period when school attendance is not complete and large percentages of students drop out after a few years, this midday meal can be an important factor in maintaining attendance and, for some of the children from the poorest families, will definitely improve performance at school.

A program aimed at reducing the wave of juvenile delinquency ordinarily associated with rapid urbanization and social change is also likely to be oriented to the school system. Complete programs for providing mental therapy for potential delinquents at a time when it may do the most good are far too expensive even for the most advanced and the richest societies. Therefore various strategies are required for the reduction of cost. One of them is to attach the program to the educational system in such a manner that it is possible to use the teacher's experience with the students to best advantage and at the same time help the teacher by paying attention to those "problem children" who seem destined to become worse rather than better.

In other countries schools and the schoolteachers may aid in census taking, in the conducting of elections, in the actions of local courts, in the elimination of malaria, etc. Often they become much too burdened with extra duties, and teaching performance suffers. The best principle to apply here seems to be that extra routine duties which do not tend to improve the quality of education should be avoided. Special projects that require no repetitive labor might well be assigned to teachers because very likely some local educational reinforcement is necessary for successful completion. If the teachers are given a small bonus for their cooperation in such projects as the census, the task is likely to move more quickly and surely. However, in general, planners should resist exploiting the educational system and to that end should support efforts of those government departments that claim to need a comprehensive system of town and village clerks, postmasters, etc. Only programs that directly help the children, the schools, or the teaching ought to be permanently grafted to the educational system.

SUMMARY OF OPERATING PRINCIPLES

Education is a prerequisite for development, but the education normally available in a newly developing country must be liberalized and modernized as well as expanded. Schools have a bewildering variety of objectives before them which must be translated into programs that are consonant with the image of the future of the nation. The ordering of these objectives and their transformation into attainable goals for the educational system are tasks that require the concentrated attention of a small group of leading educators, scholars, philosophers, and politicians for years at a time. The education that proceeds outside the school system must fit into these also, even though the goals are less explicit. The outcome of such studies should be a series of guides for the formulation of education plans through the combined efforts of the planning commission and the department of education.

The realistic recommendations that would follow upon a broad-gauge analysis would probably include at least the following:

1. A program for reorganizing the teaching of teachers
2. A program for expanding the elementary school enrollment
3. A formula for producing the most crucial skills that are needed for high priority projects in the development plan

At the same time, or a little later on, other subsystems would be added which include:

1. Secondary school programs
2. Comprehensive development of institutions for higher education
3. Adult and community education
4. Vocational education

If several independent subsystems are introduced for each of these undertakings, the resultant development of the society should be more flexible and able to withstand a greater variety of upsets. Thus there may be public schools and church schools, classical and modern curricula, and outlooks that may be either provincial or national-international in their scope of interest. The financing may be handled according to different formulas in each system so as to take advantage of diverse means of support.

The new programs are almost always based upon the prior experiences of other developed or rapidly developing countries, modified, of course, to suit the indigenous requirements. They are built up with borrowed technology and often manned initially with foreign experts or local citizens who went abroad to obtain such training. Many new educational subsystems will contain organizations which operate in the private sector, some of them as profit-making firms. The government has less authority over the latter type of educators, but it still can wield a great deal of influence by applying the following procedures:

1. Introduce incentives for the initiation and promotion of the desired kind of private organizations.
2. Set up prizes and awards for various kinds of high-quality performance.
3. Establish and supervise a system of licenses, examinations, health standards, safety standards, and the like which tend to set the minimums for the quality of the services.
4. Create within the department of education, or elsewhere in the government, prestige or "yardstick" operations which would experiment in various ways that seem likely to improve the quality of the services.
5. Split off new and independent bureaus and agencies which collaborate with the organizations in the private sector and expedite their various requests for governmental cooperation.

The best example of a plan that has been constructed in this manner and on this scale is that provided by the United Nations Economic Commission for Africa (*Final Report,* Conference of African States on the Development of Education in Africa, Addis Ababa, 1961). These educational planners were conscious of the economics of education, the need for data, and the requirements for growth. They recommended, for example, lower standards for school structures than in Europe or America (lower also than many African states which have been prone to make the buildings into inflexible public monuments). They also came out for research in teaching methods and for more emphasis on science and its applications, and they believed that some means of financing education with loans could be developed. The conference programmed a rapid growth of expenditure on education so that it would reach 6 percent or more of national income in the 1970s, which is about double the present rate.

There are repercussions from this scale of investment that cannot be overlooked. The widespread borrowing of ideas and techniques from the outside world, the bootstrap process that pulls ever-increasing numbers of persons out of the morass of ignorance, and the visibly improving economic conditions combine to create a society with a new self-image. Its relationships with other societies change, so that it begins to serve as a mentor of less rapidly developing countries; it starts regarding countries with long and illustrious histories as cultural equals, and it begins to assert its viewpoints on the international scene. Such a society occupies a new and more influential niche in world affairs mainly because it has become confident that it can meet standards required by the role.

In many societies, particularly those in Latin America and South Asia, the struggle for social status will lead many families to direct their children into studies that are not very useful for development. Unemployment and underemployment in the educated classes result, and a huge potential for disturbing the social order is created whenever the discontents of this group are mobilized. The solution proposed in Chapter 16 was a retraining program for the positions that were not being filled. An alternative is that of establishing higher standards, preferably set by international educational groups, which require further study of a general-purpose character, e.g., competence in other international languages, methods of social investigation, statistics, accounting, psychological tests, or elements of design, which are useful in both large bureaucracies and small enterprises. Then the highest prestige agencies would tend to draw their recruits from among those who meet international standards of competence. Since much of this oversupply of graduates has advanced to the stage where they can study by correspondence, the availability of programmed instruction (see Chapter 15) can become a very significant factor in further education. The availability of skills at international standards also makes possible the rapid buildup of new organizations which can exploit the best opportunities available to the society.

At an even later stage in the development process a cultural flowering may be expected. Ideas and concepts are promoted from within the society that no longer can be traced either to classical tradition or to something borrowed from beyond the borders. They are not even direct offshoots or hybrids with traceable ancestry but products of complex cultural synthesis. At first this maturation may be evident in only a few directions among all those possible (e.g., mathematics, physical science, biological science, psychology, engineering, architecture, painting, drawing, sculpture, music, poetry, fiction, literary criticism, drama, history, philosophy, etc.). After the first creative successes have been recognized and accepted outside of the society, many other channels of cultural activity are likely to be affected. Such an outcome is one of the long-range results that are continually sought through the educational planning, but little is known about efficient means for achieving them.

Because there is so much that cannot be ascertained prior to the commitment of time, money, and materials, despite a smoothly functioning information-gathering service, the guiding philosophy in planning for education should be that of freeing individual intellectual choice. Within a wider range of tools and concepts from which to choose and a greater sophistication in the techniques for arriving at a good choice, the society is then better prepared for whatever future it must face. The most that educational planning can do is to release human potentials. What is done with the extra potentials is a matter for the people who possess them to decide.

BIBLIOGRAPHY

Erasmus, C. J.: *Man Takes Control,* The University of Minnesota Press, Minneapolis, Minn., 1961.
> An appraisal of the technique of foreign-aid administration, particularly those with a heavy educational component, from the point of view of a participating social scientist.

United Nations Economic Commission for Africa: *Final Report,* Conference of African States on the Development of Education in Africa, Addis Ababa, 1961.
> An excellent example of analysis, proposals for reorganization and balance, and programming, but still too far from the procedures for implementation to show many of the necessary compromises with national politics.

PART FOUR

FURTHER INTEGRATION OF PLANS

21

RATIONALIZING URBAN DEVELOPMENT

THE CONCERN THUS FAR has been limited to the initiation, direction, and expansion of the lead sectors of a socioeconomic system. This approach was chosen in the belief that the other sectors would follow by adopting the precedents that had been established and by making adjustments according to principles that were already becoming familiar. Education and industrialization have been emphasized because they constitute the principal forms of productive investment that enable a modern society to grow; they are activities which need comprehensive planning in most societies at a relatively early stage in development.

Planning elsewhere in government has been reviewed and analyzed in like manner. Each branch of the government is expected to foster its own specialized modern institutions; each must therefore assemble data, evaluate alternative proposals for additions, lay out a capital budget, etc. The statements about what must be done become quite repetitious. They employ the same reference systems for collecting and interpreting data, but suggest the addition of one other (which could be called the *dietary*) for countries likely to encounter periods of severe food scarcity. The goals of the other governmental departments represent elaborations of points already raised, and the concrete targets for their plans are determined by the achievements in the lead sectors. In general, they are able to borrow administrative procedures and technologies from more advanced countries. However, all these branches of national government encounter their greatest mystification in ascertaining what course is best in the largest urban areas. The big city represents a major investment in physical equipment, but it is also the arena for the struggle between tradition and mod-

379

ernism. It provides the greatest challenge for the integration of agency master plans.

Cities in developing countries have lost the initiative they held prior to the takeover of nationalism and are, almost without exception, incapable of planning their own future. City governments do not possess the power to control the influx of population or direct the rate of investment in physical equipment. They must therefore swim with the tide of change, moderating the evils of overcrowding, congestion, and *anomie* with the rather puny resources left to them. The real urban development planning must for a long time to come be carried out at the provincial or national level, whichever holds and uses land controls, police powers, and capital allocation. Yet most of the information—the raw material from which projects are synthesized—can only be obtained on the scene, usually in the heart of the city. The spatial separation of the facts from the political interaction involved in plan making results in simplistic approaches to problem solving.

Such mistakes can be costly. Conditions of life in cities can deteriorate to the point where development is stifled. When that happens, the urban communities are disorderly, makeshift, congested, diseased, and ugly. Strong efforts are then made, in a few countries at least, to employ civic design as a means of ameliorating such conditions, but most design efforts (as in Brazilia, Caracas, Lima, or Chandigarh, for example) result in expenditures for housing and other structures which strain the economy without significantly improving the welfare of the inhabitants. Urban development must get things done which lie behind external appearances. Design questions need to be considered after a project has been justified on economic grounds, and the final configuration should contribute to efficiency as well as aesthetics.

A city destined to become large in the course of economic development faces a series of problems. Measures for alleviating these problems are known. Therefore some arm of the planning and administrative system responsible for the city must be given responsibility for preventive action, and a recommended procedure was elaborated earlier (see Chapter 4). The tasks of the transitional period are those of creating an orderly environment, so that residents are permitted to develop an elaborate set of expectations which enable them to calculate what is best for themselves, their families, and their neighbors. The trains must run on time, the voltage should remain steady on the power lines, and water should run when the faucets are opened. The sewage must be treated, and the air must remain clean enough to maintain health. There must be space to live and opportunity for work. The planning and management of these services are most easily implemented initially by controlling the land that is accessible to the urban centers, but as development proceeds, the information-collecting apparatus becomes an increasing significant instrument for guidance. The arguments that explain this transfer of dependence are worth considering in greater detail.

COPING WITH URBAN GROWTH

The treatment of urban growth in contemporary long-range developmental planning often contains hidden biases. Either some of the most embarrassing long-range consequences are not mentioned (i.e. the build-up of the *favelas* in the shadow of Brasilia and the effect of its monumentality upon the national fiscal system) or excessively critical evaluations of inconsistencies in the plan are made (the "flaws" often represent conflict-reducing compromises between factions which must be found before any long-range commitment can be made). It is best to choose as an example a country where a serious attempt to face up to urban growth has been made by government, where criticism from all professional viewpoints has been aired freely, and where serious, fact-oriented reconsideration has been under way.

The dimensions of the urban-growth problem in India are as staggering as any in the world except those of China. A convenient many-sided review is found in the reports from a recent symposium (Turner, 1962). In it Kingsley Davis shows that the urban population of India must be expected to increase by a factor of six (low estimate) to eight (high estimate) during the last half of the twentieth century. The first quarter of this period is now past, and it appears that even the high estimate may be conservative because overall population growth is not constant but seems to be accelerating. At the beginning of the twenty-first century the urbanization process would even then be only partially complete, so that cities must be expanded several times more during the latter stages of development. If India conforms to world experience, the largest urban center should be roughly twice the size of the second largest, and three times the size of the third ranked, etc. Thus past trends suggest that Greater Calcutta would be 66 million in the year 2000, Delhi would be 33 million, and Bombay 22 million, with all of them still growing at a rate of 3 to 5 percent per year. Actually, however, more detailed analysis reveals that partition has cut off part of the hinterland of Calcutta, so that about a third of its growth potential is likely to collect around Dacca, the capital of East Pakistan. Bombay has severe land reclamation problems (or transport problems, if it decides to settle agricultural land at some distance from the existing center) which should inhibit its growth. Therefore other centers may expect to expand much more rapidly, and some as yet unspecified urban regions must accommodate five to ten times the population that is presently found in the New York, Tokyo, London, and Moscow complexes.

The alternative, that of creating ideal-size communities in all locales where cities could possibly be sustained, does not help very much because it requires continuous enforcement of authoritarian measures for settling emigrants from the countryside. Any breakdown in the central authority results in the appropriation of the most desirable land by squatters. Therefore the resulting settlement pattern, which normally occupies the roadsides between centers, soon gives the appearance of continuous urbanism. From the air it would appear weblike, with green, brown, and gray occlusions. Thus a realistic assessment of urban-growth policy leads us inevitably to a distribution of city sizes, and some cities will have unprecedented dimensions.

Size is not an evil by itself. Its principal threat is that of congestion. Nevertheless, large numbers intimidate civil servants; they refuse to face the facts. Therefore most official metropolitan plans in developing countries seriously understate the rate of population growth, and these errors lead to an inappropriate allocation of scarce resources. Again, in *India's Urban Future,* Albert Mayer points out that the regional plan for Delhi aimed at accommodating 5.5 million by 1981, whereas a realistic appraisal of the growth pressures suggest at least 1 to 2 million more by that date (the projections by Davis propose about 3 million more), and there is no hope for leveling off at that date despite rapidly increasing marginal costs for providing housing and basic services.

The planners' concern with numbers results from experience showing that many commodities, such as land, water, living space, and transport services, must be allocated at some minimum per capita level that is established by the culture. The hard core of the capital-improvement budget for the metropolis is obtained by multiplying the population increase by the unit requirements of basic facilities. (It is necessary that the national planning must accelerate the introduction of the family-limitation process, but acceptance will be slow in the traditional sector of the population; therefore the cessation of growth cannot be accomplished for decades.) Existing technologies, as they have evolved in Western countries and Japan, are often inadequate to meet the demand; therefore the newly developing countries are forced—much more in the development of cities than elsewhere—to utilize promising technological and organizational innovations that have not yet been applied on a large scale. Such cost-reducing innovations are likely to be adopted by growing cities regardless of size.

Some new devices are available for the allocation of *urban land* to the respective public and private uses. It is now much more feasible to maintain a market. The users bid for the title or for a long-term lease, and the maximum price offered serves as a first approximation of value. It is no better than a crude indicator, because land in older countries also has many symbolic values and groups sharing such values are rarely organized well enough to make a high bid. Sanctified land occupied by temples or shrines often falls into this category. Violations cause the values to be expressed in terms of political agitation or rioting.

The planners must acquire information about the strength of both these varieties of values and consider, in addition, some long-term aesthetic components of value. They are then ready to construct a course of action as far in advance as it is possible to make projections with confidence. Master plans—complete proposals designating urban form for some rather distant date in the future—are clearly a mistake for rapidly growing urban regions.[1] Growth brings many unexpected crises and opportunities which change the values attached to particular sites so that their rational development is then very much out of line with the plan. The proper decision, then, is to revise the plan.

Since urban land use is indissolubly linked to accessibility to population (the greater the accessibility, the greater the number of alternative uses to which the tract can be put and, with few exceptions, the greater the economic rent that can be paid) the *urban transport* network plan can be used as the principal control for urban land development. At present the administration of land controls and of the transport services is quite independent, and radically different policies are pursued. It is crucial that their aims harmonize. Transport tariffs should be sensitive indicators of cost, preferably marginal cost, so that a strong motive exists for converting the most accessible land to urban uses first. Mechanical procedures for the fine adjustment of fares to cost are now much more feasible than they have ever been in the past. Therefore land-planning effort is often more usefully expended in the improvement of transport management than in the construction of land-use maps and an elaborate system of land-use controls.[2]

[1] This assertion is still heretical in many parts of the world where urban planners are trained. However, none of the scores of master plans which have come to my attention, each of them put together at a cost of dozens of man years of professional effort, could actually be implemented. Critics will admit that such plans serve as heuristic devices, but there are more economical devices for illuminating the problems of creating order; the master plan seems best suited to slow growing areas, if any at all.

[2] In Turner (ed.), *India's Urban Future,* in Meier, *Science and Economic Development,* and elsewhere, the writers have argued that automobiles must, for reasons of land-use efficiency, have a minimal role in internal transport. The bulk of the trips and shipments must move by electric railway, pedestrian ways, and

One of the gravest limitations upon very large cities is the shortage of *water* in the drought years. It is much too expensive to desalinate sea water and pump it inland if the demand is only for one year in five or ten. Obviously, the polluted water that is available must be reprocessed until it either evaporates or becomes unusable. Nevertheless, a very dry year will create a distressed population that seeks to settle near guaranteed sources of water supply. Therefore we may conclude that, in the long run, water supply, as much as land or accessibility, will be a determinant of the urbanization. The largest aggregations of people will cluster around protected openings to the high seas because these supply both access to raw materials and emergency supplies of fresh water at reasonable cost.

URBAN SOCIAL PLANNING

The foregoing arguments are pointed at the physical elements of urban growth but do not attempt to employ strictly physical concepts. The social problems of urbanization already appear even more overwhelming.

The greatest single problem, perhaps, is that of finding productive roles for the immigrant masses. The disguised underemployment of the villages becomes visible unemployment in an urban environment. The most important set of tools for meeting the need may be classed as *education,* and the various procedures for organizing education have been reviewed.

In the urban planner's point of view the elementary school becomes the focus of the urban neighborhood during the period of settlement and socialization. The common language is learned, and the population is prepared for exposure to the mass media. A cluster of other facilities must be planned for in the vicinity of the school, including a medical clinic, a market, some shops, perhaps some light industry, and administrative offices. About a dozen small firms and other organizations need to be founded in each neighborhood.

The secondary and vocational schools serve larger aggregates and must be spatially coordinated with a wider range of facilities. Hospitals, factories, intensive gardening, parks, distribution centers, and clubs must be integrated in a fashion that fits the climate and culture. The object in planning is to conserve human effort in carrying out routine behavior and to maximize the interaction that occurs under mutually rewarding

---

bicycle-scale vehicles, with buses and trucks serving the less organized, growing periphery. No major inventions can be found in theory or prototype that would change this expectation. Important innovations seem likely, however, for linking urban centers together at express speeds. This mode of transport becomes the basis for megapolitan linkage.

circumstances. Quite a bit of local data needs to be collected concerning urban behavioral trends before adequate judgments can be reached regarding adequate sites and sizes of facilities. Scores of small firms and minor institutions must be founded and developed for a completed community of this magnitude (10,000 to 20,000 persons).

The *housing* must be regarded as part of the educational process. Newcomers should be taught how to build and improve their own dwelling units. Neighborhoods should be able to improve their living conditions as their skills and savings increase. Stimuli for redevelopment should be built into the community charters. The extended family of the rural settlement must be converted into an urban household—a social unit that motivates people to acquire skills and take advantage of the varied opportunities provided by a metropolitan environment. Several thousands of such micro institutions must be initiated for each such community.

Looking away from face-to-face interaction to predominantly formal, impersonal transactions, the uniquely urban phenomena come to the fore. The public utilities must be expanded to meet the demand. The pattern for the distribution of energy is quite routine by now and is not likely to change significantly, but the links between telephone, radio, television, newspapers, mail, libraries, and recordings are far from fixed. It is quite likely that some of the radically new combinations in the technical journals will provide greatly improved services at less cost. The design of cities at this level becomes an exercise in systems analysis. Communications utilities must be used to regulate and coordinate transport, and later, once the various firms and organizations have been established, messages will be increasingly employed as economical substitutes for trips. A few large multifunction monopolistic institutions with many branches need to be created to service the metropolitan region.

The public recreation services must also be viewed as having valuable socializing and training functions. The capacity to organize teams in outdoor sports, to reach human physical capabilities in a controlled situation, to become familiar with visual artistic abstractions, and to read for pleasure are closely connected to the ability to live well in cities. Most of the organizations created in the pursuit of recreation are *ad hoc* and transitory, but a few, such as those that operate parks, museums, libraries, and stadia, require technical expertise and may live on for decades.

URBAN PLANNING INSTITUTIONS

Most, but not all, important cities have an office for the recording of deeds of land and property. The land parcels have undergone a careful survey, and the boundaries between plots have been marked. Even if some lines are destroyed, a relatively inexpensive resurvey from bench marks can replace them because comprehensive records are kept. These systems of records are a fundamental prerequisite for any kind of effective urban planning.

Associated with such block-by-block and tract-by-tract data are the maps which describe precisely the location of the services to the land office—water mains, sewers, streets and walks, power lines, telephone cables, gas mains, and many other less common uses of the land reserved to the public. The plans for installation of new facilities within an old city require this detailed information. These detailed maps and specifications are normally kept in the city engineer's office, which is usually given responsibility for seeing that the installation job is done correctly. Most of these services are buried in the streets and roads and are dug up only when local improvements are installed. The city engineer's office initiates most of the smaller proposals for change and the short-term adjustments in the urban services, and it supervises contractors who carry out all changes.

A majority of the cities in developing areas have instituted a system of land-use controls which attempt to keep the neighboring uses compatible with each other. Thus stables for animals are no longer permitted in the most densely settled portion of the city, nuisance industries are segregated, small parks and plazas are created for the neighborhoods, and the like. Normally this procedure is incorporated in the laws regulating building, and they fulfill the function of *zoning regulations* in countries borrowing American legal instruments.

Zoning carried out in a growing city can work only as long as the effort required to enforce it remains reasonable. A zoning plan cannot change completely the direction that a city is growing; it can only assist and rationalize the strong trends already at work. When the effort required to bring about compliance to law becomes excessive, a tract of land should be allowed to revert to uncontrolled uses. This is better than making exceptions, for too many exceptions to specific zoning provisions result in disrespect for the law. Most often the pressure occurs when the most valuable uses for the land turn out to be worth much more than the prescribed categories, that is, when the plan incorporated in the zoning provisions deviates furthest from the natural sequence of changes during a period of growth. Zoning for orderly land use thus needs to be revised every ten to twenty years.

The most effective device to regulate land use is building permit control. New buildings and improvements placed upon the land which are valued beyond a minimum figure ($100 to $200 is appropriate for a newly developing area) must be approved by an appointed group, which operates under various names in different parts of the world. Plans may be rejected for not conforming to prescribed use, for not meeting safety standards, or even (in some societies) for not following a desirable architectural style.

An administrative follow-up procedure is necessary to make building permit control truly effective. A cadre of building inspectors with some technical training must make on-site visits to see that the approved plans are not being modified after approval. An adverse finding on their part, when brought to court, would result in a substantial fine for the builder or owner, whichever was responsible. The building inspectors are also employed to investigate citizens' or other complaints (mainly governmental) concerning violation of building regulations, including zoning. These building inspectors are particularly useful for the urban redevelopment programs where slums and obsolete structures are removed or reconstructed and the land is put to modern uses. Since there is a tendency for law enforcement to be somewhat relaxed in all societies, strict enforcement as effected by these inspectors can be a harassing device that makes landlords willing to accept radical changes. So many private interests must be overcome in favor of long-range public gain that the successful strategy for redevelopment of the chaotic parts of growing cities must employ every tool available to the government. Most developing cities, particularly those having British and French influences at the start, do not have an effective system of inspection. The inspection technique will probably be adopted quite uniformly over the next decade or two.

Each city may be expected also to develop a planning office. If it has politically independent suburbs, the latter will also create planning offices, and the upper-middle-class suburbs would almost certainly lead the rest. The planning office finds itself becoming involved in increasingly complex programs for urban growth and reorganization as development proceeds. Initially its principal tasks are primarily those of guiding new settlement at the fringes of the metropolitan area. The planners see that the allocations of space are balanced and that the pattern for neighborhood organization is more open and flexible than that which would be chosen naturally by tradition-oriented immigrants or by profit-oriented landlords. Although modern services may not be installed simultaneously with the construction of homes, space is provided so that they can be laid down as soon as the incomes rise to a point where they can be supported.

These practical tasks will often be frustrated for lack of explicit projections of growth over the long run. City planners are greatly dependent upon *perspective planning,* with horizons fifteen to thirty years in the future. Within the context of national perspective planning, urban planners must determine the scale of the new services that need to be installed in their locale and what pattern is most economical and desirable. The function of the forecasting effort is to identify new problems created by growth which have not been encountered before in that city.

The city planning office is often presented with an unexpected opportunity, also. It could be a new industry, a major benefaction, or the technical feasibility of some public work like a bridge, a telecommunications center, or a large instrument for research purposes. Then the challenge is to make the most of the opportunity. Again, special studies must be undertaken to discover the best location, the best integration with existing services, the nuisances and other costs, and the further opportunities likely to be generated. These are the externalities associated with a new project.

A further responsibility of the planning commission for a metropolitan area is that of plotting the regrowth of the settled area. There is a strong tendency for a city to expand into a new area by building first a few scattered structures, then ribbons, followed finally by a filling in of interstices. The period of settlement of any large tract of land may take ten to twenty years. The structures are amortized, and the functions become obsolete perhaps twenty to sixty years later. This means that a part of the city, totally surrounded by urban settlement of various kinds, then needs to be rebuilt and reorganized.

Such a task requires a deep involvement in urban politics and administration, as well as analysis and design. Many established social and cultural interests will be disturbed by redevelopment of their part of the city, so that various efforts to amend the plan to suit the respective interest groups will be undertaken simultaneously. The threats of disorganization associated with redevelopment and renewal programs, which transform a neighborhood from one set of specialized functions in the metropolis to others, ordinarily cause city officials and property owners to ask for plans and programs of conservation and spot renovation so as to postpone the painful surgery needed for the welfare of the city as a whole. Hence the implementation of the programs which reconstruct, renew, and conserve parts of the city draws the planning commission directly into the political and administrative conflicts. There its expertise in architecture, engineering, economics, sociology, and statistics is less important, and a capacity for leadership, cooperation, and education makes the difference between success and failure.

Typically, a variety of agencies and authorities created for special purposes will take over some of these strategic functions of a planning commission to go along with the tactical operations such new agencies normally undertake. One of the major threats to the effectiveness of urban planning is that this involvement in politics can cause a paralysis of the planning function itself on many occasions. When recommendations are made upon technical considerations, people in the city then seek some political pretext that might lie behind them. This degree of suspicion of motives is unhealthy; yet if plans were proposed without regard for political feasibility in the vortex of special interests that makes up a large city, those plans would be meaningless.

Capital saving is a primary function of urban planning. The program of projects and the land-use controls are calculated to extend the life of structures and facilities that otherwise would become prematurely obsolete and to keep the cost of land for public purposes from becoming prohibitive. Thus the *physical* capital is used efficiently to serve a rapidly growing and shifting population. The *human* capital—the skills and knowledge acquired as a result of investing human time in learning situations—is conserved by keeping one skill accessible to another with minimum time lost in getting together. The battle against congestion in transport and communication, along with the improvements of accessibility brought about by these public projects, operates so as to conserve human resources. Programs for recreation have the same purpose but are less immediately utilitarian.

THE EVOLUTION OF URBAN PLANNING

When developmental planning begins, it is almost always conducted on a national or provincial scale. Hence projects for the improvement of cities are formulated in the same agency as projects for the development of natural resources. While the need for much decentralized planning is recognized, the shortage of competent staff and the difficulties in obtaining access to data prevent devolution to the city itself for a long time.

The vacuum in local planning during a period when the urban leaders are girding themselves for expansion often results in the creation of a circle concerned with the orderly development of the city. They are unpaid amateur planners and promoters, who in America are called *boosters*. They form clubs and associations, hire staffs, and engage in the political process. By the time the national planning or the regional planning feels it can afford to assign a group to be responsible for a city and to allow it to work on the scene with funds and powers at the disposal of the city government, the group will have a counterpart supported by the business and other private interests. Sometimes conflict develops between these two—the official planners and the amateurs. When that happens, the more complex projects for the development of the city may have to be postponed for lack of cooperation. Usually, however, some kind of compromise is found.

One of the most formidable obstacles to city planning created by the business and private interests is that of the independent suburb. Members of a professional and managerial class find they can obtain the services that their families need and desire by resettling in communities of their own making on the urban fringe. Similarly, the white-collar workers discover that they have more in common with people of their own status than with the ethnic communities of immigrants from which they had emerged and within which they had grown up. While the needs of this class for housing, education, recreation, and transport are more modest than those of the professional and managerial class, the white-collar workers are more numerous and so will create larger and more numerous suburbs. If permitted by law, these single-class communities will incorporate as cities and villages in their own right, or set up their own administration and urban services, thus creating a girdle of special interests around the growing city which prevent it from expanding outward or effecting transformations in the circulation system.

In all but a few American states, Canadian provinces, and Western European countries, the independence of the suburbs has prevented the evolution of comprehensive urban planning. What has resulted at best is metropolitan coordination of all those projects which assure that the gain in welfare of each such community should be roughly equal to that of the others. Regionwide developments which give one suburban community a boost without directly assisting the others tend to be ruled out, unless there are so many of these that they will affect a majority of the individual communities in the region. Most of the best ideas for improving the city, including the siting of a new industry, the levying of a new tax, or the establishment of an institution for higher education, can be blocked by a handful of small communities that feel they would get nothing from a project for themselves, or fear that it might "hurt" them at some time in the future. The predominant Western pattern of suburbanization should not be imitated in developing countries.

It is necessary, nevertheless, that specialized communities, set apart by social class, source of employment, or religious teaching, exist in the growing metropolis. Their boundaries, however, should not be formalized in the political sense, so that these communities may expand or contract in response to shifts in settlement, according to the pressures experienced. Such boundaries as separate them should be amenable to change as part of a plan and not allowed to be defended to the last dollar by local interests intent upon building a protective wall around themselves.

Conflicts which occur among plans when urban communities border upon each other cannot be avoided for long. They may first occur in miniature when villages, towns, and small cities must be annexed as the metropolis grows. Progress seldom is brought to a halt at this point, however, because the influences of the metropolis infiltrate the smaller community and change it substantially. The old community is submerged (perhaps after some struggle), and a new set of interests dominate decisions about its future. Representatives of these old interests should be persuaded to abandon the defenses at the boundaries and allow change to take its course, but this strategy will not always succeed. Some enclaves may have to be tolerated.

Eventually, too, one spreading metropolis will meet another of its own kind. These contacts between the growing edges of large cities have occurred in recent years, but the consequences are still difficult to foresee. They presage a new development in city form—the *megalopolis*. A megalopolis evolves around one or two major axes; it is made up of a constellation of urban centers. The residential areas depending upon each center begin to interpenetrate and overlap. Many cities will be forced by national pressures to abandon previously established local plans and accept those laid out for the urban region as a whole.

Some developing countries, such as India, Egypt, Indonesia, Korea, Argentina, and perhaps the Philippines, must consider megalopolis problems very soon. Japan is omitted from this list only because it has already been seriously engaged in analyzing the complications arising from the continued growth of the Tokyo-Osaka belt. China's urban agglomeration problems are expected to be the most severe of all, but the whole society there has taken a path of development which creates problems even more serious than those associated with orderly, efficient urban expansion.

All the megalopolises presently forming as a result of industrialization and overall development border upon the sea and therefore contact a frontier that may be settled in the not too distant future. The value of the water surfaces close to the megalopolis is already bringing about the reclamation of submerged lands. Within two decades it is anticipated that marine technology will reduce the cost of floating settlements to a point where some water surfaces will be competitive with the land. These possibilities introduce new complications. In the law courts, for example, should a floating community beyond the eight-mile limit be regarded as a fleet on the high seas? How is it to be governed? Mobilization of both water surfaces and land surfaces to accommodate the necessary growth leads to quite a different sort of urban planning than has existed up to the present. Institutions controlling recording of deeds, the mapping of surface use, zoning, transport development, recreation, food production and distribution, pollution control, and urban renewal would require drastic reorganization of procedures after they have been established.

These revolutionary changes in opportunities for metropolitan and megalopolitan development will affect the planning organization. Coordination with national, provincial, and hinterland planning should result in a free interchange of specialized personnel among the respective governmental agencies. An urban economist, sociologist, engineer, or architect planner should move from one office to another to accumulate experience for undertaking more responsible posts. Where civil service regulations do not permit this lateral movement, some informal means must be introduced. Many countries accustomed to using foreign consultants may develop consultant firms made up of local talent. Administrative systems modeled after the British and French can "second" personnel without loss of seniority or perquisites. In this manner a cadre of geographically mobile, broadly experienced personnel can be built up who employ informal methods for getting a job done, often by exploiting personal relationships with other experienced people in and out of government. This mode of professionalization assures a rapid spread of innovations and a capability for launching large complex projects in a short period of time. It would be expedited by a separate institutionalization of data acquisition regarding urban operations.

USEFUL STATISTICS

The technological revolution in data gathering and processing is at hand, so nations must proceed to build systems based not on present costs but on the much lower future costs. The Rand Corporation authors E. F. R. Hearle and R. J. Mason, in *A Data Processing System for State and Local Governments* (1963), are the first in this field to incorporate change and growth into total system planning.

Their categories include (1) environmental data, (2) real-property items, (3) person data, (4) personal-property data, and (5) operations records. Behind all these they need a reference system for *addresses and locations* with a minimum of ambiguity, so a comprehensive *census* can be founded on this framework. It has been suggested elsewhere that many complications in urban measurements can be avoided by using latitude and longitude in minutes and fractional seconds instead of the present practices for numbering residences and structures. The sampling frame for *social surveys* is also greatly simplified.

From such data it is possible for planners to formulate a *space budget* for an urban region. In many parts of the world the *water budget*—derived mostly from environmental data and internal operations reports—will become crucial and must therefore be given high priority. The *energy budget*, conversely, is giving fewer headaches as nuclear energy enters the picture.

Hearle and Mason assumed that the private sector, as well as the national government, would independently accumulate their own data. The national economic accounts would wish to install as quickly as possible a continuous set of reports on business transactions. From such data the urban planners would be able to estimate *income distribution and expenditure*—presently the most useful indicators of welfare. The availability of such comprehensive indexes makes it possible to compute cost-benefit ratios for projects that are competing for inclusion within the capital budget.

The improvement in data gathering should make it possible to prepare an as yet unobtainable index of urban development—*the number of public transactions* of an economic, social, cultural, and political nature. Very likely it would be assembled by combining surveys with comprehensive operating data on turnover tax, stamp taxes, and taxes on entertainment; vehicular trips, telephone, "exposures" to mass media, and workplace interactions all add partially overlapping transactions. The stream of these transactions, each of them an adjustment of one urban resident or organization to the physical environment or to others of its own kind, must be subjected to analysis, so that the relationship to the building of the major urban institutions becomes apparent. Another reference system, the *allocation of time to public purposes,* is closely linked to the transaction aggregate. Since all transactions have a time component, a strong indicator of the value attached to the transaction is the amount of human time devoted to it. Attempts to assemble a time budget for a city are just now beginning; later it should be possible to gauge institutional efficiency by increases in the number of transactions completed per unit time.

A *cultural index* should express the long-run contribution of the city to society; it should epitomize the richness of the imagery that is exchanged as a consequence of the plans. In its simplest form it would aggregate the information component of the transactions. Such an index cannot yet be assembled as a full accounting system; nevertheless, because the flow of information depends so heavily upon the transmission of written or taped materials, it is quite possible to combine all the ready sources and compute annual estimates of cultural interaction. Increase in information flow, it was argued in Chapter 3, makes possible subsequent growth in the social and economic indicators.

In the long run it is hoped that the "per capita income" figure that can now be provided for almost any region would be balanced by several income-distribution parameters, by a "transactions per day per capita" statistic, and by a "cultural interaction" estimate. The extra figures would remove a lot of nonsense from the arguments concerning comprehensive planning. The findings would affect project design in the plans at all governmental levels, but especially in cities.

THE SEARCH FOR NEW STYLES OF LIFE

The basic aim of all this analysis of opportunities and coordination of developmental effort should not be overlooked. It is intended to achieve the most valued social condition possible from a limited supply of physical and human resources.

It may be observed that when people are offered a choice between a traditional and undeveloped state of existence or a modern and developed one, a large share of their number will return to the society to which they are most accustomed, despite its limitations, but among those who choose to shift, the transitions are virtually all in one direction.

The principal dissatisfaction with the traditional society is that it offers rewards for too restricted a range of cooperative behavior. In other words, the worthwhile jobs are limited in both number and scope. The principal threat of modern society is that changes come too quickly and unexpectedly; the individual is not given time to integrate his behavior so that it makes sense to himself in the new situation before he is asked to make other major new changes.

Therefore, the concept of "development" in this work has been taken in its broadest possible sense. *Development is intended to create a wider range of choice for individuals and groups.* By making this possible it is anticipated that practically all individuals will also make many more conscious choices in a lifetime. Increased money income will make this wider choice possible as long as commodities and services are provided by a relatively free market. The economic institutions for dealing with variety in demand work reasonably well. The most modern forms are adapted not to equilibrium in accord with simple theory but to moderate rates of economic growth. However, the choice of roles and human associations within a modern society is not yet as free and open as it could be. Similarly, the range of possibilities for becoming familiar with images is highly restricted, so that opportunities for cultural choice are unnecessarily limited. The developmental societies, once they have achieved steady growth, must not be satisfied with current concepts of modernity. They must create something that goes beyond it.

It is already evident that for 95 to 99 percent of the population, the new styles of life that need to be synthesized must be urban in character. It is only through the organization made possible by cities that the productivity of labor can achieve the levels which permit greater freedom of choice. Much of agriculture will be urbanized as well. Factories are now displacing fields in the production of fibers; the most efficient meat and milk production is now being concentrated upon the urban fringe, and work in the experiment stations suggests that family farming will become obsolete.

Many urbanites, particularly those with romantic notions about smiling peasants and the simple pleasures of life, will resist this transformation. The peasants themselves, however, and their children, when given the chance, seem almost everywhere to prefer urban life, even if this means moving into a slum for a while. The flow of city people to the country to replace them exists, but it is not a very significant movement. The net result to be anticipated is, first, the movement of the landless rural surplus population to the cities, then the marginal rural population with land, and finally a regrouping of the parcels of land so as to permit efficient production by mechanical means. At that time the refugees from the city, most of them top professionals who wish to escape the stresses they had been subject to when residing in the city, will start resettling the countryside.

Some planners with backgrounds in the advanced social sciences will consider seriously the preferences for varied "ways of life" as revealed in the studies by Charles Morris, particularly in *Varieties of Human Values* (1956). In that study he formulated thirteen different ways of life and then collected the scaled preferences of students and other relatively un-committed persons in China, India, and Japan, as well as in more devel-oped countries. It was demonstrated that each population contained some individuals who preferred each of the distinguishable ways of life, but that the culture and the contemporary stresses affecting young people influenced the choice that was expressed. Morris's technique might be fitted to the design of the social institutions and the physical equipment of an urban society so as to satisfy the most people. However, the transi-tion from rural to urban, and from traditional to modern, is known to affect human values strongly. In the United States, where social change has been perhaps most rapid, Morris found an unwillingness to make firm commitment to *any* way of life, so that the way which reflected flexi-bility—the greatest degree of noncommitment that is possible—prevailed in the random sample of United States college students. It seems likely that each developing society will go through this stage.

It is still possible for urban communities to specialize, however, so that the minor preferences can be satisfied as well as the dominant ones. What is a mosaic of ways of life for the individual becomes a "style of life" for an urban environment.

One style of life that suggests itself is that of nonfarm residence com-bined with intensive agriculture of various kinds. There are people who have a psychic need for space but also have needs for the most advanced urban services. They are willing to pay a high price for spaciousness, even if they do not own or control the land. For them small exurban settle-ments, containing a few thousands of persons altogether, would seem to be the best solution. Perhaps some complementarity can be worked out between these ideas. For example, tree crops provide intensive use of land that is highly compatible with urban settlement of the kind envisaged here. The same roads that serve agriculture can also carry express buses to urban centers. It is entirely possible to imagine a predominantly agricultural area containing up to 10,000 persons per square mile in some of the Oriental cultures, and up to 3,000 per square mile in Western cultures. There are many variants of this style to be developed, depending on crop types and land forms.

Another direction for a style of life to evolve leads to an active urban public life at high-population density. The two street floors of structures would provide a variety of public services, and the upper stories either residence or office space. Schools would be combined with indoor swimming pools, gymnasiums, libraries, programmed-instruction tapes, studios, and clubrooms, but not playing fields and parking lots. Each residential structure would have its own nursery, perhaps in connection with a roof garden which was used for adults socializing at night. The entertainment of friends would be sustained in various cafés, tea shops, bars, and clubs, rather than at home. Much time could be devoted to the achievement of excellence in science or the arts. Life could be organized so that the consumption of power was small, and that of materials was also small, once the basic structures were in place. Changes in cultural style and appearance could be effected by changing wall hangings, floor coverings, and furnishings. Temporary interior walls could be created with modular panels and insulated with foam plastic so that isolation from the sight and sound of the city without, while still remaining in it, could be much more satisfactorily effected than it is today. Atmospheric conditions in large-scale urbanization would be vastly improved by eliminating internal-combustion vehicles and going over to an all-electric system for internal transport. This picture of urban life at densities of 50,000 persons per square mile (200 per hectare) or greater suffers from being overexplicit; many interesting potentials exist which could be adopted, but presently they may seem as bizarre as the cultures found in faraway places by missionaries and anthropologists. This portrayal has focused upon the main trends in the international urban culture associated with the downtown areas. Actually, the physical environment here would be of little consequence to its inhabitants, as long as it worked reasonably well, because they would be deeply involved in a multiplicity of institutions which carry on the affairs of various kinds of corporate enterprises— government, business, cultural, and religious. The planner's task is to devise an environment of physical *equipment and services* which facilitates the widest possible exploration of these ways of life.

Another way of life will have to be found for living on and with the sea, particularly on the edges of Asia, where so much of the world's population will be concentrated. Urban settlement need not be quite so dense in such areas; the whole Indian and Pacific Oceans are there to expand into. They represent another kind of frontier. The physical equipment for life on the sea so far is developed only for vessels and not for prolonged residence. A whole new urban technology is needed for house-boats, apartment units, floating platforms; for gardens, domesticated live-stock, and ways of making a living. An amphibious style of life has been developing for some time along every continental shore line. In the past few years the introduction of improved communication techniques and new materials of construction has made relatively safe and rewarding the occupation of protected water surfaces in the vicinity of the large cities. Very likely the subtropical and tropical regions will be preferred. The seas provide the last fertile "no man's land" for the venturesome individuals and families in the society of the future. It is possible that specialized communities will literally "cast off" from a coastal metropolis, each of them intent upon creating a style of life all its own. The possibilities for planning many different ways of life within an aquatic environment are very great.

Developing societies in their later stages also need communities de-voted to research and development, perhaps as an adjunct to communities devoted to postgraduate education. These are small social systems requir-ing the highest standard of welfare services in education, medicine, and recreation. The amenities are expected to be the highest for the imme-diate region, but the technical facilities are unique (as evidenced by Harwell, Oak Ridge, Cape Kennedy, Cambridge, and the Stanford-Berkeley axis, to provide a few contemporary examples). Whereas pre-vious research communities have been organized primarily to solve prob-lems in physical science and technology, it seems quite possible that in the newly developing countries analogous groupings will have to be formed to prepare educational materials that are demonstrated by ex-periment to minimize the amount of student time to reach given levels of competence, and still others to handle the data processing of economic and social statistics. Research and development communities now need access to a modern airport and a modern communications system, high-capacity computers, and a large variety of skilled technicians. A diversi-fied library is important. Public life in such a community is extraordi-narily rich in imagery because the best in many foreign cultures is blended with selected local cultures.

Interdependent with the research and development community is another style of life based upon the needs of the technical entrepreneur. As solutions to national problems begin to appear, often even before sug-gestions are published in technical journals, entrepreneurs should be form-ing new organizations to exploit them. These organizations may be offices in the government that are relatively free of budgetary control ("crash programs"), divisions of existing organizations that deal with new prod-ucts and processes, or independent enterprises. Most are led by scientists and engineers with organizing ambitions. The subsidiary problems are formulated and speedily solved, whereupon the organization goes into production of new goods or services. Perhaps one out of ten will succeed and grow into a large-size unit, mainly by absorbing and amalgamating with those that are less successful. Those scientists and engineers who dislike the discipline of the large organization will seize upon a still more recent idea, and then build an organization of their own to exploit it. In this environment the ordinary semiskilled and skilled worker will not be employed all his lifetime by one or two firms, where the workplace itself might change addresses three or four times, as in the typical industrial city. Instead he may change his employer every five years or so.

Mobility among organizations has become a healthy way of life for an important stratum of London and Tokyo society; a similar element has become the principal source of dynamism in Los Angeles, California. The mobility of the household is an important adjunct of organizational mobility, so that moving from one address to another must be made relatively easy for all members of the family. An extremely flexible urban transportation system is also required, so that one can move from a single home address to many potential sources of employment. A standardized educational system, effecting school-to-school transfers with ease, aids the rest of the family in its adaptation to changes in address.

These descriptions of special environments for urban life could easily be elaborated further. However, the essential instances, as far as they can be foreseen from present experience, have been set forth here. They comprise altogether the greatest challenges for careful, yet imaginative, developmental planning that yet remain.

All the external economies of enterprise that economists refer to, but are rarely able to measure, must be identified and knit together with social and cultural opportunities in a manner that is not only accepted but preferred by the inhabitants of the community. The planning must take into account the present distribution of preferences for way of life in the community; it must also leave room for adjustment by succeeding generations. Some of the adjustment can be accommodated by migration from one kind of urban environment to another, but when a serious amount of emigration from a single community seems likely, it will be necessary to undertake a redevelopment and reorganization program.

Most urban communities constructed during the period of exponential growth of cities must become obsolete within a generation or two. Thus, even before world population reaches some equilibrium level and virtually all the rural immigrants have been accommodated, a huge integrated program of redevelopment involving adaptations to new styles must be under way. Planning for growth and development of the poorer parts of the world can be only a temporary phase in world history; it must gradually be replaced by a still more complex program for achieving a state of development everywhere that is compatible with the still growing body of cultural, social, and physical knowledge. Those challenges are already being faced by the most affluent societies of the world.

BIBLIOGRAPHY

Gottman, Jean: *Megalopolis,* Twentieth Century Fund, New York, 1961.
Describes the evolution of the world's leading megalopolitan complex (along the American Atlantic seaboard) and identifies the knowledge-oriented quaternary activities which it supports.

Hearle, Edward F. R., and Raymond J. Mason: *A Data Processing System for State and Local Governments,* Prentice-Hall, Inc., Englewood Cliffs, N.J., 1963.
Although based upon American methods of government, this system illustrates a typical structure to be expected by 1975, with the scale of operations and prospective costs indicated, but does not anticipate the new uses to which the data might be put.

Morris, Charles: *Varieties of Human Value,* The University of Chicago Press, Chicago, 1956.
A quantitative analysis of the preferences that students hold for ways of life and the identification of five underlying factors and their relation to existing theories of action and the physiological bases of behavior.

Turner, Roy (ed.): *India's Urban Future,* University of California Press, Berkeley, Calif., 1962.
A review of the results of recent urban analysis in India, with projections of city growth and the planning needs of major urban agglomerations.

NAME INDEX

SUBJECT INDEX

Higher education, planning for, 303–
304, 326
site selection, 362–363
standards, 319
Highway system, improvement of, 248
Hindus as ethnic entrepreneurs, 157
Honduras, natural resources, 15
per capita income, 20
Hong Kong, economic development,
28–30, 161
level of education, 30
Households, survey of, 111
Housing in educational process, 385
Hubit, definition of, 95
Human resources, analysis of, 279–283
for construction industry, 285
definition of, 279
in Fomentarian revolution, viii
government contribution, 353–354
for industrial planning, 187, 189–190
investments in, 280, 343, 347, 349,
353–354
optimal development of, 142
reallocation of, 283–288
as reference system, 189, 277–278
Hungary, agriculture in, 27
planning program in, 32
Hydroelectric power, quantities by nation, 14–16

Iceland, fisheries, 18
natural resources, 14–18
per capita income, 20
Identity, need for, 56, 266–267
Image, definition of, 69
and Plan, 68
Images, in advanced societies, 98–100
of future, viii, 253
in industrial promotion, 159
intangible elements of, 77
national, x, 53, 55–57, 76
and organization, 76–79
repertoire of, 88–90
Immigrants, productive roles for, 384
Incentive programs, in education, 373
for entrepreneurs, 175, 179, 205
for industrial promotion, 159–161
for small industries, 175
Incentives, cost of, 202
Income, education and, 265, 345–346,
348

Income, estimated, in educational planning, 352
in urban development, 392–393
minimum family, 142
national, per capita, 20
Indexes for development, 393
India, certificates and degrees in, 266
five-year plan, 140
import substitution, 253
institutions for, 128
Japanese technical work in, 31
life style preferences, 395
megalopolis potential, 391
natural resources, 15
per capita income, 20
planning agencies, 34
political development, 58
prospective planning, 184–185
small industrial centers, 239
soil resources, 18
urban growth, 381
Indonesia, economic development, 23
information flow, 95
megalopolis potential, 391
national language development, 93
natural resources, 16
petroleum resources, 23–25
political development, 58
Industrial categories in census, 192
Industrial complexes, formed by families,
228
and harbor cities, 148–149
input-output table of, 188
petroleum-plastics-packaging, 189
in Soviet planning, 32
Industrial data sheet, 192–197
Industrial development, definition of,
135
Industrial economy, models of, 239
Industrial estates, on metropolitan periphery, 242
standards for, 220
Industrial location, 238–249
and urban plans, 206–207
Industrial planning, 135–155
education and, 118, 184, 259, 284
goals, 137–138, 140–142
incentives for, 159–161, 175
procedures, 181–200, 206, 208
proposals, screening of, 203–208
sources of, 157–159